The International
Money Markets

THE INTERNATIONAL MONEY MARKETS

by

JOHN T. MADDEN

and

MARCUS NADLER

GREENWOOD PRESS, PUBLISHERS
NEW YORK   1968

TO

ALLAN M. POPE

OF THE COUNCIL OF NEW YORK UNIVERSITY

Foreword

PERHAPS never before in peace time has the international money market been subjected to such stresses as during the period 1931–1935. The banking crises in many countries; the abandonment of the gold standard by Great Britain, the United States, and other nations; the declaration of transfer moratoria; the institution of rigid foreign exchange restrictions—all have left indelible marks on the financial machinery of the leading monetary centers of the world. The gold standard, which operated successfully for several decades before the war and under which the economic and financial relations of the various nations developed to their mutual benefit, broke down under the impact of the world-wide depression and was made by many the scapegoat for the ill-advised economic and financial policies of the post-war period.

So far no definite standard has taken the place of the gold standard. Managed currency, although advocated by many, has not been adopted by any country. The sterling bloc and the United States gold standard of 1934 are at best makeshifts intended to bridge over a difficult period until the international horizon becomes clearer and a return to more normal currency conditions is possible. The revolutionary changes that have taken place during the past few years in the field of international banking and in the money market machinery of the principal financial centers are but a reflection of the underlying economic philosophy that dominates the world at the present time.

The gold standard in its broader aspect presupposes an international division of labor embracing a moderately free interchange of commodities, services, labor, credit, and capital. The international financial machinery was the outgrowth of the closer economic intercourse among nations which it was intended to facilitate and finance. But in an era of extreme economic nationalism when every nation is endeavoring to become economically independent of the rest of the world at any cost, obviously there has been no room for a currency standard which of necessity is international in character. Thus, since finance is merely a handmaiden to industry and trade, the machinery created for the purpose of financing such international transactions has had to undergo serious and important changes.

The purpose of this volume is to analyze the changes in the rôle of gold and the causes of its collapse in the postwar years; to study the functions and operations of the international money and capital markets; and, above all, to describe the organization and operation of the leading international financial centers. The latter occupies the greater part of the volume. Although limitations of space have made necessary the omission of minor details, the authors have endeavored as far as possible to present an up-to-date description of the banking systems of the principal countries, to analyze the functions and operations of the leading money markets, and to describe the rôle in international finance played by each market.

The authors have drawn their material from a number of sources and owe a debt of gratitude to many who have furnished them with information. Special acknowledgment is due to Dr. Sipa Heller and Mr. Harry C. Sauvain, both of New York University and the Institute of International Finance, who have assisted in the research work and otherwise aided in the preparation of this volume; to Professor J. I. Bogen and Miss A. G. Corrigan, both of New York University, who have assisted in various phases of the work; and to Mr. W. A. Sholten of the First Boston Corporation, who has read most of the foreign sections and made numerous suggestions. Mr. Ernest Schwarzenbach prepared the section on the Swiss Money Market.

JOHN T. MADDEN
MARCUS NADLER

New York University
New York, February 1935.

Contents

Contents

Contents

The International
Money Markets

CHAPTER I

Gold and the Rôle of the Gold Standard

DURING the last quarter of the nineteenth century and up until the outbreak of the World War, the monetary systems of most of the western nations of the world were linked to gold, and the gold standard in varying forms functioned in a relatively satisfactory manner in both Europe and America. Silver did not play an important rôle in the currency systems of the western nations. In the narrower national sense, the gold standard meant two things: (1) a free gold market; and (2) often, although not always, the unrestricted and unlimited redemption of notes in gold.[1]

In the broader international sense, however, the gold standard meant much more than this. It was a part of the pre-war international economic system which was based on the principle of the division of labor and a moderately free interchange of commodities, services, and labor. In this system gold was the common denominator of the

---

[1] The variations in the types of gold standard in operation before the war were numerous. In respect to convertibility of notes, there were three types, namely, the gold specie standard, the gold bullion standard, and the so-called limping standard. Under the latter, bank notes were convertible either into gold or into one specified silver coin, such as the five-franc silver écu in France. In respect to reserves against notes in circulation, there were other variations. These included: (1) a reserve requirement of 100 per cent in gold, as for example in Peru and some other South American countries; (2) a minimum requirement of 30 to 40 per cent in gold, as in Germany; (3) a fixed fiduciary issue with the balance of notes secured entirely by gold, as in England; (4) a fixed note issue regardless of the metallic reserve, as in France; and finally (5) the gold exchange standard, which permitted the holding of a part of the metallic reserve in foreign exchange of countries on the gold standard (although notes were convertible only into gold), as in Belgium, Bulgaria, Finland, Russia, and Italy.

1

various national currencies and, in fact, served as an international currency. The free movement of gold between countries not only assured stable exchange rates, but also permitted a correspondingly free international movement of funds which tended to equalize interest rates and price levels and, consequently, to maintain a certain degree of adjustment between the national economies of the principal commercial countries.

Prerequisites of the gold standard. While the gold standard in any particular country can be established only by national legislation, its successful functioning as an international standard depends upon the existence of conditions too broad to be defined or to be regulated by the domestic legislation of any one country. There are several well-defined rules, or prerequisites, for the operation of the gold standard which all the countries must observe if the standard is to operate satisfactorily. The first requirement is freedom from legislation restricting the free movement of gold from one country to the other, such, for example, as laws that may nullify clauses covering convertibility of notes, the imposition of embargoes on the export of gold, and interference with the ordinary procedure for the purchase and sale of gold. Since the primary purpose of gold movements is to facilitate the international transfer of funds, it follows that dealings in foreign exchange must also be free of restrictions.

The second requirement is a state of international economic equilibrium, a condition which can be brought about and maintained only by a reasonably free movement of commodities, services and capital, which tends to create a comparatively stable balance between the international income and outgo of each individual nation. Often equilibrium in the international accounts is achieved by capital transactions, and the free movement of long-term capital is just as essential to the maintenance of the gold standard as is the free movement of gold and short-term funds. Countries with a consistently favorable balance of payments which are unable or unwilling to make foreign loans and investments can be paid the balances due them only in gold, and the continued accumulation of gold by some countries at the expense of others must sooner or later force the losers to abandon the gold standard.

A third prerequisite to the successful functioning of the international gold standard is a willingness on the part of central banks to permit gold movements to exercise their full effect on the credit structure of their countries. If central banks counteract the effects of gold movements through open market operations, the semi-automatic adjustments which normally correct the conditions giving rise to gold movements do not take place, and a situation of disequilibrium is maintained.

The fourth prerequisite is political in nature. The gold standard operated successfully before the war because, then, political hazards interfered with the movements of funds, short-term as well as long-term, much less than in the postwar period. Political uncertainties not only interrupt the normal movement of short-term and long-term capital to the countries affected, but often give rise to a "flight of capital" which may cause the collapse of one country's currency system and create abnormal conditions in the money markets of other countries.

The international gold standard and the international credit system built upon it are a delicate mechanism which is very easily thrown out of adjustment. Since the war, nations have tended more and more to adopt policies of national self-sufficiency which, in violation of the fundamental prerequisites, involve restrictions of the international movement of gold, capital, commodities, and services. The result has been an almost complete breakdown of the international gold standard and a collapse of the international credit structure. Superficial observers have hastily concluded that the defect lies in the gold standard itself; actually it lies in the impossible conditions under which the gold standard has been expected to function.

4   The International Money Markets

Use of gold. Under the international gold standard as it existed in the pre-war period, gold was used as a basis for currency and credit and, to a lesser extent, for the settlement of temporary marginal deficits in the international balances of payments. In this connection, a careful distinction must be made between temporary deficits and more permanent maladjustments. In the latter case, equilibrium was generally achieved by means other than gold shipments, namely, by long- and/or short-term borrowing until such time as the fundamental causes for the deficit could be rectified. Before the war, gold was not ordinarily used as a medium for the actual payment of international debts; it was an instrument of commerce but not a commodity of commerce. The use of gold for settling marginal balances before the war was comparatively small, because the international accounts of the principal countries were much better balanced than in the post-war period. In the first place, foreign trade was better adapted to the international economic status of each country. The great creditor nations, as a rule, had an unfavorable trade balance, thereby enabling the debtor countries to pay their debt service in commodities. The debtor countries were young and economically undeveloped, and therefore attracted a more or less steady stream of foreign capital for use in the exploitation of their natural resources. It was this equilibrium in the balance of payments of the various countries of the world which prevented gold from becoming a means of debt payment and which brought about a more or less satisfactory international distribution of gold.

The usefulness of gold in settling balances was due to the fact that, as a commodity with a world market and a relatively stable value, it was universally acceptable. Furthermore, since the monetary units of most countries were defined in terms of gold, the movement of gold provided an automatic check on fluctuations in foreign exchange rates. Whenever a monetary unit on the gold standard fell below a certain point in the exchange market, gold exports immediately rectified the situation. The export of gold for such purposes, however, was as a rule small. If it assumed very large proportions, it caused a contraction of credit and an increase in interest rates, which in turn led to an influx of short-term funds from abroad and a rise in the exchange value of the currency.

The direct effect of gold movements on interest and exchange rates gave rise to the view that the operation of the international gold standard was automatic. This view was only partially correct, since the central banks could, and at times did, influence interest rates and thereby affect the movement of funds regardless of gold movements. However, in the pre-war period the central banks rarely used open market operations to influence credit conditions and counteract the movement of gold. The control over the money market was effected chiefly by manipulation of the discount rate; but discount rates as a rule were determined chiefly by the movement of gold, and it was the gold position of a central bank which determined its discount policy. Thus, while central banks even in the pre-war era were able to influence and counteract the movement of gold, in most cases the effects of gold imports or exports on the money market were direct and immediate.

Up to the outbreak of the World War the gold standard functioned with relative success in most of the countries of Europe, in the United States, Australia, and Japan, and in several countries of South America. Although gold moved freely from one country to another, actual shipments were not large. Furthermore, the yellow metal was fairly well distributed throughout the world, the amount of gold corresponding more or less to the economic or political needs of each country.

War period. One of the first moves of the belligerent nations upon the outbreak of the war was to sever the connection between their monetary systems and gold. This general suspension of gold payments shows clearly the extent to which the gold standard depends upon political stability and normal international economic intercourse among the nations of the world. It also revealed the fallacy of the theory that gold reserves are maintained to protect the stability of currencies in emergencies—although the truth should be evident without such a demonstration, since it is obviously impractical for a country to maintain a sufficiently large monetary stock of gold to permit the conversion into gold of any very appreciable portion of its bank deposits. A great political upheaval such as a war inevitably leads to a flight of capital, and if free conversion of notes and a free gold market should be maintained by the various central banks, the gold stocks would very soon be exhausted.

While the export of gold by private individuals and corporations was prohibited during the World War, the governments and the central banks exported large amounts of gold to the neutral countries and also to the United States, in payment for merchandise and military supplies. The war thus had two serious effects on the world's monetary gold stock. It drove gold out of circulation in most countries and caused an international maldistribution of gold. Although serious efforts were made to redistribute the yellow metal, little progress has been made in the post-war atmosphere of economic nationalism.

Post-war period. The end of the war found Europe in a financial chaos. When the artificial pegging of the exchanges ceased, currencies depreciated rapidly and the world was faced with a series of monetary crises which affected almost all countries except the United States. The problem of currency stabilization was one of the most important in the post-war program of economic reconstruction, for currency depreciation and exchange fluctuations constituted one of the most serious impediments to the restoration of sound state finances and the revival of world trade.

By 1928 the stabilization of the currencies of the world on a gold basis was virtually completed, and once again the monetary units of the principal countries were tied to gold. The gold standard, however, had been subjected to such strain that it came back in a form greatly altered and containing within itself the germ of its future destruction. In the first place, no provision was made in the new currency laws for the circulation of gold coins, and except in the United States and a few other countries where bank notes had long been convertible into gold, the specie standard was a thing of the past. The removal of gold from circulation facilitated the concentration of gold in the hands of central banks, but this development was of little importance as compared with the far-reaching changes brought about by the wide adoption of the gold exchange standard. The introduction of the gold exchange standard in a number of European and South American countries modified to a considerable extent the operation of the gold standard, both in the narrower legal sense and in the broader economic sense, and it had a decided influence on economic developments throughout the world in post-war years.

The gold exchange standard. The essential features of the gold exchange standard in post-war years were the inclusion of foreign exchange on gold standard countries as part of the legal reserve of the central banks and the conversion of bank notes, at the option of the central bank, into either gold or foreign exchange. Thus, while adhering to the principle of gold as the standard of value, the gold exchange standard used claims payable in gold in one country as the equivalent of gold in the credit base of another, and hence made possible the double use of the yellow metal for currency and credit purposes. Variations in the application of this standard were developed in different countries. In Austria and in Hungary, for instance, the entire legal reserve of the central banks against notes in circulation and demand deposits might consist of foreign exchange payable in gold, while the central banks of Germany, Poland, and Belgium were permitted to hold only 25 per cent of their legal reserves in foreign exchange. The term *foreign exchange* itself was applied generally to demand and short-term deposits with well-known banking institutions, short-term bankers' bills arising out of commercial transactions, and bank notes of central banks on the gold standard. Some central banks were also permitted to include short-term government securities as part of their foreign exchange holdings which were eligible for note cover.

Effects of the establishment of the gold exchange standard. The original motive for the establishment of the gold exchange standard was to effect an economy in the use of gold. It was based on the erroneous belief that the world was confronted with a shortage of gold, a premise strengthened at the time by the prospect of a decline in gold production. The assumption of a shortage of gold was partly the result of a comparison of two sets of figures which were not comparable; namely, the liabilities of the central banks expressed in depreciated currencies, and the gold reserves at the pre-war parity. If the depreciated liabilities had been stated in terms of gold or if the gold had been stated in terms of depreciated currencies, it would have been apparent that there was no serious shortage of gold and that there was no immediate need for economy in the use of gold. As a matter of fact, at the end of 1922 —before the various currencies had been stabilized—the monetary stock of gold in the vaults of the central banks and government treasuries of the world amounted to $8,-402,141,000, as compared with $4,856,712,000 at the end of 1913: an increase of 73 per cent. Moreover, at the end of 1922 the total volume of production and trade was still below the pre-war level. The idea of a shortage of gold arose partly from the fact that existing stocks were so poorly distributed that some countries had very little gold; yet it should have been obvious that it was just as difficult for those countries lacking adequate gold reserves to acquire gold exchange as to acquire the gold itself. In fact, if they could get gold exchange, the conversion of the exchange into gold was a very simple matter. It is safe to say that the double use of gold which the gold exchange standard permitted was responsible in a measure both for the tremendous inflation which took place from 1924 to 1929 and for the ultimate breakdown of the gold standard in 1931.

The gold exchange standard also interfered with the proper functioning of the international gold standard, in that it largely eliminated, as far as the gold exchange standard countries were concerned, the corrective movements of gold which contributed so much to international financial equilibrium before the war. Formerly a central bank in a gold standard country which acquired an unusually large amount of foreign exchange of another gold standard country would reduce its holdings to more normal proportions by converting a part of them into gold, since foreign exchange was not eligible for its legal reserves. The gold shipment would increase the credit base of the country receiving it and decrease that of the country losing it, with little or no net change in the amount of credit available in the international money market. The central bank of a country on the gold exchange standard which acquires a supply of foreign exchange, however, would have no incentive to convert its exchange into gold, since the exchange serves the same purpose as gold in its legal reserves. The acquisition of foreign exchange expands the credit base in the same manner as do gold imports in a gold standard country, but, because there is no loss of gold, there is no corresponding contraction of the credit base in another country. The gold in a gold standard country serves as the basis for its own currency and credit structure, and at the same time claims on its gold may serve as a basis for currency and credit in another country.

Illustration of operation of gold exchange standard. This double use of gold under the gold exchange standard may be illustrated by the following example: An Austrian corporation issues a long-term loan in New York, the net proceeds of which are $1,000,000. The corporation, which needs Austrian currency (schillings), sells the proceeds of the loan to a Viennese bank. The latter in turn sells its dollar deposits with the banks in New York to the Austrian National Bank. Since Austria is on the gold exchange standard, this move immediately increases the "metallic" reserve of the central bank and enables it to increase its notes in circulation or demand deposits by about $3,000,000, or about 21,000,000 schillings, assuming a reserve ratio of 33⅓ per cent (the actual legal requirement at present is lower). At the same time the money market in New York is practically unaffected, except that, if the bonds of the Austrian corporation were purchased with newly created bank credit or were purchased by investors in other parts of the country who remitted funds to New York, the sale of the bonds may have led to some increase in deposits of the New York banks. If, on the other hand, the bonds of the Austrian corporation had been purchased entirely by investors in New York and solely out of existing deposits, this entire transaction would have resulted merely in a shift in the ownership of deposits on the books of some New York banks. But while the credit base in the United States is unchanged, since there has been no export of gold, and the volume of credit is little affected, the Austrian National Bank is in position to increase its currency or deposit liabilities by three times the amount of the loan.

Thus, the operation of the gold exchange standard not only contributed to maintaining the maldistribution of the world's gold stocks, but also made possible a pyramiding of credit on gold. There is no doubt that, but for the gold exchange standard, there would not have been such a great expansion of bank credit in the United States as took place in the years 1927 to 1929, because gold exports would have contracted the credit base.

Other weaknesses of gold exchange standard. While the inflationary effects of the double use of gold might have been foreseen, the gold exchange standard has certain other weaknesses which have become apparent only as the system has been subjected to practical tests. These weaknesses affect the gold exchange standard countries as well as the gold standard countries whose exchange is held as a part of the metallic reserve of the former. Before going into a discussion of these weaknesses, let it be said that the gold exchange standard is not without its advantages. The principal advantage derived from the gold exchange standard is economy; first, because the reserves held in foreign exchange earn interest, and second, because the expense of storing and handling gold is largely eliminated. In addition, the gold exchange standard has at times been psychologically advantageous in that changes in foreign exchange holdings of a central bank may be practically unnoticed by most people, while an outflow of gold would cause wide concern.

The chief disadvantages to countries on the gold exchange standard are the risk of loss in case the country in which their reserves are held goes off the gold standard, and the possibility of the confiscation of these reserves in event of war. The seriousness of this risk was realized when England abandoned the gold standard in September 1931, and a number of countries which held large balances in London suffered heavy losses and, consequently, were themselves forced to suspend gold payments. In addition, the central banks of certain gold standard countries which had large sterling balances—as, for example, the Bank of France and the Nederlandsche Bank—sustained such heavy losses that they had to apply to their governments for assistance.

The gold exchange standard and its effect on gold standard countries. From the standpoint of the country on the gold standard, the holding of the reserves of other countries involves the now questionable advantage of increased gold holdings. However, the central bank authorities of countries on the gold standard that held substantial amounts of the reserves of central banks of countries on the gold exchange standard generally recognized that a portion of their gold reserves was held by them in trust for other nations. This view was clearly expressed in the annual report of the Federal Reserve Board for the year 1926, which stated:

> Dollar balances in New York have been built up not only by foreign industrial corporations and commercial banks but also by European and South American central banks, which in many instances are authorized by law to keep a portion of their reserves in the form of foreign exchange in countries with stable currencies. These dollar balances of foreign central banks, whether they are invested or kept on deposit, are in liquid form and subject to immediate withdrawal at any time. If they were to be withdrawn in gold, in whole or in part, the demand for the gold, though it would first be felt by the commercial banks, both member and non-member, would promptly reach the Federal Reserve Banks as the only holders of gold in any considerable amount. These balances are, therefore, potential sources of demand upon the Federal Reserve Banks for gold out of their reserves, the central banking reserves of the United States, which have thus become indirectly a part of the reserves against bank credit and currencies in other countries. The existence in America of these foreign balances consequently presents a condition in the banking situation to be taken into account in determining the Federal Reserve System's credit policy with a view to maintaining the country's banking system in a position to meet demands for gold from abroad without disturbing balances and credit conditions in this country.

In accepting their responsibility as trustees for the reserves of the gold exchange standard countries, the gold standard central banks, by means of open market operations, often followed a policy of preventing gold imports from having their normal effect on the credit system. In financial parlance, the gold imports were "sterilized." Thus, when large stocks of gold were accumulated in the United States and the reserve banks were reproached for hoarding gold and thereby preventing the free operation of the gold standard, they replied with the obvious answer that the gold sterilized through open market operations was held in trust for foreign countries, who might withdraw it whenever they saw fit. While the policy was severely criticized at the time, subsequent events have demonstrated that the position of the reserve banks was well taken.

The full disadvantage of this system, as it affects central banks of gold standard countries in which foreign balances were accumulated, did not become apparent until 1931, when the general movement to convert these balances into gold was one of the principal influences which forced England to abandon the gold standard and was an immediate cause of the breakdown of the international currency and credit system. Central banks may attempt to formulate their policies so as to permit the withdrawal of foreign bank reserves in the form of gold, but when a concerted withdrawal develops it creates an atmosphere of fear and uncertainty which causes other foreign creditors to become panicky, and may easily lead to such a large outflow of gold as to necessitate suspension of gold payments.

Structural changes in the use of gold. The introduction of the gold exchange standard on an extensive scale was perhaps the most important innovation in the use of gold. Strangely enough, however, at the same time that such emphasis was being placed upon devices to economize in the use of gold and great concern was being voiced over its scarcity, changes were made in the statutes of the central banks in a number of countries which tended to increase greatly the demand for gold for monetary purposes.

The most important of these changes was the wider adoption of fixed minimum gold reserve requirements against deposit liabilities. Before the war, Holland was probably the only country in which the central bank was required to hold metallic reserves against demand deposits. A similar legal requirement was adopted in the United States when the Federal Reserve Act stipulated that the reserve banks must maintain reserves, in gold or lawful money, equivalent to at least 35 per cent of their demand deposits. After the war most of the European countries which revised their monetary systems followed the example

of the United States and Holland. This practice not only
increased the demand for gold but gave it a rôle of increased
importance as the basis of credit. The amount of gold
held by a central bank came to be considered, at least
theoretically, as an index of the potential credit expansion
of the country. The question of whether this view is warranted is discussed later in this chapter.

The second change tending to increase the demand for
gold was the adoption of higher minimum reserve requirements against notes in circulation. Before the war the
statutory requirement for minimum reserves where the
system of flexible currency was in existence was generally
33⅓ per cent. In the post-war reconstruction of currencies
this minimum was generally raised to 40 per cent, partly
under the influence of the higher percentage adopted by the
United States and partly to reassure the public as to the
future soundness of the currency. In many instances provisions were made to permit the reserve to fall below the
minimum in case of emergency. This emergency provision,
however, was of doubtful value, because as soon as gold
reserves fall below the legal minimum, confidence in the
currency is undermined and it is usually necessary to resort
to foreign exchange restrictions in order to prevent a flight
of capital and to maintain the stability of exchange rates.

Changes in the operation of the gold standard. In addition to the legislative changes in the structure of the gold
standard, there has been considerable modification in central bank practices affecting the operation of the international gold standard. The pre-war policies of the leading
foreign central banks, particularly those of England, France,
and Germany, had been directed primarily to the maintenance of stable exchange rates, the prevention of an excessive gold movement, and the regulation—in so far as was
deemed necessary—of the domestic money market. Aside
from these policies, the central banks as a rule did not
interfere with the free operation of the gold standard, nor

did they attempt to counteract or offset the effects of an inflow or an outflow of gold through open market operations. Such operations, practically unknown in the prewar period, have now not only become major instruments of domestic credit control but are often used to offset and counteract the international movements of gold, thereby preventing the equalizing influences which such movements would exercise on the money market.

A movement of gold to a country on the gold standard broadens the credit base of the country and would normally be reflected in an increase in the volume of bank deposits with the central bank. If, however, the central bank sells government securities or permits its portfolio of acceptances to decline, there is an offsetting reduction in the central bank balances of the commercial banks and the gold movement has no effect on the credit structure or on conditions in the money market. Conversely, an outflow of gold under the normal operation of the gold standard causes a narrowing of the credit base which, in turn, may lead either to increased borrowing at the central bank or to the calling of loans by the commercial banks, and eventually to an increase in interest rates with resultant effects on business and prices. But if the loss of gold is offset through the purchase of government securities or acceptances by the central bank, the effect of the outflow of gold on the money market is nullified.

The use of open market operations as a major instrument of credit control by the central banks brought to an end whatever automatic readjustments had been caused by international gold shipments before the war. By offsetting the effects of gold movements, these operations led to the accumulation of large quantities of gold in some countries without creating monetary and credit conditions favoring an outflow of funds. Experience has now shown that they contributed considerably to the breakdown of the gold standard during the depression. Even during the short post-war period when most currencies were linked to gold, there was no international gold standard such as existed before the war.

Effects of post-war economic changes. The numerous modifications of the gold standard introduced in the post-war period, and the changed practices of the central banks, so completely altered the standard that its free operation on an international scale was made, if not impossible, at least very difficult. The establishment of the gold exchange standard and the open market operations of the leading central banks, notably of the Federal Reserve banks in the United States, largely eliminated the effects which movements of gold had formerly had on the money markets.

But while these factors were important, they were overshadowed by post-war economic developments. The international gold standard can operate successfully only when the balance of payments of the individual nations adhering to it is more or less in equilibrium, and when gold is used only for the settlement of marginal international balances. Once the balance of payments of a country becomes seriously maladjusted, the country is forced to use gold as a means of payment and, sooner or later, either to abandon the gold standard or to impose rigid foreign exchange restrictions—which is, in practice, the equivalent of abandoning the gold standard. Now, during the post-war period one of the fundamental prerequisites of the international gold standard was generally ignored, namely, that there must be a reasonably free movement of goods and services between nations. The spirit of nationalism, intensified by the war, was reflected in the economic sphere in increased governmental interference with the movement of trade and through higher tariffs, import quotas, and subsidies—in brief, the adoption of policies designed to make nations more economically self-sufficient. These obstacles to the normal development of trade prevented many countries from properly adjusting their imports and exports to their economic circumstances, and greatly contributed to the maladjustment of their balances of payments. During most of this period equilibrium was maintained in the international accounts by foreign borrowing, on either long- or short-term account. But when the international flow of capital came to an end during the depression, the debtor countries were suddenly confronted with a greater demand for foreign exchange than they could supply, and were thus forced to draw on their monetary stocks of gold until they were seriously depleted.

These conditions, and not the shortage of gold or some inherent defect in the gold standard, were responsible for the abandonment of the gold standard by so many countries during the last few years. They destroyed the foundation upon which the international gold standard and the delicate money market machinery are based. They will continue, while they operate, to make a return to the international gold standard of the pre-war era impossible.

The alleged shortage of gold. The maldistribution of gold, resulting from the maladjusted balance of payments of a number of countries, has given rise to the belief that the world is confronted with a shortage of gold which is bound to affect prices and general economic conditions. As the depression deepened and as prices in the gold countries continued their precipitous decline, the gold shortage theory became more widely accepted and the depression was attributed, by many, solely to this factor. It is therefore necessary to consider more carefully the theory of a gold shortage and to examine closely the rôle played by gold in the financial and economic structure of the individual countries.

Professor Cassel is perhaps the best known of the economists who maintain that an annual increase in gold production of from 2 per cent to 3.1 per cent is necessary to sustain the normal increase in the volume of the world's business activity. If this increase does not take place, it is held, the monetary stock of gold will not be sufficient to support the necessary volume of currency and credit, and prices will decline. In support of this theory it is pointed out that between 1850 and 1910 industrial production increased at the rate of about 3.1 per cent each year, while the monetary stocks of the world increased at approximately the same rate. There are, of course, differences in the estimates of industrial production and the growth of gold stocks, owing to the fact that accurate statistics for the entire world are not available. Nevertheless, on the surface it appears more than a coincidence that the gold supply and industrial production increased at approximately the same rate while commodity prices remained relatively stable. Within the period, of course, there were fluctuations in prices, in gold production and in industrial expansion, but the averages for the entire period are taken as the basis for this theory.

Fallacies of the gold shortage theory. In an analysis of the argument of the gold shortage economists, several points become apparent. In the first place, the statistical data cited cover a period during which silver was being gradually demonetized while the gold standard was being more widely adopted throughout the world, thus creating an additional demand for gold. Furthermore, the entire period was marked by a tremendous expansion of industry, trade, and agriculture throughout the world. A number of European countries went through an economic revolution which converted their national economies from an agricultural to an industrial basis. This change brought with it an increased demand for credit and currency which, in turn, caused an increased demand for gold. At the same time the western hemisphere experienced a vast development. New territories were opened and settled with millions of immigrants, both agricultural and industrial production expanded rapidly, and the total volume of business rapidly increased. The entire period was one of economic expansion at a pace probably unprecedented in the history of the world. It is true that there was an increase in the number of commercial banks and in the use of bank credit instead of currency, and that the development of a credit economy and the establishment of central banks afforded considerable economy in the use of gold; but these economies certainly did not offset the increased need for gold in the monetary systems of the world.

If under these conditions the gold supply proved adequate to maintain a relatively stable price level, why should one anticipate that it will fail to be adequate in the future? It is highly doubtful whether economic expansion in Europe and the United States will continue at the same rate as during the last quarter of the nineteenth century and the first three decades of the twentieth century, and there is little prospect of a decline in gold production. In fact, gold production has actually increased appreciably in the last few years and will probably continue to do so in the near future.

The theory, moreover, that there must be an increase of about 3 per cent per annum in the world's monetary gold stocks in order to permit the maintenance of a stable price level assumes that no further changes can be made in the world monetary and credit system to economize in the use of gold. The nature of future changes is, of course, subject to much controversy at present. The most likely possibilities include: (1) the abandonment of reserves against central bank deposits; (2) the abolishment or reduction of the fixed minimum reserves against notes outstanding; and (3) the remonetization of silver. The last remedy has been strongly advocated in the United States, where steps have already been taken to broaden the credit base through the inclusion of silver as part of the metallic reserve. The merits of these possible reforms must be analyzed carefully.

Gold reserve against central bank deposits. The requirement of reserves in gold against deposits held by central banks has been described above as a post-war development. The maintenance of such reserves is based on the theory that these deposits are liabilities of the same category as notes in circulation, and reserves against them are just as necessary as reserves against notes. It is also argued that such reserves constitute a check against the expansion of central bank credit.

At this point a distinction must be made between those countries which have followed the American system of compelling the commercial banks to maintain fixed reserve balances with the central banks against their own deposits, and those countries where the banks are not required to maintain such fixed reserves. The commercial banks in the latter countries merely maintain balances with the central banks for clearing purposes or as a convenient way of holding their cash resources.

Banks with fixed reserve requirements. In countries where the commercial banks must maintain certain fixed reserve balances with the central banks, these balances are not actually reserves, for the banks cannot reduce them below the required limit without incurring certain penalties. The only way in which a bank can avail itself of its reserve balances with the central bank is by reducing its own demand deposits. In the United States, for example, taking the banking system as a whole, the member banks must reduce their own deposits by about $10,000 in order to be able to reduce their balances with the Federal Reserve banks by $1,000. This fact clearly indicates that member banks are able to draw on their deposits at the Reserve banks only to a very limited extent, and that the Reserve banks are required under normal conditions to pay out in cash only a small amount of the member-bank deposits which they hold. In periods of panic, such as during the banking crisis in the United States in the early part of 1933, when there is a concerted movement by depositors to convert their deposits into gold, specie payments are usually suspended. The term "reserves," therefore, is not properly applicable to these deposits, since they do not represent cash which the member banks can withdraw in full at any time. In practice they serve merely as instruments to facilitate the control of bank credit by the central banks. Consequently, there is no need for the central banks to maintain gold reserves against the deposits of the commercial banks.

Banks with no fixed reserve requirements. In countries where there are no fixed reserve requirements for the commercial banks it is even more apparent that gold reserves against the deposits of the central banks are unnecessary. The banks in France, for example, maintain only small deposits with the Bank of France, because the latter, like all other central banks, does not pay interest on deposits. Deposits with the Bank of France are not considered as reserves but serve merely to facilitate clearings, and there is a more or less definite relationship between the amount of the deposits of individual banks and the volume of their clearings through the central bank. Thus, so long as a bank continues to clear through the central bank, these balances cannot be withdrawn. They may decrease slightly in periods of depression, and invariably increase whenever business expands and the velocity of circulation of bank credit rises. Therefore they are not reserves in the strict sense of the term, and there is no need for the central bank to maintain gold reserves against them.

This argument is, of course, applicable only to the deposits of commercial banks with central banks, but as a matter of fact most European central banks accept deposits from ordinary business concerns. The principal argument for gold reserves against central bank deposits in general is that, in a gold standard country, these deposits are convertible into gold in the same manner as bank notes. This is a fiction which has survived for many years, although it is only too well known that it is actually impossible for deposits to be converted into gold on a large scale. The $16,400,000,000 of demand deposits of all banks in the United States at the end of June 30, 1932, were theoretically convertible into gold upon demand. Nevertheless, subsequent events proved that when the depositors of the country lose confidence in the banks and endeavor to withdraw any substantial portion of their deposits, there is a complete collapse of the banking structure and the banks are forced to close their doors. Even the huge gold reserves of the United States could not withstand a widespread public panic which resulted in heavy withdrawals of bank deposits. When the conversion of deposits into notes becomes impossible, it follows conclusively that the conversion of deposits into gold is impossible.

Reserve against notes. The fixed reserve requirements against notes in circulation may also be questioned. The term "reserve" implies a fund which can be used in an emergency. For example, if a country is confronted with a temporarily unfavorable balance of payments, in theory it should use the reserve to maintain the stability of the exchange. However, in post-war years central banks have become accustomed to consider some minimum amount of gold reserve as fixed and untouchable. When reserves decline to this minimum, they cease to perform the function for which they are intended, and the government usually authorizes the central bank to suspend gold payments. Under these circumstances, the real reserves consisted of the amounts of gold or foreign exchange over and above the legally fixed minimum.

The holding of gold as cover against notes in circulation is a remnant of the old metallistic theory to the effect that money must have a value in itself. When paper money was adopted it was supposedly given an intrinsic value by providing for the free redemption of notes in specie. The gold exchange and the gold bullion standards deviated further from the old theory. Under the gold bullion standard the central bank is obligated to sell gold at a fixed price in certain minimum quantities, but such sales are made chiefly to meet international obligations or to make payments abroad whenever a shipment of gold becomes more profitable than the buying of foreign bills. Such a standard practically precludes, so far as domestic use is concerned, retention of the idea that currency has an intrinsic value. Under the gold exchange standard there is not even an absolute obligation to redeem notes in gold.

Thus the legal requirements of certain minimum gold reserves against notes in circulation and against demand deposits of central banks have, under modern conditions, considerably outlived their purpose. If the gold standard is to be reëstablished, a change in reserve requirements will have to be made, in order to avoid tying up the credit structure of the world too closely to a metal the output of which is uncertain and the distribution of which is subject to the hazards of international economic conditions. The credit and currency system must be flexible enough to adjust itself readily to the volume of business, and should increase or decrease in accordance with business conditions irrespective of the amount of gold available in individual countries. A country with a stable balance of payments which plays an unimportant rôle in the international money market can get along with little gold, regardless of its domestic demands for credit and for currency. On the other hand, a country where an important international financial center is located ought to have a comparatively large monetary stock of gold.

It is often stated that fixed reserve requirements serve as a barometer for the central banks that aids them in the formulation of their credit policies. It is said that the lowering of the reserve ratio of gold to notes and demand deposits of a central bank is a signal for the contraction of credit and for the raising of interest rates. This, no doubt, was the case before the war, but in the post-war period gold has played only a minor rôle in determining the credit policies of the central banks. With the exception of 1928 and 1929, when the high call rate in the United States attracted a large volume of gold here, the loss of gold by the central banks was often caused by fear and uncertainty rather than by differences in interest rates. Furthermore, during practically the entire post-war period, when the Reserve banks dominated the international money market, their discount policy was determined not by the amount of gold held in the country or by the ratio of gold to notes and demand deposits, but by other considerations. In recent years the central banks have developed, to guide them in their credit policies, other and much more important indices than the ratio of gold to demand liabilities.

Statistical position of gold. Aside from the possibility of effecting economies in the use of gold by modifying reserve requirements, a statistical examination of the gold supplies reveals that the world's monetary gold stock is more than ample to support the necessary volume of credit and currency. The gold holdings of the central banks and treasuries of fifty countries amounted to $11,930,000,000 at the end of 1933, as compared with $4,856,712,000 at the end of 1913—an increase of 148 per cent.[2] Part of this increase represents new gold and part is gold which was formerly in circulation or being hoarded. While the withdrawal of gold from circulation caused an increase in the amount of notes outstanding, thereby necessitating an increase in the amount of gold held as reserve against these notes, it is clear that gold in the vaults of central banks can support at least twice its amount in notes. Furthermore, the fact should not be overlooked that, since the end of the war, substantial progress has been made in the development of the checking system, through which bank deposits are substituted for currency with a resultant decrease in the demand for gold.[3] One may therefore conclude that even before the abandonment of gold by the United States there was no world shortage of gold, and that the monetary stock of gold is still large enough to sustain even a very rapid growth of industrial activity.

---

[2] In terms of the new devalued dollar these stocks amounted to $21,163,-000,000 at the end of July 1934.

[3] In the United States, for example, one dollar in gold can support only about $2.50 of Federal Reserve notes but approximately $28 of bank deposits.

In fact, the devaluation of the dollar and of other currencies has so changed the situation that today one is more justified in speaking of the problem of an *oversupply* rather than a shortage of gold. In the United States, for example, on August 29, 1934, the amount of gold certificates held by the Reserve banks was equivalent to 70.2 per cent of their notes in circulation and demand deposits. On the same date the Treasury held $2,678,178,788 of gold in its various funds, free of all liabilities, which if spent would result in a corresponding increase in member-bank reserve balances on which a much larger volume of bank credit could be based. This condition prevailed at a time when the member banks already held about $2,000,000,000 of excess reserve balances. It is obvious that if all the unused gold and surplus reserve balances of the member banks were used to the fullest extent for credit expansion, there would be a credit inflation on a scale hitherto unknown in the history of the United States.

In other countries a similar situation prevails. On August 30, 1934, the Bank of England held £192,335,992 of gold carried at the statutory price of 77s 9d per standard ounce. This gold was actually worth, at the market price of 140s 3d per fine gold ounce prevailing on the same date, approximately £318,000,000, or $1,594,500,000 at the rate of $5.01⅜ per pound. Also, it is a well-known fact that the British Exchange Equalisation Fund holds considerable amounts of gold, while large quantities of the yellow metal are hoarded by foreigners in the vaults of the British banks. Once the pound is stabilized and confidence returns, the hoarded gold will be sold in the open market and still further increase the gold supply of the Bank of England or of other central banks. These stocks, together with the newly mined gold from the British Dominions and the outflow from the hoards from India, will give Great Britain a supply of gold far beyond its needs. Evidence that similar conditions exist in France, Holland, and Switzerland is shown in Table 1. Furthermore, the legal devaluation of the sterling bloc currencies and the possible devaluation of the currencies of some of the gold bloc countries would greatly increase the value of the central banks' gold reserves in relation to the amount of their notes in circulation and of other demand liabilities.

TABLE 1

RESERVE POSITION OF THE CENTRAL BANKS OF FRANCE, HOLLAND, AND SWITZERLAND

End of		Gold	Notes in Circulation	Ratio of Gold to Notes
	BANK OF FRANCE (In millions of francs)			
1931		68,863	85,725	80.3
1932		83,017	85,028	97.6
1933		77,098	82,613	93.3
September 1934		82,281	81,479	101.0
	NETHERLANDS BANK (In millions of florins)			
1931		887	1,023	86.7
1932		1,033	962	107.4
1933		922	912	101.1
September 1934		864	882	98.0
	NATIONAL BANK OF SWITZERLAND (In millions of francs)			
1931		2,347	1,609	145.9
1932		2,471	1,611	153.4
1933		1,998	1,510	132.3
September 1934		1,808	1,400	129.1

The above discussion clearly indicates that, although the world is suffering from a maldistribution of gold caused by a maladjustment of international balances of payments, the amount of gold is, if anything, too large, and if fully utilized would cause serious credit inflation. The maldistribution of gold, however, has nothing to do with the alleged gold shortage. The former was caused by the faulty economic policies adopted after the war and can be remedied only by the restoration of sound international economic conditions.

Remonetization of silver. In spite of the huge increase in the monetary gold stocks caused by the devaluation of the dollar, the increase in gold production, and the return of gold from hoarding, the demand in the United States for remonetization of silver has continued to be as vociferous as ever, even since the passage of the Silver Purchase Act in June 1934. The advocates of silver remonetization still maintain that the amount of gold is not adequate to serve as a basis for the country's credit and currency structure and that a broadening of the metallic base is necessary in order to bring about an increase in prices and restore business prosperity. This demand for remonetization does not arise in those countries whose gold supplies are small or in the great silver-using countries such as China, for it is realized that since they are not silver producers it would be as difficult for them to acquire silver as gold. These nations, therefore, have shown no interest in the silver legislation in the United States and have indicated no desire to increase their silver stocks or to consider silver as part of their metallic reserves. On the contrary, several of the continental European countries whose gold supplies are nearly exhausted have reduced the silver content of their subsidiary coins and have exported the white metal.

The large silver-using countries, notably China, which is the only country of importance on the silver standard, have on the other hand looked askance at the proposals for the remonetization of silver and the increase of its value in terms of gold. China in particular has taken the position that the higher silver prices resulting from the silver legislation in the United States are having a deflationary effect on that country. In a note of protest to the United States the Chinese Government pointed out that "the rising of silver value in terms of foreign currency has involved severe deflation, economic losses to China, and has dislocated China's balance of payment." Failing to obtain any assurance from the United States that its silver buying program would be modified, the Chinese Government imposed a flexible tax on silver exports which in effect meant the abandonment of the silver standard by that country. So long as there was a free market for silver in Shanghai, the rate for the Shanghai tael was based on the world price of silver, notably the price in the London bullion market. However, since the imposition of the export tax, the Shanghai tael has steadily declined to considerably below its silver parity. Thus, as far as the silver-using countries are concerned, the silver legislation in the United States merely resulted in upsetting the Chinese currency.

It is indeed surprising to find a country like the United States, with more than 2½ billion dollars in gold idle in the Treasury and with more gold in the country than can safely be used as a basis for currency and credit, nationalizing silver and issuing silver certificates at the statutory price of $1.29 per ounce. It is clear that the move to broaden the metallic base of the United States currency, as embodied in the legal provision that silver stocks shall be increased until they represent 25 per cent of the total metallic reserves of the country, either is based on ignorance as to the rôle which gold plays in modern economic society or, more likely, was dictated by political expediency. Certainly it was not justified by any inadequacy of the gold stocks.

One may therefore conclude as follows:

1. The world at large, although faced with the problem of the maldistribution of the yellow metal, is not confronted with a shortage of gold. On the contrary, the world's monetary stock of gold is so large that the real problem is to prevent the gold from causing serious credit inflation.

2. This being the case, there is no need for the remonetization of silver. In fact, with the exception of the United States, where the use of silver is a political question, leading countries of the world have shown no great interest in silver legislation.

3. Events since 1929 have shown that gold in most countries has ceased to be the basis for currency and credit, and the credit policies of some of the large central banks are determined without regard to their gold position. In view of these developments, and particularly in order to dissociate the credit structure of the individual countries from the hazards of gold production and of gold movements caused by abnormal and erratic international economic developments, abolishment of minimum required gold reserves against the demand deposits of central banks seems advisable.

4. In view of the almost complete withdrawal of gold from circulation and of the fact, demonstrated by the experience of the United States and other countries, that notes cannot be converted into gold on a large scale, it would seem advisable to modify the gold reserves held by central banks against notes in circulation and to coördinate them with the international financial position of each individual country.

5. Once gold ceases to be a factor in the volume of credit and currency, all fears of a gold shortage will disappear and the demand for devaluation of gold and/or for remonetization of silver will lose one of the most popular arguments advanced in their favor. Credit policies should then be determined, without regard to gold, by the central bank authorities or, more accurately, by the governments.

The rôle of gold in the future. Recent monetary legislation in the United States has been based to a considerable extent on the erroneous idea that the gold standard, as it has operated in the past, has been responsible for most of the economic ills from which the world is suffering. It has been repeatedly stated that there is a definite relationship between the price of gold and commodity prices, and the devaluation of the dollar was based on this premise. Is this premise sound? In the following paragraph it will be analyzed.

In our modern currency and credit system gold serves: (1) as a standard of value; (2) as a basis for currency; (3) as a basis for credits; and (4) as a medium of settling marginal balances among the various economic political units.   Gold as a standard of value is described in every elementary textbook and needs no further discussion.   It is the metal in terms of which currency units are defined by the laws of the individual nations, and its price in terms of local currency remains unchanged so long as the country remains on the gold basis.   In this way the various currencies of the world are coördinated and maintained in a certain definite relationship with each other which is determined by the quantity and fineness of the gold content of each currency unit.   Experience has shown that no other metal can better perform this function and that the complete abandonment of gold would lead to currency chaos.

Since gold forms the basis for currency values, it has also become the standard of measurement through which prices of all other commodities and of all services are expressed.   It is this function of gold which has given rise to the belief that there is a definite relationship between gold and commodity prices.   When prices are high, it is said that gold is cheap; and, vice versa, that when prices are low gold is high or dear.   In fact, gold figures in few if any national or international transactions.   It is merely a symbol, the actual transactions being carried out through currency or bank deposits.   The price of gold as measured by other commodities in modern society, where purchasing power is chiefly represented by bank deposits, affects no one except the gold producer, to whom the yellow metal is merely a commodity.   Yet the belief prevails, and it has found its way into the laws of the United States, that since commodity prices in a country on the gold standard are expressed in terms of gold, the lowering of the gold content of the currency unit will result in higher commodity prices in terms of the devalued or depreciated currency unit.   To the uninitiated layman, this seems on the surface to be logical and correct. Yet even a superficial analysis soon proves the fallacy of this reasoning.

The devaluation of the dollar did not increase the volume of currency and credit outstanding in the country and, hence, it did not affect the purchasing power of the people. By far the largest part of the population, if they had no access to the newspapers, would never have known that there had been any change in the gold content of the currency. Since the devaluation of the dollar did not increase the purchasing power of the country, it could have no influence on the demand for commodities, except a psychological one, and hence no influence on prices or on services. It cannot, of course, be denied that the devaluation of a currency has a psychological effect in that it encourages speculation in commodities and securities. This psychological influence, however, is only temporary in character and lasts only so long as the currency fluctuates. Once the currency is stabilized, either *de facto* or legally, this influence disappears.

The only prices which are directly affected by currency depreciation are those of imported commodities and, to a lesser extent, of exported commodities. It is but natural that, since the unit of the devalued currency is worth less in terms of a given foreign currency, a larger number of the units must be paid for the same quantity of goods. Countries which depend to a large extent on foreign trade therefore feel immediately the effect of currency devaluation, while nations such as the United States, whose foreign trade represents only a small fraction of the total volume of commodities produced and consumed in the country, are but little affected by a decrease in the gold content of the currency. Gold can, however, exercise an influence on economic conditions if, through its functions as a basis for currency and credit, it affects the volume of purchasing power.

Gold as a basis for currency. In all countries on the gold standard the laws establish a more or less fixed relationship between the volume of currency outstanding and the amount of gold, or its equivalent in foreign exchange, held in the vaults of the central bank and/or the Treasury. A decrease in the amount of gold, unless counteracted by open-market operations, leads to either a decline in the amount of notes in circulation, a reduction in the deposits of the commercial banks with the central bank, or an increase in borrowing by the former from the latter. This consequence is due to the fact that gold, as a rule, can be obtained only from the central bank, and that in order to pay for it, the banks must do so either with currency, with their own deposits kept with the central bank, or with a loan from the latter. Once this takes place, however, the interest rate rises, banks curtail their loans, and business conditions are affected. Such was the case in the pre-war period when the international gold standard operated successfully.

However, in the post-war period, and particularly since 1931, gold has ceased to exercise a major influence on currency and on credit. Whenever a country was confronted with a serious loss of gold, it invariably imposed foreign exchange restrictions or abandoned the gold standard, and the reduction in the monetary stock of gold was not permitted to affect the currency and credit policy of the central bank. Germany is a good case in point. Although the stock of gold and of foreign exchange declined from RM 2,685,000,000 [4] at the end of 1930 to RM 77,000,000 at the end of June 1934, the amount of Reichsbank notes fluctuated only between RM 4,778,000,000 and RM 3,777,000,000 during the same period, a fluctuation determined by business conditions and not by the movement of gold. As a matter of fact, the Reichsbank was authorized by law to substitute certain securities for gold as a reserve against notes in circulation. Thus, while there is a relationship between gold and currency under the normal operation of

---

[4] This does not include all foreign exchange, but only that used as reserve against notes in circulation.

the gold standard, this relationship is severed whenever the supply of gold of an individual country is exhausted or materially reduced, because under such conditions laws or decrees are immediately passed which make the central banks entirely independent of their metallic reserves.

Gold as a basis for credit. If, under present conditions, the influence exercised by gold on the volume of currency is only of nominal importance, the influence of gold on credit is still further removed. Even under normal conditions, the amount of gold needed to support a given volume of bank credit is very small. In the United States, for example, where the member banks are required to maintain fixed reserves with the reserve banks, $1,000 of deposits kept with a member bank require a reserve in the reserve banks of only $35. Even this small amount need not be in gold; it may be in lawful money. In some countries, such as England, no gold reserve against the central bank's deposits is necessary. Furthermore, in the case of reserves against central bank deposits, as also against notes, the prescribed requirements are maintained only so long as the reserve is ample, and when the reserve is reduced or depleted the requirements are suspended.

Moreover, gold loses its influence over the credit and currency policies of the central banks not only when the metallic reserves are depleted but also where there is too large a supply of gold. The sterilization of gold during the entire post-war period through open market operations, and the acquisition by, or the shifting of gold to, the British Exchange Equalisation Fund and the Stabilization Fund in the United States, are good examples of the efforts made to prevent gold from exercising its full influence on credit and on the credit policies of the central banks. While this development has been regretted by many, it is not without benefits. Credit and currency are merely a handmaid to industry and trade, and their volume in the post-war period was determined not by a given amount of a certain precious metal held by the central bank, but rather by business conditions and often by the policies of the central bank authorities. Gold as a basis for currency and credit, under these circumstances, could not exercise any material influence on the volume of credit and of currency, and hence had little influence on the movement of prices.

Gold as a medium for settling marginal international balances. While gold has lost much of its importance as a basis for currency and credit, it continues to perform the very important function of an instrument through which individual nations are enabled to settle marginal international balances. Although it is possible that at some future time a satisfactory mechanism may be established to facilitate international clearings, it is still an open question whether even such a mechanism would entirely eliminate gold shipments. It is the shipment of gold, in the absence of foreign exchange restrictions, which keeps the various currencies at par and prevents violent currency fluctuations.

Although deprived of its influence on currency and credit, gold in the future will act as an international standard of value and as a medium of settling international balances. Restricted to these narrow functions, it will permit the restoration of stable currency conditions without interfering with the credit policies of the various central banks. A return to gold on this basis would mean the restoration of the gold standard in its narrow nationalistic sense but also the end of the standard in its broad international aspect, since gold movements would cease to affect credit conditions. In this respect, however, the gold standard would merely be adapted to present-day circumstances. When the world economy was based on the principle of division of labor, with a comparatively free interchange of commodities and labor, the gold standard could operate internationally and act somewhat as an equalizer of economic conditions throughout the world. But in an age of nationalism, based on the principle of economic self-sufficiency, the gold standard cannot operate on an international scale and must give way to the narrow nationalistic concept.

CHAPTER II

The International Money Market

Introduction. The economic organization of modern society, with its division of labor and interchange of commodities and services, together with increased facilities for communication, has brought the nations of the world much closer together than ever before. This economic integration of nations has given rise to a multitude of transactions which are financed through what are termed the *international money and capital markets*. The rôle of each of these markets is distinctly different, although it is frequently impossible to draw a sharp line of demarcation between them. Each market must be discussed separately before the inter-relationships of all the markets can be clearly understood. The international money market will be dealt with first.

International money market defined. The term *international money market* refers, in its narrower technical sense, to the leading financial centers of the world in which monetary transactions are constantly conducted on an international scale. It embraces those markets which are so closely knitted together by the constant shifting of funds that the effect, normally, is the equalization of interest rates in such centers. The international money market is not a separate organization but is to be understood as embracing the entire monetary machinery of the principal financial centers of the world. Notwithstanding its far-flung operations and its heterogeneous composition, it is efficient in the accumulation of the short-term funds of the world and in the employment of such funds in those quarters where they are needed most and where they will earn the most favorable rate of interest.

In the broader sense, the international money market embraces the interrelations of the individual money centers of the world and the totality of their activities, including all types of short-term financial transactions, which constitute the great body of what is commonly called international finance. Reflecting as it does the economic relations among the various nations, the international money market is a good current indicator of the political and economic status of the civilized world. Political stability combined with economic equilibrium brings about a greater measure of economic intercourse among nations. This, in turn, stimulates the movement of funds from one center to another and tends to increase economic activity. Similarly, an economic breakdown, particularly if combined with or resulting from a political crisis, results in stagnation in the international flow of funds, which in turn adversely affects prices as well as economic conditions throughout the world.

Political instability resulting in money market stagnation. As a general rule, stagnation in the international money market develops only after a period of hectic activity caused, chiefly, by the desire to liquidate existing outstanding commitments in the disturbed market or even in other markets. Impending stagnation is reflected principally by the decline in new lending operations. A panicky repatriation of funds sets in, resulting in wide fluctuations of exchange rates and in a movement of gold, not only from debtor to creditor countries but also from the leading financial centers where these funds have been temporarily employed. If this crisis does not abate, it invariably leads to the imposition of foreign exchange restrictions and, ultimately, to the legal or technical abandonment of the gold standard by the countries most affected by the withdrawals of funds.

These developments may be illustrated by the events that took place at the outbreak of the war in 1914. The international money market was plunged immediately into great disorder. Bankers and others having funds in foreign countries endeavored to withdraw them as fast as they could, and governments, fearing a loss of gold, imposed gold embargoes. Thereafter the international money market became stagnant, and remained so until conditions warranted the resumption of the international flow of capital and credit.

A similar chain of events took place in the summer of 1931, when the financial crisis of that year resulted in an unprecedented withdrawal of foreign funds which, for several years previously, had been used as working capital on the continent of Europe, particularly in Germany. The rapid withdrawals of funds were stopped by the abandonment of the gold standard by Great Britain and a number of other countries, by the widespread adoption of exchange restrictions, and by "standstill" agreements on foreign credits. Afterwards the international money market quieted down for a short time, but the banking crisis in the United States in the early part of 1933 caused a huge exodus of funds from this country, only to be followed by a return of the funds after the passage of the Gold Reserve Act of January 30, 1934. After each of these convulsions, the movement of international funds came almost to a complete standstill and at present, for all practical purposes, the international money market is non-existent.

Prerequisites of an international money market.—*Stable currencies.* Until the abandonment of the gold standard by England in September 1931, a stable currency was thought to be one of the first prerequisites of a financial center of international importance. But London has continued since then to be an important international money market, and hence, while the conclusion is unwarranted that a stable currency is no longer a necessity, yet it is evident that in the present chaotic state of the world currency stability has become more of a relative matter.

London has maintained its position chiefly because a number of countries followed the example of Great Britain in abandoning the gold standard and formed what has come to be known as the "sterling bloc." Their currencies are linked with the British currency and have moved more or less in unison with the pound sterling. The prestige of London as an international money market has grown in spite of the fact that the pound sterling is unstable in relation to gold.' Two reasons may be assigned for this development: (1) the British Equalisation Fund has skillfully and conservatively managed the exchange market with a view to preventing sharp fluctuations in exchange rates; and (2) there has been no loss of confidence in the pound. On the other hand, New York failed to attract foreign funds on a large scale even after the passage of the Gold Reserve Act.

The reason for this apparently inconsistent development is not far to seek. In the first place, Great Britain abandoned the gold standard under circumstances of economic necessity which made this act justifiable, and furthermore, she did not adopt a definite policy of currency depreciation after the abandonment of gold. The abandonment of the gold standard by the United States, on the other hand, was not dictated by economic necessity and was not justified, at least in the eyes of foreigners who had balances in the United States or who held American securities stated in gold. In the second place, the United States Government required all private gold holdings in the country to be turned over to the Treasury, and dealing in gold was made subject to the regulations of the Secretary of the Treasury. But no such drastic action was taken by the British Government, and the London gold market is still free and unrestricted, thereby permitting the free withdrawal of gold from London. Thus the monetary policies of the United States, when contrasted with the conservative policies of Great .Britain, were not calculated to inspire confidence in the future of the dollar. This combination of factors enabled London, in spite of the handicap of a fluctuating currency, to preserve its position as an international money market while New York declined in importance in international finance.

A free exchange market. A free exchange market—that is, the complete absence of restrictions upon the conversion of local currency into foreign exchange, and vice versa—is the second prerequisite of a market forming part of the international money market. Laws themselves are never entirely effective in preventing the flight or the export of capital; actually, absolute freedom in this matter is essential to the intricate financial operations of an international money center. Individuals or institutions placing their funds in foreign countries wish to be certain that they will be able to withdraw these funds quickly and without inconvenience at any time they may desire. Thus, at the present time, although the German currency has remained stable and interest rates in Berlin are substantially higher than in other important financial centers, foreign banks are unwilling to make further commitments in Germany because, among other things, of the restrictions placed upon all payments in foreign exchange.

A sound banking structure. A third prerequisite for any center constituting a part of the international money market is a sound banking structure with banks of international repute and with international connections. In the absence of such banks, foreign institutions or nationals of a foreign country are unwilling to place short-term funds at the disposal of another country. For example, the acceptance business, which—as will be seen later—constitutes an important part of all the transactions of the international money market, depends entirely upon the credit of the individual banks accepting bills. In such transactions the international standing of the bank is of primary importance, since an exporter or his bank would not be willing to receive a draft on the importer's bank unless the latter were well and favorably known to the exporter's bank. Similarly, banks located in leading financial centers often will not finance transactions between two foreign countries unless a bank of standing in one of the two countries guarantees the transaction.

A discount market. In addition to the conditions of a sound and stable currency, a free exchange market, and a banking system of international repute, in order to be a part of the international money market a financial center must afford adequate facilities for the investment of short-term funds. The most favored type of credit instrument for this purpose is the banker's bill, or banker's acceptance. Before the war, sterling bills were the most popular type of credit instrument for the investment of the liquid funds of the world. After the war, dollar acceptances rivaled sterling bills in international importance, while mark and franc bills practically disappeared. Recent financial events, particularly the departure of England and the United States from the gold standard, have greatly altered the policies of the banks concerning the investment of their liquid reserves. Instead of holding a large portion of their reserves in foreign markets, even in such a liquid form as bankers' acceptances, they have preferred to keep most of their reserves at home and to hold in the form of gold such funds as they may place abroad. It is said that many millions of dollars in gold are held by foreigners in the vaults of British institutions. This situation, however, is temporary and merely reflects the prevailing economic and financial uncertainties. It will disappear as soon as more normal conditions are established. Surplus funds kept in the form of gold are idle funds and an economic waste; if they are employed in a leading money market, they will not only earn a return but will also aid in the financing of international trade and other transactions.

Not every financial center has developed an acceptance market strong enough to attract foreign funds, but each important money market has its own machinery developed in accordance with economic conditions and financial practices peculiar to its own country.   Thus, in New York, the call money market under normal conditions absorbs a substantial amount of foreign funds, while in Germany, from 1925 to the middle of 1931, deposits with the large banks and the discount of domiciled bills constituted favorite forms of investment for foreign funds in that country.

In addition to the above-mentioned prerequisites of an international financial center, the country in which the center is located must enjoy a certain degree of political stability.   The international money market is extremely sensitive to political events, and any disturbing development in the sphere of politics invariably causes a withdrawal of foreign funds, often on such a scale as to disrupt the money market seriously and jeopardize the stability of the currency.

Operation of the international money market.   The primary function of the international money market is the constant shifting of funds from one center to another. Frequently this is an end in itself, in that the movement of funds arises from the desire to profit by the variations in interest rates prevailing in different centers.   But for the most part the reasons are deeper than this.   International commerce and all other international economic activities necessitate the transfer of funds either to cover individual transactions or to settle balances between nations.

Every item that enters into the balances of payments of nations is potentially the cause of a movement of funds in the international money market.   Shipments of commodities, rendering of services, emigrant remittances, and purchases by foreigners of the internal securities of a country all have the same effect as the movement of short-term funds from country to country caused by differences in interest rates.   The method of remitting funds is the same irrespective of the purpose of the remittance, and the transactions are usually executed by a comparatively small group of banks engaged in international business. Aside from the movement of gold, either through actual shipments or earmarking, the settlement of practically all international accounts is done through bankers' bills or cable transfers. Unless effected through a movement of gold, the transfer of funds from one center to another is accomplished simply by bookkeeping transactions showing changes in the ownership of the funds.

Illustrations of shifting of funds. Let us assume, for example, that a London bank with a deposit in a New York bank desires to place funds in the New York call money market. It may instruct the New York bank to place part of its deposits in the call money market, in which case there is an increase in the broker's loans of New York banks for the account of others. In this instance, there has been no transfer of new funds but simply a change in the manner in which existing funds are employed. Or, suppose the London bank asks its New York correspondent to sell some of the acceptances, Treasury notes, or Treasury certificates of indebtedness held for its account, and to place the proceeds "on call." In this case, the ownership of the acceptances or Treasury obligations changes hands, and the British bank, which was formerly a creditor of a bank (the acceptor) or of the United States Government, becomes a creditor of a broker. In these two cases, the British bank already had funds in New York and merely shifted them from one individual market in New York to another. Such transactions have the same result as if executed by any American owner of short-term funds.

But suppose the London bank has no funds available in New York and decides to transfer funds for investment in the New York money market. Suppose it is desired to transfer £100,000 to New York, and that the rate for demand bills on London in New York is $5.00. The New York bank acting as its correspondent will be instructed to draw a demand draft on the London bank for £100,000. The draft will then be sold in the open market for about

$500,000, which amount the New York bank will place in the call money market for the account of the London bank. In this case, too, there was no actual inflow of funds, for the sterling bill was purchased in the United States with New York funds by a person or concern who had occasion to remit this amount to London. Hence, the entire transaction was merely a bookkeeping entry to record a shifting of the ownership of funds. Before the transaction, the owner of the dollar funds was an American resident; after the transaction, the owner is a British bank.

It is obvious, therefore, that the statement so often made that the New York money market is influenced by the inflow or outflow of foreign funds is inaccurate. As far as international transactions are concerned, only an outflow or an inflow of gold can affect the New York money market or any money market in a country on the gold standard. But the international movement of funds may, of course, affect the *individual markets* of a money market.

While the shifting of funds through the drawing of bankers' bills or cable transfers has no effect on the credit structure of a country on the gold standard unless it reaches the point where gold is shipped, it does have a decided effect upon the exchange market. The more bills that are drawn on London in order to place funds in the New York money market for the account of British banks or others, the greater is the supply of sterling bills; and if the supply increases in relation to the demand, the sterling exchange rate tends to decline.

Central banks and the international money market. Since the movement of funds in reality involves merely a change in the ownership of funds, the central banks are directly affected only when exchange rates vary from par sufficiently to cause gold movements. In this case, an increase in the central bank discount rate or the tightening of credit conditions at home through open market operations, or a combination of these measures, are used to halt the outflow of funds and check the loss of gold. Reversal of these policies under normal conditions tends to discourage gold imports. Manipulation of discount rates and open market operations are used chiefly by central banks on the gold standard. In recent years London has relied more on the Equalisation Fund, while in New York the reserve banks have had, since March 10, 1933, the power to supervise and regulate transfers of capital abroad.

Since the movement of gold exercises an influence on the money market of each individual center, it is obvious that in normal times the discount policy of the central banks of countries on the gold standard is often affected by conditions prevailing in other financial centers. Central banks in those countries where financial centers operate as part of the international money market must, under normal conditions, take into consideration the situation of other international money markets in formulating their policies. This, however, has not always been the case, and the failure of an important central bank to consider the international financial situation has created difficulties for the other important money markets.

Discount rate and open market operations. Many instances of the raising of the discount rate to end an outflow of gold may be cited in the cases of England, Holland, and to a lesser extent the United States. When the discount rate has not proved an effective measure, open market operations have frequently been undertaken by those central banks that are permitted by law to engage in such operations with a view to tightening or easing the local money market, and thus influencing interest rates sufficiently to reverse the movement of funds and, consequently, of gold. Thus, in 1927 the Federal Reserve banks bought securities in the open market, and this easy money policy led to a substantial outflow of gold during 1927.

The experience of the reserve banks in 1927, 1928, and 1929 demonstrates how difficult it is at times to reconcile the internal money market situation of an individual country with that of the international money market. The lowering of the discount rate and open market purchases by the reserve banks in 1927 favorably affected the international money market, but created artificially low rates of interest in the United States which, in turn, tended to stimulate speculation here. Vice versa, the raising of the discount rate by the reserve banks in 1928–29 was intended primarily to tighten the domestic credit situation in order to curb excessive speculation, but it forced all other central banks to raise their rates in order to prevent serious gold losses. The conflict between the individual market and the international markets has been due chiefly to the fact that, in the United States, domestic business conditions invariably overshadow the influence exercised by foreign developments.

Foreign exchange operations of central banks. Prior to the collapse of the international money market in 1931 some central banks, besides making changes in the discount rate and operating in the open market, engaged in foreign exchange operations in order to exercise an influence on the movement of short-term funds. This method has been used quite often and with considerable success by the central banks on the continent of Europe. By selling foreign exchange, a central bank could bring about an appreciation in the exchange value of its own currency and make the inflow of funds less profitable, since more units of a foreign currency are then required to buy a stated amount of local currency.

For example, the par of exchange of the German reichsmark was 23.82 cents in United States currency prior to the devaluation of the dollar. If, through its own initiative, the Reichsbank brought about an appreciation of the mark to 23.85 cents, it became less profitable for a German to borrow dollars abroad, because in converting his dollars into marks he suffered a loss. Vice versa, when a central bank depresses the exchange value of the currency, it becomes more profitable for banks in that country to borrow abroad. To continue with the same example: if the

Reichsbank, through actively buying dollars, brought about a decrease in the value of the mark from 23.82 cents to 23.77 cents, then borrowers of dollars would obtain more marks for their dollars.

While the international flow of funds and of capital may affect the policies of all central banks of countries which are a part of the international money market, its influence has been particularly marked in the case of the central banks of debtor countries, particularly those on the continent of Europe which borrowed heavily abroad on short-term. As a matter of fact, one may safely state that the discount policies of the Reichsbank, the Austrian National Bank, and the Hungarian National Bank, from 1924 to the middle of 1931, were to a large extent determined by the inflow and outflow of short-term funds. In the more normal periods before the war, the balance of payments of the various countries was more or less adjusted, and the international flow of funds and of gold merely acted as a stabilizer of interest and exchange rates. But in the post-war period the flow of funds became largely one-sided—that is, to those countries which lacked working capital. These funds therefore, although short-term in character, had all the earmarks of long-term loans.

After the collapse of the international money market in 1931, the methods of control over the international flow of short-term funds changed. Most of the debtor countries established foreign exchange restrictions and placed all international transactions under government or central bank supervision. In England and in the United States, the abandonment of the gold standard removed the obligation of the central banks to sell gold, and thus, particularly after the establishment of the Equalisation and Stabilization Funds, the movement of funds ceased to exercise an influence on the central bank policies. At present, the discount policy of almost every central bank is determined by domestic considerations exclusively—a clear indication of the stagnation prevailing in the international money market.

Short-term loans in the money market. The flow of funds from country to country for short-term investment under normal conditions depends chiefly upon the movement of interest rates. If interest rates are higher in New York than in London, Americans having funds in London will tend to withdraw them, and the British banks and others having funds to invest will be inclined to place them in New York. The fluctuation in interest rates that took place in the post-war years was chiefly responsible for the huge movement of funds from New York, London, Zurich, and Amsterdam, and to a smaller extent from Paris, to the Continental European countries such as Germany, Austria, and Hungary. Short-term loans made by the banks in the leading financial centers to governments, political subdivisions, or corporations of other countries were motivated by the same factors and belong to this class of transaction.

The essential quality of a short-term investment from the standpoint of the money market is liquidity. This quality is found to a marked degree in acceptances, call loans, short-term government securities, and loans made to finance self-liquidating transactions. Short-term loans and investments, however, are liquid only if they do not become part of the necessary working capital of the nation. If, on the other hand, foreign short-term funds are used for transactions which should be financed by long-term loans, or if they become part of the permanent working capital of a country, then their quality of liquidity disappears and the debtors are not able to repay their loans on short notice. This was particularly the case in Germany, where short-term credits were used for purposes which should have been financed with long-term capital.

Similarly, in order to preserve their liquid character, short-term funds placed in foreign financial centers must bear a certain relationship to the gold and foreign exchange reserves of the central bank and of the leading financial institutions. It is obvious that if the volume of foreign short-term funds placed in one market is much larger than the liquid foreign assets owned by this market, any withdrawal on a large scale results either in abandonment of the gold standard or in the "freezing" of these short-term funds through subsequent arrangements between the creditors and debtors, such as the "standstill" agreements of Germany, Austria, and Hungary. Under more or less normal conditions, a change in the discount rate by the central bank of the debtor country can prevent too heavy an inflow or outflow of foreign funds. In the abnormal post-war period, however, the shortage of funds in some countries and the discrepancy of interest rates between debtor and creditor countries were so great that the discount policy of the central banks in debtor countries was without effect in preventing the inflow of funds, and the political and financial crises which marked this period made impossible any central bank policy intended to stem a too rapid withdrawal of foreign funds.

Abnormal movements of funds. In contrast to the shifting of funds caused by the difference in interest rates, there is the movement of funds caused by political motives, monetary uncertainty, and exchange speculation. In such cases the movement of funds is abnormal and is due only to the unusual conditions prevailing at the moment.

International movements of funds designed to promote national political policies are not unusual, and in fact such tactics were often used in pre-war days by the foreign offices of the leading countries. In the post-war period, however, the use of financial measures as a political weapon reached such a point that it may reasonably be said that the collapse of the international money market and the financial panic of 1931–32 were to some extent the result of "too much politics in international banking."

One of the many instances of the shifting of funds for political reasons was the withdrawal of French funds from

Germany during the negotiations on the Young Plan in
1929.   Dr. Schacht, then president of the Reichsbank and
chief German delegate to the Experts' Conference in Paris,
relates in his book, *The End of Reparations,* how the French
authorities endeavored, through ever-increasing withdrawals of funds from Germany during the negotiations, to
weaken the resistance of the German delegation to the
French proposals.

> At first slowly, then at an increasing tempo, the Reichsbank,
> which had entered the Paris negotiations with an unusually
> large gold and foreign exchange reserve, began to note a with-
> drawal of foreign exchange. . . . After the German memo-
> randum, with its proposals for the solution of the reparations
> problem, had been met by a complete unwillingness on the
> French side to discuss its suggestions, throwing the Conference
> into a crisis, the withdrawal of foreign exchange suddenly in-
> creased at such a pace that the Reichsbank to maintain the
> stability of the currency could not further delay raising the
> discount rate.   This was done on April 25, 1929. . . . Simul-
> taneously the big banks of Berlin received from various French
> financial institutions letters . . . referring in unmistakable
> terms to the Paris negotiations, announcing a curtailment of
> the credits which had been put at Germany's disposal.
>
> This was followed by such a heavy withdrawal of foreign
> exchange that on May 7, 1929, the coverage in gold and ex-
> change had, at 41%, almost reached the legal minimum. . . .
> This French attack, during the Paris Conference of experts,
> upon the German currency was the seed of that evergrowing
> lack of confidence which today (1931) hangs heavy over the
> entire economic world.[1]

The movement of funds motivated by political and not
by economic considerations is unsound.   It tends not only
to withdraw funds from where they are needed for sound
economic purposes, but also to create abnormal money
market conditions in the country affected and to upset the
functioning of the entire international money market machinery.

---

[1] Schacht, Hjalmar, *The End of Reparations* (tr. by Lewis Gannett),
Robert O. Ballou, New York, 1931, pp. 88–91. Reprinted by permission
of the publishers.

Movement of funds caused by speculation. The movement of funds caused by exchange speculation has played an important rôle in post-war years and has resulted in sharp fluctuations of the exchanges of the countries affected. Exchange speculation is international in character and it may be carried out through any one or more of several centers, depending upon the point of operation which offers a greater advantage.

Aside from the exchange battles which took place in Amsterdam over the German, Austrian, and Hungarian currencies shortly after the war, the most notable cases of exchange speculation were in the French franc during the summer of 1926 and in the American dollar during 1933. Owing to the belief that the French currency was about to collapse completely, an international speculative raid was made on the franc during the summer of 1926. Speculators in the United States and in practically every country on the continent of Europe participated in this raid. A credit of $100,000,000 granted by a group of financial houses in New York and elsewhere to the French government brought this speculation to a halt, with disastrous results to those who had sold the franc short. Then, after the reorganization of the French budget and the *de facto* stabilization of the franc at approximately 3.92 cents in September 1926, the speculators reversed their operations and bought francs heavily in the belief that the French currency would further appreciate. It was only the law of 1926 which enabled the Bank of France to issue notes over and above the maximum previously fixed, provided they were secured 100 per cent by gold and/or foreign exchange, the latter clause preventing international speculation from bringing about a rapid upswing in the franc.

The banking crisis in the United States during the early part of 1933, and the agitation for the abandonment of the gold standard, caused considerable short selling of the dollar. This time, however, the subsequent acts of the American government justified the calculations of the speculators, and they reaped huge profits when gold payments were suspended. Speculative raids on various currencies were numerous during the eventful years 1931–34, and they resulted in an uneconomic criss-cross movement of funds. But, by the middle of 1934, speculation in foreign exchange was practically checked by the rigid foreign exchange restrictions imposed in a number of countries, by the successful operation of the British Exchange Equalisation Fund, and by the firm stand of the central banks of the gold bloc countries against currency depreciation or devaluation. Towards the end of 1934, however, the gold bloc currencies weakened again.

Movement of funds caused by flight of capital. The flight of capital has also been an important factor in the movement of funds and of gold, and it has left a deep mark on the international money market. During the war, there was a flight of capital from some of the belligerent countries, such as Germany, Austro-Hungary, and Russia. After the war, the movement was accelerated and it affected most of the formerly belligerent countries. The flight of capital was caused either by the fear of the depreciation of the currency, by political uncertainty, or by high taxation. But irrespective of its causes, the effects were the same. It resulted in large offerings of currencies or securities of countries from which a flight of capital was taking place, and it brought about an increase in the demand for the exchange of those countries in which the capital was seeking refuge. In the post-war flight of capital, the United States, Great Britain, Switzerland, and Holland were the principal recipients of foreign funds. The effect of the inflow of funds caused by the flight of capital was felt in England, for example, during 1926, when in spite of adverse economic conditions in that country caused by the general strike and the coal strike, the pound sterling remained stable, chiefly because the pound was supported by the demand for sterling arising from the flight of French capital.

Just as the flight of capital from France to England and the United States strengthened the currencies of the two latter countries, similarly the return or repatriation of French capital exercised an adverse influence on these currencies and, in the case of England, was partly responsible for the decline of the pound in the fall of 1931. The collapse of the international money market in 1931, following the banking crisis in Austria and Germany, set in motion another flight of capital. While almost every nation suffered from this movement, the United States and Great Britain were more affected than any other countries. At first the United States had been the recipient of capital from Great Britain. Soon, however, the tide changed and the United States witnessed a considerable flight of capital, which was reversed only after the passage of the Gold Reserve Act on January 30, 1934. The magnitude of this movement of capital can best be gauged from the huge criss-cross movement of gold. (See Table 2.)

TABLE 2

GOLD MOVEMENTS TO AND FROM THE UNITED STATES
(In thousands of dollars; total net imports (+) or net exports (—).)

	1932	1934
January	—72,950	—2,767
February	—90,567	+452,571
March	—24,671	+237,336
April	—30,239	+54,784
May	—195,514	+33,583
June	—206,047	+63,705
July	—3,437	+52,346
August	+6,103	+37,225
September	+27,897	—18,670
October	+20,613	+10,837
November	+21,740	+120,889
December	+100,859	

Difference between normal and abnormal movement of funds. While the effect of the abnormal movement of funds on the exchanges of the various countries is the same as that of the movement of funds caused by the difference of interest rates, the economic effect is quite different. In the latter case, funds are shifted from centers where they are not needed to those places where the demand for funds or shortage of working capital has resulted in high rates of interest. Even when the movement of funds is caused by a great speculative boom, as was the case in the United States during 1928 and 1929, the inflow of foreign funds performs a certain economic function, for ultimately funds used on the stock market find their way into business. Such an inflow of funds may denude the international money market of funds needed for other purposes, such as the financing of foreign trade, but at least it creates temporary prosperity in the country drawing the funds and provides a high return to the owners of the funds.

A movement of funds caused by abnormal factors, on the other hand, usually results in the accumulation of capital where it is least needed and where the return on the money is consequently very low. Thus, the withdrawal of funds by France from Germany during the Young Plan Conference, and again the withdrawal of funds from England prior to the abandonment of specie payments in 1931, resulted in the accumulation of funds in France, where they were not needed; at the same time it deprived the countries from which the funds were drawn, of capital which could be usefully employed at rates much higher than those prevailing in France. The movement of funds and of gold from and to the United States during 1932–34 is a further example of the harmful effects of such movements caused by uneconomic factors.

Similarly, the international movement of funds caused by exchange speculation is economically unsound and harmful. Where the speculation is based on an expected appreciation of a currency, as was the case in England and the Scandinavian countries in 1925, it leads to an inflow of funds which may not be needed and to a rapid appreciation of the currency, which in turn has adverse effects on economic conditions in the country affected. Selling exchanges "short" for speculative purposes does not lead to a movement of funds from one country to another, but is one of the most harmful operations on the international money market. It is often responsible for sharp, erratic movements of the exchanges and is, in itself, often an important factor in the depreciation of currencies. Economically it has no justification, for it does not tend to act as a stabilizing influence in the manner claimed by the proponents of "short-selling" on the security exchanges. It not only tends to disorganize the economic structure of the country involved but may, as in the case of the short selling of the French franc in 1926, bring ruin to banking institutions and individuals participating in the speculation.

While a flight of capital may be justified as far as the individual owner of the capital is concerned, it also constitutes an uneconomic movement of funds. It invariably produces an outflow of capital, from centers where it is needed and where it brings a higher return, to those centers which already have more funds than can be economically used. The flight of capital often coincides with the withdrawal of foreign funds, and thus not only denudes the country affected of working capital but also creates a serious currency and exchange problem. The flight of capital from Germany from September 1930 until rigid foreign exchange restrictions were imposed is a good example of the uneconomic effects of such a movement. It resulted in the placing of German funds in Switzerland, Holland, and the United States, countries which already had an abundance of gold, at a time when Germany was suffering severely from a lack of capital and when interest rates were abnormally high. While the flight of capital from the United States during the latter part of 1932 and up to March 1933 did not deprive this country of capital needed at home, yet it accentuated the banking panic and increased the distrust of Americans with regard to their own currency.

The abnormal movement of funds is not the cause of abnormal business and political conditions, as is often claimed; on the contrary it is the result of the uncertain political and economic conditions prevailing in one individual market or in the international money market as a whole. The movement of funds and the fluctuation of interest rates are merely barometers reflecting the more fundamental conditions prevailing in one or several countries. The movement of funds caused by differences in interest rates reflects more or less normal conditions prevailing in individual markets or in the international money markets as a whole. On the other hand, the movement of funds caused by political motives, exchange speculation, or fear reflects an abnormal economic and political situation prevailing in one or several countries, or in the international money market generally.

Financing of world trade. The international shifting of funds caused by differences in interest rates normally attracts funds to places in which they can find profitable investment and from which, as it is believed, the funds may be withdrawn at the option of the owner. In the post-war period up to 1931, a part of the funds available in the international market found their way into such markets as Berlin, Vienna, and Budapest, where they were used chiefly for financing domestic trade and industry; but as a general rule the liquid funds of the world are placed in stronger financial centers, such as London, New York, Amsterdam, and Zurich, in which they can find safe temporary employment. A considerable part of these funds, as well as the liquid funds of the individual centers themselves, represent the short-term working capital of the world. Through the facilities offered by the large financial centers, either individually or collectively, the international trade of the world is financed and the production and marketing of staple commodities in countries with less developed banking facilities are financed.

In financing these transactions, the international money
market performs internationally the same functions that a
local money center performs for an individual country.
It acts as a bank, in that it collects deposits from a number
of nations and uses them to finance economic activities
throughout the world. And just as an important bank
failure disrupts local industry and trade and creates runs
on other banking institutions, bringing ruin to depositors,
so the collapse of an important international financial
money center through the abandonment of specie payments
or the introduction of foreign exchange restrictions has
disturbing effects all over the world. The rigid foreign
exchange restrictions imposed by Germany not only hurt
the principal money markets which had placed funds in
Germany, but also adversely affected all countries which
had close trade connections with Germany.   The abandonment of specie payments by Great Britain and the United
States has had its repercussion on such widely scattered
countries as France, Greece, Siam, and Ecuador, while the
collapse of the international money market and the stop-
page of the flow of credits and of capital have resulted in
a great shrinkage of internal industry and trade throughout the world.

Importance of foreign trade financing.   Of the various
economic activities financed through the international
money market, the financing of the movement of commodities among the countries of the world is perhaps the
most important.   Without the machinery and the facilities
of the international money market, foreign trade would
have to be conducted on virtually a barter basis.   As a
matter of fact, during 1931 and 1932, when a number of
countries instituted foreign exchange restrictions and the
international flow of credit almost ceased, barter transactions again reappeared in international trade and several
companies were organized to effect exchanges of goods
without the aid of banking institutions or of credit.

Although all types of international financial transactions increased considerably from 1920 to 1930, the financing of the international movement of trade has remained the chief function of the international money market. The magnitude of this activity can best be gauged from Table 3, which shows the annual value of the world's foreign trade. From this table it may be seen that, in the postwar period of prosperity, the total value of the world's foreign trade ranged from about $62,000,000,000 to more than $68,000,000,000 annually. Obviously, this activity necessitated a huge shifting of funds through innumerable transactions in the international financial system.

TABLE 3

WORLD'S FOREIGN TRADE
(In millions of gold dollars)

Year	Imports	Exports	Total Trade
1913	19,465	18,332	37,797
1926	32,117	29,770	61,887
1927	33,740	31,308	65,048
1928	34,652	32,728	67,380
1929	35,606	33,035	68,641
1930	29,083	26,492	55,575
1931	20,847	18,922	39,769
1932	13,996	12,902	26,898
1933	12,485	11,694	24,179

These figures, large as they are, do not indicate clearly the predominant rôle which foreign trade plays in the international business relations of the world. This rôle becomes more evident if the foreign trade of the various countries is compared, as in Table 4, with the total of all the items entering into their international balances of payments. From this analysis, it is evident that trade as a factor in the total of all current transactions is very considerable even in the case of a great creditor country like the United States. As compared with the total of all international transactions, including capital items, the percentage is of course lower, but in most countries it amounts to about two-thirds of the total. As a matter of fact, with the exception of certain services, such as tourists' expenditures, charitable and immigrant remittances, etc., most international financial transactions are either directly or indirectly connected with the movement of goods. Shipping earnings, insurance, banking commissions, and to a large extent foreign loans, are the direct result of movements of commodities in international trade.

TABLE 4

TRADE AS A FACTOR IN TOTAL BALANCES OF
PAYMENTS OF VARIOUS COUNTRIES

	Percentage of Trade to Total Current Items		Percentage of Trade to Total Items	
	1927	1930	1927	1930
United States	68.6	59.4	51.9	41.4
Germany	75.0	78.2	66.6	62.9
France	75.3	64.3	70.4	60.0
Hungary	86.0	74.3	84.2	67.8
Argentina	82.8	75.0	77.3	65.7

Bankers' acceptances in foreign trade. The financing of foreign trade is not only the oldest but also one of the safest of the transactions carried out on the international money market. This safety factor in foreign trade financing is due to the fact that most transactions, particularly those arising out of the shipment of raw materials and agricultural commodities, are self-liquidating in character. The shipment of commodities from one country to another is usually financed through bankers' acceptances which give the buyer between thirty and ninety days to obtain funds to repay his bank, the acceptor, for the invoiced amount of the shipment. In this respect, the importation of merchandise does not differ materially from a domestic transaction financed through a bank credit. The only difference is that an importation of goods usually involves payment in a foreign currency. However, in times when the movement of funds runs smoothly, the acquisition of foreign exchange is only a technical detail, since local currency can be converted without any difficulty into foreign exchange. It is only when the machinery of the international market breaks down that the transfer problem, the problem of converting local currency into foreign exchange, arises.

One of the greatest advantages of the banker's acceptance, particularly if stated in an internationally recognized currency, is that it can be sold without difficulty in the open market, with the result that the burden of financing the movement of trade is shifted to institutions or markets which can most easily bear it. For example, in normal times a dollar draft drawn on a New York bank to finance a shipment of wool from Argentina to Germany may be sold to a bank in Argentina. The latter, in turn, may sell it in the New York market, and ultimately the draft may find its way to the Reserve bank, which may hold it, say, for the account of the Bank of France. Thus the burden of financing the particular shipment of goods has been carried by Argentinian and American banks, by the Reserve banks, and by the Bank of France, through the utilization of the liquid funds of these institutions.

Misuse of acceptance credits. So long as bankers' acceptances are employed for self-liquidating transactions arising out of foreign trade, they retain their liquidity and perform a most useful function. Frequently, however, acceptance credits are misused; *i.e.,* the credits obtained are not used for financing transactions of a self-liquidating character but, instead, are employed in providing working capital which should have been obtained through the issue of securities. An example of such a misuse of acceptance credit occurred in Germany in 1930–31, when, on account of the inability to obtain long-term loans, acceptance credits were utilized for working capital purposes. The misuse of acceptance credits is dangerous both to the lender and to the borrower. The lender suffers because funds which are supposed to be liquid and easily withdrawn become frozen.

The misuse of acceptance credits also constitutes a danger to the individual debtors and may jeopardize the currency system of their country. The debtor banks operate under the constant threat that the credits granted to them may be withdrawn. In order to meet these withdrawals, the banks must call the loans of their debtors, and since the credits are not based on self-liquidating transactions, it is obvious that they cannot be repaid. The use of foreign short-term credits to finance long-term transactions was one of the chief causes of the difficulties of the Darmstaedter und Nationalbank (Danat) of Germany in 1931. When the foreign banks began to withdraw their funds, this bank was unable to liquidate some of its own loans and was therefore unable to obtain cash with which to buy foreign exchange.

The danger to the currency of the debtor country from the misuse of foreign acceptance credits or foreign short-term credits in general arises particularly when the underlying transactions on which these credits are based do not create a supply of foreign exchange. When the foreign creditors begin to withdraw their loans, the debtor banks are forced to borrow from the central bank in order to obtain the necessary foreign exchange. This, in turn, leads not only to a tightening of credit and to higher interest rates, but also to a reduction in the central bank's gold and foreign exchange reserves. The weakening of the currency then may lead to further foreign withdrawals and even to a flight of domestic capital. If withrawals of foreign funds are beyond the capacity of a country to meet, the result is either a suspension of specie payments or the imposition of foreign exchange restrictions.

Choice of market to finance international trade. Under normal conditions, the foreign trade of the world can be financed through any one of the various financial centers of the international money market, such as London and New York and the lesser centers, such as Zurich, Amsterdam, and Paris. The choice that the individual or corporation makes depends to a considerable extent upon: (1) the rate of interest on acceptances prevailing in these markets; and (2) the banking connections and credit facilities extended to the exporter or importer—whichever is to assume the burden of financing—in one of these markets. If the drawer or drawee has good banking connections in all these centers, his choice will depend entirely upon the prevailing rate of interest on bankers' bills and/or the credit facilities offered to him.

If, for example, a Brazilian exporter has shipped coffee to Germany, he may demand under normal conditions that the shipment be financed by a banker's bill drawn on a bank in either New York or London. Since the exporter will sell or discount the draft immediately with his own bank in Brazil, the choice of the market will depend upon the rate of interest prevailing in each market. The difference between the ninety-day dollar rate and the cable rate will depend on the rate of interest on bankers' acceptances prevailing in New York. Similarly, if the exporter sells a ninety-day pound sterling draft, the difference between the ninety-day draft and the cable transfer will depend upon the rate of interest on prime bankers' acceptances prevailing in London. Therefore, if interest rates in New York are lower than in London, the difference between the price of the ninety day draft and the cable draft on New York will be smaller than the difference between the ninety-day draft and the cable transfer on London. This means that the exporter will receive a larger amount of dollars for his dollar draft than he would receive pounds for his pound sterling draft. Under these circumstances, it would seem that whenever interest rates are lower in New York than in London, the volume of acceptances in New York arising out of the financing of trade of foreign nations will be greater; and vice versa, when the rate of interest on bankers' acceptances in New York is higher, the volume of such acceptances in New York will decrease. The interaction of supply and demand, however, tends to maintain relative stability in the rates on acceptances unless other factors affect money rates.

The fact that the volume of bankers' acceptances outstanding in one country depends to a considerable extent on the bill rate prevailing in that country enables the various central banks, under normal conditions, to exercise an influence on the movement of the exchange rates. If, for example, through an increase in the bank rate of the Bank of England, the bill rate becomes higher in London, the number of sterling acceptances will tend to decrease, while those stated in dollars will tend to increase. This condition, in turn, will result in a decline in the supply of sterling exchange and an increase in dollar bills, thereby removing an important source of supply of sterling bills and tending to improve the value of the pound in relation to foreign currencies.

Financing of services. Partly as a result of the international movement of goods, and partly as the result of cultural and social relationships among nations, a large number of financial transactions arise which require the shifting of funds from one country to another. In addition, the movement of long-term capital entails the shifting of short-term funds, chiefly in the form of payments of interest and amortization charges. These transactions may be classified as follows:

I. Those resulting chiefly from trade movements:
　　1. Freight charges;
　　2. Insurance transactions;
　　3. Cablegrams, telephone service, etc.;
　　4. Bankers' commissions, etc.

II. Those resulting from cultural and social relationships:
　　1. Tourist expenditures;
　　2. Ocean travel or railway passenger traffic;
　　3. Immigrants' remittances;
　　4. Missionary and charitable contributions;
　　5. Motion picture royalties, etc.

III. Those resulting from capital movements:
　　1. Interest on foreign bonds;

2. Repayment of principal of foreign loans;
3. Earnings of direct investments in foreign countries, or payments of dividends and profits.

Some of these transactions are settled between two countries without the aid of a third country or the international money market, while others are carried out through the aid of a third market, usually an important international center. For example, the owners of Greek vessels carrying Russian grain to Italy are, under normal conditions, not paid in drachmae or lire but rather in pounds sterling or in Dutch florins. Therefore, the exporter or importer, as the case may be, has to appear in the market as a buyer of pounds or florins. Similarly, American missionary societies, in remitting funds to India, may find it more desirable to buy rupees in England, thus causing a shifting of funds from the United States to London and, in turn, from Great Britain to India.

Some of the items arising out of social and cultural relationships are of considerable importance both in the movement of funds and in the balances of the international accounts of several countries. Thus, expenditures abroad by American tourists during 1930 amounted to over $800,-000,000, an amount only slightly less than the total earnings of American investments abroad. France, on the other hand, received $330,000,000 in tourists' expenditures during the same year. The effect of the movement of these funds on the exchanges is the same as that of the shipment of commodities or the movement of long-term capital. As far as the United States is concerned, tourists' expenditures create claims on the United States throughout the world, while in the case of France, they provide the French banks with claims on many countries. There is, however, a difference between financing foreign trade and financing transactions arising out of cultural and social intercourse among nations. In the former, the burden of financing is either carried by the institutions located in the large financial centers or is shifted from one market to another to obtain the most advantageous rate of interest. In the latter case, no financing through banks is involved, and the international money market, either collectively or through individual centers, provides the facilities for exchanging one currency into another, or furnishes clearing facilities whereby one claim is offset by a counterclaim.

Clearing or offsetting claims. The clearing, or offsetting, of claims was effected until a few years ago almost exclusively through the large financial institutions. In recent years, the central banks of the various countries have developed a system of clearing among themselves, and the establishment of the Bank for International Settlements has given a substantial impetus to the creation of a well-organized international financial clearing system. If the efforts of the Bank for International Settlements along these lines are successful, they not only may result in a saving to those who are required to make international remittances, but will undoubtedly exercise a stabilizing influence on the movement of the exchanges. Realization of such an ideal, however, presupposes more or less adjusted balances of payments of the various countries and greater political and economic stability than has existed during the period 1931–34.

Capital transactions and the money market. The movement of funds arising out of capital transactions, although originating on the capital market, falls into the sphere of the international money market. The payment of interest on outstanding foreign obligations gives rise to a demand for foreign exchange just as a demand is created by the importation of goods or the payment of freight charges. Therefore, as far as their effect on the foreign exchanges is concerned, these transactions do not differ from others previously described. There is, however, some difference in the manner in which this movement of funds affects the countries concerned. A large part of the outstanding foreign obligations is government debts, and the local currency for the payment of debt service is obtained through taxes or from revenues of enterprises owned by the state. These funds are often concentrated in the hands of the central banks. The latter; however, knowing in advance how much must be remitted annually on account of debt service for the state or its political subdivisions, can arrange for the acquisition of the necessary foreign currencies so as not to disorganize or, even temporarily, adversely affect the exchange market.

Funds remitted for interest payments usually arrive in the creditor country about thirty to sixty days prior to the coupon date, and are temporarily invested in the market before being distributed to the bondholders. Then, too, the funds arising out of the payment of principal and interest are frequently handled by investment bankers and not through the ordinary commercial banking channels. Since these transactions are closely interwoven with capital transactions, they will be dealt with in the following chapter.

CHAPTER III

The International Capital Market

Introduction. The international money market and the international capital market are so closely interwoven that it is very difficult to differentiate between the two. Capital transactions such as the flotation of foreign loans, or direct foreign investments, have the same effect on the borrowing country as an exportation of goods, and the same effect on the lending country as an importation of goods. After a long-term loan has been negotiated and sold in the open market, short-term funds are placed at the disposal of the borrower and can be withdrawn in the same manner as any other short-term funds. On the other hand, short-term transactions in the money market are often merely a preliminary to long-term loans, with the creditor expecting repayment only after the debtor has later obtained a long-term loan or sold a stock issue in the capital market.

But in spite of the close connection between the two markets, each performs certain definite functions and possesses a separate machinery organized for the purpose. Just as the function of the money market is to finance short-term transactions and to facilitate the movement of short-term funds from country to country, so the function of the capital market is to finance long-term capital transactions and to facilitate the shifting of long-term capital from country to country.

Operation of market. Transactions in the international capital market are of two main types: (1) the flotation of new foreign securities and (2) the transfer or redistribution of previously issued securities among investors in various countries. On the surface, it may appear that

66

the international. capital market provides merely a one-way stream of funds from capital-rich to capital-poor countries, and in the view of some observers this constitutes the greatest distinction between the capital market and the money market.

The one-way movement of capital on the international capital market, however, is more ostensible than real. The movement is in one direction only when new foreign issues are floated, because in that case the funds move from the richer to the poorer countries. In the case of securities already outstanding, the movement is quite often in the opposite direction. This latter shifting of capital arises often out of the buying of securities issued in capital-rich countries by residents of capital-poor countries, either in order to obtain greater safety, larger yields, better diversification, or because of the expectation of speculative profits. It may also at times be the result of a flight of capital caused by the fear of currency depreciation or a desire to avoid high taxation. These factors are chiefly responsible for the purchase of securities originally issued in the United States, England, and Holland, for either foreign or domestic issuers, by investors in such countries as Greece and Uruguay.

The second source of the flow of capital from debtor to creditor countries is the payment of principal and interest by debtor countries on their outstanding external obligations. While such transactions are carried out in the international money market like payments for merchandise as described in the previous chapter, the fact should not be overlooked that these funds, once they reach the creditor country, are likely to be used for the purchase of other securities and thus remain in the capital market. In addition, international arbitrage in securities causes a continuous shifting of securities from one country to another. Thus, while the flotation of new foreign securities represents a one-way flow of capital from creditor to debtor nations, the other transactions of the international capital market cause a continuous shifting of capital in both directions.

Criticisms of the international capital market. While the international money market is generally recognized as essential to satisfactory international economic relations, the international capital market has been often subjected to severe criticism and even to parliamentary and congressional investigations. This critical attitude has resulted in direct or indirect regulation of the capital market by governments for many years. Thus, the United States Government did not interfere with the granting of short- or medium-term credits to the Soviet Union, but for a number of years it has opposed the flotation of Soviet bonds in the United States. There is, however, no economic distinction between the two classes of Soviet loans, because the short-term credits were used by the Soviet Union almost exclusively for the purchase of capital goods.

It is not difficult to ascertain the reason for the criticism of the international capital market. Short-term foreign loans are for the most part made by banks, and the loss, if any, is borne by the banks and only indirectly, and usually unknowingly, by the bank's stockholders or depositors. Bank failures do not change this situation, because banks which engage in the granting of international credits are usually the larger and stronger institutions among which failure is rare. However, in the case of long-term loans obtained through the issue of bonds, the loan is actually made by a large number of individual bondholders, and any loss that may occur because of a default or a decline in market value of the securities falls directly on the holder of the bonds and not on the institution that issued them. In addition to this factor, political considerations often play an important rôle in governmental control over the issue of foreign securities.

Importance of the market. In spite of the severe criticism to which international capital transactions have been subjected recently in the United States, the international capital market is just as important to the economic development of the world as the international money market is to the international movement of commodities and services. Economic progress would have been greatly impeded, and certain areas could not possibly have been developed, without the aid of foreign capital. In the past, practically every nation has at one time been a borrower of long-term capital, and foreign capital is still urgently needed for the further development of many countries. Dutch capital was employed for the development of British industry and trade. British capital in turn was employed for the economic development of many countries on the continent of Europe. The economic progress of the United States during the nineteenth century was accelerated by the inflow of capital from Great Britain and the continent of Europe. More recently, American capital has been used for the development of South America and of the Far East, and for the rehabilitation of the industrial plants of a number of European countries.

While it cannot be denied that serious mistakes have been made in the granting of loans, and that the history of the movement of long-term capital in practically all countries contains examples of mismanagement, over-lending, misuse of proceeds of the loans, bribery of officials, and so forth, these incidents in the international field do not differ materially from similar ones in the field of domestic long-term financing. The experience of bondholders in the early history of American railroads and, lately, in real estate financing in the United States, to mention only two examples, has been more disastrous than the experience of investors in foreign financing.

Economic development and capital loans. The economic development of new countries and the industrialization of agricultural countries can be financed in either one of two ways. A new country may either rely on its own resources and wait until sufficient capital has accumulated to finance its development, or it may obtain the necessary capital from abroad. Under the first method, the process of development is very slow. Abyssinia is, perhaps, a good example of a country which has followed this policy; but even there most of the new developments, particularly in the railroad field, have been financed with the aid of foreign capital. A more striking instance is that of the Soviet Union, which under the Communist régime has endeavored to carry out industrialization on a large scale chiefly through its own resources. Such a procedure invariably means a substantial decrease in the consumption power of the country, because everything that can find a market abroad is exported in order that the capital goods needed for industrial development may be obtained. On the other hand, the industrialization of Canada and the reorganization and modernization of German industry have progressed very rapidly without pressure on the standard of living of the population, since both countries have financed the acquisition of capital goods by foreign borrowing.

The course that a nation follows in the development of its natural resources or in the process of industrialization has important consequences not only for the country itself but for other countries as well. When a country is utilizing foreign capital on a large scale, it normally has an excess of imports over exports. In other words, the borrowing country consumes more than it produces, and this consumption leads to greater industrial activity in other countries supplying the imports. As the natural resources of the country are developed, the increase in production not only permits an improvement in the standard of living of the people, but also enables the country to export more than it imports, and the surplus used to pay interest and dividends on foreign capital tends to raise the standard of living of other nations.

On the other hand, when a country develops its natural resources or its industries either entirely or to a large extent through its own resources, the saving of capital required leads to under-consumption within that country, and consequently to forced exports, which in turn have an unfavorable effect on the countries affected by these forced sales. It is well known that the Soviet government has exported wheat, dairy products, and other consumption goods greatly needed at home in order to obtain foreign exchange with which to pay for imported capital goods. Such forced exports not only have lowered the standard of living within Russia but also have tended to demoralize commodity markets in other countries and to depress prices throughout the world. The international capital market, therefore, in transferring capital from one country to another, not only accelerates the economic progress of the world but also prevents the ruthless competition and dumping in foreign markets which takes place when countries are forced to develop their natural resources without access to the international capital market.

The favorable effect of the international flow of capital becomes more apparent when economic and/or political conditions bring the flow to a halt. When this takes place, countries which have to make substantial payments abroad in the form of principal and interest on their outstanding obligations, and which to a considerable extent depend upon the continuous inflow of foreign capital, are required to curtail their imports greatly, and endeavor by all means to increase their exports. This activity occurred in Germany, beginning in the fall of 1930, when the international flow of capital came to a halt and Germany was forced to provide for the payment of its external obligations out of its own resources. Germany's imports declined, and every possible measure was adopted to increase exports. This tendency continued until other nations, in self-defense, adopted measures to curtail their imports from Germany, and ultimately Germany defaulted on its foreign obligations.

Over-lending. Just as a well-regulated flow of international capital has a beneficial effect both on the lending as well as on the borrowing country, a too rapid movement of capital adversely affects both creditor and debtor nations and may ultimately cause injury to other countries. So long as a country limits its exportation of capital to the surplus in its current international accounts, exclusive of capital items, its currency and banking system is not jeopardized. Thus, for example, if in a given year the current accounts of the United States show a surplus of $500,-000,000, not only may this amount be safely invested abroad but it becomes economically desirable to do so, since otherwise foreign countries will either have to curtail their purchases of American goods and services, ship gold to this country, or default on their outstanding obligations.

On the other hand, if a country exports more capital than its actual current earnings from abroad, it may endanger its own currency and banking system. Such a situation sometimes arises when a nation utilizes foreign short-term funds for the making of long-term foreign loans. The danger arises out of the fact that the short-term funds can be withdrawn practically at will, while long-term loans cannot be recalled and it is usually very difficult to dispose of a large volume of foreign securities in the markets of other nations without causing a substantial decline in prices. The investment of foreign short-term funds in foreign long-term obligations was a contributing factor in the abandonment of specie payments by Great Britain in 1931.

Over-borrowing.   Just as over-lending may have adverse effects on the lending country, over-borrowing invariably creates a difficult situation for the debtor country and often leads to default. Theoretically, any nation can absorb an unlimited amount of capital; such capital can be used for all kinds of projects, whether economic or uneconomic. However, if default is to be avoided, the amount that a country can borrow is limited by the amount which it is able to provide and transfer for the service of its foreign obligations under adverse economic conditions.

The payment of the debt service on foreign loans involves two problems: (1) the accumulation of funds in local currencies, and (2) the transfer of these funds into the currencies of the creditor countries. These two requirements set definite limits to the borrowing capacity of a nation. Of course, it is not always easy to ascertain when these limits are reached, because at the time when a country is able to borrow abroad, it is usually enjoying a considerable measure of prosperity—which creates the impression that additional debts may safely be contracted. The over-borrowing does not become clearly apparent until economic depression develops. If a country has heavily over-borrowed, as did Chile, Peru, and Bolivia in the 1920's, the debt service becomes a heavy burden on the budget when business activity declines, and eventually a point is reached where the service cannot be met even if foreign exchange is available. Thus, for example, the service of the external debt of the Bolivian government, if paid, would have absorbed about 75 per cent of its total revenues during the year 1931. It is obvious that even if these funds could have been converted into foreign exchange, the balance left to the government would have been totally inadequate to finance even the most essential governmental functions.

The transfer of local currency into foreign currencies for the payment of external debt service has proved to be even more difficult in many cases than the problem of providing funds in local currency. As a matter of fact, all of the European and many of the South American defaults during the last few years have been caused by the inability to effect transfers. The experience of Hungary, Germany, and Austria demonstrates the seriousness of this problem. Practically all foreign loans made to the governments, political subdivisions, banks, and most corporations of these countries may be considered as sound in the sense that the borrowers are in a position to accumulate in local currency the necessary funds for the payment of the external debt service. However, the total amount of foreign exchange required for the external debt service of all the individual borrowers is so large that, under the conditions prevailing since 1931, the central banks have been unable to meet the demand for foreign exchange, and transfer moratoria have been declared. Furthermore, while the amount of funds available in local currency can be increased to a certain extent by a government, either through increased taxation, domestic borrowing, or curtailment of expenditures, there is little that an individual country can do to solve the transfer problem other than to impose foreign exchange restrictions.

Organization of the international capital market. In contrast to the international money market, which operates through the well-established money market machinery of all the leading financial centers of the world, the operation of the international capital market requires only the machinery, established in the individual lending countries, for issuing and distributing securities. Obviously, no special financial facilities are required in the borrowing countries. Thus, a description of the organization of the international capital market is limited to the facilities in the principal lending countries for the flotation of foreign loans. The mechanism differs from country to country, and is described later in the chapters dealing with individual financial centers.

As a rule, the principal institutions of the international capital market are the investment banking houses, organized as either partnerships or corporations. In some countries, as on the continent of Europe, the commercial banks also engage in the underwriting of securities; while in others, such as England, the flotation of foreign securities is handled almost exclusively by a few well-known investment banking institutions. In the United States, since the passage of the Banking Act of 1933, the investment business has been restricted to firms not affiliated with member banks and not engaged in the private banking business.

The number of institutions engaged in the flotation of foreign loans or in the buying and selling of securities on an international scale is comparatively limited. This is because the flotation of foreign issues requires a broad knowledge of economic and political conditions in the borrowing countries, accurate judgment of the domestic money and capital markets, and large financial resources. In some capital markets, the various institutions have divided the field among themselves in order to avoid the too keen competition which, in the long run, causes over-lending or the granting of doubtful loans.

However, some time must elapse before a financial center develops to a point where the issuance of foreign securities becomes concentrated in the hands of a few well-known and responsible institutions. Usually, when a country first begins to lend abroad, a number of firms with limited resources, and without adequate facilities to investigate economic and political conditions in the borrowing countries, are attracted by the large potential profits to the business of underwriting foreign issues. This was the case in England in the early part of the nineteenth century, and again in the United States in the post-war period. Not having the necessary facilities and not being familiar with this type of financing, such houses compete with the more experienced and responsible firms by offering too liberal terms to the borrowing countries. The result, of course, in England as well as in the United States, was over-lending and subsequent defaults. Only after there have been numerous defaults does the investing public become more discriminating, and the discrimination usually results in a gradual reduction in the number of houses engaged in the underwriting of foreign loans.

In addition to investment banking houses engaged in the origination and distribution of new foreign issues, the international capital market includes a number of organizations engaged in the secondary international distribution

of outstanding foreign securities. These are principally
dealers and brokers with international connections. In
addition to actually distributing securities, these institutions engage in arbitrage transactions.

Arbitrage in securities. International arbitrage is conducted in securities which are traded in the markets of two
or more countries. The object of the arbitrageur is to buy
a security in one market and immediately sell the same
security in another market at a higher price; or, vice versa,
to sell a security in one market and cover the sale by a
purchase in another market at a lower price. Simple as
this may seem, it is complicated by the great dissimilarity
in the practices of the various stock exchanges. An arbitrageur, to be successful, not only must know his own
market but must also be familiar with the technique and
operation of foreign markets. He must know the general
trend of prices of the security dealt in and, above all, he
must know whether or not there is an active market for a
particular security, so that it can be bought and sold at
any time.

The regulations and practices of the stock exchanges in
the various countries differ widely. In contrast, for instance, to the New York market, where transactions are
settled daily, most foreign stock exchanges have biweekly
settlements. The arbitrageur, therefore, must know when
delivery is to be made and must be sure that he will be
in a position to make delivery in time. He must also
be familiar with the methods of quoting the various American certificates representing foreign shares. To illustrate,
one American Roan Antelope certificate represents four
English shares, so that if an American sells 100 American
certificates of Roan Antelope in New York and he wants
to meet this delivery through a purchase in London, he
must buy 400 shares there. Furthermore, an arbitrageur
must know that, in London, shares are quoted on the basis
of a percentage of par. Thus, if U. S. Steel Common is
sold in London at 150 per cent, that means 150 per cent of

$100, or the equivalent in sterling. In addition, he must be familiar with the various charges that are involved in the buying and selling of securities, because these charges form a part of the total cost. Only after considering all these charges will the arbitrageur be able to determine whether or not a proposed transaction will be profitable.

The basis of arbitrage is the figuring of the price parity; that is to say, the calculation to determine the answer to the question: If a share is selling abroad at a certain price, for what must it sell in New York in order to make an arbitrage transaction profitable? To arrive at this figure, the arbitrageur must be familiar not only with prices abroad and with the various costs involved, but also with foreign exchange rates, for each arbitrage transaction involves the conversion of one currency into another.

Joint account transactions. Arbitrage can be carried out either for the account of an American house alone or for a joint account. In the former case, the American institution bears all the risks, retains all the profits, and has to pay commissions to its foreign correspondent. If a firm in New York and a foreign institution operate a joint account, they share the risks and profits equally, and no commission is charged one party by the other. Usually the American house and the foreign institution set aside a certain stipulated sum for the purpose of arbitrage operations. At fixed intervals, as at the end of each month, an accounting is made, and after the deduction of all expenses the profits or losses are shared equally or in accordance with the agreement.

Turning of position. In a number of countries, the delivery of securities involves the payment of a stamp tax. In countries where settlements are made only fortnightly, the arbitrageur will often turn his position before the settlement date in order to avoid the stamp tax. Such a transaction is often made even when there is no profit to be realized. If after figuring out the parity, for example, the arbitrageur finds it profitable to sell International

Nickel in London and to buy it in New York, the correspondent of the American house must make delivery in London. If actual delivery is made, a stamp tax on the securities must be paid. In order to avoid the payment of the tax, the arbitrageur in New York may instruct his correspondent in London to buy International Nickel and cover the sale by a corresponding sale in New York. Of course, if the loss which would result from turning the position is greater than the stamp tax, then it is clear that the transaction would not be carried out.

Although arbitrage transactions are carried out primarily with the view of deriving a profit from the difference in prices in two different markets, the effect of such operations is to equalize the price of securities in the several markets. Like all other international financial transactions, the arbitrage presupposes free and unrestricted markets in the countries involved. Fluctuating exchange rates are not a deterrent to arbitrage transactions; they increase the risk but also enhance the possibilities of profit. Arbitrage, of course, involves little or no international transfer of funds, since the buying of securities in one market is offset by the selling of securities in another market.

International coöperation. In pre-war years, international capital movements concerned only the individual borrowers and the private lenders. In only rare cases did a government aid in the flotation of a loan for another country, and then only when the borrower was under the protectorate of the guarantor. Similarly, the coöperation of a group of countries to restore the credit of another sovereign nation or to enable the latter to float a loan on the international capital market was a very rare occurrence. As a rule, countries with an unsatisfactory credit standing abroad could not obtain any loans in the international capital market and had to help themselves as best they could.

In post-war years, under the pressure of the conditions created by the war and the treaties of peace, a new practice was instituted which made it possible for even weak nations, without credit standing at home or abroad, to obtain loans on relatively favorable terms in the international capital market. This practice was inaugurated in the flotation of the so-called League of Nations loans, or loans issued under the auspices of the League of Nations. The work of the League in restoring the credit standing of weaker countries, and thereby enabling them to have access to the international capital market, is well known and needs no detailed discussion. The principal work of the League in these cases consisted in the examination of the economic and financial status of the prospective borrower, in the preparation of a plan of financial rehabilitation, and in the appointment of foreign experts to supervise the execution of the plan. The supervisory powers were vested in a high commissioner in both Austria and Hungary, and in the trustees of the loans for Bulgaria. These officials also had the power to supervise the expenditure of the proceeds of the loans and to administer the revenues pledged as security for the loans. The flotation of loans under the auspices of the League was an innovation of considerable importance, for it opened up the capital markets to countries which otherwise could not have obtained the foreign loans which were so essential to the economic reconstruction of these countries.

The defaults which have occurred on some of these loans, in spite of supervision by the League authorities, have dealt a blow to the prestige of the League which will make it difficult for that body to continue to play its rôle of the past in the future economic reconstruction of weaker nations. In the future, the sponsorship of the League in connection with international loans will afford little assurance to investors, who have learned that even the greatest goodwill on the part of a debtor country and the closest supervision over its finances cannot overcome the transfer problem, which is the most important cause of defaults on foreign loans.

The international capital market, 1931–34. As has happened many times in the past, the severe economic depression of the 1930's caused a complete cessation in the flotation of new foreign loans. In the face of adverse economic conditions, investors refused to risk new capital abroad. Furthermore, the shrinkage of governmental revenues and the decline in foreign trade made it impossible for many countries to continue the full payment of external debt service, and widespread defaults brought foreign securities into general disfavor. Defaults began on a large scale in the early part of 1931, and by the latter part of 1934 approximately $3,000,000,000 of foreign dollar bonds, or about 40 per cent of all foreign loans outstanding in the United States, were in default. However, many foreign borrowers continued to make partial interest payments in cash, some issued funding bonds or scrip in lieu of cash payments, and some used a combination of these methods.

The losses incurred by many purchasers of foreign bonds have created an unfavorable attitude on the part of investors toward foreign securities in general, and there has been considerable agitation for governmental restriction or supervision of foreign lending. This feeling has found expression in the Johnson Act, which prohibits loans to foreign governments in default on their debts to the United States Government, and in the provisions of the Securities Act of 1933, which requires the registration of foreign issues with the Securities and Exchange Commission.

The experience of Great Britain has been similar to that of the United States. According to the estimates of Sir Robert Kindersley, the total income of Great Britain from its foreign investments—both direct and portfolio investments—has declined from £230,900,000, in 1929, to £154,900,000, in 1933. However, the British, more experienced in foreign lending, have taken their losses with more equanimity than has this country. Since 1931 the British Treasury has maintained an unofficial embargo on foreign loans, but this measure was not adopted so much for the protection of investors as for the protection of the British balance of payments. In 1934 this embargo was modified to permit the refunding of certain foreign loans, and the flotation of new foreign loans for the purpose of financing purchases of British goods or increasing the sterling assets of the sterling bloc countries. Incidentally, the tying up of foreign loans with the purchase of goods in the lending country is economically unsound in that it interferes with the normal movement of international trade, which is usually multilateral rather than bilateral.

What rôle the United States will have as a foreign lender in the future is difficult to foretell. It appears that the next phase in the development of the United States as a creditor nation will involve a measure of refunding by those countries which have come through the depression with improved credit standing, and of readjustment by those which have been obliged to default. Already a number of foreign issuers have offered bondholders temporary readjustment plans. In any case, it will undoubtedly be some years before the capital market of this country will be receptive to new foreign loans on any very large scale. The experience of other creditor countries, however, indicates that when economic conditions are favorable foreign lending is invariably resumed after a period of depression and default. Certainly, as long as the balance of international payments of the United States remains favorable, the export of capital in some form is necessary if even those claims on foreign countries arising in the ordinary course of business are to be collected.

In contrast to the stagnation in the market for new foreign capital issues, the international market for outstanding issues has been quite active during the last few years. There has been a great deal of shifting of securities between countries and, in particular, there has been large scale repatriation of securities issued in creditor countries by the debtor countries.

The Department of Commerce estimates that in 1933

Americans purchased $685,000,000 of foreign securities through the securities markets, and repurchased some $580,000,000 of American securities from foreigners. On the other hand, foreigners repurchased about $565,000,000 of foreign stocks and bonds from American holders and also bought $760,000,000 of American securities. Similarly, in the first six months of 1934 alone, foreigners purchased about $850,000,000 of securities in this country, of which about $490,000,000 were American. In the same period Americans purchased $625,000,000 of securities from foreign holders, of which $370,000,000 represented American stocks and bonds.

Thus, during both 1933 and the first half of 1934, foreigners purchased more securities in the United States than Americans bought abroad—a situation which tended to reduce the creditor position of the United States. This tendency, in view of the consistent favorable trade balance of the United States and the large amounts of debt service which foreigners have to make in this country, indicates clearly the abnormal international financial position of the United States. A creditor nation as a rule should have an excess of current expenditures abroad over current income from abroad, or it should continue to export capital. If neither of these conditions exists, debtor countries can liquidate their obligations to the creditor country only by shipping gold. The economic position of the United States is such that a resumption of foreign lending is almost imperative. The experience of the United States with foreign securities has not differed materially from that of the older lending nations, notably Great Britain. Yet in spite of defaults and losses to individual bondholders, the British have again and again returned to this type of business, and only recently the restrictions imposed on foreign lending have been modified so as to permit a resumption of the export of capital.

The future of the international capital market, as regards both new issues and secondary distribution, depends to a very large extent on the economic policies pursued by the lending countries of the world. If they return to a policy of international coöperation based on the principle of the division of labor, the international capital market will revive. On the other hand, if they insist on pursuing policies of national economic self-sufficiency, the international lending of capital, if possible at all, must be materially reduced and will be carried out chiefly through governmental agencies.

CHAPTER IV

The Restoration and Collapse
of the International Money Market

Effects of Treaties of Peace

THE World War wrought havoc with the economic
and financial structure of Europe. But in spite of
the exhaustion of Europe and the great losses in manpower
and capital goods, the reconstruction of the war-torn world
and the establishment of a solid economic foundation could
still have been accomplished within a reasonably short
time, if the economic insanity of the treaties of peace and
their aftermath had not prevented such a course. Instead
of honestly and intelligently recognizing the weakened
condition of the defeated Central Powers or attempting to
mitigate the ill effects of the war, the Allies dictated economic measures in their treaties that were bound to hamper
world recovery. Large economic units were split up, an
action which in itself was certain to disrupt seriously the
trade of the areas affected; but in addition, the financial
demands of the Allies in the form of reparations made impossible the economic recuperation of the defeated Central
Powers. To these factors there was added a growing spirit
of economic nationalism, expressed in a desire for national
economic self-sufficiency, which together with the war debts
contracted by the various governments both during and
after the Armistice, was a deep-rooted source of evil.

No permanent solution of the European financial question could be found while such factors as these were operating. And yet, in spite of the great economic and financial
difficulties which confronted them at the end of the war,

the European nations did make a gallant fight to restore their currencies, and to return to those conditions which they had known before the war. That their success was of a temporary character only was due chiefly to the fact that they applied pre-war methods to post-war conditions. The economic consequences of the war and of the treaties of peace were hurdles too high to be overcome by such measures.

The Restoration of Currencies

Among the first of the many problems that pressed for solution were the restoration of the budgets in a number of countries, the halting of currency depreciation, and above all, the arrest of inflation. The disastrous effects of inflation were described by the Financial Committee of the League of Nations in its report on Austria in the following terse words:

> All those whose assets were expressed in terms of currency were ruined; persons with fixed incomes, the middle classes, have been utterly crushed and are in extreme poverty. Everyone therefore has attempted to make provision against this continual fall in the krone. Any loan or deposit represents a ruinous operation.

The problems of inflation and currency depreciation were the subject of discussion at a number of international conferences, the most important among them being those at Brussels and Genoa. The Brussels Conference, duly recognizing the danger, stated that the first reform in Europe and the one on which all others depended as a means of avoiding ruin, was to arrest inflation. The unhesitating acceptance of money as an absolutely stable measure of value is indispensable to the smooth working of the modern industrial and financial machine. It was felt that fluctuation of the currency made industry and trade speculative, destroyed the money and credit economy, and caused the reappearance of the primitive method of barter in international as well as in domestic transactions. The recom-

mendations of the Brussels Conference took a more con-
crete form in the resolutions of the Genoa Conference of
1922, which indicated the general steps to be taken in stabilizing a currency.

Genoa Conference. Among the recommendations of the
Genoa Conference concerning the restoration of currencies
and the return to financial stability was the statement that

> all European currencies should be based on a common stand-
> ard; that gold is the only common standard which all Eu-
> ropean governments could at present agree to adopt; that it
> is in the general interest that European governments should
> declare now that the establishment of a gold standard is
> their ultimate object, and should agree on the program by
> way of which they intend to achieve it.

The conference declared that stability of currencies is a
sine qua non of economic equilibrium; that so long as budget deficits are met by the creation of paper money or bank
credit, currency reform is impossible; and that the central
banks should be independent of political influence. The
desirability of effecting a devaluation of existing currencies
was felt to be a matter for the individual governments to
decide, as internal conditions would determine whether it
were either possible or desirable to return to the pre-war
gold parity or whether a new parity in the neighborhood
of existing values should be agreed upon. It was, however,
feared that if currency reform should be simply a return
to pre-war conditions, the value of gold might possibly be
raised by "the simultaneous and competitive efforts of countries to secure metallic reserves." In order to obviate an
undue demand for gold, there must be devised a method of
economizing in the use of gold as currency. The Genoa
Conference recommended the gold exchange standard as a
panacea. The gold exchange standard—which had been
in operation in a few countries even before the war—
enabled a country to maintain its monetary unit at par with
the unit of a country on a gold standard, without necessitating the maintenance by it of a monetary stock of gold.

Under this standard the currency, instead of being convertible into gold, was convertible at par into the currency of countries on the gold standard.

In effecting the stabilization of their currencies, the various countries were faced with the alternative of a return to par or the devaluation of the currency. While the majority of the representatives at the Genoa Conference decidedly favored a restoration to pre-war values, they lacked the resources to back up such ambitious plans. Where a currency had lost one-third or more of its original value, it was not only impossible but not desirable to restore it to its original parity, because of the danger of severe economic and social repercussions. It would have involved a redistribution of wealth, favoring the relatively small class of creditors while imposing a crushing burden on debtors and taxpayers. Furthermore, a return to the previous parity would have had these results: (1) a gradual appreciation of the currency; (2) falling prices as expressed in local currency; (3) decreasing production; and (4) increasing unemployment. Since modern business is financed to a large extent with borrowed money, a definite policy of currency appreciation and price reduction would necessarily bring ruin to many business enterprises, particularly those with fixed monetary obligations. Of all the belligerent nations, Great Britain and Japan alone restored their currencies to pre-war parity, but the wisdom of this step may readily be criticized in the light of the ensuing financial and economic woes of the two countries.

Devaluation meant the stabilization of a currency at a lower level and a decrease in the gold content of the monetary unit. It was camouflaged repudiation, since the victims were not directly aware of the effect of the act of the government. Devaluation could be accomplished through an exchange of old notes against a smaller number of new notes, or through the adoption of a new gold unit representing approximately the gold value of the paper money at the moment of stabilization. The second method was followed by practically all countries which devalued their currencies after the war.

Defects of stabilization. In retrospect, it appears clearly that those who were responsible for the stablization of the various currencies, including the financial experts of the League of Nations, were more concerned with the stabilization of the budgets and the setting up of central banks independent of the Treasury than with the fundamental economic position of the countries affected or the status of their balances of international payments. Apparently it was believed that, once a currency was stabilized and a foreign loan obtained to strengthen the gold and foreign exchange holdings of the central bank, the maintenance of stability would present no difficulties so long as the government had no recourse to the central bank for additional credits in large amounts. The changed economic status of the world in general and of the individual countries in particular seems to have been of little concern. Thus, at the Genoa Conference, which dealt with the stabilization of the currencies, such vital questions as reparations and war debts were ruled out. In dealing indirectly with these questions the Conference merely stated that, in some countries which suffered from inflation and were compelled to make heavy outside payments, external loans would be necessary because of the unfavorable balance of payments. "Without such a loan, comparative stability of the currency upon which the balancing of the budget largely depends may be unattainable," was the finding of the Genoa Conference.

Indeed, the stabilization of the currencies of several countries in Europe was based on the continuance of foreign loans. The fact that such loans tend in the long run to aggravate the balance of payments, and that the cessation of foreign loans endangers the stability of the currencies, seems to have given no great concern at the time. The leaders (or directing forces) of post-war Europe were motivated by their deeply rooted pre-war concepts.

The latter were reflected in political and economic opinion and action; they resulted in the adoption of measures and remedies which would have been suitable to conditions before the war but which were unworkable under the changed circumstances. The belief was still cherished that once a country had stabilized its exchange, the mere raising of the discount rate would suffice to cause an inflow of funds and readjust the balance of payments. This conclusion was based on pre-war conditions, when the international economic position of the various countries was more or less well adjusted and when a change in interest rates was sufficient to attract funds from abroad. It failed to recognize the economic effects of the war and of the treaties of peace and, above all, the existence of reparations and war debts which were to play such an important rôle in later developments. The payment of reparations and war debts both constituted a one-sided stream of capital for which there was no present economic consideration or *quid pro quo,* and although each was based on a different legal foundation, their economic effects were identical. In essence, war debts constituted huge payments by Germany to the United States, since a considerable part of the funds paid by Germany to the victor nations in the form of reparations was, in turn, remitted to the United States by those countries in payment of their war debts due to the United States. Since the payment of war debts depended upon the receipts from reparations, these two problems were always considered as one by the debtor nations, and the financial rehabilitation of Europe depended to a considerable extent on their settlement.

Fallacy of stabilization methods. The stabilization of the European currencies was carried out in disregard of the changed economic structure of the world, and in the face of involved international financial problems which made a return to normal currency and credit conditions impossible. From the beginning it was clear that countries which were burdened with reparations and war debts, and which, though not complete economic units, still adhered to a policy of economic isolation, could maintain the stability of the exchanges only so long as the capital-rich countries were willing to supply the necessary funds, both long and short-term. It was this willingness, chiefly on the part of the United States, to invest huge amounts abroad which gave the world in general and Europe in particular the appearance of prosperity; and it was American capital to a large extent that kept the various currencies stable for a number of years.

The rise of the United States to a position as the most important creditor nation of the world carried with it, however, complications which became apparent at the moment when this country ceased pouring its capital abroad. The national policy of the United States, which had formerly been a debtor nation, was based on the doctrine that an import surplus was detrimental to the country. Obviously a continuance of this policy must have disastrous consequences under the altered status of this country. The attempt to export as much as possible and to restrict imports to a minimum by high tariffs does not lend itself to the best interests of a creditor country. Such a policy invariably leads to the default of the debtors, the disruption of their credit standing, and the disorganization of their currencies. A nation which discourages imports through high tariffs and which has a continuously favorable balance of trade deprives the debtors of the means of repayment of their debts. This fact was illustrated in the case of the United States, which had been a debtor on the international capital markets before the war but which acquired her creditor position with amazing speed under the pressure of abnormal conditions. During the fifteen-year period from the beginning of the war in 1914 through 1929, the United States showed an excess of exports over imports amounting to $25,909,381,000. During the same period, the stock of monetary gold in the United States showed a net increase of $2,166,096,000, while the purchase of foreign securities, the repurchase of American securities, direct investments abroad, and loans made by the United States government exceeded 25 billions of dollars. In 1929 this movement came to a halt. The decline in the volume of foreign loans, coupled with the unsound tariff policy adopted by the United States in 1930 and followed by other countries, was one of the strongest indications that the period of post-war stabilization had come to an end.

The influence of short-term funds. Another important development in the post-war period which constituted an element of danger to the stability of the exchanges was the accumulation of huge volumes of short-term debts. This accumulation received its impetus partly from the great discrepancy in interest rates prevailing in various centers; partly from the reluctance of certain countries, notably France, to make foreign long-term loans, and from their preference for short-term lending; and finally from the inability, due to unsettled domestic conditions, of Continental European countries at certain times to obtain long-term loans. This accumulation of short-term balances was further accelerated by the extensive adoption of the gold exchange standard, which permitted certain central banks to maintain the whole or part of their required gold reserve in sight balances in countries on the gold standard.

While these short-term funds performed a useful function, the possibility of their withdrawal either on demand or at very short notice constituted a constant menace to the financial equilibrium of the debtor countries and to the stability of their exchange. The owner of short-term funds had in his hand an effective and dangerous weapon against the debtor; but this weapon is doubled-edged for, if used unwisely, it could hurt the creditor as well as the debtor. The results of the maintenance of this unwieldy mobile reservoir of short-term funds is now evident in the depreciation of a number of currencies, in the foreign exchange restrictions that have been imposed, in the necessity for various standstill agreements, and in the frozen nature of most of the funds themselves.

Conclusion. The post-war stabilization failed because it was based on the quicksands of foreign loans, both short-term and long-term, and not on the rock of economic equilibrium in the individual countries. The post-war economic and political leaders saw in the unbalanced budgets of the various nations the greatest danger to the stability of their currencies, and therefore concentrated their efforts on rehabilitation of the public finances; but they relied too much on orthodox central bank policy to rectify the maladjusted balance of payments. So long as confidence prevailed, the capital-rich nations, notably the United States, were willing to place funds abroad and thereby enable the stability of the currencies to be maintained. However, once confidence was destroyed, the creditors ceased lending money and withdrew their foreign balances, and the entire system collapsed.

The Collapse of 1931–1932

It was not surprising that the first warnings of the upheaval to come should be sounded from Austria, which was crippled both politically and economically. On May 11, 1931, came the shocking revelation that the Oesterreich-ische Credit-Anstalt für Handel und Gewerbe in Vienna, the largest banking institution in Austria, had applied for assistance to the Austrian Government and to the Austrian National Bank when the closing of the accounts for 1930 revealed losses of about 140,000,000 schillings, or an amount equal to its entire capital. The Credit-Anstalt was an old and highly regarded institution which had never failed to earn its dividends since 1857, and its difficulties were not due so much to its losses as to the lack of liquidity resulting from the "freezing" of large short-term funds. The imminent financial disaster, with its unavoidable repercussion on the entire economic life of the country, was so serious that the Austrian Government felt compelled to take action to save the institution. The desired help was so promptly given that, when the embarrassing position of the Credit-Anstalt was made public a few days later, it was possible to announce at the same time that arrangements had been made for its reorganization.

The Credit-Anstalt crisis destroyed to a great extent the results of the international financial reconstruction scheme of Austria. This had been heralded as one of the great achievements in European politics since the war, and the crisis demonstrated again the difficulty, if not the impossibility, of maintaining Austria as an independent unit under the existing economic and political conditions in Europe. The Austrian crisis was an alarm signal to all who had short-term loans in Europe. The delicate chain of international credits was broken at its weakest link. It was the starting point of a credit crisis, unprecedented in peace time, which spread rapidly throughout Central Europe, finally crossing the channel to grip London and, ultimately, the United States.

Germany. Germany was the first major country to feel the shock of the Austrian crisis. After the stabilization of the currency, Germany had managed to accumulate huge short-term foreign debts, and during a brief interval of two years—1929 and 1930—she was twice subjected to large withdrawals of foreign credits. These events had left the country unprepared for the huge internal as well as external run on the banks of the country that was thereafter to follow. According to the report of the Basle Committee of Inquiry under date of August 20, 1931, during the first seven months of 1931 the withdrawals of foreign credits from Germany, together with the selling by foreigners of German internal securities and the flight of German capital abroad, amounted approximately to 3,500,000,000 marks. The effect of these withdrawals can be seen from the fact that during the three-week period from May 30 to June 23, 1931, the Reichsbank lost 1,075,000,000 marks of gold and foreign exchange held as part of the metallic reserve.

The German banks thought at first that they could withstand the pressure by liquidating their foreign assets, and as a last resort by rediscounting at the Reichsbank, which in its turn was believed to be able to stand the strain. Events swiftly disproved this optimism, for by June 19 the Reichsbank was faced with the dilemma of either putting into effect the extreme measure of credit rationing or abandoning its legal minimum ratio of 40 per cent gold and foreign exchange as cover for its notes in circulation.

The English Government, which had been well informed of the precarious state of the German finances, supported the German Government in its efforts. These developments culminated on June 30, 1931, in President Hoover's historic proposal for a one-year moratorium on reparation and war debts. If the Hoover declaration had been adopted immediately and unreservedly by all countries concerned, the financial crisis might have been brought to an end. Unfortunately, France put obstacles in the way of the Hoover moratorium by insisting on the payment of the unconditional annuity and on the inviolability of the Young Plan. Up to that time France had been only mildly affected by the world crisis and did not comprehend the seriousness of the situation. With the exception of a few political loans of moderate amounts made to its allies, and a small participation in the Dawes and Young Loans, France had refrained from making long-term loans, while the huge short-term balances maintained abroad placed that country in a strong position. When an agreement was finally reached between France and the United States on July 6, two weeks after the proposal for the moratorium had been made, it was too late to stem the avalanche of domestic and foreign withdrawals. The closing of the German banks became unavoidable. The delay in accepting the moratorium destroyed the last vestige of confidence at home and abroad and accelerated the run on the German

banks. Under the credit restriction policy of the Reichsbank, the banks were unable to meet the withdrawals of
the frightened public; and when it became evident, on the
same day after a meeting of the directors of the Bank for
International Settlements, that no adequate assistance to
Germany would be forthcoming from abroad, the Government felt itself compelled to close all the banks—*i.e.*, to
suspend cash payments and inter-bank clearing by emergency decree.

Although no moratorium was declared, the closing of all
banks was tantamount to a complete bank moratorium.
The temporary closing of the whole banking system of the
country was the first event of its kind in the history of
modern German banking, so drastic a step not having been
taken even under the desperately chaotic monetary conditions of 1922 and 1923.

The steps taken by the German government to reor-
ganize the German banking structure are described in Chapter XIV.

England. When the financial crisis broke out in Central Europe, London—true to its traditions as a great international money center—did all in its power to prevent
the spread to other countries. The Bank of England extended a credit of about $21,000,000 to the Austrian gov-
ernment to help to tide over the critical situation, and
later, in conjunction with the Bank of France, the Federal
Reserve banks, and the Bank for International Settlements,
extended $25,000,000 as its share of a joint credit of $100,-
000,000 to the Reichsbank. These steps were taken at a
time when it was already clear that at least a portion of
the large British commitments in Central Europe could
no longer be considered as short-term in character nor be
withdrawn at the option of the lenders. The immobiliza-
tion of foreign credits in Central Europe and in Germany
caused apprehension concerning the liquidity of the international money markets, particularly of London, the international clearing house of the world, which was known to

have had in Germany about £100,000,000 of frozen short-term credits. As such fears grew, the banks throughout the world thought it advisable to strengthen their liquidity by recalling from London part of their balances, both sight and short-term, so that during the months of July and August London repaid on this account a total of £200,-000,000.

Although the foreign balances maintained in England represented only a fraction of its investments abroad, the City found itself in difficulties because it could not realize on its long-term nor on most of its short-term investments abroad and because the foreign creditors were not at the same time debtors to London.   Between the middle of July and the first of August, 1931, the gold holdings of the Bank of England declined by £32,000,000 ($155,520,000) to a total of £133,800,000 ($650,268,000), the lowest since November 1929.   Of these withdrawals, $100,000,000 went to Paris and the balance to Amsterdam and Zurich.   In an attempt to check the run on its gold reserves, the Bank of England raised the discount rate from 2½ per cent to 3½ per cent on July 23, and then to 4½ per cent on July 30. Following the report of the Committee on Finance and Industry (Macmillan Report) which exposed the weakness of the international position of the London market, the report of the Parliament's Economy Committee (May Committee) was issued on July 31, predicting, in the absence of special measures, a budgetary deficit of nearly £120,-000,000 for the year 1932–33.   The publication of these reports was followed by further withdrawals of funds from England.   The Bank of France, realizing the imminent danger of suspension of the gold standard in England, and having in mind the safety of the French balances in England (estimated at that time to be about £150,000,000), tried to prevent a further outflow of gold from London by absorbing any amount of sterling offered by the French banks.   In the meantime, the Bank of England resorted to all means at its disposal to maintain the stability of the pound. On August 1, it contracted with the Federal Reserve Bank of New York and the Bank of France a credit of £25,000,000 (from each institution) in the currency of the two respective countries, hoping that the mere arrangement of such a credit would suffice to stem the flight from sterling. At the same time the Bank of England procured permission from the Exchequer, in accordance with the provisions of the 1928 Currency and Bank Notes Act, to increase the fiduciary note issue from £260,000,000 to £275,000,000. These measures were inadequate to allay the fears of the creditors or to restore confidence, for by the end of August the proceeds of the above-mentioned credits had been exhausted.

Great Britain did not surrender, but continued the desperate fight to save the pound through the contraction of new foreign loans. On August 28 the Treasury obtained credits for £80,000,000 in New York and Paris, although even this credit postponed only for three weeks the step that was inevitable in the face of the incessant run. On September 20 the Cabinet ratified the resolution to suspend the gold standard provisionally for a period of six months, the resolution to become effective the following day. At the same time the bank rate was raised to 6 per cent. Sterling exchange was left unprotected to find its own level.

The events preceding the abandonment of the gold standard by Great Britain revealed the danger inherent in holding large short-term foreign funds which, when confidence is destroyed, can be hastily repatriated without any concern for the effects on the country losing them, or which can be used by the owners to attain selfish political or economic aims. The fact that a reduction of not even 20 per cent in the gold holdings of the Bank of England forced the pound off the gold standard is a clear indication of the narrow margin of safety with which the City, as the most active international financial center, carried on its operations. London's ratio of liquidity, based on the practical experience of a century, would have been adequate under "normal" conditions, but it is problematical whether the highest liquidity compatible with the function of a bank could have saved the pound in the face of the general distrust shown by nations all over the world.

Other countries. The pound sterling did not fall alone. The announcement of the suspension of the gold standard was followed by the immediate closing of the stock ex-

TABLE 5

RATE OF EXCHANGE IN PERCENTAGE
OF FORMER GOLD PARITY

European Currencies	Jan. 1931	Dec. 1931	June 1934
Austrian schilling	100.00	99.11*	78.27
Czechoslovakian koruna	99.96	99.99	83.33
Danish kroner	99.72	69.36	49.93
English pound	99.76	69.32	61.59
Finnish mark	99.94	67.25	52.59
German reichsmark	99.79	99.15*	95.63
Greek drachma	99.73	99.24*	43.23
Hungarian pengo	99.92	99.82*	98.70
Italian lira	99.47	97.08	97.00
Norwegian kroner	99.73	68.97	56.17
Polish zloty	99.04	99.75	99.94
Portuguese escudo	100.00	73.02	62.07
Swedish kroner	99.87	69.82	57.64
Swiss franc	100.32	100.96	99.99

* The more rapid depreciation of these currencies was prevented through the introduction of rigid foreign exchange restrictions.

changes in some countries. The suspension weakened the currencies in a great number of countries which had maintained large balances in the London market, and proved beyond doubt the interdependence of the various money markets.

The abandonment of the gold standard by England was followed by similar action elsewhere, culminating, as may be seen from Tables 5 and 6, in the devaluation of the dollar.

Among the British Empire currencies, the South African pound was the only one to remain for a time linked to gold, but this relation ceased on December 29, 1932. The Irish Free State, India, Egypt, Palestine, and those British colonies in which the pound is the unit of account, abandoned the gold standard with Great Britain. Canada suspended free gold exports without formally abandoning the gold standard. The Scandinavian countries, owing to their great dependence upon Great Britain as an outlet for their products, followed Great Britain closely in suspending the gold standard, and at brief intervals still other countries made the same decision or introduced foreign exchange regulations. With the exception of a few nations such as

TABLE 6

RATE OF EXCHANGE IN PERCENTAGE
OF FORMER GOLD PARITY

Other Currencies	Jan. 1931	Dec. 1931	June 1934
Argentine peso	72.25	60.66	46.81
Bolivian boliviano	100.69	97.95	42.07
Brazilian milreis	75.83	51.83	39.85
Canadian dollar	99.79	82.71	59.52
Chilean peso	99.18	99.18	49.59
Indian rupee	98.45	69.48	61.34
Japanese yen	99.19	97.20	35.42
United States dollar	99.93	99.87	59.39

France, Holland, Switzerland, Belgium, and Poland, which demonstrated their ability to remain on the gold standard, practically all other countries which remained nominally on the gold standard were forced to surround themselves with foreign exchange restrictions. Contrary to the general trend, however, Poland returned to the gold bullion standard. On February 9, 1933, by a vote of the stockholders of the Bank of Poland, which was later ratified by the government and the parliament, Poland discarded the gold exchange standard and adopted the gold bullion standard. The legal minimum reserve ratio was reduced from 40 to 30 per cent; and the minimum reserve ratio, which under the old law applied to note circulation plus sight liabilities, in the future will apply to note circulation only, plus any amount of sight liabilities in excess of 100,-000,000 zlotys.

United States. It is only natural that a banking panic which gripped the European nations should have repercussions in the United States. The collapse of the pound had caused considerable losses to a number of central banks and other institutions, which now hastened to withdraw their balances from the United States. From the end of September 1931 to the end of June 1932, the United States witnessed an outflow of gold amounting to $898,000,000. However, during the summer of 1932 there was hope that the crisis in the United States had passed and that this country would be able to weather the storm. The dollar became once again the favorite currency throughout the world and sold at a premium in all markets. The export of gold stopped, and a return flow set in. This improvement, however, was only of short duration. The increasing number of bank failures soon caused another confidence crisis, resulting in a tremendous outflow of gold and in gold and currency hoarding which came to an end only on March 5, 1933, when the banks of the country were closed by Presidential proclamation.

The banking holiday in the United States ended the bank panic, but it also resulted in the abandonment of the gold standard. The subsequent monetary developments in the United States are fresh in recollection and need not be described. The gold-buying policy, the devaluation of the dollar, and the silver legislation have been criticized by many competent experts. Although the dollar was legally stabilized on January 30, 1934, at 59.05 per cent of its previous parity, this does not necessarily mean final stabilization, because under the amendment to the Agricultural Adjustment Act, the President has the power to devalue the currency up to 50 per cent of its original parity—a factor which is threatening stability of the dollar at this writing. Czechoslovakia soon followed the example of the United States, and on February 17, 1934, reduced the gold content of the crown from 44.58 milligrams fine to 37.15 milligrams fine, or 83.34 per cent of the old parity; but she otherwise adhered to the gold standard.

Effects of the Collapse on the International Money Market

These developments brought the international financial situation back to where it was shortly after the war, but with this important distinction: that, in addition, the world in 1934 was confronted with new problems and with the task of liquidating the huge volume of short-term and long-term foreign debts contracted prior to 1930. The disruption of the international money market could have been localized if creditors had not become panic-stricken or if politics had not played an important rôle in determining the withdrawal of funds. The fearful creditors completely disregarded the fact that, in international transactions, only comparatively small marginal amounts can be transferred in the long run, and that even within the same country only marginal amounts can be transferred from one form of investment to another without causing considerable havoc. The amount that a country has available for payment abroad depends upon its economic structure and, chiefly, upon its balance of payments and the liquid short-term resources that it has abroad. Beyond that margin, no real transfers short of exports of goods can be made without causing a breakdown of the currency of the debtor. Up to 1930, few debtor countries could meet even the service on their foreign debts without a simultaneous inflow of short- or long-term credits. The international flow of credit abruptly ceased in 1931, and the fall in the prices of raw materials and agricultural products that ensued further aggravated the plight of the debtor nations. Short-term or long-term international payments are made through the sale of commodities and services in the absence of new foreign loans; hence, a drop in commodity prices is particularly disastrous to debtor nations, for they must ship more commodities in order to obtain the necessary foreign exchange. Foreign debts contracted in the years shortly after the war were about twice as burdensome in 1931–32 as at the time they were incurred, if measured in the volume of goods which had to be sold to meet the debt services or to liquidate the debts. The situation was further aggravated by the protectionist policy of certain creditor countries, notably the United States, in their attempt to avoid the import surplus which is an essential condition in the creditor nations. Under these circumstances, the various countries of the world, particularly the debtor nations, were forced to adopt measures which prevented the creditors from collecting their just debts. The measures most commonly introduced to this end were foreign exchange restrictions, transfer moratoria, standstill agreements and, as a last resort, the default of principal and interest on outstanding foreign obligations.

Foreign exchange restrictions. One of the first steps taken by governments confronted with a sharp withdrawal of funds from abroad or with a serious transfer problem, is the institution of foreign exchange control. The main objects of this measure are the protection of the domestic currency, the prevention of the flight of capital, and the regulation of imports. In countries which institute such restrictions, foreign exchange allotments are made by the government or the central bank only for imports that are considered absolute necessities, and such allotments are often accompanied by the imposition of obstacles to imports in the form of tariffs or import quotas. In this way it is hoped to bring the balance of trade into equilibrium and to improve the external position of the currency. Foreign exchange control not only imposes restrictions on trading in foreign currencies but also regulates all financial transactions between the country affected and the rest of the world.

Other countries, by organizing "clearing arrangements" for the purpose of offsetting import debts against claims resulting from exports in the same market, endeavored to overcome some of the trade obstacles caused by the foreign exchange restrictions. Although clearing arrangements may temporarily facilitate the trade between the two countries, they are generally harmful in that they prevent triangular trade arrangements and thereby tend to reduce the volume of international trade. Exchange control in its various forms and degrees interferes with economic freedom, and although it furnishes a weapon temporarily helpful in an emergency, it is not a fundamental solution of the problems but tends rather to restrict further the movement of funds and commodities. By the middle of 1934, the majority of the countries of the world had instituted foreign exchange restrictions.

Standstill agreements. A new arrangement called into life by the credit crisis of 1931 is the so-called "standstill" agreement. It is the English equivalent for the German word *stillhalten* and may be legally defined as a moratorium on outstanding foreign short-term debts by mutual consent of the creditor and debtor. It is a makeshift consisting of an agreement between creditor and debtor designed to avert an unavoidable default by the latter. It has been applied chiefly in the case of short-term inter-bank debts and in the case of short-term loans made by banks to large foreign industrial and commercial enterprises. Standstill arrangements were the best solution under the existing conditions, for in most cases the debtors were large institutions which could have repaid the debt if local currency had been acceptable. However, since the final liquidation of the debt required a transfer of local funds into foreign exchange which was not available, the standstill agreements prevented some of the largest banks on the continent from becoming technically bankrupt. It was relatively easy to form creditor committees empowered to evolve and sign a binding agreement with the debtors, because the creditors were chiefly international banking institutions. The rigid foreign exchange control introduced in the debtor countries offers assurance that, so long as the parties to the standstill agreement do not receive further repayments of capital, no payments will be made to other short-term creditors outside the agreement. The foreign exchange regulations also protect the interests of the foreign creditors against the export of capital by citizens of the debtor country.

While standstill agreements freeze short-term credits and may cause considerable embarrassment to creditors, they have certain advantages both to debtors and to creditors. They prevent repayment by the debtor country to one or several creditors who are more aggressive or who have better connections at the expense of other creditors. Secondly, they do not entirely deprive the debtor country of foreign credits essential to the financing of its foreign trade, and they provide for liquidation through gradual repayments or through conversion into long-term debts. Standstill agreements, however, do not remove the root of the evil, which lies in overborrowing and in the maladjusted balance of payments of the affected countries.

Transfer moratorium.   Another measure at the disposal of governments to protect the exchange is the transfer moratorium on the external debt.   The term *moratorium* means a period during which an obligor has a legal right to delay meeting an obligation which has become due.   A sovereign state may declare a partial or general moratorium. General moratoria have been authorized by law during times of war, national emergency, or financial distress.   An example of a partial moratorium was the one granted by the Swedish Government to the Kreuger & Toll Company. A moratorium suspends all or certain legal remedies against debtors and is applicable only in relations between citizens of the same state.   A unilateral moratorium on foreign obligations, *i.e.,* the suspension of fulfillment of contractual obligations towards other states or citizens of other states, is a breach of contract, a non-performance of obligation, and is tantamount to default.   The transfer crisis of 1931–

1932 resulting from the great volume of international long-term debts and from the disproportionately huge short-term indebtedness, coupled with a precipitous decline in prices, gave rise to a special moratorium characteristic of the present international economic and financial conditions—the so-called "transfer moratorium." As the word *transfer* indicates, such a moratorium affects obligations that are to be met abroad and can be liquidated only through foreign media of payment. The peculiarity of this "transfer moratorium" lies in the fact that, while the individual debtors must meet their obligations in domestic currency to be deposited with a trustee within the country, yet the funds can be remitted in foreign currency only upon termination of the transfer moratorium or with the special permission of the government. The debtor thus discharges his obligation so far as the payment is concerned, but owing to the foreign exchange restrictions imposed by the government, he is unable to pay in the currency stipulated in the loan contract and thus is in default. In some cases, the foreign creditors may use the domestic currency deposited to their account for certain specified purposes within the debtor country. The transfer moratorium is the logical sequence to government monopolization of foreign exchange transactions, and creates a serious problem which must be solved before normal conditions on the international capital market can be restored.

Blocked accounts. The institution of transfer moratoria and the adoption of standstill agreements resulted in the development of a system of "blocked" accounts, *i.e.*, accounts stated in local currency which could be used within the respective country but which could not be transferred abroad. The foreign owner of such accounts has funds at his disposal which he cannot use; but, on the other hand, there are always other individuals and corporations who can utilize such funds within the country. A market for "blocked" accounts is thus developed in which the funds are traded at a substantial discount.

In countries where this development occurred, there are thus two types of currencies: the "free," which sell at the regular exchange rate, and the "blocked," which sell at a material discount.   In Germany the blocked accounts are again subdivided into several groups according to their origin.[1]   The sharp depreciation of the blocked currencies not only enabled the debtor countries to repay a substantial part of their short-term debts but also put them in a position to finance supplementary exports at the expense of their foreign creditors.   In this manner Germany, although adhering to a stable currency, was able to compete with countries with depreciated currencies.   Since, however, exports financed through blocked accounts do not create foreign exchange but merely result in a decrease in foreign debts, their use has been gradually restricted and their value in the exchange market has declined sharply.

The creation of blocked accounts arising out of transfer moratoria on external debts raised a number of important questions concerning the use of funds.   Under the transfer moratoria in existence in several European countries, the individual debtors were under obligation to pay principal and interest in local currency into a special account at the central bank.   If these funds were not used by the bank, a substantial contraction of credit would have followed; if, on the other hand, the central banks used these funds to their full extent for commercial or other purposes, such action was tantamount to the making of new foreign loans to the respective countries, which would have led to rapid credit expansion within the country.   In most cases, the latter procedure was followed, and as a matter of fact, the recovery that became noticeable in a number of countries in default on their external obligations was financed with funds due to foreign creditors.   Thus, against their will, bondholders in the capital exporting nations were called

---

[1] See Chapter XIV, p. 376.

upon to help to lay the foundation for a new recovery and a new business cycle.

Conclusion. The institution of the above-described restrictions and regulations concerning the international flow of capital and of credit made the existence of an international money market impossible. So long as these restrictions exist and so long as the leading currencies continue to fluctuate, there is no hope of restoring the money and capital markets on a broad international basis. But in spite of the great pessimism, the many handicaps and difficulties that have to be overcome, the signs of a revival on a restricted scale are already noticeable. The London market is beginning to extend financial assistance to the countries of the sterling bloc. The establishment of the export and import banks by the United States Government is a clear indication that in this country, too, the importance of the international flow of capital is being recognized. Among the debtor nations the necessity of liquidating the past-due debt is also being recognized, and several of the nations in default have already taken steps to arrange settlements with their creditors. However, before a sound basis for the international money market is created, the nations of the world must again revert to the principle of the international division of labor and abandon the doctrine of economic self-sufficiency.

CHAPTER V

The Money Market—General
Comparative Analysis

Definition. The banking and credit system of a country is designed to finance its business in the most efficient manner possible and must, therefore, be closely adapted to its economic structure. The development of banking facilities in a country is concomitant with the growth of its production, distribution, and consumption, and the increasing intricacy of its economic structure is reflected in the greater elaboration of its credit facilities. The tendency for commerce and industry to concentrate in certain trade centers has its natural counterpart in the development in those centers of the particularly elaborate and specialized credit machinery which constitutes the money market.

A money market is a mechanism through which short-term funds are loaned and borrowed and through which a large part of the financial transactions of a particular country or of the world are cleared. Broadly conceived, it includes the entire mechanism employed in financing business of all types. In the narrower sense in which the term is generally used, however, a money market includes only dealings in more or less standardized types of loans, such as call loans, and in credit instruments, such as acceptances and treasury bills, in which personal relations between lender and borrower are of negligible importance. In this sense a money market is distinct from, but supplementary to, the commercial banking system.

In a certain sense a money market is a reservoir of short-term funds; it is a center where funds seeking temporary investment are accumulated and made available to those of the business and financial community desiring short-term accommodation.   A money market of international scope in normal times attracts funds from all over the world and redistributes them among borrowers in many countries. Since these funds are short-term in character, they require highly liquid investments, which are provided by the acceptance market, the commercial paper market, the short-term treasury bill market, and the call money market. The first two markets—the commercial paper and the acceptance markets—utilize these funds for the purpose of financing domestic and foreign trade.   The short-term government security market employs the funds to finance the deficits of governments, while the call money market is used to facilitate marginal trading on securities already outstanding in the market or to facilitate the issue of new securities before they have reached the ultimate investor. Under normal conditions the money market operates in a highly efficient manner.   Thus, for example, it has been estimated that the amount of short-term funds employed in the London money market in normal times is about £900,000,000.   The fact that a large part of these funds mature within thirty to ninety days is an indication of the great liquidity of the London money market.

Composition of market.   Frequently a money market is referred to as a highly centralized organization functioning more or less in the manner of an organized security or commodity exchange.   But this is not the case.   A money market is a loosely organized affair with a number of divisions and subdivisions, each devoted to a particular type of credit operation and each constituting a separate market in itself.   Each division of the market, however, is closely related to the others, and conditions in one often affect the others.   The various divisions of the money market proper, although differing in organization and technique, have one common characteristic—namely, that they are all engaged in the borrowing and lending of short-term funds.   In a broader sense, the money market embraces a number of independently organized markets, which directly or indirectly are related to the money market proper.

An important money market, such as London or New York, in its broader aspect is composed of the following individual markets:

A. The money market proper, which includes:
    1. The commercial paper market;
    2. The acceptance market;
    3. The collateral loan market, particularly the brokers' loan market in New York;
    4. The carry-over (contango market) in London;
    5. The market for short-term government securities;
    6. The federal funds market (only in New York).

B. The capital market, which in turn may be divided into:
    1. The market for new securities;
    2. The market for secondary distribution of securities, including the stock exchanges and over-the-counter markets;

C. The commodities markets, *i.e.*, the organized exchanges for cotton, rubber, grain, silk, coffee, cocoa, metals, etc.

D. The foreign exchange market;

E. The bullion market (in London);

and, to a lesser degree,

F. The shipping market;

G. The insurance market.

On the surface it may appear that there is little connection between the money market proper on the one hand and the commodity markets, the capital and the foreign exchange markets, on the other. But these markets are the pillars on which the money market rests, because in them are centered to a large extent the business transactions which the money market is called upon to finance and without which there would be no occasion for a money market to exist.

The most obvious relationship is between the money market and the stock market. When the stock market is active and prices of securities are rising, more funds are borrowed to finance trading, and this increased demand is usually reflected in rising interest rates in the money market. As a matter of fact, without a money market there could be no capital market. Similarly, trading in commodities is financed to a large extent by short-term borrowing on the money market, and therefore is dependent on the existence of the latter. The existence of these various markets creates a continuous demand for funds and thus provides employment for the funds offered in the money market proper.

It is evident that the greater the number and the larger the size of the directly or indirectly related markets in a financial center, the greater will be the demand for funds and the broader the foundation of the money market. The secondary rank of such financial centers as Paris, Amsterdam, and Berlin, for instance, as compared with London and New York, is due largely to the absence of important commodity, shipping, and insurance markets in the former centers. The predominance of the London center, aside from efficient organization and specialization of the market proper, is attributable in no small degree to the existence of the great international commodity markets and to the vast shipping and insurance interests of Great Britain.

Distinction between money and capital markets. Although a technical distinction can be made between the money market and the capital market, the two are, in practice, very closely inter-related, and transactions originating in one market are often completed in the other. Capital transactions, such as the flotation of securities, are often financed by means of short-term loans obtained in the money market; and payments of interest and dividends on securities, although having their origin in capital transactions, have the same effect on the money market as the repayment of commercial paper or the retirement of outstanding acceptances. Similarly, the proceeds of a loan floated on the capital market, once deposited to the account of the issuer, may be and often are used by the latter in the same manner as the proceeds of a short-term bank loan.

In spite of the close relationship between the capital and money markets, they perform separate functions. The money market is concerned primarily with short-term funds used for the financing of current business operations, domestic and foreign, and/or the primary and secondary distribution of securities, while the capital market deals in long-term funds obtained by the sale of stocks and bonds for capital purposes or for financing the deficits of governments and political subdivisions.

Functional organization of the money market. The technical organization and operation of the principal money markets of the world differ widely, since each has been developed so as to accommodate best the country or the economic area which it serves. Thus, for example, the brokers' loan market was the most important market in New York up to the end of 1930, and overshadowed all the other short-term money markets. In London, on the other hand, the acceptance market has been the principal subdivision of the general money market. This position was the natural result of the long and extensive activity of the London market in financing international trade, which is carried out chiefly through bankers' acceptances. In postwar years, however, important changes have taken place, and today, in both New York and London, the short-term government-security market is larger than the brokers' loan and acceptance markets. In the continental European financial centers, as in Paris and Berlin, the trade bills arising out of domestic commercial transactions and bearing two or three signatures have been and still are the most important instruments of the money market.

Institutional organization of the money market. The organization of the money market may be analyzed also on the basis of the different types of financial institutions engaged in the borrowing and lending of short-term funds. While it is impossible to classify borrowers and lenders accurately, since an institution may at one time be a borrower and another time a lender, the following classifi-

cation indicates the usual position of the chief types of
institutions. The positions of the individual institutions,
however, are not uniform in the various countries.

Lenders.—*The central bank.* The central bank, under
normal conditions, is the ultimate source of credit and
currency. In the United States the Federal Reserve Banks
extend credit, except under provisions of recent emergency
legislation, only to the member banks and to a few dealers
in bankers' acceptances and government securities. The
Bank of England, on the other hand, while free to do
business with anyone, deals chiefly with the bill brokers
and financial institutions. On the Continent of Europe, on
the other hand, the central banks usually conduct a general
banking business and deal with the public as well as with
banks through a more or less extensive system of branch
offices. Whereas in the United States and in England the
central bank is primarily a bankers' bank, on the Continent
of Europe and particularly in France and in Belgium, the
central banks deal more with individuals than with banks.
However, in contrast to the United States, where it is the
established practice for the member banks to borrow directly from the Reserve banks, in London the joint stock
banks almost never borrow directly from the Bank of
England, and the influence of the central bank on the
money market is exercised through the bill brokers, who
stand as a buffer between the central bank and the commercial banks.

Commercial banks. The commercial banks constitute
the most important single class of lenders. In the United
States they frequently appear as borrowers at the Reserve
banks or in the federal funds market. The manner in which
the commercial banks place funds at the disposal of the
money market differs in various countries. In the United
States before the war the brokers' loan market, and to a
lesser extent the commercial paper market, were considered
as the most important outlets for short-term funds. However, the development of the acceptance market during the

post-war period provided a new medium for short-term investments, and during the past few years Treasury bills and certificates of indebtedness have become the most important outlet for bankers' short-term funds. In England the joint-stock banks put funds in the money market chiefly in the form of loans to bill brokers and discount houses, and through the purchase of acceptances and Treasury bills. On the Continent, in addition to the financing of stock market transactions, the chief outlet for funds of commercial banks is the purchase of trade bills bearing two signatures, which upon endorsement by the banks become eligible for discount at the central bank.

The unit banking system in the United States, in contrast to the well-developed branch banking system of the leading European countries, also exercises an influence on the relationship of the commercial banks to the money market. In England and on the Continent, the banking assets are concentrated to a large extent in a few large institutions operating numerous branches. These banks are thus able to shift surplus funds from one market to another or from one center to another where the funds are most needed. In the United States a much smaller proportion of the country's banking resources are held by the half dozen or so larger banks, and owing to the absence of nation-wide branch banking, these institutions are unable to transfer their funds efficiently to those parts of the country where they may be most needed. The correspondent system, which serves as a substitute, is much less flexible than the European system, since the movement of funds is only partially subject to the control of the large banks.

The legal status of the commercial banks also differs in the various countries. In the United States every phase of banking activity is subject to governmental regulation, to which is added the supervision of the Federal Reserve banks over the member banks. In Great Britain, on the other hand, the banks are practically free from governmental regulation, and banking is governed primarily by long-established traditions which are so respected as to have almost the force of law. That these unwritten laws have proved more successful and effective than the multitude of federal and state laws in the United States is best demonstrated by the record of bank failures and loss to depositors in the United States even during prosperous years. The degree of governmental regulation of banking institutions and of financial transactions on the Continent of Europe differs. In recent years, however, and particularly during the depression, the tendency toward governmental supervision has been more pronounced, and in several countries new legislation has been enacted providing for increased powers of the governmental or central bank authorities over the banks. The world-wide depression has also strengthened the movement to nationalize banks; in some countries the governments have acquired control over a number of banking institutions through the purchase of stock. Thus, in Germany the government owns directly or indirectly a majority of the shares of some of the largest banking institutions, and even in the United States the government, through the Reconstruction Finance Corporation, has invested several hundred millions of dollars in the preferred stock and capital notes of banks throughout the country. In spite of the gradual recovery from the depression, the tendency to nationalize the banks, particularly central banks, still persists.

The business conducted by the commercial banks in the various countries varies considerably. The joint stock banks in England and the *banques des depots* in France are typical commercial banking institutions engaged only in the financing of commerce and industry and in the operation of the money market. As a rule they do not engage in the underwriting of securities and have no financial interests in the industrial establishments other than to finance their current transactions. In these countries the earnings and assets of the commercial banks are less dependent upon the status of the capital market or upon the movement of security prices. However, in some European countries, notably Germany and Holland, the banks are of a mixed type, engaging in both commercial and investment banking. In the United States, too, the commercial banks until recently engaged in investment banking through security affiliates.

In recent years, however, there has been a marked tendency to segregate commercial from investment banking, and in several countries, such as Italy, Belgium,. and the United States, legislation has been enacted or measures adopted to separate the two functions. The depression has clearly indicated the dangers inherent in the mixed type of banking. The collapse of the Austrian Credit-Anstalt and of the Danat Bank in Germany were partly caused by the fact that these institutions were too deeply involved in long-term financing.

Business enterprises. Business enterprises such as large corporations and, particularly, insurance companies often appear as huge lenders of money. During the stock market boom of 1928 and 1929, several billions of dollars were loaned on. call to brokers and dealers in New York by such non-banking corporations, chiefly through the agency of the large commercial banks. However, since the latter part of 1931 the large New York banks have refused to make loans for the account of others, and recent laws have prohibited such transactions. In London the surplus funds of the large corporations and insurance companies are often used for the purchase of acceptances and thereby create a continuous demand for such credit instruments. In post-war years the Treasury bills have to a large extent replaced bankers' acceptances. During the latter part of 1933 and the first half of 1934, the large insurance companies in England, owing to the low rate of interest on gilt-edged securities, have adopted the practice of making direct loans to business concerns and to political bodies, thus entering a field which hitherto was served by the investment banking

institutions. In Holland it has long been the practice of
the large business enterprises to place part of their surplus
funds in prolongatie, or renewal, loans and thus aid in the
financing of security transactions.

Borrowers. The borrowers in the money market consist
of a group of institutions and enterprises which operate to
a greater or lesser extent with the funds obtained in the
market. In the New York money market the stock exchange brokers, investment houses, and security and acceptance dealers constitute the most important group of
borrowers in normal times, while in London the chief
borrowers are the bill brokers, or dealers in bankers' acceptances and Treasury bills, and the discount houses. In
the leading centers on the Continent of Europe, security
dealers and the smaller financial institutions are the chief
borrowers of short-term funds in the open market.

The different types of borrowers and their relationship to
the central banks, perhaps more than anything else, indicate
the fundamental difference between the London and New
York money markets. In London the bill brokers and discount houses borrow money on call or on short notice from
the joint stock banks in order to finance the carrying of
their portfolios of acceptances and Treasury bills. In New
York the brokers borrow from the banks, pledging stocks
or bonds as collateral, for the purpose of financing the purchase of securities on margin. The loans may be payable
on call or may be contracted for a definite period of time,
usually thirty to ninety days.

In London the rate on "loans at call" or "short notice"
stands in a definite relationship to the discount rate of the
Bank of England, and the former can not go above the
latter. This situation is due to the fact that, whenever
the joint stock banks call their loans from the bill brokers,
the latter can have recourse to the Bank of England, which
stands ready to discount their acceptances or Treasury bills
at the official discount rate. In New York, on the other

hand, the securities (with the exception of government securities) which the brokers pledge as collateral for loans
are not eligible for discount or purchase at the Reserve
banks. Hence there is no direct connection between the
rate on call loans and the discount rate, and often, particularly in times of active security trading, the call rate is
substantially above the discount rate of the Federal Reserve
banks. The fact that the most important open market in
London—namely, the bill market—has direct access to the
Bank of England gives the London money market, at
least theoretically, a greater degree of liquidity than that
possessed in the United States, where the liquidity of the
security loans depends primarily upon the marketability of
the securities pledged as collateral for loans. This difference in liquidity, however, is of little practical importance,
because in the United States the member banks borrow
directly from the Reserve banks. In periods of stress,
therefore, the member banks can obtain funds from the
Reserve banks by discounting their eligible paper or pledging government securities.

The different relationship between the leading individual
money markets and the central banks is of particular importance from the international standpoint. In the case
of the London money market, particularly before the war,
a large inflow of foreign capital placed more funds at the
disposal of the bill brokers, but since the volume of bills
could not increase automatically to the same extent, the
result was a decline in bill rates which, in turn, tended to
check a further inflow of funds or resulted in an outflow
to centers where interest rates were higher. In New York,
on the other hand, a large part of the foreign funds coming
into the market during the period 1927–29 was used for the
financing of stock exchange transactions, thereby further
stimulating speculation in securities and creating a further
demand for funds. Since the demand for funds for stock
exchange speculation during a boom period knows practically no limit, the inflow of foreign funds from abroad

did not bring about a decline in interest rates and thereby prevented the automatic adjustment which usually took place in England.

There has been considerable change in recent years in the relative importance of the individual money markets in the principal international financial centers. Whereas before the war the acceptance market in London and the call loan and commercial paper markets in New York were the largest of the individual markets, at present the market for short-term government securities overshadows all the other markets in both centers. At the end of August 1934, there were outstanding in the United States $520,000,000 of bankers' dollar acceptances and $188,000,000 of commercial paper, as compared with $5,394,000,000 of government obligations maturing within one year. In England the situation is very much the same. This shift to short-term government securities indicates that the leading money markets are today being called upon to finance the governments rather than private trade and commerce. Such a development, deplorable as it may be, is but the natural result of the economic and financial conditions prevailing during an economic depression. It reflects partly the great shrinkage of foreign trade and partly the cessation of the international flow of credit and capital caused by foreign exchange restrictions and fluctuating currencies. The growth of the short-term government securities market, however, is undoubtedly a temporary situation. Sooner or later the governments will refund their short-term obligations, and then the question of finding a suitable outlet for the short-term funds of the market will become an important problem. In the United States the Securities Exchange Act will no doubt tend to prevent any marked expansion in the volume of brokers' loans, while the increased trend toward policies of economic self-sufficiency by so many countries during the past few years must have an effect on the supply of acceptances.

Government. The United States Government, and also the governments of other countries, very often appear in the money market as borrowers of short-term funds. In this country governmental borrowing takes the form of the sale of Treasury notes with a maturity of one to five years, of certificates of indebtedness with a maturity of thirty days to one year, and of Treasury bills with maturities of less than one year. The British Government has in post-war years made it a practice to issue every week a certain amount of Treasury bills, which are absorbed by the market. To a considerable extent, therefore, money market conditions in London are affected by the amount of Treasury bills offered and redeemed. It is obvious that when the Treasury redeems more bills than it offers, there is a tendency for money rates to decline; and, vice versa, when the Treasury increases its demands upon the money market, there is a tendency for rates to rise. Short-term Treasury bills and certificates of indebtedness did not play a dominant rôle in the New York money market until 1930, but since then the amount of short-term government securities outstanding has been greater than that of any other type of short-term credit instrument. In all the leading money markets, with the exception of Paris, the central banks engage in open market operations in government securities, but in no country has the central bank engaged in open market operations on such a large scale as have the Federal Reserve banks in the United States.

Relationship of various markets. Although the money market proper consists of a number of separate individual markets, each dealing with a special type of credit instrument or loan, the rates prevailing in the various markets are closely related. In London this is the result of the close relationship between all open market rates and the Bank of England discount rate. As a rule, the Bank of England rate is the highest, followed by the rates on prime bankers' bills and Treasury bills, which as a rule are higher than the rates on loans at call or short notice. Thus, in England, under ordinary circumstances any change in the Bank of England rate immediately affects all other rates, and only very seldom is the rate structure changed. The same applies to the countries on the Continent of Europe, where the central bank discount rate under normal conditions is higher than any other open market rate.

In the New York money market two distinct rate structures are in existence: (1) rates which stand in a definite relationship to the discount rate of the Federal Reserve bank, and (2) rates which are not directly related to the central banking system. In the first class are the rates on acceptances, commercial paper, short-term government securities, and federal funds. These rates invariably move in close harmony with the discount rate and, as a rule, are somewhat lower, since the transactions to which they apply may be shifted to the Federal Reserve banks in one manner or another. Entirely distinct from these rates is the rate on brokers' loans, which are not shiftable to the Reserve banks. Consequently, this rate has no definite relationship to the discount rate and often moves entirely independently of it. However, in spite of the independence of the call rate, there is a definite relationship between it and the other rates in the New York money market. If the call rate is higher than the other open market rates, it is only natural that lenders should place their funds in this market, with the result that the demand for acceptances, Treasury bills, and commercial paper is reduced, and rates of interest on the credit instruments traded in these markets rise. Similarly, a decline in the call rate tends to cause a shift of funds to other markets, thereby resulting in a lowering of other rates. Whether or not the control over the volume of stock exchange loans vested in the Federal Reserve Board by the Securities Exchange Act will alter the situation is as yet impossible to predict.

Relationship of the central bank to the money market. Every money market is, to a greater or lesser extent, subject to the control or domination of the central bank. The relationship of the central bank to the market, however, is different in the various countries, and depends to a large extent upon the laws and statutes governing the central banks. In the United States the sphere of activity of the Reserve banks is definitely prescribed by law and by the rules and regulations of the Federal Reserve Board. In England, on the other hand, the operations of the Bank of England are not subject to any legal restrictions, but are determined solely by the decisions of the "court" or the board of directors. Hence the latter has often engaged in such transactions as the purchase of stocks of foreign banks or of subsidiary banks, and in other domestic and foreign transactions which are prohibited to the Federal Reserve banks. The activities of the central banks on the Continent of Europe are, like those of the Federal Reserve banks, subject to the strict provisions of their respective statutes.

As a rule, the operations of the central banks are not shrouded in secrecy, and their activities can easily be followed from the weekly statements or from their annual reports. The principal exception is the Bank of England, which does not publish an annual report and whose weekly statement reveals comparatively little. Since the establishment of the Equalisation Fund the situation has been further complicated, because of the close relationship of the fund to the Bank of England and the secrecy with which its operations are conducted. Yet in spite of this secrecy it is known that the Equalisation Fund plays an important rôle not only in the buying and selling of foreign exchange and gold but also in the Treasury bill market, and thus exercises a powerful influence on the money market proper. In fact, the function of central banking in England is now performed by both the Bank of England and the Equalisation Fund. The former is concerned chiefly with regulation of the domestic flow of credit, while the function of the latter is to regulate as far as possible the international movement of funds and to prevent any unwarranted inflow or outflow of funds, into or from the country, from exercising an influence on domestic credit conditions. If the Equalisation Fund in Great Britain and the Stabilization Fund in the United States remain as permanent institutions, they may succeed in making credit conditions in their respective countries independent of the international movement of funds, so that the central banks in exercising their control over credit could be guided only by domestic considerations.

The control of the central bank over the money market is exercised through the discount rate, which, as was pointed out before, has in several markets a direct and often an immediate effect on all other rates and/or on open market operations in government securities or acceptances. Open market and discount policies of central banks are usually coördinated with the view of making the discount rate effective. The effect of open market operations in the various markets differs. In the United States the selling of securities by the Reserve banks, unless offset by other influences, reduces the amount of member banks' reserve balances and may force them to increase their borrowings at the Reserve banks, which event may be, and usually is, accompanied by an increase in the discount rate. In England, on the other hand, a reduction in bankers' balances caused by the selling of government securities by the Bank of England forces the joint stock banks to call loans from the bill brokers, forcing the latter to borrow from the Bank of England. Since the central bank rate is usually higher than the acceptance rate or bill rate, the forcing of the bill brokers into the Bank of England penalizes them and results in a general increase in the market rate on acceptances, often followed by an increase in the discount rate of the Bank of England. Some central banks, however, as for example the Bank of France and the Nederlandsche Bank, have no or only limited authority to engage in open market operations; credit control there is exercised exclusively through the discount rate.

Open market operations are of two types: (1) ordinary operations intended to offset seasonal factors such as an increase in the volume of currency during the summer months and before certain holidays, or to offset gold movements; and (2) extraordinary operations intended to broaden or to narrow the credit base of the country in order to influence business conditions. Ordinary open market operations have been conducted as a matter of course by both the Federal Reserve banks and the Bank of England. On the whole, such activities on the part of the central banks, particularly if intended to maintain the volume of credit on an even keel, are justified. On the other hand, extraordinary open market operations undertaken for the purpose of influencing business conditions or the international money market have been subject to severe criticisms. In discussing this phase of the Federal Reserve banks' activity before a Senate Investigation Committee, Dr. Adolph Miller, a member of the Federal Reserve Board since 1914, stated:

> In the year 1927, if the committee will look at the curve which relates to Federal reserve holdings of United States securities, you will note the pronounced increase in these holdings in the second half of the year. Coupled with the heavy purchases of acceptances, it was the greatest and boldest operation ever undertaken by the Federal reserve system, and, in my judgment, resulted in one of the most costly errors committed by it or any other banking system in the last 75 years. I am inclined to think that a different policy at that time would have left us with a different condition at this time. That is not an easy or a pleasant thing for me to say, but in the atmosphere of this committee, where you are undertaking to find out what can be done to control the use of Federal reserve credit for certain purposes, I feel it ought to be said.
>
> You notice that as the volume of these securities voluntarily purchased by the Federal reserve banks increases, in other words, as the Federal reserve puts money into the market, not because member banks asked it by offering paper for rediscount, but in pursuance of an affirmative policy of its own, which in effect said, "We shall not wait to be asked to provide increased money through rediscounts; we will operate on our own responsibility and through our own instrumentality, to

wit, the purchase of United States Government obligations"—
there followed immediately an increase in the reserve balances
of the member banks. . . . That was a time of business reces-
sion. Business could not use and was not asking for increased
money at that time. But the banks do not want to, and in
fact do not, carry uninvested moneys or idle reserves. Here,
then, in 1927 came an accession to their reserves for which
they had to find a use.

In spite of the severe criticism, in 1932 and again during
1933 the Reserve banks engaged in heavy open market
operations with the view of bringing about an expansion of
bank credit, but with little success. Under the Bank Act
of 1933 and the Securities Exchange Act of 1934, the powers
of the Reserve banks have been broadened, and in the
future they will in all probability depend on these powers
more than on open market operations, particularly in order
to prevent the use of credit for speculative purposes. The
granting of powers to the Reserve Board to control by order
(direct action) the flow of funds is a new departure in
central banking. Although this measure of control was
used successfully by the Reichsbank in 1927 to stem the
rapidly rising speculative activity in securities, and unsuc-
cessfully by the Federal Reserve banks in 1929, neither were
directly authorized by law to adopt such measures. These
new powers granted to the Federal Reserve Board increase
their responsibility to the money market and to the national
economy as a whole. If the Board is guided only by economic considerations, its new powers may be of great help
in checking credit inflation and in preventing the abuse of
bank credit. If, however, the banking authorities should
be guided by political motives, they may use these powers
to work great hardship on the money market and on the
country as a whole.

Management of credit and currency. The open market
operations of the central banks have already constituted a
serious breach of the rules of the international gold standard
as it existed before the war. They have enabled central
banks to broaden or to narrow the credit base of the country

irrespectively of the international movement of gold or the amount of gold available within the country. This management of credit, however, was not considered sufficient, and during the depression the theory was advanced, chiefly in the United States, that the management of the international value of the currency is more important in fighting a depression and in restoring good business conditions.

TABLE 7

MOVEMENT OF THE KRONOR—STERLING EXCHANGE RATE
(Par of exchange, 18.16 kronor per pound sterling)

	1932	1933	1934
Annual average...	19.01	19.20	19.40
January	17.91	18.38	19.40
February	17.96	18.77	19.40
March	18.32	18.92	19.40
April	19.72	19.06	19.40
May	19.69	19.45	19.40
June	19.52	19.46	19.40
July	19.51	19.41	19.40
August	19.48	19.40	19.40
September	19.50	19.40	19.40
October	19.40	19.40	19.40
November	18.81	19.40	19.40
December	18.32	19.40	19.40

The adoption of a managed currency would introduce an element into the money market which before had been considered as a great hindrance to its normal functioning. While the management of credit through open market operations weakened the international character of the gold standard, the introduction of the managed currency would destroy it entirely and would make the international movement of funds practically impossible. Briefly stated, the theory of a managed currency in its narrow sense means the shifting of the gold content of the currency in accordance with the movement of prices. An increase in prices would be checked by an increase in the gold content of the currency; a falling tendency would be halted by a lowering of the gold content.

The success with which Sweden fought and overcame the depression was generally ascribed in the United States to the operation of a managed currency. This belief is erroneous. After the suspension of specie payments by Great Britain, the Swedish kronor moved in unison with the pound sterling, as may be seen from Table 7. Through the entire period the fluctuations of the kronor in terms of the pound sterling were relatively very small. It is therefore inaccurate to state that the Swedish banking authorities have regulated the movement of the currency with the view of assisting business. The assistance given to business by the Swedish central bank consisted chiefly in open market purchases. The holdings of government securities by the latter increased by about 256,000,000 kronor from March 1932 to June 1933. Open market operations by a central bank, however, cannot be considered as the management of the currency. It constitutes rather the management of credit, which had been practiced in the United States by the Reserve banks throughout the entire post-war period.

It is not necessary to discuss the fallacies of the managed currency theory. If adopted by several leading countries, it would deal a last blow to the international money market and would mean the adoption of the theory of economic self-sufficiency in the flow of credit and of capital. The international movement of funds is predicated on the idea that the lender will receive the amount in local currency which he has lent. If, however, his own currency or that of the debtor is subject to constant changes, international lending would become a speculation in foreign exchange. Ordinarily the gold 'clause could eliminate the danger of currency fluctuation and depreciation, but Public Resolution No. 10 of the 73d Congress, which abrogated the gold clause as far the United States is concerned, makes the insertion of such a clause practically valueless.

The adoption of the managed currency system with a fluctuating currency would terminate all international financial transactions with a country or countries adhering to this standard. The international money market in the past, particularly before the war and during the period 1925–30, has been a useful mechanism through which funds have been shifted from one nation to another and to those centers where they have been most needed. In this capacity it was instrumental in the post-war recovery of Europe. The abuses of the short-term funds and their use for capital purposes finally led to the breakdown of the money market.

After the beginning of 1933 the international money market had practically ceased to exist, and the banking difficulties in the United States in March 1933, followed by the depreciation of the dollar, destroyed the last vestige that remained. Various suggestions have been made for the revival and reorganization of the international money market, some of them involving the use of the Bank for International Settlements to facilitate international movements of funds. However, a restoration of the international money market can take place only when the currencies of the leading countries are again on a common standard and when economic and political conditions again permit the free shifting of funds from one center to another. It is obvious that the adoption of the managed currency would not furnish the basis for the restoration of the international money market.

Importance of the money market. Each individual money market plays an important rôle in the national economy of the country which it serves and facilitates the financing of transactions, domestic and foreign, which cannot be conveniently financed by the banks individually. It offers the banks of the country the means of temporarily employing their funds in liquid investments and constitutes a reservoir from which funds are obtained when special demands arise. The money market thus performs for a nation or a given area the same function that a bank performs for a locality.

By the accumulation of funds, the money market facilitates the flotation of long-term loans for governments, political subdivisions, and corporations. Conditions in the money market, therefore, influence the rate of interest on long-term capital and have a direct bearing on the movement of funds into long-term capital investments. The existence of a capital market is therefore dependent upon the existence of a well-organized money market, and the two together have played an important rôle in the economic development of the world. The money market is of importance to the government particularly in periods of budgetary deficits, since it enables the treasury to obtain funds to meet temporary needs when it does not wish or is unable to increase its funded debt.

The service which the money market renders to governments is of the utmost importance. Where a money market does not exist, a government in need of short-term funds can finance itself either through the issue of fiat money or through borrowing directly from the central bank. Such methods of financing the needs of the government, however, are inflationary in character and, if carried too far, invariably lead to a debauching of the currency and credit system of the country. On the other hand, the existence of a well-organized money market enables the government to shift this burden onto the open market without interfering with the normal functioning of the credit and currency system. Thus in August 1934 the British market held about £850,000,000 of short-term Treasury bills, while in the United States the market held over $5,000,000,000 of government obligations having a maturity of less than one year. Without the assistance of the open market the governments of these two countries would be forced to have recourse to the central banks or the printing press.

Not only the domestic government and its political subdivisions, but also foreign governments, are in a position to finance their short-term needs through the money market. This was particularly the case before the breakdown of the international money market, but even during the collapse strong governments at times had recourse to a foreign market for short-term financing.

Through the money market, therefore, the financial resources of the country are mobilized and utilized for the benefit of the country as a whole.   The fact that the facilities of the money market have been abused at times in the past is not a reflection on the money market itself, but is the fault of individuals who abuse the market.

CHAPTER VI

New York—Institutions of the Market

Introduction. Although relatively young in comparison with London and some of the European financial centers, the New York money market has been important in international finance during the last two decades and, in spite of the setback caused by the bank crisis in 1933 and the subsequent abandonment of the gold standard, is bound to remain one of the leading financial centers of the world. In contrast to the other European money markets, which have reached a stage of maturity wherein their characteristics have become fairly well crystallized and well defined, the New York money market had to adapt itself to the rapidly changing conditions during the first two decades of the century and, more recently, has been subjected to far-reaching reforms under the New Deal legislation. The Bank Act of 1933, the Securities Act of 1933, and the Securities Exchange Act of 1934 have necessitated such extensive modifications in both the operation and the institutional organization of the market that the ultimate effects cannot yet be accurately appraised. It is axiomatic that the financial machinery of a country is merely a handmaid to industry and trade and must be so constituted as to meet its needs adequately. The profound changes in business that have occurred in the United States since 1929 are, therefore, even aside from the effects of new legislation, bound to cause material changes in the operation of our financial system.

It is clear that under existing conditions many observations regarding the New York money market must be tentative. The purpose of the present discussion is (1) to describe the institutions which provide and utilize the facilities of the money market, (2) to describe the operation of the various divisions of the money market, and (3) to analyze New York's position as an international financial center. An effort will be made to evaluate the effect of recent legislation on the money market and to point out possible future trends.

The principal institutions related to the New York money market are:

1. *The Federal Reserve banks,* which are the ultimate source of credit and currency for the member banks and therefore play an important rôle in the money market. The Reserve banks are invariably lenders.

2. *The commercial banks and trust companies* constitute the most important single group of lenders. They occasionally appear as borrowers from the Federal Reserve banks or in the Federal funds market.

3. *Business enterprises* are important borrowers, but the larger corporations have in the past invested excess cash reserves in the money market.

4. *Brokerage houses* are the chief borrowers in the collateral loan market.

5. *Investment banking houses* customarily borrow large sums to finance security syndicate operations, but at times they also loan funds in the money market.

6. *The United States Government,* and also the state and municipal governments, are large borrowers through the sale of short-term notes and certificates of indebtedness.

7. *A miscellaneous group of financial institutions,* including insurance companies, investment trusts, and discount houses, are sometimes borrowers and sometimes lenders.

The Federal Reserve System

The Federal Reserve banks, constituting the central banking system of the country, are the most important single institutional factor in the New York money market.

The policies of the Reserve banks at times influence to a large extent the credit policies of the member banks and therefore have a very important effect on the volume of credit outstanding and on interest rates in the money market. The organization and operation of the Reserve banks have been so well described that no detailed discussion is required in this volume. A comparison of certain characteristics of our central banking system with those of European central banks and a description of the new legislation insofar as it affects the money market may, however, be profitable.

Decentralization. In the United States there are twelve Reserve banks coördinated through the Federal Reserve Board, while in every other country, including small countries such as Holland as well as large countries such as the Soviet Union, there is but one central bank. However, the central banks in other countries have branches, sub-branches, and agencies, varying in number from nine, in Great Britain, to several hundred, in France, while the Federal Reserve banks have twenty-five branches and two agencies. Closer examination of the operation of the Federal Reserve banks, however, shows that the decentralization of our central banking system is more legal than actual, since the policies of all the Reserve banks are largely dominated by the Federal Reserve Board. Thus, although each Reserve bank fixes its own discount rate, changes are subject to review and determination by the Reserve Board, which insures harmonious credit policies. Furthermore, the open market operations of the entire system, the most powerful instrument of Federal Reserve credit policy in the past, are directed by a single committee, the so-called Federal Open Market Committee, created by the Banking Act of 1933. In accordance with the provisions of this law, no Federal Reserve bank may engage in open market operations except in accordance with regulations adopted by the Federal Reserve Board and transmitted to the Committee and to the Federal Reserve banks.

If any Federal Reserve bank decides not to participate in
the open market operations recommended by the Committee, it must within thirty days notify the latter and the
Board of its decision.

The same act also centralized in the Federal Reserve
Board all international relations of the Reserve banks.
The law now requires that: (1) all relationships and transactions between Federal Reserve banks and foreign banks
shall be subject to the supervision and regulations of the
Federal Reserve Board, (2) no officer or other representative of any Federal Reserve bank may conduct negotiations
with any foreign bank without first obtaining the permission of the Board, (3) the Board shall have the right in its
discretion to be represented in any such negotiations, and
(4) a full report of all conferences or negotiations and
understandings or agreements, together with all relevant
material facts, shall be made in writing to the Board.
Thus, in spite of the theoretical and legal decentralization
of the system, in actual practice and as far as its major
policies are concerned, it works as a single bank with a
number of branches.

Powers of Reserve banks to control credit. The Federal Reserve Board and banks probably have greater power
to regulate credit than any foreign central bank, but at
the same time they are subject to greater restrictions than
many of the foreign institutions. The original Federal
Reserve Act and the early amendments intended that the
control of credit should be exercised primarily through
the discounting of eligible commercial and agricultural
paper for the member banks and through open market
operations in government securities and bankers' acceptances. While these instruments enabled the Reserve banks
to exercise a very considerable influence on the money market, they proved to be inadequate to check the tremendous
expansion of bank credit for speculation in securities during 1927–29. Consequently, new legislation has been enacted which greatly increases the power of the Reserve

banks to control loans on securities for speculative purposes.

The Banking Act of 1933 amended the Federal Reserve Act to authorize the Federal Reserve Board, upon the affirmative vote of not less than six of its members, to fix for each Federal Reserve district the percentage of individual bank capital and surplus which may be represented by loans secured by stock or bond collateral by member banks within the district. The percentages so fixed may be changed from time to time upon ten days' notice. The Board is also authorized to direct any member bank to refrain from further increasing its loans secured by stock or bond collateral for any period up to one year, under penalty of suspension of all rediscount privileges at the Federal Reserve banks.

The Federal Reserve Board's control over collateral loans was greatly increased and extended by the Securities Exchange Act of 1934. Section 7 of this act provides that, for the purpose of preventing the excessive use of credit for the purchase or carrying of securities, the Federal Reserve Board shall prescribe rules and regulations with respect to the amount of credit that may be initially extended and subsequently maintained on any security, except exempted securities, registered on a national securities exchange. These rules and regulations apply not only to members of national securities exchanges and brokers, and to dealers transacting a business in securities through the medium of such members, but also to all loans extended or arranged by other persons for the purpose of purchasing or carrying any security registered on a national securities exchange. However, the provisions regarding persons other than members of a national securities exchange, or brokers and dealers doing business through them, do not apply (1) to a loan made by a person not in the ordinary course of his business, (2) to a loan on an exempted security, (3) to a loan to a dealer to aid in financing the distribution of securities to customers and through the medium of a national securities exchange, (4) to a loan by a bank on a security other than an equity security, or (5) to such other loans as the Federal Reserve Board shall exempt.

In addition, Section 8 of the act requires that members of a national securities exchange, or any broker or dealer who transacts a business in securities through the medium of a member, may borrow on securities registered on a national securities exchange only (1) from a member bank of the Federal Reserve System, (2) from a non-member bank which has filed an agreement with the Federal Reserve Board to comply with all provisions of legislation applicable to member banks regarding the use of credit to finance transactions in securities, or (3) in accordance with such rules and regulations as the Federal Reserve Board may prescribe.

This legislation obviously gives the Federal Reserve Board a very extensive power to control collateral loans. Sufficient time has not elapsed to permit an evaluation of its effect on the money market, but the Board has indicated that its guiding principle in administering the law will be the prevention of the excessive use of credit for speculation in securities. In a statement issued on July 5, 1934, the Board emphasized that insofar as banks are concerned, the law does not apply to loans made solely for industrial, agricultural, or commercial purposes, regardless of how they may be secured. It took the position that "The determining factor is the purpose of the loan and not the nature of the security offered." The Board also pointed out that a very large group of securities are exempted from the provisions of the law and that its power is further limited by the special exemption allowed bank loans on bonds.

Limitations on powers of Reserve banks. In contrast to their broad powers to control credit for speculation in securities, the Federal Reserve banks are more limited as to the scope of their business than most European central banks. Whereas the Bank of England is free to engage in any kind of legitimate business except "dealing in merchandise or wares of any description," the Federal Reserve banks may engage only in those transactions and with such other parties as are stipulated in the Federal Reserve Act. With certain exceptions, the Reserve banks may deal only with member banks, while the foreign central banks ordinarily deal not only with financial institutions in general but also with business enterprises and private individuals. The principal exception from the standpoint of the money market is the power of the Reserve banks to buy and sell bankers' acceptances and government securities in the open market.

Until 1932 the Reserve banks were permitted to extend credit through discounts and advances only to member banks, to Federal intermediate credit banks, and, in the case of notes secured by adjusted service certificates, to non-member banks. However, recent banking legislation has somewhat enlarged the scope of their lending activities. First, the Emergency Relief and Construction Act of July 21, 1932, provided that "in unusual and exigent circumstances" the Federal Reserve Board may authorize any Federal Reserve bank to discount for any individual, partnership or corporation, notes, drafts and bills of exchange eligible for discount by member banks. Second, the Emergency Banking Act of March 9, 1933, authorized the Reserve banks, subject to the regulations of the Federal Reserve Board, to make advances to individuals, partnerships, and corporations secured by direct obligations of the United States Government. An amendment to this act, approved on March 24, 1933, provided that for a period of not more than one year the Reserve banks could, under certain conditions, make loans to non-member banks. This period has now elapsed.

Finally, an Act of Congress approved June 19, 1934, authorized the Reserve banks to make loans on a sound and reasonable basis to, or purchase the obligations of, any established individual or commercial business. The law provides that such credit be extended only (1) in exceptional circumstances, when it appears that the applicant is unable to obtain requisite financial assistance on a reasonable basis from the usual sources; (2) only for working capital purposes; and (3) for a period of not more than five years. The Reserve banks are also authorized to purchase from banks and other financial institutions obligations created in accordance with the above requirements, or to make loans secured by such obligations, provided the seller or borrower assumes liability for 20 per cent of any loss which may be sustained. The amount of loans which the Reserve banks may have outstanding at any time under this act is limited to approximately $280,000,000.

These amendments to the Federal Reserve Act constitute a serious breach of the principle that the Federal Reserve banks are primarily bankers' banks, and considerably extends the scope of their lending operations. However, the volume of credit which has been extended under this legislation is comparatively small, and the Reserve banks still remain much more restricted, as to the type of borrower with whom they may deal, than are most foreign central banks.

Discounting. The practice of the Federal Reserve banks in discounting certain types of credit instruments also varies in several important respects from the practice of foreign central banks.

The Reserve banks afford credit accommodation to the member banks in two ways: (1) member banks may discount commercial paper from their portfolios provided it meets with certain requirements as to eligibility, or (2) they may obtain advances for a maximum period of fifteen days on their own promissory notes secured by eligible commercial paper or by such securities as the Reserve banks are authorized to purchase. Up to 1932 the Reserve banks, with certain minor exceptions, had only one rate, which applied to all classes of eligible paper discounted by the member banks as well as to the fifteen-day advances. The central banks in Europe, on the other hand, ordinarily have two rates, *i.e.*, a "discount rate" which is applied when banks or individuals discount certain well-defined paper with the central bank, and a "lombard rate" which is applied to loans collateralled by certain types of securities. However, the difference is more legal than real. Actually the Reserve banks also have two different rates—namely, the rate at which they buy acceptances in the open market and the discount rate. The former is always lower than the latter. The rate at which the Reserve banks buy acceptances corresponds more to the discount rate of the Bank of England, while its discount rate, particularly applying to advances against government securities, is more like the lombard rate of the latter.

Recent banking legislation has necessitated abandonment of the principle of a uniform discount rate. The Glass-Steagall Bill, which became law on February 27, 1932, amended the Federal Reserve Act by adding sections 10*a* and 10*b*. Section 10*a* authorized the Federal Reserve banks, with the consent of the Federal Reserve Board, to make advances to groups of five or more member banks [1] not having "adequate amounts of eligible and acceptable assets available to enable such bank or banks to obtain sufficient credit accommodations from the Federal Reserve Bank through rediscounts or advances" under the provisions of the act. Section 10*b* authorizes loans under similar conditions to individual member banks having a capital not exceeding $5,000,000. The law requires that the rate of interest charged on loans under both of these sections be not less than one per cent above the regular discount rate. Section 10*b* was originally limited to one year from March 3, 1932, but has since been twice extended for periods of one year, and now expires March 3, 1935.

In addition to the separate rate on 10*a* and 10*b* loans, the Reserve banks also have different rates on (1) discounts

---

[1] Advances may be made to groups of less than five banks if their deposits amount to at least 10 per cent of all deposits in the Federal Reserve district.

for individual partnerships and corporations under the Emergency Relief and Construction Act of July 21, 1932; (2) on advances to individuals, partnerships, and corporations secured by United States Government obligations under the Emergency Banking Act of March 9, 1933; and (3) on loans and discounts for established industrial and commercial enterprises under the Act of June 19, 1934. Thus the Federal Reserve banks now have different rates for different transactions. However, most of these rates apply to loans and discounts authorized by legislation of an emergency nature and may not be permanent features of the central banking system. At any rate, the volume of credit extended under these special provisions is quite small, and the rates have little effect on the money market.

Reserve requirements. One of the most significant relationships between the Reserve banks and the member banks, from the standpoint of the money market, arises out of the requirement that the member banks maintain deposits with the Reserve banks equal to a fixed percentage of their net demand and time deposits. This requirement also varies from foreign practice. In Europe the commercial banks customarily keep balances with the central bank, but such balances are not required by law and are maintained chiefly as cash reserves and for clearing purposes.

The section of the Federal Reserve Act defining reserve requirements divides member banks for this purpose into three classes. Member banks in central Reserve cities, *i.e.*, New York and Chicago, are required to maintain deposits with the Federal Reserve banks equivalent to not less than 13 per cent of their net demand deposits. In Reserve cities, which include the larger commercial and industrial centers, the requirement is 10 per cent of net demand deposits, while banks in all other localities must maintain reserves of only 7 per cent. Against time deposits all member banks must maintain a 3 per cent reserve with the Reserve banks. No interest is paid on the deposits, which constitute the member banks' reserve balances. The reserve requirements are strictly enforced and penalties are levied on banks whose reserves become temporarily deficient.

Title III of the Agricultural Adjustment Act of May 12, 1933, authorized the Federal Reserve Board, upon the affirmative vote of not less than five of its members and with the approval of the President, to declare that an emergency exists by reason of credit expansion, and during such emergency to increase or decrease from time to time, in its discretion, the reserve balances required to be maintained against either demand or time deposits. This amendment to the Federal Reserve Act further strengthened the control of the Reserve banks over the money market, for an increase in the reserve requirements would have the same effect as an outflow of gold, an increase of currency in circulation, or the sale of government securities by the Reserve banks. This is a particularly effective instrument of credit control at a time when the member banks have large surplus reserve balances and when the Reserve banks are unable or unwilling to sell government securities.

Federal Reserve control of credit. The Federal Reserve System has in the past relied principally on two instruments of credit control; namely, manipulation of the discount rate and open market operations. By raising or lowering the discount rate, the Reserve banks make it more or less expensive for member banks to increase their reserve balances by borrowing. By buying acceptances and/or government securities in the open market, the Reserve banks increase the volume of Federal Reserve credit outstanding and consequently increase member bank reserves. Sale of government securities or failure to replace maturing acceptances has the opposite effect.

These two instruments of control are generally used together. For example, if the Federal Reserve authorities wish to check expansion of member bank credit, they may sell government securities and/or reduce their portfolio of acceptances. Payment for securities sold or bills matured is generally made by checks on member banks. The checks are debited to the deposit accounts of the member banks, thereby reducing their legal reserves. If reserves fall below the legal requirements, the member banks must replenish them by borrowing. If at this point the discount rate is raised, borrowing at the Reserve banks becomes more expensive, and member banks are encouraged to reduce the amount of their deposits by contracting their loans or by liquidating some of their investments. Since the operations of the Federal Reserve banks under normal conditions have a decided influence on the money market, the Federal Reserve statement is watched carefully in the financial district.

Federal Reserve Credit

The changes in the amount of Reserve bank credit outstanding and the causes thereof can best be observed from the table issued each week along with the regular Reserve bank statement, showing the factors of increase and decrease in the volume of Federal Reserve bank credit outstanding. This statement for the week ended January 9, 1935, is reproduced in Table 8.

TABLE 8

FACTORS OF INCREASE AND DECREASE IN VOLUME OF FEDERAL RESERVE BANK CREDIT OUTSTANDING

(In millions of dollars; (+) Increase, (—) Decrease)

	1935		1934
	Jan. 9	Jan. 2	Jan. 10
Bills discounted	7	...	—97
Bills bought	6	...	—107
U. S. Government securities	2,430	—1	—2
Industrial advances*	15	+1	+15
Other Reserve bank credit	9	+6	+2
Total Reserve bank credit	2,467	+6	—188
Monetary gold stock	8,258	+15	+4,222
Treasury and national bank currency	2,508	—6	+206
Money in circulation	5,420	—114	+23
Member bank reserve balances	4,283	+193	+1,506
Treasury cash and deposits with Federal Reserve banks	3,094	—70	+2,741
Non-member deposits and other Federal Reserve accounts	436	+6	—31

* Not including $10,000,000 of commitments on January 9.

A brief explanation of each item will be helpful to the understanding of the significance of this Federal Reserve statement:

1. *Bills discounted.* This item represents the borrowing of the member banks from the Reserve banks. Member banks borrow only to replenish their reserve balances. An increase in borrowing may be caused by one or several factors, such as (*a*) an increase in deposits of member banks; (*b*) the sale of securities or acceptances by the Reserve banks; (*c*) the export or the earmarking of gold; (*d*) an increase of currency in circulation; (*e*) an increase in the deposits of non-member banks with the Reserve banks. The other items in the statement help to explain the causes of increases or decreases in member banks' borrowings from the Reserve banks.

2. *Bills bought and United States Government securities.* These two items reflect the open market operations of the Reserve banks. An increase in the holding of acceptances or of government securities places Federal funds at the disposal of the member banks; a decrease, on the other hand, reduces the volume of Federal Reserve credit. The movement of these two items as a rule indicates the open market policies pursued by the Reserve System. An increase in open market purchases usually indicates a desire on the part of the Reserve banks to create easy money market conditions.

3. *Industrial advances* consist of loans to private business enterprises made under authority of the Act of June 19, 1934. As far as the money market is concerned, such loans do not differ from bills discounted.

4. *Other Reserve bank credit.* This represents several items, including the so-called "float" arising out of the Reserve banks' system of collecting checks and drafts for commercial banks. "Float" is the difference between "uncollected items" and "deferred availability items"; or, in other words, it is an amount for which the Reserve banks have given the commercial banks credit, but which the

latter have not yet collected. It also includes the Reserve banks' holdings of Federal intermediate credit bank debentures, Federal land bank bonds, municipal warrants, and sums due from foreign central banks.

5. *Total Reserve bank credit* is the combined total of the above five items and shows the total amount of Federal Reserve bank credit outstanding..

6. *Monetary stock of gold* represents the total amount of gold held by the Treasury. An increase in the gold stock through either imports, release from earmark, or production of new gold tends to increase member bank reserve balances. This tendency is due to the fact that all gold must be sold either to the Treasury or to Reserve banks, and the checks which they issue in payment are, in the ordinary course of business, deposited at the Reserve banks to the accounts of the member banks.

7. *Treasury and national bank currency.* This item represents the amount of credit which the Treasury has contributed to the financial system through putting into circulation currency for which it is directly responsible. An increase in this item means that the Treasury has put out more money, which in turn results in an increase in member bank balances with the Reserve banks.

8. *Money in circulation.* This item represents the total amount of currency of all kinds actually in circulation. Any increase in the volume of currency in circulation tends to decrease the volume of the member bank reserve balances, because the currency is obtained by member banks from the Reserve banks and, in order to pay for the notes, the former draw on their reserve balances. Conversely, a decrease in the volume of currency in circulation results in an increase in member bank balances as the member banks return the unneeded currency to the Reserve banks.

9. *Treasury cash and deposits with the Federal Reserve banks* represent cash funds available for expenditure by the Treasury, other than deposits with commercial banks on account of the sale of government securities. It includes

these they could sell in the open market and thereby wipe out the member banks' excess reserves. However, such a measure would have an extremely depressing effect on the government bond market. In view of the tremendous amount of new financing and refunding which the Treasury must execute to meet the needs of the government's recovery program, any such course of action is practically out of the question.

As a matter of fact, control over the reserve balances of the member banks has been largely shifted to the Treasury. This development is chiefly the result of the revaluation of the country's monetary gold stocks consequent upon the devaluation of the dollar, which yielded the Treasury a profit in gold of about $2,800,000,000. Of this, $2,000,000,-000 was set aside as a stabilization fund, and the balance was added to the gold already in the general fund. However, this distinction is of little importance as far as credit is concerned. The significant point is that the expenditure of this gold by the Treasury in any manner other than by gold exports would cause a corresponding increase in member bank reserve balances.

The Treasury has already utilized a portion of its gold to meet the current expenses of the government by depositing gold certificates with the Reserve banks. This action increases the Treasury's reserve bank deposits, against which it draws checks to meet obligations. The checks so issued are deposited with the commercial banks and eventually, find their way back to the Reserve banks for payment, usually to the credit of member bank accounts. Through this mechanism the reserve balances of the member banks are increased in the same manner as by gold imports. The Treasury, on September 19, 1934, had more than $3,000,-000,000 in free gold and in deposits with the Reserve banks, and if this entire amount were disbursed, there would be a corresponding increase in the excess reserve balances from the present level of about $2,000,000,000 to some $5,000,-000,000. Although such a development is only remotely possible, it is clear that the status of member bank reserves is now entirely in the hands of the Treasury rather than the Federal Reserve banks. As a matter of fact, since the stabilization of the dollar took place the Reserve banks have acted merely as instruments through which the Treasury has increased the member bank reserve balances.

The Act of Congress providing for silver purchases at home and abroad until the amount of the white metal represents 25 per cent of the total monetary gold stocks, constitutes another source through which the Treasury is able to increase the reserve balances of the member banks. As the silver is acquired by the Treasury, the latter is under obligation to issue silver certificates; this, of course, represents an increase in the volume of currency. Since there is no real need for additional currency it will not remain in circulation, but will be returned to the banks and deposited by the latter with the Reserve banks, thus increasing the member bank balances with the Reserve banks. This is another mechanism through which the Treasury may interfere with the normal operations of the Reserve banks.

In spite of the increased powers of the Treasury over the money market, the Reserve banks are not powerless to control the expansion of member bank credit. In the first place, they have the very extensive power to regulate collateral loans, conferred on them by the Banking Act of 1933 and the Securities Exchange Act, which we have previously discussed. This in itself is adequate to prevent any such expansion of loans on securities to finance speculation as occurred in 1928 and 1929. Second, and probably even more important, is the provision of the Agricultural Adjustment Act of May 12, 1933, authorizing the Federal Reserve Board, with the approval of the President, to proclaim that an emergency exists by reason of credit expansion and during such emergency to increase or decrease from time to time, in its discretion, the reserve balances required to be maintained against either demand or time deposits. This power alone opens the way for the Federal

Reserve Board to eliminate the existing huge excess reserve balances of the member banks and regain its normal control over the money market.

However, there is an additional factor to be taken into consideration. In the past, any very aggressive move by the Federal Reserve Board to check credit expansion has met with serious opposition from certain political and business interests. This was true in 1920 and again in 1929. The Board has always been under the influence of the Treasury, and this influence has recently been greatly increased. It is, therefore, unlikely that the full powers to check credit expansion conferred on the Board could be exercised without the approval and support of the Administration, which in turn makes the future of credit control by the Reserve banks a matter of politics.

Treasury financing and the money market. In addition to the influence of the Treasury on Federal Reserve policy and its ability to affect member bank reserve balances through utilization of its free gold and through the issue of silver certificates, the Treasury under normal conditions exerts an important influence on the money market through its ordinary financial operations. On the 15th of the months of March, June, September, and December each year, the Treasury has the task of collecting taxes, calling in funds from depositary banks all over the country for payment of interest on government obligations, selling new Treasury notes, bills, certificates of indebtedness and often long-term bonds, and redeeming or refunding matured issues. In spite of the magnitude of the transactions, the technique of Treasury financing has been so highly developed that ordinarily they cause little or no disturbance in the money market, and it is seldom that interest rates are even temporarily affected.

The technical details of this financing, and the amounts involved, vary considerably from one quarterly date to another. They are governed by a number of factors, including the amount of the Treasury's cash balances, the financial needs of the government for the next quarter, the amount of revenue expected to be collected, the condition of the government securities market, and the amount of maturing obligations to be redeemed or refunded. The quarterly financial operations of the Treasury begin with the disbursement on the 15th of funds for payment of interest on the public debt, for redemption of short-term Treasury securities, and for special purposes—*e.g.*, the loans to veterans, as on March 15, 1931. Payment is made by checks drawn on the Reserve banks which are immediately deposited by the recipients with commercial banks and sent by the latter to the Reserve banks for credit to their accounts, thus resulting in an increase in member bank reserve balances. At the same time that these disbursements are being made, the Treasury is also receiving checks drawn on commercial banks in payment of taxes and for new issues of Treasury obligations. As these checks are collected, member banks' balances at the Reserve banks are debited, so that the effect is just the opposite of that of disbursements.

If disbursements and collections exactly coincided, they would offset each other and there would be little change in the total of member bank reserve balances. However, in practice, collections lag several days behind disbursements, and in order to cover the deficit the Treasury resorts to borrowing from the Reserve banks. This borrowing takes the form of a purchase by the Reserve banks of a special one-day certificate of indebtedness for amounts up to several hundred millions of dollars. The certificate is renewed each day in decreasing amounts as collections come in.

The amount borrowed in this manner is, of course, credited to the Treasury's account at the Reserve banks and is drawn on to cover the Treasury's disbursements. Consequently it results in an expansion of Federal Reserve bank credit outstanding and causes an increase in member bank reserve balances which, under normal conditions, would create a temporary condition of artificial ease in the market. Several measures are used to prevent the latter condition. In the first place, the Reserve banks sell participations in the special Treasury certificate of indebtedness to the member banks (mainly in New York), and their reserve balances are debited by the amount of their participation. A second method whereby the Reserve banks, under normal conditions, may counteract the effect of Treasury borrowing, is the sale of government securities in the open market together with a reduction in holdings of acceptances by a failure to replace maturities. However, this method is not always feasible. During 1934, for example, it would have been inconsistent with the government's financial policies for the Reserve banks to affect adversely the quotations for government securities by selling even a small part of their holdings. At the same time their portfolio of acceptances was so small that failure to replace matured bills would have had little effect on the member banks' reserve balances. Finally (the third method) some of the slack is taken up by permitting the reserves of member banks in New York City to fall temporarily below requirements, so that, just prior to the Treasury operations, a deficiency accumulates which is corrected by the excess reserves during the next few days.

Although the greater part of the Treasury's operations are concentrated about the quarterly tax collection and interest payment dates, it is constantly carrying on financial dealings with the banking system which often have a more pronounced effect on credit conditions than the quarterly financing. The Treasury is, of course, constantly collecting revenues from various sources and making disbursements to cover governmental expenditures. It is the established practice of the Treasury to keep most of its cash balances on deposit with the commercial banks throughout the country, but its checks are drawn on its deposits at the Reserve banks. Funds in the commercial bank depositaries are transferred to the Reserve banks at such times as they are needed.

Thus, the Treasury's current operations set up a two-way movement of funds between the Reserve banks and the commercial banking system. On the one hand, the Treasury withdraws funds from the Reserve banks by checks which are deposited with the member banks and eventually credited to their accounts at the Reserve banks. On the other hand, it transfers funds from bank depositaries to the Reserve banks, which action results in debits to member bank accounts. Consequently, unless the amounts of debits and credits are the same, member bank reserve balances are affected. In the week ended September 26, 1934, for example, the increase in member bank reserves of $81,000,000 was due chiefly to a net decrease of $63,000,000 in the Treasury's cash and balances with the Federal Reserve banks.

Commercial Banking System

Standing between the Reserve banks and the ultimate users of credit are the commercial banks of the country. These institutions directly finance a large part of the nation's business. One characteristic of the American commercial banking system which differentiates it from that of any other country is its dual nature. In Europe banks are created either under one general banking law, or under the laws governing ordinary business enterprises without being subject to any special banking legislation. In the United States banks may be chartered by both the national and the state governments. Thus, we have national and state banks existing side by side, but subject to different laws and different supervision.

The Federal Reserve Act was a step in the direction of a more homogeneous banking structure, in that it required national banks to become members of the Federal Reserve System and permitted state banks to do so provided they complied with certain requirements. The fact that membership is optional for state banks, however, constitutes a serious obstacle to strong centralized banking control, since member banks can evade national legislation which they consider prejudicial to their interests by giving up their national charters, becoming state banks, and withdrawing from the Federal Reserve System. The provision of the Banking Act of 1933 whereby after July 1, 1937, only member banks may have their deposits insured by the Federal Deposit Insurance Corporation was interpreted as a move to induce the non-member banks to join the Reserve System. It is questionable, however, whether the bank deposit insurance scheme will remain in force as a permanent measure.

Elimination of security affiliates. The provisions of the Banking Act of 1933 imposing drastic restrictions on national and member bank affiliates has necessitated considerable reorganization among the banking institutions of the larger financial centers. The law requires that after June 16, 1934, no certificate representing the stock of a national bank shall represent the stock of any other corporation,[2] and that its ownership or transfer shall not be conditioned upon the ownership, sale, or transfer of a certificate representing the stock of any other corporation, except a member bank. More particularly it provides that after June 16, 1934, no member bank shall be affiliated by interlocking management with any corporation or organization engaged principally in the issue, flotation, underwriting, or distribution of securities. Another section stipulates that after January 1, 1934, no officer or director of a member bank shall be an officer, director, or manager of any firm engaged in the securities business, and no member bank shall maintain correspondent relations with such firm, except as authorized by a permit issued by the Federal Reserve Board.

In accordance with this law, all member banks have either liquidated or divorced their security affiliates. Some of the

---

[2] Except a member bank, or corporation existing on June 16, 1934, which is engaged solely in holding the bank premises.

affiliated security companies were merged with other firms, and some were reorganized as independent concerns. As a result, the commercial banks have withdrawn from the investment banking field, in which they were an important factor during the boom period, and are now restricted to buying and selling securities for the accounts of their customers and purchasing investment securities for their own portfolios.

By far the most important financial institutions in the New York money market are the large New York commercial banks and trust companies which do a commercial banking business. These institutions are the chief lenders in the collateral loan market, the leading creators of bankers' acceptances, and the principal buyers of short-term government obligations. Most of the large New York institutions are members of the Federal Reserve System. The great importance of the New York banks in the banking structure of the country is evident from the fact that, at the end of 1933, the loans and investments of the New York reporting member banks alone represented 16.7 per cent of the total loans and investments of all banks in the country. If the resources of the other member banks, the non-member state banks, the private banking houses, and the branches of foreign banks are taken into consideration, the preponderant importance of New York is still more apparent. Nevertheless, the degree of banking concentration in New York is, of course, much less than in London and Paris, where a comparatively few large banks conduct the greater part of the total banking business through extensive, nation-wide systems of branches.

In addition to the large banks there have been a number of smaller banking institutions in New York which do not directly participate to any large extent in the New York money market. Their main function is to facilitate local trade, and their surplus funds have been placed in the money market usually through larger banking institutions. As far as the money market is concerned the small banks, although located in New York, are in the same category as out-of-town institutions. During the past few years a large number of these banks have disappeared, partly through absorption by larger banks and partly through failures.

Investment banks and private banks. In the past many financial institutions, generally referred to as investment banking firms, have conducted both a security underwriting and distribution business and a private banking business. In this dual capacity they have been among the more important institutional elements in the New York money market. As private bankers they accepted deposits from their clients and placed the funds chiefly in securities, short-term credit instruments, and collateral loans. In addition, they created bankers' acceptances, issued letters of credit, and dealt in acceptances, commercial paper, and foreign exchange. In connection with their security origination and distribution business, they sometimes appeared in the money market as borrowers to finance syndicate operations and often extended short-term loans to their clients to be refunded through the sale of long-term securities. Also, they frequently acted as fiscal agents for foreign governments, domestic and foreign political subdivisions, and corporations for whom they had been instrumental in marketing securities. In this rôle they received large sums from the issuers prior to interest and redemption dates, and these they temporarily invested in the money market. The strong influence which these firms exercised in financial affairs was due not only to their own great financial strength and prestige, but also to the fact that they held substantial interests in many commercial banks and were often represented on the latters' boards of directors. Furthermore, their operations in floating securities for business enterprises gave them representation on the boards of a large number of our biggest corporations and permitted the bankers to have an important voice in formulating their financial policies.

However, during the last few years the investment banking business has been subject to a most thorough reorganization. With the collapse of the market for new capital issues, many smaller firms were liquidated, and there were mergers even among the larger ones. But it was the Banking Act of 1933 which necessitated the greatest changes. As previously described, this law required member banks to divorce their security affiliates, and these affiliates, which in 1929 did a considerable portion of the total security underwriting business, have now been reorganized as independent firms or have been merged with other organizations.

In addition, the Banking Act prohibited any firm engaged in the underwriting or distribution of securities from accepting deposits subject to check or to repayment upon presentation of a passbook or certificate of deposit, or upon the request of the depositor. This meant that the investment bankers could no longer carry on a securities business and a private banking business at the same time. If they chose the private banking business, they had to take into consideration a further provision of the law requiring that firms receiving deposits must submit to examination by either the state banking authorities, the Comptroller of the Currency, and the Federal Reserve banks, and must publish periodic reports showing assets and liabilities in detail. This requirement made the secrecy in which the private investment banking houses had long clothed their affairs no longer possible. However, many firms elected to abandon the securities business for private banking, including such houses as J. P. Morgan & Co., Drexel & Co., Brown Brothers, Harriman & Co., and A. Iselin & Co. On the other hand, Kuhn, Loeb & Co., Speyer & Co., and Dillon, Read & Co., to mention only a few of the larger firms, relinquished their deposit business and continued in the securities business.

Capital issues and the money market. The investment banking houses influence the money market chiefly through the flotation of new issues of securities in the capital market. The sale of any new issue of securities involves two distinct movements of funds, which must be considered separately in an analysis of effects of the operation of the capital market on the money market. First, there is the movement of funds from the purchasers of securities to the underwriters, and second, the transfer of these funds from the underwriters to the issuer.

The principal investment banking firms are located in New York and Chicago, but any large issue of securities is usually distributed widely all over the country. Consequently, the sale of securities tends to cause a movement of funds to the larger financial centers. If the underwriters are located in New York, there may be a decrease in the deposits of out-of-town banks with their New York correspondents. If the out-of-town banks replenish their balances by transferring additional funds, the deposits and reserve balances of the New York banks are increased, and there is consequently a tendency toward greater ease in the money market.

In those cases in which an issue of securities is distributed locally, there is of course no geographical movement of funds, but merely a change in the ownership of deposits in the same locality. However, regardless of whether there is any transfer of funds to the financial center where the investment bankers are situated, a new capital issue may affect the money market by increasing the demand for brokers' loans to finance the purchase of securities by investors or the carrying of securities by the investment bankers.

The money market may again be influenced when the proceeds of a new issue are turned over to the issuer by the investment banker. However, this effect is likely only if the issuer wishes the funds accumulated by the investment bankers to be transferred to banks in another city. In that event, assuming that the funds are held in New York, there is a decrease in the balances of New York banks with banks in some other city, and this decrease may be accompanied, or followed by, an actual transfer of funds. The effect on the money market is just the reverse of that resulting from the accumulation of funds in New York, and it may tend to cause some withdrawal of funds from the market. Very often, however, the funds raised by a new issue of securities are left on deposit in New York by the issuer and are gradually utilized for corporate purposes as the need arises. In this case there is no perceptible effect on the money market.

Institutions engaged primarily in the open market. In addition to the large banking institutions described above, there are a number of specialized financial institutions in New York which engage primarily in open market transactions. The most important of these are (1) acceptance houses which engage chiefly in granting acceptance credits, (2) discount houses and acceptance dealers which buy and sell acceptances and commercial paper, (3) dealers in Federal funds, (4) dealers in short-term government securities, such as Treasury bills and certificates of indebtedness, and (5) foreign exchange dealers who act as intermediaries in the foreign exchange market. Several of these various types of business may be carried on by one firm. Thus, a firm dealing in acceptances may also deal in short-term government securities, Federal funds, and commercial paper.

Finance companies. In recent years, new types of financial institutions have arisen which exercise some influence on the money market. Such institutions include investment trusts, holding companies, and finance companies. All of these organizations perform certain financial functions in that they accumulate funds and endeavor to find profitable employment for them. The main function of an investment trust is to sell its own securities and reinvest the proceeds in other securities. The management may have free choice in the handling of its security portfolio or may be limited by charter provisions as to the securities that may be purchased.   The former are known as general management trusts, and the latter as fixed trusts. Investment trusts appear at times as borrowers, but more often as lenders—particularly in the call money market.

CHAPTER VII

New York—Individual Markets

Introduction. The New York money market is not a single homogeneous market but a combination of several separate markets, each dealing in a different type of short-term credit and all closely related. Some of the individual markets, such as the collateral loan and commercial paper markets, date back a number of decades and have developed in response to the financial needs of the country. Others, such as the acceptance and Federal funds markets, are the outgrowth of the Federal Reserve Act.

The individual markets are still in a state of flux. While the commercial paper market has decreased in importance, the acceptance market, in spite of the setbacks it has suffered during the last few years, has shown remarkable strength and will no doubt expand considerably with any revival of international trade. The collateral loan money market, on the other hand, will probably have a much less important rôle in the future than in the past, since the regulations embodied in the Banking Act of 1933 and the Securities Exchange Act of 1934 are expected to prevent any such expansion of this type of credit as occurred in 1928 and 1929. The short-term government security market has expanded to tremendous proportions in the last few years and now overshadows all the other markets. However, the Federal Government's policy of financing a part of its needs through short-term treasury bills and certificates of indebtedness must be regarded as temporary, and it is expected that as soon as money market conditions permit, a considerable portion of the government's short-term obligations will be converted into longer maturities.

160

The basic function of the money market is to bring together those who have short-term funds available for investment and those having need of such funds. So long as the market is able to perform this function, it makes no difference, as far as the general market is concerned, in which of the individual markets funds are employed, although the economic effects of the employment of the short-term funds in the various markets differ. An understanding of the nature and operations of the various individual markets, however, is essential to the interpretation of current money market developments. The following is a brief analysis of the various short-term markets that at present constitute the New York money market proper.

Acceptance Market

The market for bankers' acceptances in the United States is of comparatively recent development. Prior to the passage of the Federal Reserve Act in 1913, national banks were not permitted to accept drafts, and only a comparatively small amount of acceptance credit was created by some of the state banks, the larger investment banking houses, and private bankers. The framers of the Federal Reserve Act, however, appreciated the advantages of bankers' bills as a means of financing trade, and realized that a broad acceptance market would contribute to the strength and flexibility of the banking system. This law therefore authorized member banks to create acceptances subject to certain restrictions and to the rules and regulations of the Federal Reserve Board. It also made acceptances eligible for discount at the Federal Reserve banks, subject to the eligibility requirements, and authorized the Reserve banks to buy and sell eligible acceptances in the open market.

It was to be expected that such a technical and highly specialized business as acceptance financing should develop slowly. At the end of 1917, however, there were already about $450,000,000 of acceptances outstanding. As bankers and business men became more familiar with the technique of acceptance credits, and as the provisions of the Federal Reserve Act were liberalized, the volume of acceptances steadily increased to a peak of $1,732,000,000 at the end of 1929. Business depression, and the accompanying decline in prices and the shrinkage of international trade during the next few years, brought about a steady contraction in the amount of acceptances outstanding, and at the end of December 1934 the total was only $543,385,000. The development of the acceptance market is illustrated in Table 9.

TABLE 9

BANKERS' ACCEPTANCES OUTSTANDING
(In thousands of dollars)

End of		End of	
1917	450,000	1926	755,360
1918	750,000	1927	1,080,581
1919	1,000,000	1928	1,284,486
1920	1,000,000	1929	1,732,436
1921	600,000	1930	1,555,966
1922	600,000	1931	974,059
1923	650,000	1932	709,730
1924	821,418	1933	764,111
1925	773,736	1934	543,385

Classification of acceptances. The banker's acceptance, or banker's bill, is primarily an instrument for financing the movement or storage of merchandise. The Federal Reserve Act originally permitted member banks to create acceptances only to finance imports and exports, but was later amended to include other types of transactions. Table 10 shows acceptances outstanding at the end of 1926, the end of 1929, and August 31, 1934, classified according to purpose.

For many years acceptances drawn to finance imports and exports have constituted the bulk of the bills outstanding in this country. Bills of this character have long been regarded as inherently sound, because the transactions they finance are self-liquidating in character. The same is true of bills drawn to finance domestic shipments insofar as they represent actual sales of goods.

The use of bankers' acceptances to finance goods stored in or shipped between foreign countries increased rapidly during the latter part of the last decade, and at the end of 1930 the amount of this type of acceptance credit outstanding was $561,442,000, as compared with $40,313,000 at the end of 1926. It was to be expected that an important international money market such as New York should be

TABLE 10

CLASSIFICATION OF BANKERS' ACCEPTANCES OUTSTANDING
(In thousands of dollars)

	End of		
	1926	*1929*	*August 1934*
Imports	283,587	383,015	88,509
Exports	260,713	524,129	139,704
Domestic shipments	28,686	22,830	8,871
Domestic warehouse credits	115,882	284,919	137,838
Dollar exchange	26,179	76,285	4,248
Based on goods stored in or shipped between foreign countries	40,313	441,258	140,833
Total	755,360	1,732,436	520,003

called upon to finance the foreign trade as well as some internal transactions of foreign countries, but it was inevitable that unless the strictest standards were maintained unsound practices would develop, with disastrous results to both drawer and acceptor. The "freezing" of a substantial amount of such acceptance credits under the German standstill agreements clearly revealed the dangers inherent in this type of financing.

Another type of acceptance credit which has come to be of major importance is that based on staple commodities in warehouses (domestic warehouse credits). During the recent years of business depression there has been proportionately less decline in the amount of outstanding acceptances of this kind than in any other category. The use of acceptance credits to finance the holding of goods in warehouses prior to shipment or sale is generally regarded as a sound practice, but unfortunately it lends itself to misuse, particularly to the holding of goods for speculative purposes.

Acceptances drawn to create dollar exchange are peculiar to the United States and are used by bankers in certain countries whose exports are of a decidedly seasonal character, notably Central and South America, to create dollar balances during the season when exports are small. The drawer is obligated to provide the accepting bank with funds to pay the acceptance at maturity, and obtains the funds to do so from the proceeds of merchandise sold in the United States during the exporting season. Inasmuch as acceptances drawn to create dollar exchange are not based on the actual shipment of goods, the Federal Reserve Board has established strict rules and regulations governing their creation by member banks.

Accepting institution. The passage of the Federal Reserve Act did not cause an acceptance market to spring immediately into being. It merely paved the way for an acceptance market, and there remained the development of the machinery and technique essential to such a market. There are three primary institutional elements in the acceptance market: namely, the accepting institutions which create the supply of bills, the bill dealers who "make the market," and the purchasers who provide the demand.

The member banks of the Federal Reserve System are the most important single group of acceptors. The Federal Reserve Act authorized member banks to create acceptances in an amount equal at any one time to not more than one-half of their paid-up capital stock and surplus. However, with the permission of the Federal Reserve Board and subject to its regulations, member banks may create acceptances to the full amount of their capital and surplus. In addition, under regulations prescribed by the Federal Reserve Board, they may accept bills drawn to create dollar exchange to the amount of 50 per cent of their capital funds. Besides the member banks there are a number of private banking firms as well as foreign banking corporations and American agencies of foreign banks engaged in creating acceptances.

The acceptance business has in the last fifteen years come to be concentrated more and more in the hands of a comparatively few leading financial institutions located in New York City and, to a lesser extent, in other large Eastern cities. When the Federal Reserve System was first established, a considerable number of banks were attracted to the acceptance business, and in the period 1918–21 there were about 500 institutions, many in small interior cities, reporting acceptance liabilities. However, many banks found that the amount of acceptance financing which they could undertake was insufficient to warrant maintaining the specialized facilities required, and they withdrew from the business. On August 31, 1934, only 112 institutions reported acceptance liabilities. The geographical concentration of the acceptance business in New York is indicated by the fact that approximately 80 per cent of all acceptances outstanding on that date were created by banks in the New York Federal Reserve District.

Table 11 shows the kinds of institutions engaged in creating acceptances.

TABLE 11

CLASSIFICATION OF BANKS AND BANKERS
REPORTING ACCEPTANCE LIABILITIES
ON AUGUST 31, 1934

National banks	59
Trust companies and State banks	33
Private bankers	9
Foreign banking corporations	1
American agencies of foreign banks	10
Total	112

Bill dealers. The bill dealers consist of a group of private bankers and financial firms which do a general business as middlemen in the money market. They usually deal in securities as well as acceptances, while some act as brokers for commercial paper and as intermediaries in placing collateral loans and Federal funds. Most of them are located in New York. Less than a dozen firms do the bulk of the acceptance business.

The function of the dealer is to purchase bills from the drawers, accepting institutions, or other holders, and to distribute them to investors. Usually the dealer sends to prospective buyers a daily offering sheet listing the acceptances offered with the name of the accepting bank, amount offered, due date, number of days to run, denomination and lot number, and rate at which offered. The dealers buy bills outright and derive their profit by selling them at a slightly higher price, usually one-eighth to one-quarter of one per cent above the buying rate. They are required to add their endorsement on bills sold to the Federal Reserve banks, but do not endorse bills sold to other buyers unless especially requested to do so. Bills bearing a dealer's endorsement command a slightly lower rate. The dealers ordinarily quote uniform rates on eligible bills accepted by banks of first-class credit standing. Somewhat higher rates are quoted on ineligible bills and bills accepted by less well-known banks.

Purchasers. The principal buyers of bankers' acceptances are the commercial banks, the Federal Reserve banks, and to a lesser extent, savings banks, insurance companies, and other financial institutions. Bills drawn in accordance with the regulations of the Federal Reserve Board are generally recognized as among the safest and most liquid of short-term credit instruments, and it is a general practice among the commercial banks to include some acceptances among their secondary reserves. Legislation has been enacted in a number of states permitting savings banks and insurance companies to invest in bankers' acceptances.

The Federal Reserve banks have long been the mainstay of the acceptance market. They not only buy bills for

their own account at regularly quoted rates, but also buy
bills for account of their foreign correspondents, and purchase bills from dealers under repurchase agreements
whereby the dealers undertake to buy back their bills
within fifteen days. The readiness of the Reserve banks to
buy bills during periods of heavy liquidation by bankers
and other holders has been a stabilizing influence on the
market and has enabled the bill dealers to carry adequate
inventories with a minimum of risk. As a rule the Reserve
banks purchase acceptances after they have been held by
banks, dealers, or other holders for some weeks. It is
estimated that they purchase from one-third to one-half
of their bills from dealers and the remaining bills from
banks, although, if bills bought under the repurchase agreement are excluded, the proportion purchased from banks is
about three-quarters of the total.

The purchase of bills by the Reserve banks for their
own account is, like discounting for member banks, a pas-
sive operation in that they merely buy part or all of such
bills as are offered to them at their published buying rate;
they neither bid for bills in the market nor sell bills from
their portfolios. However, expansion of reserve credit
through this channel is much more closely under the control of the Reserve authorities than discounting, since by
fixing the buying rate below the bill market rate they induce large offerings; and conversely, if the reserve buying
rate is above the market rate, few bills will be offered and
the maturing of bills already held will result in a decrease
in the Reserve banks' bill holdings.

On the other hand, in buying bills for account of their
foreign correspondents, the Reserve banks are active bidders in the acceptance market. In order to execute
promptly the orders of the foreign central banks, the Reserve banks usually offer a rate about 1/8 of one per cent
lower than the buying rate for their own account. When
requested to do so, the Reserve banks add their endorsement to such bills, for which they make a charge of 1/8

of one per cent. By far the greater part of the bills bought
for foreign correspondents are obtained directly from the
bill dealers. The buying of bills for foreign account has
in the past been an important element in the market; at
times as much as one-third of all the bills outstanding have
been held by the Reserve banks for their foreign correspondents. However, during the past few years of disturbed monetary conditions, purchases by foreign central
banks have steadily declined. In the fall of 1934 the Reserve banks held less than $1,000,000 of bills for account of
foreign correspondents.

Since the Reserve banks are such large purchasers of
acceptances, it is natural that their buying rates should
have a very considerable influence on open market rates.
Ordinarily, the open market rate on prime 90-day bills in
New York is the same as, or slightly higher than, the Reserve banks' rate, but this relationship is often affected by
changes in the Reserve banks' buying policy and in the
demand from other sources. If the Reserve banks are not
buying freely, it may be necessary to raise the market rates
in order to stimulate demand from other buyers. Similarly,
if there is a strong demand for bills by banks, market rates
may fall below the Reserve banks' rate.

The distribution of bankers' acceptances among the various types of buyers is determined largely by prevailing
market conditions. In periods of credit stringency and
high interest rates, the banks reduce their holdings of acceptances in order to have funds available for other purposes. At such times a large part of the bills outstanding
are shifted to the Reserve banks. On the other hand,
during periods of low money rates when the banks have
difficulty in finding profitable employment for their funds,
they prefer to buy bills they have accepted from the drawers and to increase their bill holdings by purchases in the
open market.

Thus, at the end of July 1929 the Reserve banks held
(both for their own account and for the account of foreign

correspondents) about 47 per cent of all bills outstanding. Conversely, at the end of July 1934 the Reserve banks held only a little more than $1,000,000 of acceptances, of which less than $500,000 was for their own account, while the accepting banks held 91 per cent of all the bills outstanding. In April 1934 the supply of bills offered in the market was so small that the bill dealers instituted discriminatory rates against banks which made a practice of buying their own bills from the drawers and withholding them from the market. The rapid shifts in the distribution of outstanding acceptances during recent years are illustrated in Table 12.

TABLE 12

DISTRIBUTION OF BANKERS' ACCEPTANCES
(In millions of dollars; end of July)

Held by	1929 Amount	1929 Per Cent of Total	1931 Amount	1931 Per Cent of Total	1934 Amount	1934 Per Cent of Total
Federal Reserve banks:						
a. For own account	72	6.4	39	3.2	(*)	....
b. For account of foreign correspondents	459	40.7	243	19.8	1	0.2
Total, Federal Reserve	531	47.1	282	23.0	1	0.2
Accepting banks:						
a. Own bills	24	2.1	232	18.9	222	43.1
b. Bills accepted by others	66	5.9	436	35.5	250	48.4
Total, accepting banks	90	8.0	668	54.4	472	91.5
Others	506	44.9	278	22.6	42	8.2
Grand Total	1,127	100.0	1,228	100.0	516	100.0

* Less than $500,000.

Federal Funds Market

Federal funds are sight claims on the Reserve banks or the United States Treasury, and consist of checks drawn on the Reserve banks, cashiers' checks of the Reserve banks, and checks of the United States Treasury. The Reserve banks give immediate deposit credit for such claims. Thus, a bank which is deficient in reserves may temporarily increase its reserve balance by exchanging its own cashier's check for a check on a Federal Reserve bank drawn by another bank having excess reserves. Deposit of the check on the Federal Reserve bank (Federal funds) immediately increases the reserve balances of the borrowing bank, while the latter's own cashier's check must go through the clearing house and is not debited to its account at the Federal Reserve bank until the next day. In practice it is not necessary for the lending bank actually to draw a check on the Reserve bank; it may simply ask the Reserve bank to debit its account for the amount of the loan and credit that of the borrowing bank. The borrowing bank actually obtains a loan of Federal funds for one day which is repaid when its cashier's check for the same amount, plus one day's interest, is cleared and credited to the account of the lender at the Reserve bank. In case a loan of Federal funds is made on Saturday or on the day before a holiday, the borrower's check is not cleared until the second day, and the loan is actually for two days.

Since the establishment of the Federal Reserve System, a regular market for Federal funds has been developed in New York by a few large financial institutions which act as intermediaries in arranging the exchange of checks and charge a small commission for their services. Member banks ordinarily do not like to maintain deposits with the Reserve banks in excess of the legal requirements, since these deposits earn no interest, and consequently they usually seek to dispose of their excess reserves. On the other hand, whenever a member bank's reserves fall below the legal requirement they must be replenished. The most obvious method of increasing reserve balances is by direct borrowing from the Reserve banks, but member banks are often reluctant to do this and prefer to obtain temporary additional reserve balances through the Federal funds market.

The market rate on Federal funds is generally lower than the discount rate, being higher only in periods when the Federal Reserve banks are endeavoring to restrict the volume of reserve credit outstanding, and when member banks are unwilling to apply for discounts or advances at the Reserve bank. A rise in the rate for Federal funds is generally an indication of higher rates in the money market. It is obvious that, in periods when the member banks throughout the country have large surplus balances with the Reserve banks, the demand for Federal funds disappears.

Short-Term Government Securities

Closely related to the capital market but, from the financial standpoint, a division of the money market, is the market for short-term government securities. These include Treasury bills and Treasury certificates of indebtedness. Both are short-term credit instruments maturing in one year or less, and both are exempt from all Federal and state income taxes but not from estate and inheritance taxes. Treasury bills bear no interest and are traded in on a discount basis, while certificates of indebtedness are interest-bearing and are, like long-term bonds, traded on a price-plus-accrued-interest basis. In addition, longer-term obligations of the government currently having a year or less to maturity have the characteristics of short-term credit instruments and are regarded in the money market as in much the same category as Treasury bills and certificates.

Since shortly after the United States entered the war, the Treasury has regularly issued certificates of indebtedness to cover its temporary financial needs. In normal times the amount outstanding has not fluctuated widely from year to year. Treasury bills did not become a regular instrument of Treasury financing until December 1929, after an act of June 17, 1929, amended the Second Liberty Loan Act to authorize their issuance; but they have since been used more and more extensively to supplement the certificates. Both types of government obligations are offered for public subscription through the Federal Reserve banks. The certificates bear a stipulated rate of interest and are offered at par and accrued interest, while bills bearing no interest are sold to the highest bidders. Obviously, the fixing of the interest rate on the certificates at such a figure as to obtain subscriptions for the full amount at the lowest possible cost to the Treasury requires very accurate judgment of money market conditions. The bills, on the other hand, are a more flexible instrument of financing. By offering them for competitive bidding, the Treasury is assured of the best terms warranted by the condition of the money market at any given time.

Since Treasury bills and certificates possess the attributes of safety and marketability to a high degree, they constitute an excellent medium for the investment of short-term funds by banks and other financial institutions. During the last few years, when the commercial banks have been confronted with a dearth of opportunities for making sound business loans, they have turned more and more to the purchase of short-term "governments" in order to employ their surplus funds. Holdings of Treasury bills and certificates by all member banks, which represent about two-thirds of the total banking resources of the country, have increased from $258,637,000 on June 30, 1930, to $1,427,343,000 on June 30, 1934. The total amount held by all banks on the latter date was probably about $2,000,000,000.

Bills and certificates are eligible for purchase by the Reserve banks, and in furtherance of their easy money policy, these institutions increased their holdings from $218,166,000 at the end of 1929 to $1,133,577,000 at the end of 1932. Since that time they have converted a part of their short-term securities into longer-term government obligations. On June 30, 1934, their portfolio of bills and certificates had declined to $742,105,000. In view of the fact that the amount of bills and certificates outstanding at the end of June was $3,039,000,000, it is apparent that the combined holdings of the banks and Reserve banks represent a very large portion of the total. Table 13 shows the movement of the banks' investments in bills and certificates during the last few years.

TABLE 13

BANK HOLDINGS OF TREASURY BILLS AND CERTIFICATES
(In thousands of dollars)

End of	Federal Reserve Banks	All Member Banks	Total
1929	218,166	248,710	466,876
1930	339,209	368,994	708,203
1931	423,553	678,595	1,102,148
1932	1,133,577	795,095	1,928,672
1933	935,850	927,057	1,862,907
1934, June 30.	742,105	1,427,343	2,169,448

Banks and other investors obtain a substantial part of their bills and certificates by subscription or by bidding at the time of the initial offering. However, there is also an active secondary market for outstanding issues in which investors may purchase securities or liquidate their holdings. The firms which act as dealers in short-term governments are much the same as those which constitute the acceptance market. At the time of the initial offering they ordinarily subscribe for substantial blocks of securities for distribution to their customers, and stand ready to buy or sell bills and certificates in the market at a very small price differential. Their object is to obtain a large turnover on a comparatively small profit margin. It is of course to the interest of the Treasury to have an active and orderly market for its short-term securities, and the Federal Reserve Bank of New York has arrangements with several of the leading dealers whereby it undertakes to buy securities from them under repurchase agreements. Such arrangements protect the dealers from losses due to temporary price declines, and enable them to carry adequate inventories of securities.

In the past the short-term government securities market has at times been overshadowed by the collateral loan mar-

ket and even by the acceptance market. However, during
the depression the situation has been reversed. The volume of collateral loans and acceptances outstanding has
declined sharply from the peak of 1929, while the amount
of short-term government securities has greatly increased;
and at present the latter market is by far the most important of the individual money markets.

The expansion of the market for Treasury bills and certificates is a direct result of the large budget deficits incurred by the Federal Government during the last few
years. In order to meet the financial needs of the government at the lowest possible cost, during the early years of
the depression the Treasury resorted more and more to the
use of short-term securities. The amount of Treasury bills
outstanding increased rapidly, and there was also a substantial increase in the amount of certificates. The total
of the two rose from $1,640,000,000 on June 30, 1929, to
$3,447,000,000 on June 30, 1932. Since then some of the
certificates have been refunded into longer-term obligations,
but the amount of bills outstanding has continued to increase. On June 30, 1934, the combined total still
amounted to $3,039,000,000.

The development of the government's short-term debt
since 1929 is shown in Table 14.

TABLE 14

SHORT-TERM GOVERNMENT SECURITIES OUTSTANDING
(In millions of dollars)

Date	Treasury Bills	Certificates of Indebtedness	Total
June 30, 1929	....	$1,640	$1,640
" " 1930	$ 156	1,264	1,420
" " 1931	445	1,923	2,368
" " 1932	616	2,831	3,447
" " 1933	955	2,200	3,155
" " 1934	1,404	1,635	3,039

The yields on Treasury bills and certificates, by reason
of the high credit standing of the government and the tax-

exempt features of these securities, are ordinarily the lowest of all the rates in the money market. Although the Treasury had to offer an interest rate of 4 ¼ per cent on an issue of nine-month certificates of indebtedness offered March 12, 1933, owing to the abnormal conditions prevailing during the bank holiday, it has ordinarily been able to obtain oversubscriptions during the last few years on certificates bearing rates as low as ¼ of one per cent. The cost of borrowing through Treasury bills has been even lower. The average price of accepted bids on 91-day bills has often afforded a yield of less than 1/10 of one per cent. During 1934 these securities were for months quoted in the market to yield only .07 per cent.

Commercial Paper Market

The commercial paper market is the oldest of the short-term money markets and the one most indigenous to this country. It is the market for promissory notes of all well-known business concerns of high credit standing, usually unsecured and unendorsed. Commercial paper is usually issued in denominations of $2,500 and multiples thereof, ordinarily matures in four to six months, and bears interest at some stipulated rate. Usually it is based solely on the credit of the maker, but occasionally paper is endorsed by a parent or affiliated concern or by an individual of considerable wealth, and it is sometimes secured by collateral.

The use of commercial paper is limited, for the most part, to well-established firms engaged in the manufacture or sale of staple commodities and capitalized at $250,000 to $10,000,000. Smaller firms are not sufficiently well known for their paper to be widely acceptable, and larger concerns have access to the securities market and banking connections which make the use of commercial paper unnecessary. Unlike trade bills and bankers' acceptances, commercial paper is not drawn to finance a specific sale or transaction. To a large extent, it is used to provide additional temporary working capital for meeting payrolls, purchasing materials, and paying general operating expenses during periods of seasonal business activity. It is estimated that about 60 per cent of the commercial paper drawn is of a seasonal character. Thus it supplements the regular lines of credit of the issuers at their banks and often enables them to obtain additional funds at lower cost than at the banks.

Commercial paper is marketed through the so-called commercial paper houses, which buy the paper direct from the issuers. There are some three dozen firms in the country handling commercial paper, along with other types of short-term credit instruments, and of these seven do more than 50 per cent of the business. These firms do not, except in rare instances, endorse the paper they sell, but they carefully investigate and constantly check the credit standing of the makers, since their own business reputation depends on the quality of the paper they handle. Their income is derived from the commission of ¼ of one per cent charged the seller for distributing the paper.

The commercial banks, and particularly the country banks, are practically the sole buyers of commercial paper. Although less liquid than acceptances, since it is not usually eligible for discount at the Reserve banks, and not so safe as Treasury bills and certificates, commercial paper is attractive to banks by reason of the higher yield obtained. During periods of seasonal decline in the demand for loans in their localities, many country banks make it a regular practice to invest a portion of their surplus funds in this type of credit instrument. Some banks include commercial paper in their portfolios in order to obtain geographical diversification of credit risks.

In order to reach the buying banks in various parts of the country, many of the commercial paper houses have branches in a number of leading cities. Various methods of selling are used. Some houses employ salesmen to make personal calls on client banks; others rely on telephone solicitations; and most of them circularize their customers with offering-lists giving the details of paper available for sale. Ordinarily customers are allowed an option period of five to twenty days in order to give them an opportunity to investigate the paper offered.

Interest rates on commercial paper vary widely with changing conditions in the money market, but they are usually the highest of the open market rates. During recent years the rate on prime paper of four to six months' maturity has ranged from 6¼ per cent in 1929 to as low as ¾ of one per cent in 1934. Rates are not uniform, but vary with the credit standing of the maker.

From the standpoint of the volume of paper outstanding, the commercial paper market is the least important of the individual money markets. Furthermore, its importance has declined steadily since shortly after the war. According to figures reported to the Federal Reserve Bank of New York by about twenty leading commercial paper houses, the amount outstanding gradually fell from a peak of $1,296,-000,000 in January 1920 to only $60,000,000 in May 1933. Since the latter date there has been some increase as a result of the expansion in business activity. The amount reported outstanding at the end of August 1934 was $188,-000,000. These fluctuations are shown statistically in Table 15.

TABLE 15

COMMERCIAL PAPER OUTSTANDING *

(In millions of dollars)

End of		*End of*	
1922	722	1930	358
1924	798	1931	118
1926	526	1932	81
1928	383	1933	109
1929	334	1934, August	188

* These figures do not represent the total amount of commercial paper outstanding, since some is handled by dealers other than those which report to the Reserve bank. On June 30, 1934, the total commercial paper held by all member banks was $200,004,000, while the amount reported by the dealers to the Reserve bank was only $151,000,000.

The decline in the importance of the commercial paper market is primarily the result of the evolution of American business and finance during the post-war period. Thus, there has been a definite tendency toward business concentration and the creation of larger business units. At the same time conditions in the security markets up to the latter part of 1929 made it possible for concerns of fair size to market readily new issues of stocks or bonds and, by building up their working capital, avoid reliance on outside sources for temporary funds. There has also been a tendency to substitute bankers' acceptances for commercial paper. However, it is probable that in the near future the commercial paper market will be more active than it has been in the last few years. Many concerns have suffered a considerable decrease in their working capital as a result of operating losses, and in the absence of a major boom in the security markets, are likely to find the commercial paper market a desirable medium for financing seasonal and other temporary working capital requirements.

Collateral Loan Market

As far back as the records of human society extend, it has been the custom for lenders to demand that borrowers pledge something of value as security for loans in order that, in the event of failure to receive interest or principal as agreed, they may be compensated by the forfeiture of the security. In earlier days the security usually consisted of real property or chattels owned by the borrower; these are still among the common forms of security. However, with the development of modern corporations and the virtually universal system of public borrowing by governmental bodies, there has come into existence a new type of property, or property right, even better suited to serve as security for loans: namely, stocks and bonds. Such securities are now one of the most important elements in our credit structure.

The market for loans secured by stocks and bonds, or collateral loans, is the most geographically diversified and most loosely organized of the short-term money markets.

In the broadest sense it includes loans, by lenders of all kinds to borrowers of all descriptions, secured by stocks and bonds. However, in the narrower and more popular sense it is the market for collateral loans to brokers and dealers in securities, either on call or for a comparatively short period of time. It is this phase of the collateral loan market in which the characteristics of an organized short-term money market are most developed, and with which this study is primarily concerned.

Purposes of collateral loans. Since the stock market boom of 1927–29, collateral, or brokers' loans, have been closely associated in the mind of the public with speculation in securities. It is true that in periods of speculative activity a large portion of the collateral loans outstanding are made to finance speculative purchases of securities, but this is only one of the several purposes for which such loans are contracted. In a study, made for the sub-committee of the Senate Committee on Banking and Currency, on the operation of the national and Federal Reserve banking systems, the chief purposes of collateral loans were summarized as follows:

> 1. Carrying of securities by dealers pending distribution to investors.
> 2. Carrying of securities with the intention of reselling them at a rise in price, to permit payment of the loan out of the proceeds.
> 3. Carrying of securities for long-term investment, the borrower expecting to liquidate the loan gradually out of income.
> 4. Carrying of securities for indefinite periods for purposes of corporate control, etc.
> 5. For business, agricultural, and commercial uses.
> 6. For consumption purposes.

In addition, it may be noted that banks often obtain from their correspondent banks loans secured by collateral.

Adequate statistical data for determining the amount of collateral loans made for each of these various purposes are not available. However, the Senate sub-committee referred to above endeavored to obtain an approximate answer to this question by means of a questionnaire sent to a group of leading banks. The replies of ten New York banks showed that in the latter part of 1930 the proportion of their collateral loans contracted for the purpose of carrying securities varied from 42.9 to 98 per cent. Similarly, the proportion made for commercial, industrial, and agricultural purposes ranged from 2 to 57.1 per cent. Reports from twenty other banks outside New York City showed approximately the same situation.

Borrowers and lenders. It is apparent from the diversity of purposes of collateral loans that there is a great variety of borrowers in the collateral loan market. The group includes not only brokers, dealers in securities, investment bankers, and financial companies, but also ordinary business concerns as well as private individuals. On the other hand, the commercial banks are almost the only lenders. At times in the past when interest rates have been unusually high, lenders other than banks placed considerable amounts of funds in the collateral loan market, but during the last few years of very low interest rates, and particularly since the passage of the Banking Act of 1933, these other lenders have disappeared.

Under these circumstances, the regular reports to the Federal and state banking authorities by the commercial banks of the country throw considerable light on the amount and nature of the collateral loans outstanding from time to time. In the Member Bank Call Report issued by the Federal Reserve Board, which includes reports of all member banks of the Federal Reserve System (owning almost two-thirds of all the banking resources of the country), loans on securities are classified into four categories: (1) loans to banks, (2) loans to brokers and dealers in New York City, (3) loans to brokers and dealers outside New York City, and (4) loans to others. Table 16 shows the

TABLE 16

MEMBER BANK LOANS ON SECURITIES

(In millions of dollars)

Date	To Banks		To Brokers and Dealers in N.Y.		To Brokers and Dealers Elsewhere		To Others		Total
	Amount	Per Cent of Total	Amount	Per Cent of Total	Amount	Per Cent of Total	Amount	Per Cent of Total	
Dec. 31, 1928	(*)	..	2,555.9	..	974.5	..	6,372.5	..	9,902.9†
Dec. 31, 1929	(*)	..	1,660.2	..	802.7	..	7,685.0	..	10,147.9†
Dec. 31, 1930	314.8	3.2	1,497.5	15.4	675.3	6.9	7,266.3	74.5	9,753.9
Dec. 31, 1931	455.2	6.2	574.7	7.9	391.0	5.3	5,899.3	80.6	7,320.2
Dec. 31, 1932	241.9	4.4	357.2	6.6	240.5	4.4	4,607.7	84.6	5,447.3
Dec. 31, 1933	157.6	3.3	839.6	17.6	166.0	3.5	3,605.7	75.6	4,768.9
June 30, 1934	52.6	1.1	1,081.6	23.3	207.5	4.5	3,308.9	71.1	4,650.6

* Loans on securities to banks were not reported separately on these dates.
† Exclusive of loans to banks.

amount of loans outstanding in each of these classes at intervals during the last five years.

Collateral loans to banks. It has long been the custom for banks to borrow among themselves to meet temporary demands for funds. Since banks often leave securities in the custody of their correspondents, it is a comparatively simple matter to arrange a loan with these securities as collateral. Loans on securities to banks differ in one important respect from other classes of security loans, in that the collateral consists almost exclusively of bonds, since banks may not own stocks except under certain special circumstances. The collateral for other loans often consists to a very large extent of stocks.

The movement of collateral loans to banks is usually from the banks in the larger financial centers to the banks in smaller communities. During periods of seasonal demand for funds, the country banks customarily borrow from their big city correspondents and at the close of the season use the funds obtained from the repayment of customers' loans to clear up their obligations to other banks. It is obvious that country banks do not borrow for speculative purposes, or make loans to customers for speculative purposes, to any great extent. Hence, this type of collateral loan is generally regarded as intended primarily for financing agriculture, industry, and commerce.

Collateral loans to banks represent only a comparatively small proportion of total loans on securities, the amount varying principally with the demand for bank credit in the interior of the country. At the end of 1931, loans to banks on securities by all member banks amounted to $455,200,-000, or 6.2 per cent of all loans on securities, while on June 30, 1934, the amount was only $52,600,000, or 1.1 per cent of the total. Usually from 40 to 50 per cent of all loans to banks on securities are made by banks in New York City, while the two central Reserve cities, New York and Chicago, normally account for more than 60 per cent of the total. Table 17 shows the distribution, on several recent

TABLE 17

COLLATERAL LOANS BY MEMBER BANKS TO BANKS
(In thousands of dollars)

	JUNE 30, 1932		JUNE 30, 1933		JUNE 30, 1934	
	Amount	Per Cent of Total	Amount	Per Cent of Total	Amount	Per Cent of Total
Central Reserve city banks:						
New York	155,032	44.9	85,301	47.6	20,314	38.6
Chicago	67,636	19.6	23,513	13.1	11,620	22.1
Total	222,668	64.5	108,814	60.7	31,934	60.7
Other Reserve city banks ..	107,788	31.2	63,320	35.3	16,764	31.8
Country banks ..	14,916	4.3	7,233	4.0	3,943	7.5
Grand Total.	345,372	100.0	179,367	100.0	52,641	100.0

call dates, of member bank loans to banks on securities, as to class of lending institution.

Loans to others. Collateral loans by banks to others than banks and brokers and dealers constitute by far the greater part of the collateral loans outstanding. In recent years, from 70 to 85 per cent of all collateral loans by member banks have been of this type. Nevertheless, the market for loans to others is not an organized open market. Each loan is a private transaction between the lending bank and the individual borrower, and the terms of the loan depend upon the relations between the parties concerned and the type of collateral offered.

Loans in this category may be divided into two broad groups: (1) loans for business purposes and (2) loans for the purpose of carrying securities. Ordinarily, business concerns borrowing money from banks to cover temporary working capital needs do so under a so-called "line of credit" arrangement which requires no collateral. However, in many cases where the credit standing of the borrower is not of the highest, banks ask that some security be pledged. Also, there are times when concerns wish to borrow sums in excess of their established line of credit and collateral is often pledged for the extra amount.   It is of course impossible to ascertain exactly what use is made by a business concern of funds obtained through a collateral loan, but it is fair to assume that by far the greater portion is devoted to regular business purposes.

Contrary to the popular impression, a large part of the collateral loans contracted for the purpose of carrying securities are not made to brokers and dealers but to "others." Where the object of the purchaser of securities is not to derive a speculative profit by appreciation in market prices in a short period, but to hold them for a longer term, it is usually more satisfactory to arrange the financing directly with a bank.   Unfortunately, the banking statistics as now published do not indicate what proportion of collateral loans to others are for the purpose of carrying securities, but it is generally believed that the amount is currently larger than the total of loans to brokers and dealers.

Brokers' loans.   Although loans to brokers and dealers in securities represent but a comparatively small portion of the total collateral loans in the country's credit structure, there is an organized open market only for this type of collateral loan, and it is only the brokers' loan market that constitutes an integral part of the New York money market.   The brokers' loan market deals in two standard types of collateral loans: (1) call loans and (2) time loans.   Call loans are made on a day-to-day basis, the lender having the privilege of demanding repayment the next business day after the loan is made.   If the loan is not called, it is automatically renewed for another day; in practice, call loans are often allowed to run for months.   Time loans, as the term indicates, are made for a specified period of time, usually three months, and provided the borrower maintains adequate collateral, they may not be called during that period.

Margin requirements.   It is obvious that lenders cannot safely advance an amount equal to the full market value of the securities pledged, since even a slight decline in market prices would result in the loan's not being fully secured. Consequently, it is the established practice to require that the market value of the collateral be greater than the amount of the loan, in order to provide a "margin" of safety for the lender. The regulations of the New York Stock Exchange have long stipulated certain minimum margin requirements which must be observed by the brokerage firms of its members, but recently the entire matter of margin requirements has been placed under the supervision of the Federal Reserve Board by the Securities Exchange Act of 1934. In accordance with this law, the Federal Reserve Board approved on September 27, 1934, and issued, Regulation T, governing the extension and maintenance of credit by brokers, dealers, and members of national securities exchanges. The regulation was to have become effective on October 1, 1934, but the date was postponed until October 15th in order that persons affected might have time to familiarize themselves with its provisions. As stipulated in the Act, the regulation establishes the general rule that the maximum loan value [1] of a registered security for the initial extension of credit shall be whichever is the higher of: (1) 55 per cent of the current market value of the security; or (2) 100 per cent of the lowest market value of the security computed at the lowest market price therefor during the period of thirty-six calendar months immediately prior to the first day of the current month, but not more than 75 per cent of the current market value.

It is provided, however, that until July 1, 1936, the lowest price at which a security has sold on or after July 1, 1933, but prior to the first day of the current month, shall be considered as the lowest market price of such security during the preceding thirty-six calendar months. Furthermore, the lowest market price which could be used under the provisions of the regulation during any calendar month

---

[1] Maximum loan value is defined as the maximum amount of credit which, at any time, may be extended by any creditor on a security.

may be used during the first seven days of the following month. For the purpose of ascertaining the current market value of a security, the creditor [2] has the option of using either the closing sale or the closing bid price for such security on the preceding business day as shown by any regularly published quotation service. In the absence of a sale on the preceding day, the creditor may use either the bid price or the price at which the last sale was recorded if such sale occurred within the current or preceding month. In the event that none of these prices are available, the creditor may use any reasonable estimate of the market price.

There are several exceptions to this general rule. First, a creditor may extend credit on any registered security, in a special account recorded separately, to any other member, broker, or dealer in an amount up to 80 per cent of the current market value of such security. However, (1) the borrower must be subject to the regulation or have places of business only in foreign countries; (2) the credit may be extended only for the purpose of enabling the borrower to carry accounts for his customers, and (3) must not be for the purpose of purchasing or carrying securities for the account of the borrower's firm or for any of his partners.

The second exception is that a creditor may extend credit, in a special account up to 80 per cent of the current market value of a security, to any dealer for the purpose of financing the distribution of an issue of securities at wholesale or retail, or to any group, joint account, or syndicate for the purpose of underwriting or distributing an issue of securities. The third is that loans recorded in a special account and used solely to finance *bona fide* arbitrage transactions in securities are exempt from the provisions of the regulation, provided that the customer maintains a margin equal to 2 per cent of any net debit balance in such account.

---

[2] A creditor is defined as any member of a national securities exchange or any broker or dealer who transacts a business in securities through the medium of such member.

A fourth exception is the provision that any member, or group of members, of a national securities exchange may, with the approval of any regularly constituted committee of the exchange having jurisdiction over the business conduct of its members, make loans to meet the emergency needs of any other member or of a broker or dealer transacting business through the medium of such member. Emergency loans may be maintained and renewed until the Federal Reserve Board determines that the emergency has ceased to exist. However, the business conduct committee approving an emergency loan made after October 15, 1934, is required to make within ten days a written report of all the relevant facts to the Federal Reserve agent of the district in which the exchange is located.

Finally, certain securities are entirely exempt from the regulations governing collateral loans by brokers and dealers. These exempted securities are defined in Regulation T as:

1. Direct obligations of, or obligations guaranteed as to principal or interest by, the United States;

2. Securities issued or guaranteed by corporations in which the United States has a direct or indirect interest, as shall be designated for exemption by the Secretary of the Treasury as necessary or appropriate in the public interest or for the protection of investors;

3. Securities which are direct obligations of, or obligations guaranteed as to principal or interest by (a) a state or any political subdivision thereof, or (b) any agency or instrumentality of a state or any political sub-division thereof, or (c) any municipal corporate instrumentality of one or more states;

4. And such other securities as the Securities and Exchange Commission may, by such rules and regulations as it deems necessary or appropriate in the public interest or for the protection of investors, either unconditionally or upon specified terms and conditions for stated periods, exempt from the operation of any one or more provisions of section 7 and/or 8(a) of the Securities Exchange Act.

The regulations of the Federal Reserve Board have been generally accepted in financial circles as fair and reasonable, and the brokerage houses have adapted their operations to the new rules with comparatively little difficulty. As a matter of fact, some of the provisions of the regulations are more liberal than the margin requirements previously established by the New York Stock Exchange. However, the provisions of the law are flexible, and the Federal Reserve Board may from time to time, as it may deem necessary, change its regulations regarding the maximum loan value of securities in order to prevent the excessive use of credit for speculation in securities.

Lenders and borrowers. As previously indicated, the commercial banks supply practically all of the funds lent in the brokers' loan market. The chief lenders are the large New York City banks, although a considerable amount is loaned by banks in other cities through the agency of their New York correspondents. In the past, and particularly during the stock market boom of 1927–29, large amounts of funds were placed in the market by others than banks and were reported as "loans for account of others." These other lenders included chiefly business corporations, investment trusts, foreign banks, and private individuals. Most of the loans for others were placed through banks in the same manner as loans for out-of-town banks, but some were placed directly by the lenders with brokers and dealers.

Past experience has shown that these loans by "others" constitute an extremely unstable and dangerous element not only in the money market but in the entire credit structure of the country. In the first place, loans of this character were not subject to control by the Reserve bank authorities. When, in 1928 and 1929, the Federal Reserve Board endeavored to check the expansion of credit for speculative purposes, it was more or less successful in preventing further increases in the volume of collateral loans by member banks to brokers and dealers, but its efforts were largely nullified by the continued increase in brokers' loans by others than banks. The inability of the Reserve banks to control this type of loan is due to the fact that loans for the account of others involve simply a transfer of deposits from lender to borrower without any additional expansion of bank credit, while an increase in brokers' loans by banks does result in an increase in deposits. Since member banks are required to maintain fixed reserves against deposits with the Reserve banks, such credit expansion is subject to some degree of control by the Federal Reserve authorities, whereas loans for the account of others are not.

In the second place, these other lenders proved utterly devoid of any sense of responsibility for the maintenance of an orderly money market. Under the stimulus of extraordinarily high interest rates, loans placed by the New York City reporting banks alone "for account of others" reached a peak of $3,941,000,000 on October 9, 1929. As the stock market collapsed and security prices declined precipitously, the other lenders hastened to call their loans, and in the course of the next four weeks loans placed "for account of others" by the New York reporting member banks alone declined by $1,542,000,000. But for the action of the New York banks in replacing these funds by increased loans for their own account, the consequences on the stock market might have been disastrous.

Under these circumstances it is not surprising that measures to restrict loans for the account of others were soon forthcoming. In the latter part of 1931 the New York Clearing House Association passed a rule prohibiting its members from making collateral loans for the account of others. The Banking Act of 1933 prohibited all member banks from acting as agent for others than banking institutions in making loans on securities to brokers and dealers. Finally, the Securities Exchange Act of 1934 provided that brokers doing business on a national securities exchange may borrow on registered securities only from member banks and non-member banks which have filed with the Federal Reserve Board an agreement to comply with all the provisions of the Act, except as otherwise permitted by the

Board. Thus, other lenders have been practically eliminated from the brokers' loan market.

The brokers and dealers in securities, who constitute the
demand element in the market, borrow for two purposes.
First, they borrow to finance the margin accounts of their
customers. Speculators in the stock market often desire
to purchase a larger amount of securities than they can
pay for with their own funds. They are able to do this
by borrowing a part of the purchase price from brokers
and pledging as collateral the securities bought. However,
brokerage houses do not usually have sufficient capital to
enable them to advance their own funds to their customers
for this purpose to any very large extent, and consequently
they borrow from the banks, using the customers' securities
as collateral. Second, dealers in securities and brokerage
houses which engage in the distribution of securities often
borrow from the banks to finance the carrying of securities
in their own portfolios pending distribution to investors.

Operation of the market. Brokers and dealers in need
of financial accommodation ordinarily borrow directly from
the banks. There is thus a closer and more personal relation between borrower and lender in the collateral loan
market than in the other open money markets. This relationship often has some influence on the terms of loan
transactions. Banks are likely to be less exacting as to
collateral and interest rates and more considerate in calling
loans, when dealing with firms with which they do a regular
banking business and which are regular borrowers, than
they are with occasional borrowers.

In periods of comparatively easy money market conditions, the borrowers and lenders have little difficulty in
arranging loans directly. However, in periods of speculative activity, when the demand for collateral loans is relatively large, there is a need for special intermediaries. In
order to meet this need there has developed a type of middlemen known as "money brokers" who, for a small com-

mission, arrange loans for borrowers. They consist chiefly of firms which act as middlemen in the other short-term money markets, although some brokerage houses occasionally act in this capacity. During the late stock market boom the money brokers did a flourishing business, but in recent years the demand for brokers'. loans has been so small in relation to the amount of funds available that their services have been superfluous. Furthermore, the outlawing of loans for "others" will undoubtedly militate against their becoming an important element in the market in the future.

The services of the money brokers as intermediaries are supplemented by the special facilities created by both the New York Stock Exchange and the New York Curb Exchange for arranging call loans. Both exchanges operate "money desks" where banks may offer funds on call, either directly or through an exchange member, and where member firms may apply for accommodation. They do not handle time loans. The principal service of these facilities is in bringing about a better adjustment of the marginal supply and demand for funds and thus minimizing fluctuations in interest rates on call loans. The daily offerings of funds and applications for loans indicate accurately to the exchange officials the condition of the market, and on this basis they are able to fix rates at such a level as to attract the necessary volume of funds. The rates fixed by the exchange officials apply to all loans made through the money desks. As in the case of the money brokers, the services of the money desks have been in little demand during the last few years, and the volume of loans arranged through them has been quite small.

Rates. Interest rates in the brokers' loan market fluctuate more widely than rates in any of the other short-term money markets. At times when there is little public interest in the stock market, the demand for loans is small and rates fall to as low as a fraction of one per cent. On the other hand, in periods of great speculative activity the demand for loans grows to tremendous proportions and rates rise to extremely high levels.

The rate structure of the brokers' loan market is rather complex. There are actually three different rates applicable to different types of transactions: (1) the rate on new call loans, (2) the renewal rate on call loans, and (3) the rate on time loans. Furthermore, there is some lack of uniformity in rates for each of these types of transactions. Rates charged by some banks sometimes vary slightly from those charged by others, and individual banks often have different rates for different borrowers. The rates posted at the New York Stock Exchange for new call loans and for renewals are usually taken as the open market rates, but these rates are often out of line with rates being charged by banks.

TABLE 18

MONTHLY AVERAGE RATES ON BROKERS' LOANS

	1929			1933		
	Time Loans 90 Days	Call Loans New	Renewal	Time Loans 90 Days	Call Loans New	Renewal
January	7¾	6.94	7.05	½	1.00	1.00
February	7½–7¾	7.47	7.06	½–1¼	1.00	1.00
March	7¾–8	9.80	9.10	2½–3½	3.27	3.32
April	8½–9	9.46	8.89	1 –1½	1.29	1.37
May	8½–9	8.79	8.91	1 –1¼	1.00	1.00
June	8 –8¼	7.83	7.70	¾–1	1.00	1.00
July	7½–8	9.41	9.23	¾–1½	1.00	1.00
August	8¾–9	8.15	8.23	1 –1¼	.98	.98
September	8¾–9	8.62	8.50	½– ¾	.75	.75
October	7 –9	6.10	6.43	⅝– ¾	.75	.75
November	4¾–6	5.40	5.44	⅝–1	.75	.75
December	4¾–5	4.88	4.83	¾–1¼	.94	.94

Similarly, it is difficult to generalize as to the differences between particular rates. Usually the rate on time loans for ninety days is less than the rates on call loans, but in times of uncertainty as to money market conditions, lenders are reluctant to commit their funds for such a long period, and the time rate may rise above the call rates. During the last few years there has been practically no difference between the stock exchange rates on call loans and those on renewals. In the past, however, when the market has been more active, the two rates have varied considerably. Thus, in 1929 the monthly average rate on renewals was higher than the average rate on new loans during five months of the year, and was lower in the other seven months. Table 18 shows the movement of call, renewal, and time rates in 1929 and 1933.

Statistics on brokers' loans. The data computed and published periodically by several agencies on amounts of security loans to brokers and dealers outstanding, together with the regularly published open market rates, afford the principal basis for observing and interpreting developments in the broker's loan market. Unfortunately, none of the statistical reports include all the loans in the market. The most comprehensive is the Member Bank Call Report issued by the Federal Reserve Board for each of the member bank call dates, of which there are three or four a year. This report shows the total collateral loans of member banks classified as to types of borrowers, as indicated in Table 16, *i.e.,* as to (1) banks, (2) brokers and dealers in New York, (3) brokers and dealers elsewhere, and (4) others.

However, for current use more frequent statistics are desirable. The New York Stock Exchange publishes regularly a report of collateral loans contracted by its members as of the first of each month. This report classifies loans as to the type of lender into two categories: (1) loans from New York banks and trust companies and (2) loans from private bankers, brokers, foreign bank agencies, and others in New York City. It also shows the amount of both time and demand loans. Table 19 shows the amount and classification of brokers' loans reported by the Stock Exchange for October 1 of each year since 1928.

The third and most frequent report on brokers' loans is the weekly statement of reporting member banks in 91 leading cities. This statement is issued on Tuesday of each week and shows the position of the reporting member banks on the preceding Wednesday. There is also a separate report for the New York City reporting member banks alone; it is issued on Friday, before the complete report for all reporting member banks.

TABLE 19

BROKERS' LOANS CONTRACTED BY MEMBERS OF THE
NEW YORK STOCK EXCHANGE
(In millions of dollars)

October 1	Total	From New York Banks and Trust Companies	From Private Bankers, Brokers, etc.	On Demand	On Time
1928	5,513	4,647	866	4,689	824
1929	8,549	7,077	1,472	7,832	717
1930	3,481	3,057	424	2,830	651
1931	1,044	932	112	802	242
1932	380	292	88	270	110
1933	897	806	91	625	272
1934	831	769	62	531	300

The weekly statement shows the total outstanding security loans to brokers and dealers of the reporting banks, the loans being classified as (1) loans to brokers and dealers in New York and (2) loans to brokers and dealers outside New York. The present form of the statement was instituted on October 17, 1934. Formerly, the statement for all reporting member banks showed only total loans on securities, and details as to brokers' loans were contained

TABLE 20

BROKERS' LOANS OF MEMBER BANKS ON NOV. 28, 1934
(In millions of dollars)

	All Reporting Member Banks	New York City Reporting Member Banks
Loans on securities to brokers and dealers:		
In New York	660	525
Outside New York	155	51
Total	815	576

only in the statement of New York City reporting member banks. The latter report formerly showed brokers' loans (1) for own account, (2) for account of out-of-town banks, and (3) for account of others as well as loans (a) on demand and (b) on time; but it is now issued in the same form as the statement for all reporting member banks. The amount of brokers' loans of all reporting member banks and of the New York City reporting member banks on November 28, 1934, is shown in Table 20.

Factors affecting volume of brokers' loans. The wide fluctuations in the volume of brokers' loans outstanding during the last few years are attributable directly to changing conditions in the security markets. It is obvious that the principal factor affecting the amount of brokers' loans is the degree of speculative activity in the stock market. If all buyers of securities paid for their purchases entirely with their own funds, there would be little demand for brokers' loans, but when the general public is trading on margin, as in 1929, a tremendous amount of funds is required by brokers to finance their customers' accounts.

A second factor, closely related to the one just mentioned, is the level of security prices. When stock prices are high, a larger amount is required to purchase a given number of shares, and the amount which must be borrowed for a margin transaction is correspondingly greater. Thus, if the common stock of the American Telephone and Telegraph Company is selling at $100 per share, a margin trader can buy 100 shares for $10,000, putting up a margin of $5,000, or 50 per cent, and borrowing the other $5,000 through his broker. However, if the price of the stock rises to $200 per share, a purchase of 100 shares would require a loan of $10,-000, assuming the same margin.

The volume of new security issues is a third factor influencing the amount of brokers' loans outstanding. Investment bankers underwriting new issues of securities, including those of the government and of political subdivisions, often have recourse to collateral loans to finance the operation during the period when the securities are being distributed. If the volume of new issues offered is large, there is a tendency for brokers' loans to increase. A fourth factor is the percentage of the market price of securities which brokers are willing to advance to their customers. A reduction in margin requirements makes it possible to borrow a larger amount on securities of the same value, and conversely, an increase in margin requirements reduces the amount which may be borrowed.

Short selling and brokers' loans. There has been in the past considerable discussion and much confusion regarding the effect of the short selling of securities on the brokers' loan market. Actually, the effect of short selling varies with the circumstances of the particular transaction. As a rule, one may state that whenever short selling requires the placing of new funds in the market by either the seller or the buyer, there is a tendency for the volume of brokers' loans to decrease. On the other hand, if a short sale results in the withdrawal of funds previously used in the market, the tendency is to increase the volume of brokers' loans.

The following examples will indicate how and when short selling tends to increase or decrease brokers' loans or leave them unchanged. The examples are based on the assumption that both the buyers and the sellers already have trading accounts with brokers.[3]

> 1. Neither the buyer nor the seller put up new funds. *A* sells short 100 shares of a market value of $10,000. *A*'s broker receives the $10,000 which he, or the broker from whom he borrows the shares, uses to repay part of his bank debts. On the other hand, the broker for *B*, the buyer, borrows $10,000 from his bank in order to finance the purchase. The repayment of one loan offsets the contracting of the new loan. Net result: Brokers' loans remain unchanged.
>
> 2. However, *A*'s broker may borrow the shares from a non-broker to whom he turns over temporarily the proceeds of the

---

[3] It is obvious that the putting up of additional margin in the form of securities does not have any effect on the money market.

sale. In this case the funds are not available for the reduction of brokers' loans, but *B*'s broker still has to borrow the $10,000 to finance the purchase. Net result: An increase in brokers' loans of $10,000.

3. Both the seller and the buyer each put up $5,000 of new money, and the selling broker borrows the shares from another broker. The broker lending the shares is able to reduce his loans to banks by $10,000. *A*'s broker is also able to reduce his loans with the new money *A* advanced, *i.e.*, by $5,000. However, *B*'s broker had to increase his bank loans by $5,000. Net result: Decrease in brokers' loans by $10,000.

4. *A*'s broker borrows the shares from a non-broker; so the purchase price is not available for the reduction of brokers' loans. *A*'s broker reduces his loans by the $5,000 which *A* advanced, and *B*'s broker has to borrow $5,000. Net result: No change in brokers' loans.

5. *B* advances the full amount required for the purchase of the stock. *A*'s broker borrows the stock from another broker. Thus, no new borrowing is required, and the purchase price is available for reduction of loans. Net result: Decrease in brokers' loans of $10,000.

6. *B* advances the full amount, but *A*'s broker borrows the stock from a non-broker. The purchase price is then not available for reduction of loans. Net result: No change in brokers' loans.

These illustrations can be multiplied many times. The principle, however, to be borne in mind is that, whenever the buyer or the lender places new funds in the market and the selling broker either has the shares in his own possession or obtains them from another broker, short selling results in a decrease in brokers' loans. On the other hand, whenever no new funds are put up by either the buyer or seller and the selling broker has to obtain the shares from a non-broker, there is an increase in brokers' loans. And, finally, when neither the buyer nor the seller puts up new funds and the shares sold are either in the possession of the selling broker or are obtained from another broker, there is no change in the volume of brokers' loans outstanding.

CHAPTER VIII

New York as an International Financial Center

The pre-war period. The rise of New York to a position of paramount importance as an international money market has been so rapid, and the period of its supremacy has been so short and marked by so many economic and political convulsions, that it is difficult to make a satisfactory appraisal of its present position or its future prospects. Before the war New York played a comparatively minor rôle in international finance. Until the passage of the Federal Reserve Act, national banks were prohibited from creating acceptances, and the volume of bankers' bills created by the state banks and by the private banking houses was quite small. Although many of the large investment houses located in New York City had excellent connections in Europe, their international business consisted chiefly of distributing American securities abroad rather than floating foreign securities in this country. Some of these investment banking concerns originated abroad as branches of foreign banking houses, and even after attaining an independent status continued to operate to some extent with foreign capital. One of the important phases of the international banking business in this country before the war was the remittance of funds abroad for individuals, which developed as a result of the large inflow of European immigrants to this country. However, this type of international transaction was handled not so much by the larger banking institutions as by small banking firms which sprang up in each locality where the immigrants settled in large numbers.

Before the war, therefore, New York's chief function in international finance was to facilitate the inflow of capital for investment in the railroads and industrial enterprises, and the handling of immigrants' remittances. As a lender of long-term capital the United States was greatly overshadowed by Western European countries. The United States was a debtor country, and although American capital had begun to flow abroad, this capital was chiefly in the form of direct investments in neighboring countries. The New York money market itself was engaged chiefly in the financing of domestic business and took little part in the financing of international trade.

The war period. The establishment of the Federal Reserve System, the concentration of the gold reserves in the Federal Reserve banks, and the modification of the banking laws to permit national banks to create acceptances, prepared New York for the problems created by the World War, which disorganized the smooth-working and well-established international money market machinery. Most of the European nations promptly went off the gold standard, and the efforts of the banks and the treasuries of the belligerent countries were directed principally to the task of financing the war. Thus there was created a vacuum in the international money and capital markets which was gradually filled by the financial resources of the United States.

Up to April 1917, when America entered the war, the Allies had raised loans in the United States through the ordinary private investment banking channels. However, after this country became a belligerent, the government assumed the burden of financing the Allies, and thereafter American capital flowed to Europe in tremendous amounts through the intermediation of the United States Treasury. Meanwhile, the foreign trade of the United States was increasing by leaps and bounds as a result of the war-time demand for American goods, and because of the abnormal conditions prevailing in the European financial centers, the responsibility for financing this trade had to be assumed chiefly by the American banks. Consequently the leading financial institutions of this country rapidly expanded their facilities for financing foreign transactions, and many established branches abroad. However, this situation was abnormal, and after the close of the war many of the overseas offices were closed.

Thus, the extraordinary conditions of the war period gave a tremendous impetus to the development of New York as an international financial center. The flotation of huge bond issues for foreign governments in the early years of the war first acquainted the general investing public in this country with foreign obligations. Similarly, the financing of American foreign trade greatly stimulated the development of the acceptance market and served to familiarize American bankers with the intricacies of international trade financing. Finally, the experiences of the war period made bankers and investors as well as business men more internationally minded and more conscious of business and financial opportunities outside the United States.

The post-war period, 1919–25. After hostilities ceased, conditions in the international money markets failed to return to anything approximating those prevailing before 1914. On the contrary, they became increasingly chaotic as, following the discontinuance of the official "exchange pegging" operations by the governments, the currencies of most of the belligerent countries depreciated. The depreciation of these currencies also affected the exchanges of some of the neutral countries, although the demoralization was not so great in the latter group. It was obvious that under these conditions neither London, Paris, nor Berlin could satisfactorily perform the functions of an international financial center, and during this period the supremacy of New York was unquestioned.

Not only was the dollar the world's most stable currency in the years following the war, but the United States was the only major country where the currency was convertible into gold and where there were no restrictions on gold exports. In addition, the United States was the only country in a position to export capital on any very large scale, and after the war it assumed the position of the chief capital lending nation of the world. However, the ascendancy of New York in international finance was primarily the result of the breakdown of the European financial centers which had formerly dominated the field, and was therefore of a temporary nature. As Europe gradually recovered from the ravages of the war and as the leading currencies were stabilized, London and some of the Continental money markets increased in prestige and importance.

The period 1925–31. By the end of 1925 most nations either had returned to the gold standard or had adopted the gold exchange standard, and the foreign exchange restrictions, which had greatly hampered the operation of the international money market up to that time, had been virtually abolished. The adoption of the Dawes Plan and the funding of the inter-allied war debts further tended to improve conditions, so that for the first time since the outbreak of the World War the international money markets operated under fairly stable conditions.

However, if the pre-war period is taken as the standard of normality, even this period was abnormal. It was marked by the tremendous outflow of American capital to other countries as the investing public absorbed billions of dollars of foreign bonds, by the growth and collapse of a great speculative boom in the American securities markets, and by large international movements of capital on account of reparations and war debts. All this involved a tremendous shifting of capital between countries which constituted a severe stress on the reëstablished gold standard. Furthermore, an additional strain was created by the accumulation of huge short-term balances in London and New York by the central banks of the gold exchange standard countries as well as by some in gold standard countries, notably the Bank of France. Thus, despite the fact that the international money market had apparently recovered and entered into a new era of progress during the years 1925–31, severe strains were accumulating; and when the further tension of a great world-wide economic depression developed, the pressure was too great for the international currency and credit structure to withstand.

The period following 1931. If the years 1925–31 are termed abnormal, the period from 1931 to 1934 must be characterized as chaotic. As the economic depression deepened, foreign lending virtually ceased and international creditors became increasingly concerned over their existing commitments. This concern developed into panic when the financial difficulties of the Austrian Credit Anstalt became known in May 1931, and there began a general movement to repatriate short-term funds employed abroad. The German banks had contracted huge foreign short-term credits, and when the lenders made concerted demands for repayment, it was only the vigorous intervention of the German Government and the coöperation of the foreign central banks that saved the entire banking and currency system of Germany from complete collapse. Then the panic swept to England, and the withdrawal of funds from the London money market finally forced Great Britain to abandon the gold standard.

This marked the end of the post-war period of currency stability. Other countries followed the British example in rapid succession and severed their currencies from gold. Foreign exchange rates fluctuated, exchange restrictions were widely adopted, and in several cases foreign credits were frozen by standstill agreements. The free movement of funds between countries became virtually a thing of the past, and when the United States abandoned the gold standard, the last blow was dealt to the international money market as it had been restored after the war. Under these conditions the volume of international transactions at New York gradually dwindled, and the latest phase of its career as an international money market came to a close.

Conclusion. Perhaps no financial center of the world was ever called upon to perform such a huge task in the field of international finance with as little preparation as New York. International finance requires not only a well-organized machinery, but long training and experience of those engaged in it. The machinery could be hastily organized, but the acquisition of experience and knowledge is a slow and costly process. A short period of less than two decades witnessed the rise and fall of New York as an important international financial center. However, in spite of recent developments, it is certain that New York will have an important part in the international money and capital markets in the future. What is uncertain is the form the movement of capital will assume and the rôle the government will play.

Position of the United States on the International Money Market

Although the United States, up to the end of 1930, was one of the leading capital exporting countries of the world, it was a debtor to foreign countries on the international money market. That is, foreign short-term funds loaned to or invested in this country exceeded the amount of American short-term funds employed in other countries. The relationship of the United States to the rest of the world on the international money market, however, has undergone marked changes in the last few years. At the end of 1933 New York was a creditor on the short-term money market.

During the boom period 1928–29, the high interest rates prevailing in this country attracted a large volume of short-term funds from abroad. At the end of 1929 the amount of foreign funds employed in the New York market totaled $3,037,000,000. However, during the next four years these funds were rapidly withdrawn as interest rates in this country declined and financial panic developed abroad. At

TABLE 21

UNITED STATES INTERNATIONAL BANKING ACCOUNTS, 1930–1933

(In millions of dollars)

	End of 1930	End of 1931	End of 1932	End of 1933	Changes During Year 1931	1932	1933
Due to foreigners:							
Deposits	1,640	1,025	715	389	− 615	− 310	− 326
Advances and overdrafts	36	26	30	20	− 10	+ 4	− 10
Short-term loans, investments, etc.	1,046	394	115	63	− 652	− 279	− 52
Acceptance credits	15	20	10	15	+ 5	− 10	+ 5
Total	2,737	1,465	870	487	−1,272	− 595	− 383
Due from foreigners:							
Deposits	294	113	144	250	− 181	+ 31	+ 106
Advances and overdrafts	212	521	377	332	+ 309	− 144	− 45
Short-term loans, investments, etc.	417	156	190	129	− 261	+ 34	− 61
Acceptance credits	879	449	342	371	− 430	− 107	+ 29
Total	1,802	1,239	1,053	1,082	− 563	− 186	+ 29
Net change in international banking accounts					− 709	− 409	− 412

the same time the amount of American short-term funds invested abroad declined, but the rate of decrease was much less. By the end of 1931 the debit balance of the United States on the international money market was almost liquidated, and during 1932 the transition from a net debtor to a net creditor on short-term account was completed. At the end of 1933 this country's short-term debts to foreigners amounted to only $487,000,000, while the amount of American short-term funds abroad was estimated at $1,082,000,-000, leaving a net credit balance of $595,000,000. The trend was finally reversed in the early part of 1934, and in the first half of the year the net credit balance was reduced by about $250,000,000. These developments are shown in Table 21, compiled by the United States Department of Commerce.

Causes of the transition. While the four-year period 1930–33 was characterized by the steady decline in the amounts due to foreigners, the magnitude and tempo of the withdrawals varied in response to financial developments both at home and abroad. During 1930 withdrawals of funds from the United States were gradual and were due primarily to the decline in interest rates and to the curtailment of business activity following the collapse of security prices in October 1929. The banking crisis in Austria and Germany in the middle of 1931, followed by the abandonment of the gold standard by Great Britain, hastened the movement to repatriate foreign short-term funds, and for the whole year there was a reduction of about $1,270,000,000 in the amount of foreign funds employed in this country. This outflow was partially offset by a withdrawal of American funds from abroad to the extent of $560,000,000, so that the net reduction in the debit balance of the United States amounted to $709,000,000.

Another avalanche of foreign withdrawals came in May and June, 1932, being caused chiefly by uncertainties as to the Federal budget and apprehension as to currency inflation in the United States. Although the foreign balances declined during 1932 by only $595,000,000, the reduction was sufficient to bring the total due to foreigners to a smaller figure than the amount due from foreigners. During this year standstill agreements and foreign exchange restrictions abroad seriously hampered the withdrawal of American short-term funds from other countries; the decline amounted to only $186,000,000. The credit balance of the United States was further increased during 1933 by heavy foreign withdrawals during the American banking crisis of January and February, 1933, and by a slight increase in American short-term claims abroad, representing chiefly a flight of capital. However, the trend was reversed in the early part of 1934, when the devaluation and stabilization of the dollar resulted in a large return flow of American funds from abroad and a corresponding decline in the amount of this country's short-term claims on foreigners. According to the estimates of the Department of Commerce, there was an increase in foreigners' banking funds in this country and a decrease in United States banking funds abroad which reduced the credit balance of this country on the international money market by approximately $250,000,000.

By far the greater part of the foreign short-term funds in this country consists of deposits with American banks and banking houses. To a large extent these deposits represent the working balances of foreign commercial banks and business concerns used to finance trade with this country. In the past a considerable percentage has consisted of balances of foreign central banks, many of which included such deposits as part of their legal reserve, and it was the general movement on the part of these institutions to convert their foreign balances into gold that was largely responsible for the decrease of $615,000,000 in foreign deposits during 1931. During the three-year period 1931–33, foreign deposits dropped from $1,640,000,000 to $389,000,000. In view of the uncertainty concerning the value of the dollar at the end of 1933, the amount on deposit at that time was probably the minimum necessary to finance current business operations. The decline in "short-term loans, investments, etc.," consisting mainly of acceptances, short-term government securities, and collateral loans, was even more marked than the decline in deposits, dwindling from $1,046,000,000 at the end of 1930 to $63,000,000 at the end of 1933.

The important rôle of the United States in financing foreign trade is illustrated by the fact that the liability on acceptance credits is the largest item due from foreigners. This importance is the natural result of the encouragement of acceptance financing by the Reserve banks and the development of the acceptance market in this country. The decline in the amount of acceptance credits during the last few years is, of course, due to the fall of commodity prices, to the shrinkage in the volume of foreign trade, and to the unwillingness of American banks to extend new acceptance credits to foreigners—as well as to the unwillingness of foreign exporters and importers to finance their transactions through dollar acceptances.

The future international position of New York. It is obvious that the sharp contraction in the amount of foreign short-term funds in this country during the last few years, and the consequent transition of the United States to the position of a creditor in the international money market, have been due to the financial chaos accompanying the economic depression. However, such conditions cannot continue indefinitely. It is reasonable to expect that the gradual recovery of business will result in the stabilization of currencies and the abolition of foreign exchange restrictions to a sufficient extent to permit the more normal operation of the international money market. Once funds begin to move freely between countries, it is more than likely that the United States will resume its position as a debtor on short-term account.

There are several reasons why, under normal conditions, the New York money market is an international debtor.

In the first place, it offers excellent facilities for the safe investment of foreign short-term funds. It has long been the practice of the central banks of a number of European and South American countries to keep a portion of their reserves on deposit or invested in the leading international financial centers. In many cases the central banks may include, as part of their legal reserves, foreign balances convertible into gold. As long as the United States was on an unrestricted gold standard, New York was an ideal center for the employment of such balances: in 1927 the Federal Reserve Board estimated the total volume of funds held by foreign central banks in this country at not less than $1,000,000,000. Since January 31, 1934, the United States has been on a "modified" international gold bullion standard; gold is exported only under license from the Treasury. However, uncertainty as to the Treasury's policy regarding gold exports, and as to further devaluation of the dollar, has tended to deter foreigners from placing any very large volume of funds on deposit in New York. In the event that these uncertainties are removed, it is probable that the balances of foreign commercial as well as central banks will show a substantial increase.

A second reason for the debtor position of New York on the short-term money market arises from the fact that the United States is a creditor nation on the capital market to the sum of many billions of dollars. Foreign borrowers which have obligations outstanding in the American market must build up balances in the United States in order to meet their debt service. Since these balances are often accumulated several weeks and, in many instances, several months prior to the dates payments are due, they amount at times to quite a substantial sum. Furthermore, the United States is one of the most important foreign trading nations of the world, and foreigners are required to maintain rather substantial balances to finance their commerce with this country.

Another factor responsible for the accumulation of balances by foreigners in the United States is the fact that the New York stock exchange market has become international in character and that, under normal conditions, a substantial amount of foreign money is placed in American securities for investment or speculative purposes. Consequently foreign investors, as well as foreign banks and other financial institutions which desire to buy and sell securities in the American market, must maintain balances in the United States. In addition, New York acts as an international clearing house where the claims of various nations are cleared, especially those of the South American countries; and in order to effect these settlements, foreign banks must maintain balances with New York correspondents.

Organization of New York as an International Financial Center

The principal institutional elements in the international money market at New York are: (1) the large commercial banks; (2) private investment houses; (3) agencies and subsidiaries of foreign banks; (4) foreign exchange dealers, arbitrageurs, and brokers; (5) the Reserve banks. The first three are most important. Foreign exchange dealers are much more numerous and active during periods when the various currencies are fluctuating widely and when the potential profits from such transactions are large. During the periods of relative stability in the exchanges, profits from such transactions diminish and the number of such dealers decreases. Since the latter part of 1931, the activity of the foreign exchange market in New York has increased and there has been a corresponding increase in the number of foreign exchange dealers.

The commercial banks. By far the most important position in the international money market is held by the commercial banks. They are the largest acceptance institutions in the country; they keep the deposits of foreign banks, make short-term loans to foreign countries, and act as paying and fiscal agents for foreign borrowers in the capital market. Through their branches, subsidiaries, and correspondents, they are prepared to transact all types of international financial business, and their activities are world-wide.

The development of extensive international banking facilities by the commercial banks dates from the passage of the Federal Reserve Act in the latter part of 1913. In 1914 the American banks had only 26 branches and subsidiaries in foreign countries. The Act authorized national banks with a capital and surplus of $1,000,000 or more to establish branches abroad or to organize affiliates to operate in foreign countries, although the percentage of a bank's capital and surplus which could be invested in the capital stock of a foreign affiliate was limited. The extraordinary expansion of this country's foreign trade during the war afforded a strong stimulus to the extension of American banking facilities abroad, and by 1920 the number of foreign offices had increased to 181, excluding the 38 offices of the American Express Co. Of this number, 100 offices were operated by seven banks doing a regular banking business in the United States, and the other 81 were branches of five American-foreign banking corporations.

New legislation was enacted in 1919 for the purpose of promoting further expansion of American banks in the foreign field. First, the McLean-Platt Act amended the Federal Reserve Act to permit, up to January 1, 1921, any national bank to invest up to 5 per cent of its capital and surplus in a foreign banking affiliate. Second, the Edge Act amended the Federal Reserve Act to provide for the organization of special banking corporations to carry on a foreign business. The so-called Edge Act corporations are authorized to incur acceptance liabilities equal at any one time to a maximum of ten times their capital and surplus— a provision more liberal than the accepting provisions that govern member banks of the Federal Reserve System.

After the war, however, the foreign banking business dwindled considerably, and little use was made of this legislation; in fact, many of the previously established foreign offices were discontinued. There was some new expansion by American institutions in the foreign banking field during the post-war period of business prosperity and growth in international trade, but the general economic depression brought this movement to a halt. On June 30, 1933, there were six member banks, with a total of 110 offices, in foreign countries; one non-member bank with one foreign office; one Edge Act corporation with six offices; and one state-chartered foreign banking corporation with nineteen offices—making in all a total of 136 foreign offices.

In addition to the branches and subsidiaries, the large commercial banks maintain representatives in all important foreign financial centers in which they do not have regular banking offices. While these representatives do not carry on a banking business, they are always on the lookout for new business, keep the main office informed of the financial and economic situation of the country in which they are located, and furnish information about the customers of the bank.

Recently the United States Government has stepped into the foreign banking field through the establishment, in 1934, of the First and Second Export-Import Banks. The capital of both institutions is held by the Treasury and the Reconstruction Finance Corporation. The First Export-Import Bank was created for the express purpose of financing American trade with Russia, but when difficulties arose in the settlement of the Russian debt to this country, it was decided to postpone operations until an agreement had been reached. The Second Export-Import Bank was intended to finance trade with the rest of the world, and particularly with Cuba, but its activities have been confined to a few comparatively minor transactions.

Investment banking houses. Although the principal business of the investment banking houses is the flotation of new security issues, most of them are important in the international money market through their activities in creating acceptances, trading in foreign exchange, investing the funds of their foreign clients at short-term, and serving as fiscal agents for foreign governments and corporations having security issues outstanding in this country. Some of these houses are affiliated or closely related with foreign institutions and, like the large commercial banks, they maintain representatives in the principal foreign financial centers. Several of the investment banking firms are also important accepting institutions.

Prior to the war most of the investment houses were private firms organized as partnerships, but in the post-war period the commercial banks entered the investment banking field on a large scale through the organization of separate corporations as security affiliates. It is estimated that during the years 1928 and 1929 these security affiliates originated about one-half of all the new securities offered in the American capital market. However, the Banking Act of 1933 required member banks to divorce their security affiliates and ordered a segregation of the securities business and the private banking business. A number of private firms were forced to abandon the investment banking field. Thus the number of investment houses has greatly decreased, but those remaining, together with the private banking firms, constitute an institutional framework which will undoubtedly play a significant rôle in the future.

Agencies and subsidiaries of foreign banks. Just as the American banks have established offices abroad to facilitate the transaction of their foreign business, so foreign banks have established offices in this country, particularly in New York. Their principal business includes dealing in foreign exchange, effecting remittances between the United States and foreign countries, and financing foreign trade. Consequently, they are more specialized in the operations of the international money market than any other group of institutions.

Foreign banks may operate in New York either through agencies or through subsidiary corporations, but in either case they must comply with the state laws. To operate an agency in New York, a foreign bank must file with the Superintendent of Banks an application for a license setting forth certain essential information, including a detailed financial statement. A license may be granted only to foreign banks having a net worth of at least $250,000. Agencies are restricted, as to the business they may transact, to buying, selling, paying or collecting bills of exchange, issuing letters of credit, transmitting money abroad, and making loans. A list of some of the foreign banking institutions operating agencies in New York follows:

Main Office

Anglo-South American Bank, Ltd.	London
Banca Commerciale Italiana	Milan
Banco di Napoli	Naples
Banco Nacional de Mexico	Mexico City
Bank of Chosen	Seoul (Chosen)
Bank of London and South America, Ltd.	London
Bank of Montreal	Montreal
Bank of Nova Scotia	Toronto
Bank of Taiwan, Ltd.	Taipeh (Japan)
Banque Belge pour l'Etranger	Brussels
Barclays Bank (D. C. and O.)	London
Canadian Bank of Commerce	Toronto
Chartered Bank of India, Australia & China	London
Dominion Bank	Toronto
Hongkong & Shanghai Banking Corp.	Hongkong
The Royal Bank of Canada	Montreal
Standard Bank of South Africa, Ltd.	London
The Sumitomo Bank, Ltd.	Osaka (Japan)
Yokohama Specie Bank, Ltd.	Yokohama (Japan)

Since agencies are not permitted to accept deposits and conduct a general banking business, a number of foreign banks have found it advisable to organize subsidiary banking corporations in the United States. Such institutions, although owned and controlled by foreign banks, are organized as domestic banking corporations under state laws and are subject to no special restrictions by reason of their foreign ownership. Most of the foreign bank subsidiaries are organized as trust companies. The principal institutions of this kind operating in New York are The Anglo-South American Trust Co., the Banca Commerciale Italiana Trust Co., the Bank of Sicily Trust Co., the Bank of Athens Trust Co., and the Hellenic Bank Trust Co.

Trading in foreign exchange. In contrast to most European countries in which the foreign exchange market is organized usually as an adjunct to the stock exchange, the New York foreign exchange market is an over-the-counter market where trading is carried on between a number of commercial and private banks, foreign exchange dealers, and agencies of foreign banks located in New York. The direct method of quotation is used; *i.e.*, units of foreign currency are quoted at so many cents per foreign unit. For example, one franc may be quoted at 6.68 cents United States currency. Only rates for demand bills and cable transfers are regularly quoted, except in the case of sterling exchange, in which connection rates for 60- and 90-day bills are also quoted.

The rate on 60-day bills is lower than on cable transfers and demand bills, because the seller has the use of the funds and is able to obtain interest thereon prior to the maturity of the bills. Similarly, the rate on 90-day bills is lower than that on 60-day bills. The difference in the rate for a time bill and a cable transfer is based on the rate of interest prevailing in the market on which the bill is drawn, and not the rate of interest prevailing in New York. Thus, for example, if one wishes to ascertain the rate on a 90-day draft on London on the basis of the rate for sterling cable transfers, one deducts from the cable rate 90 days' interest at the rate prevailing in London on prime bankers' bills.

The New York foreign exchange market embraces European countries, Canada, Mexico, China, India, the Philippine Islands, Java, Japan, Straits Settlements, and the South American countries. There is little trading in Australian pounds or in South African pounds, since the principal market for these currencies is in London.

International activities of the Reserve banks. The Federal Reserve Act conferred on the Reserve banks fairly broad powers to operate in the international money market. Section 14 of the Act authorizes any Federal Reserve bank to "purchase and sell in the open market, at home or abroad, either from or to domestic or foreign banks, firms, corporations or individuals, cable transfers and bankers' acceptances and bills of exchange of all kinds and maturities . . . eligible for discount. . . ." In addition the Reserve banks are permitted to deal in gold coin and bullion at home or abroad in accordance with regulations issued by the Secretary of the Treasury; to make loans secured by gold, with the consent of and in accordance with the regulations prescribed by the Federal Reserve Board; to open and maintain accounts in foreign countries, appoint correspondents and establish agencies abroad, and to open and maintain banking accounts for such foreign correspondents or agencies.

The Reserve banks have never fully utilized these powers. Although each Reserve bank has the same privileges under the law to transact foreign business, in practice all international operations are conducted through the Federal Reserve Bank of New York, either for its own account or for the account of the other banks. The New York Reserve Bank, moreover, has established correspondent relationships only with foreign central banks and the Bank for International Settlements. The only foreign agency is that established by the Federal Reserve Bank of Atlanta at Havana, in order to facilitate the circulation of United States money in Cuba. The business which the Reserve bank transacts with its foreign correspondents consists chiefly of buying and holding acceptances for their account, accepting their deposits and, in turn, maintaining deposits with them. In addition, the Reserve banks purchase foreign bills of exchange in the open market and sometimes, under unusual circumstances and in accordance with a special agreement, extend credit to foreign central banks by buying bills from them. The volume of dollar bills purchased by the New York Reserve Bank for the account of its foreign correspondents fluctuated widely with conditions in the money market and circumstances affecting the foreign institutions.[1] In 1930 the total was in excess of half a billion dollars, while in the latter part of 1934 it declined to only about one million dollars. When the purchase of bills by the Reserve bank results in a reduction in the deposits of foreign central banks with the Reserve bank, there is of course a corresponding increase in the Reserve balances of the member banks, and the credit base of the country is expanded. Conversely, a decline in the amount of bills held by Reserve banks for foreign account should reduce member-bank reserve balances and increase the deposits of the foreign central banks. However, since the volume of foreign central bank deposits with the Reserve banks is ordinarily quite small, and since purchases of bills are usually covered by the transfer to the Reserve bank of funds on deposit with the commercial or private banks, there is little net change in the amount of member-bank reserves. Similarly, an increase in foreign central-bank deposits due to the maturing of bills is normally offset by the transfer of deposits to the commercial or private banks.

The deposits of the foreign central banks with the Reserve bank, as well as the Reserve banks' deposits with the foreign banks, are merely minimum working balances. The Reserve banks pay no interest on such deposits, and they have never solicited foreign accounts. At times when foreign institutions are liquidating commitments in the New York money market on a large scale, foreign deposits may temporarily increase sharply, as during the international financial panic of 1931, when the total rose from $7,760,000 at the end of May to $162,205,000 at the end of August. However, the amount is usually between $3,000,000 and $10,000,000. The deposits of the Reserve banks with for-

---

[1] Technical details of these purchases are discussed on pp. 217–219.

eign central banks are even smaller, ranging from less than
a million to about $5,000,000.   Table 22 shows the move-
ment of both of these items during the last few years.

TABLE 22

FOREIGN BANK DEPOSITS WITH THE FEDERAL
RESERVE BANKS
(In thousands of dollars)

End of Month	1930	1931	1932	1933	1934
January	5,732	5,753	73,672	40,003	3,952
February	6,638	5,193	16,583	40,125	3,433
March	7,296	5,145	30,630	16,384	5,941
April	5,365	5,606	46,805	29,928	6,228
May	5,711	7,760	74,405	7,848	3,743
June	5,879	33,912	9,002	15,523	4,893
July	6,956	113,995	8,922	19,023	7,159
August	5,350	162,205	14,187	37,376	11,605
September	5,242	95,135	8,261	13,504	9,810
October	5,334	150,077	10,356	16,186	8,952
November	5,552	142,665	25,947	5,324	15,577
December	5,761	79,099	19,446	4,233	19,394

DEPOSITS OF FEDERAL RESERVE BANKS WITH FOREIGN
CENTRAL BANKS AND BANK FOR INTERNATIONAL
SETTLEMENTS

January	721	701	8,608	3,505	3,392
February	721	699	8,607	3,515	3,485
March	723	707	6,645	3,618	3,131
April	711	697	5,692	3,656	3,131
May	709	699	4,643	3,815	3,125
June	700	1,425	3,655	3,729	3,129
July	706	10,726	2,887	4,029	3,124
August	703	23,782	2,668	3,710	3,127
September	701	8,752	2,665	3,769	1,819
October	702	9,297	2,873	3,732	811
November	707	8,724	2,861	3,523	803
December	704	8,662	2,976	3,333	805

The Federal Reserve banks are permitted to purchase
acceptances without distinction as to the currencies in
which they are payable, and very often they hold a much
larger amount of bills payable in foreign currencies than
bills payable in dollars.   It is the established policy of the
New York Reserve Bank to purchase foreign currency bills
in the market in order to offset seasonal influences on the

foreign exchange market. At times when foreign currency bills are being offered in considerable volume in exchange for dollar funds, purchases by the Reserve bank tend to prevent a temporary weakening of exchange rates for foreign currencies.[2]

In emergencies the Federal Reserve banks, with the approval of the Federal Reserve Board, extend credit to foreign central banks by the purchase, under special agreement, of bills from their portfolios. Such transactions are arranged through the New York Reserve Bank, but the bills purchased are usually allocated among the other Reserve banks. Thus, in August 1931 a credit of $125,000,-000 was extended to the Bank of England in order to assist that institution in its unsuccessful efforts to maintain the pound sterling on the gold standard.

The Reserve banks' holdings of bills payable in foreign currencies at the end of each month since 1929 are shown in Table 23.

To extend credit to foreign central banks, the Reserve banks have also exercised their power to make loans secured by gold. Such loans were made in 1925 to the Bank of Poland and to the National Bank of Czechoslovakia in order to assist those institutions in stabilizing their currencies, and were made in November 1934 to the National Bank of Belgium.

---

[2] Testifying before a Sub-committee of the Senate Banking and Currency Committee on January 22, 1931, Governor Harrison, of the Federal Reserve Bank of New York, explained the bank's policy in this respect as follows: "As you know, the seasonal pressure upon the foreign exchanges usually occurs in the fall, at the time our agricultural products are moving abroad, or are ready to be moved abroad. We can almost always anticipate that that will be the season of the heaviest pressure, although in recent years there has been some disturbance to the normal movement on account of extraordinary conditions in many markets resulting from the inflation here two years ago. At the time we commenced to purchase these foreign currency bills this past fall—and I am sorry I do not remember the exact date —the foreign exchanges and especially sterling were very weak and near the gold import point. Now, we know from experience that one of the factors which influences the purchase of our goods is the fluctuation in the exchanges, and at a period when the exchanges normally would be weak on account of the movement of goods we can lend some support on the foreign exchanges through the purchase of foreign currency bills."

TABLE 23

FEDERAL RESERVE BANKS' HOLDINGS OF ACCEPTANCES
PAYABLE IN FOREIGN CURRENCIES
(In thousands of dollars)

End of Month	1929	1930	1931	1932	1933	1934
January	1,019	1,035	36,119	33,444	29,036	5,977
February	1,029	1,038	23,958	33,478	28,997	5,887
March	1,036	1,040	1,063	30,778	24,788	5,275
April	1,036	1,054	1,074	30,736	7,181	5,070
May	1,040	1,058	1,073	30,837	6,981	5,075
June	1,043	1,064	10,551	30,762	7,089	5,075
July	2,061	1,065	34,371	30,645	6,821	5,081
August	12,346	1,071	145,215	30,834	6,199	5.079
September	16,955	1,075	48,804	30,849	6,068	5,691
October	17,064	21,583	33,501	30,659	5,686	5.495
November	1,027	31,587	33,386	30,652	5,841	5.499
December	1,030	35,983	33,429	29,489	6,033	5,501

Foreign central banks acquiring gold in this country often leave it temporarily with the Reserve banks, where it is said to be under "earmark." Since the passage of the Gold Reserve Act of 1934, all imports, exports, and earmarking of gold have been subject to the regulations of the Secretary of the Treasury. Once gold is bought and paid for by a foreign institution, it is actually withdrawn from the monetary system of this country even though it may be left under earmark at a Federal Reserve bank. Hence, the exportation of earmarked gold has no effect whatever on the credit structure. On the other hand, the release of gold from earmark is equivalent to an importation of gold.

Influence of Federal Reserve banks on international money market. The discount policy of a central bank located in an important international money center should be, to a very large degree, international in scope. The discount policy of the Federal Reserve Bank of New York, however, is usually determined not by international conditions nor by international gold movements, but rather by conditions prevailing in the United States. Only in a few notable instances have international considerations influenced its discount policy.

It has been said that the only international consideration that affects the policy of the Federal Reserve Bank of New York is the position of the London money market and that of the Bank of England. However, careful study of post-war developments in the international money market reveals that the policy of the Federal Reserve Bank of New York in giving London chief consideration has been well founded. For many years after the close of the war, conditions in other financial centers such as Paris, Berlin, and Milan were far from normal, and the policy of the central banks in those centers was determined by considerations largely local in character. For example, after the stabilization of the French currency, the Bank of France was confronted with a huge inflow of funds from abroad which led to large gold imports. Since the movement of gold to France was not always determined so much by credit conditions, either in France or abroad, as by the desire of the French to repatriate funds which had previously been placed abroad in order to avoid losses from the depreciation of the franc, it would have been erroneous for the Federal Reserve Bank of New York to attempt to interfere with the movement of gold from the United States to France or to let its credit policy be influenced by the movement.

Similarly, the Federal Reserve Bank in New York could not, under conditions prevailing in the post-war period, consider the credit situation or the position of the central banks in the other countries of Europe. Germany was—and still is—suffering from a serious shortage of capital, and the discount policy of the Reichsbank up to the time of the banking crisis in July 1931 was determined largely by the movement of foreign funds to and from the country. Under these circumstances neither credit conditions in Berlin nor the policy of the Reichsbank could be considered in formulating the discount policy of the New York Reserve Bank. The other important money markets, such as Amsterdam, Zurich, and Milan, are more closely tied up with London than with New York.

Even the bearing of conditions in London on the Reserve bank's discount policy has not always been clear. It is to be expected that an international financial center of the standing of New York should usually be a leader in indicating the trend of interest rates, but since the policy of the Reserve bank has been determined in most cases by internal conditions, it could not always be readily adjusted to changed international conditions. In many instances changes in the discount rate of the New York Reserve Bank followed changes in the discount rate of the Bank of England. To what extent the close movement of the discount rates in London and New York was the result of a common agreement is a matter of conjecture. Since the abandonment of the gold standard by England and the establishment of a "modified" international gold bullion standard in the United States, the discount policy of the Reserve banks, as well as of all other central banks, has ceased to be influenced by international considerations and has been determined exclusively by domestic conditions.

CHAPTER IX

London—The Bank of England
and the Joint Stock Banks

Introduction. In spite of the vicissitudes of the post-war period and the abandonment of the gold standard, London still remains one of the most important, if not the most important, of the international financial centers of the world. This position is the natural outgrowth of the economic and financial development of Great Britain. It represents a growth of over one hundred years on the part of the institutions comprising the market, during which they have become thoroughly familiar with international financial transactions and have come to regard them, in spite of losses sustained from time to time, as an important part of their activities.

This position is in direct contrast to that of the New York market, whose international position is of recent origin and where international transactions form only a small part of the activities of the various financial institutions. In the United States, with its huge home market and the great preponderance of domestic transactions, the international aspect of the business is considered as being more or less incidental. This view is partly responsible for the erratic attitude of New York towards international business, as shown in its sudden interest at times when conditions seemed favorable and its sharp withdrawal when difficulties appeared.

The fine mechanism of the London money market is the result of the international economic position of Great Britain. In London and a few other British cities are found some of the most important commodity markets of the world, such as Manchester for cotton, Liverpool for grain, London for metals. Any commodity of world importance can find a ready sale in these commodity markets, and the transactions are financed through the London money market. The fact that under normal conditions a large number of world commodities are quoted in pounds sterling creates a large amount of sterling bills and necessitates the maintenance of banking connections in London by important merchants throughout the world. British shipping is world-wide, and the operations of the merchant marine create a continuous supply of sterling bills. In addition, shipping bills of other countries are often stated in pounds sterling. British insurance companies operate throughout the world, and their international financial transactions contribute to the activity of the London money market. The strength of London as a financial center is, therefore, based primarily upon the turnover of commodities and of services; and thus the London market differed from the New York market, which, under conditions as they existed prior to 1933, was based largely on the turnover of securities.

Characteristics of the London market. One of the outstanding characteristics of the London market is its liquidity. Most of the bills arise out of short-term transactions and are based on commodities which can be liquidated on very short notice. Arising as they do out of commercial transactions, they have direct access to the Bank of England. Furthermore, the bill market, normally the most important market in London, has direct connections with the Bank of England, which not only gives the bill brokers access to the central bank but also makes the discount policy of the latter effective. This fact, too, is in contrast to the situation in New York, where the call money market, under normal conditions the most important market, has no access to the Reserve banks and, until recently, has been but little controlled by the central banking system.

Another characteristic feature of the London market which is in sharp contrast to that of New York is the absence of legal restrictions and governmental supervision. In spite of the magnitude of the operations and their vital interest to the British government and the British nation as a whole, there are but few restrictions imposed by the government on the market and on the institutions concerned with it. The Bank of England, however, through its prestige and the force of tradition, exercises great control not only over the money market but also over the flow of long-term capital. The market, one may say, is based entirely on tradition and on the complete understanding and coöperation between the individual institutions and the Bank of England. This adherence to tradition and close coöperation are a result of the concentration of banking resources. The "Big Five" joint-stock banks, with thousands of branches scattered throughout England and their various subsidiaries and affiliates at home and abroad, control about 85 per cent of the total banking resources of the country. The once numerous private banking houses have been greatly reduced in number, and even the number of investment houses is limited. The greater the institution, the greater are the responsibility and the desire to adhere to tradition and to established practice. The London market has often been criticized for its ultra-conservatism, but this conservatism, with all its shortcomings, is the great strength of the British banking community. It is based on a division of functions whereby the individual institutions become highly specialized and acquire a thorough knowledge and understanding of their particular phase of the business.

Under ordinary circumstances London performs for the world the same function that a large commercial bank performs for a district or community. Through subsidiaries, through the Dominion and Colonial banks, through the branches of foreign banking institutions, through world-wide correspondent relationships, it collects funds from all over the world, utilizing them where the return is greatest.

The status of the City under normal conditions is a good indication of the financial status of the world. Low money rates in London, under normal conditions, usually mean low money rates throughout the world and cheap financing for international financial transactions. The wide international ramifications of the London market, however, constitute not only its great strength but also its weakness, since trouble in any important point of the world is immediately reflected in London, either because of the withdrawal of funds from London or because of the freezing of British funds invested there.

In spite of the fact that in post-war years New York has given London keen competition and has vied with it for first place among financial centers of the world, and in spite of London's setbacks in recent years, the position of London as an international financial center still remains unparalleled.

The following is an analysis of the component elements of the London money market and of its organization and operation.

The Bank of England

Historical survey. The nerve center of the London money market is the Bank of England. It is the oldest central bank in the world and, prior to the World War, was the chief mainstay of the international gold standard. Although a private corporation and practically unrestricted by law, its policies are to a large extent determined by the Treasury.

In consideration of a loan of £1,200,000 at 8 per cent to the Government of William III, a group of private bankers was granted, by an act of Parliament and a Royal Charter on July 27, 1694, the right to organize a joint stock company for doing business under the name of "The Governor and Company of the Bank of England." This is still the official name of the Bank. The loan was repayable at the expiration of the twelve-year charter. Subsequent extensions

of the charter coincided with additional loans by the Bank
to the state, so that the debt of the latter to the Bank
amounts at present to £11,015,100.   The Bank Act of 1844
extended the charter for an indefinite period, subject to
termination on a year's notice and the repayment of the
debt owed by the state to the Bank.   Up to 1826 the Bank
of England had a complete monopoly of joint stock banking
and a partial monopoly of the note issue privilege.   These
privileges were granted the Bank by an act passed in 1709,
which stipulated that no "body politic or persons exceeding
six in number, united in partnership, should borrow, owe,
or take up any sum or sums of money on their bills or notes
payable at demand at any time less than six months."   The
notes of the Bank of England were not legal tender up to
1833; they were payable to order, not to bearer.

During the war against France following the French
Revolution, the government borrowed heavily from the
Bank of England.   The large loans made to the British
government and the cost of maintaining the British troops
abroad resulted in a large outflow of gold and impaired the
liquidity of the bank.   The fears of a French invasion in
February 1797 caused a run on the country banks, which in
turn withdrew gold from the already considerably depleted
stock of the Bank of England.   The latter applied to the
government for assistance, which was granted promptly in
the form of the Bank Restriction Act of 1797.   The Act
prohibited the Bank from making payments in gold except
to the Army and Navy or by order of the Privy Council.
At the same time the notes of the Bank were made valid
for payment of taxes.   In 1819, the provisions of the Bank
Restriction Act were repealed.   From 1821 to August 6,
1914, the Bank of England adhered to the free redemption
of notes, although during the crisis of 1837–40 the suspension of specie payment was avoided only through the borrowing of gold from the Bank of France.

The Peel Act.   In 1844 the Bank Act (Peel Act) was
passed, and the principal provisions of this law still regu-

late the operations of the Bank of England. The Act gave the Bank of England the exclusive right to issue notes, subject to the then existing note-issue privileges of the country banks. The volume of notes of the country banks was limited and, in case of a bank's amalgamation with a non-issuing joint stock bank or of an increase in the number of partners over six, the note-issue privilege of the bank ceased and the Bank of England was entitled to increase its fiduciary issue by two-thirds of the total of the lapsed issue. Gradually the note-issue privilege of the other banks lapsed, and the fiduciary issue of the Bank of England was increased, in 1923, to £19,750,000.

By the Peel Act the Bank of England was divided into two departments: the Banking Department and the Issue Department, the sole function of the latter being the routine matter of issuing notes. The notes under the Peel Act, with the exception of the fiduciary issue, had to be secured 100 per cent by gold, including a limited percentage of silver bullion. By the same act the Bank was compelled to buy, at the fixed price of £3.17.9 per standard ounce, all the gold that might be offered to it. The Act also required the Bank to publish a weekly return in a specified form in the *London Gazette*.

Effects of war. On August 1, 1914, the Bank of England addressed a letter to the Chancellor of the Exchequer calling attention to the

> extraordinary demands for assistance which have been made upon the Bank of England in consequence of the threatened outbreak of hostilities between two or more of the Great Powers of Europe. . . . We fear that unless we obtain authority to issue notes against securities in excess of the amount permitted by law it will shortly become necessary to curtail the facilities . . . which we regard as essential to the trade and commerce of the country.

On August 6, 1914, the Currency and Bank Notes Act was passed. Clause 3 of the Act provided that the Bank of England and Scottish or Irish banks of issue might issue notes in excess of the legal limit to an extent temporarily authorized by the Treasury and subject to any conditions attached to that authority. In practice, this clause virtually amounted to a suspension of the Bank Act of 1844.

By far the most important provision of the Act, however, was the authority granted to the Treasury to issue currency notes in denominations of £1 and 10s, leaving the amount and manner of the issues to the discretion of the Treasury. The Treasury currency (Bradburies) superseded the gold sovereign, which disappeared from circulation. The joint stock banks also transferred to the Bank of England the gold reserves which they customarily kept as part of their cash reserves in their own vaults, and replaced them with the new currency notes. On May 10, 1917, an embargo on gold exports was proclaimed.

The Cunliffe Committee of 1918, which inquired into conditions of currency and foreign exchanges after the war, recommended: (1) the absorption of the Treasury currency by the Bank of England; (2) adherence to the principle of a legally fixed fiduciary issue as stipulated in the Bank Act of 1844; and (3) the retention of the elasticity provision of the Act of 1914, which permitted the Bank of England, with the consent of the Treasury, to issue temporarily notes in excess of the fiduciary limit. It also recommended a return to the gold standard as soon as the Bank of England could successfully maintain a stock of gold of not less than £150,000,000.

Return to gold. The recommendations of the Cunliffe Committee were generally accepted and embodied in the Gold Standard Act of 1925 and in the Currency and Bank Notes Act of 1928. The Gold Standard Act of May 13, 1925, introduced the gold bullion standard, under which the Bank of England became obligated to sell gold in quantities of 400 ounces or more at £3.17.10½ per ounce troy of standard fineness and to buy gold at £3.17.9 per ounce. The Gold Standard Act also abolished the free coinage of gold.

The Act of 1928 amalgamated the two types of notes in circulation and fixed the fiduciary issue at £260,000,000. This figure was approximately the combined amount of the actual maximum fiduciary issue of the Bank of England and the Treasury notes for 1927. The law, however, provided that the Treasury may permit a reduction or increase of the fiduciary issue by a stipulated amount for a period not exceeding six months, the reduction or increase being renewable for successive similar periods. The Treasury minutes authorizing an increase in the fiduciary issue must be laid before both Houses of Parliament, and any series of renewals by the Treasury may be extended for a total of two years only, except as otherwise determined by Parliament. All currency notes outstanding on November 22, 1928 (£230,000,000) were transferred to the Bank and amalgamated with the Bank of England notes. The Bank of England was also authorized to issue £1 and 10s notes, which are legal tender to any amount. The Act also empowers the Bank to demand the surrender of gold owned by residents in Great Britain in amounts over £10,000 at its statutory buying price. Foreign-owned gold is exempt from this provision.

The fiduciary issue was increased on August 1, 1931, to £275,000,000, in order to cope with the abnormal demands on the Bank of England caused by the banking crisis in Central Europe. When the Treasury authority for this increase expired on March 31, 1933, the Bank did not seek its renewal and reverted to its normal fiduciary issue of £260,000,000.

Abandonment of the gold standard. As a result of the financial crisis brought about by the rapid withdrawal of foreign funds from London, Parliament voted on September 21, 1931, to abandon the gold standard. The relevant part of this measure reads: "Unless and until His Majesty by proclamation otherwise directs, Subsection 2 of Section 1 of the gold standard act of 1925 shall cease to have effect notwithstanding that Subsection 1 of the said section remains in force." The suspended Subsection 2 of the Gold Standard Act of 1925 reads as follows:

> The Bank of England shall be bound to sell to any person who makes demand in that behalf at the head office of the Bank during office hours of the Bank, and pays the purchase price in any legal tender, gold bullion at the price of £3 17s 10½d per ounce troy of gold of the standard of fineness prescribed for gold coin by the coinage act of 1870, but only in the form of bars containing approximately 400 ounces troy of fine gold.

While the Bank of England was released from the obligation to sell gold at the fixed price, yet no embargo was placed on gold exports. This policy is in contrast to the war-time suspension, when gold exports were prohibited but convertibility of the currency into gold was theoretically maintained, and it differs from that of most other countries, where the suspension of the gold standard usually means an embargo on gold exports besides unconvertibility of notes. Since the suspension of convertibility automatically precludes withdrawals of gold from the bank of issue, the imposition of an embargo on gold exports is ostensibly intended to prevent the shipment abroad of hoarded and newly mined gold. Great Britain deliberately abstained from that measure and maintained the freedom of gold exports, thus retaining the world gold market in London, while, at the same time, protecting the monetary gold stock of the country.

Organization and operation. The Bank of England enjoys the prestige of a government institution and the freedom of action of a private bank. It is a private institution, organized as a joint stock company under a charter and various Acts of Parliament. The capital stock ("Proprietors' Capital"), in the amount of £14,553,000, has remained unaltered since 1816. The government exercises no supervision over the Bank, with the exception of the control over the note-issue power. The Bank is at liberty to engage in any kind of transaction; the only limitation imposed on it by law is contained in the Tonnage Act of 1694, by which the Bank of England "is to be debarred for all time from using any of its funds in dealing in merchandise or wares of any description." Such restrictions on the operations of the Bank as do exist are self-imposed and may be changed or removed at the discretion of the court of the Bank. The Bank publishes only the weekly statement—no other information about its activities is made public.

The Bank is administered by a board (court) of 24 directors, a governor, a deputy governor, a comptroller, and a chief cashier. The office of comptroller was created in 1918 in order to assure continuity of policy. The directors are elected by vote of the stockholders. To be eligible to vote, a stockholder must have held a minimum of £500 of capital stock for at least six months; and each stockholder has only one vote. Directors' qualifications are £4,000 stock for governor, £3,000 for deputy governor, and £2,000 for other directors. It is a well-established tradition that no director of any of the large joint stock banks shall be elected a director of the Bank of England. Ordinarily the offices of governor and deputy governor are given in rotation for a period of two years, the deputy governor succeeding the governor, with the oldest director who has not yet been in office usually becoming deputy governor. However, in difficult times there have been deviations from this practice, and the governor has remained in office for a longer period. (The present governor, Mr. Montagu C. Norman, has held the office since 1920.) The governor is the chief executive. The "court" meets once a week, at which time the weekly statement of the Bank is drawn up and changes in the Bank rate are decided upon, although on exceptional occasions the Bank rate has been changed by the governor without convening the "court." The latter then ratifies the change at its next meeting.

The first weekly return of the Bank of England on September 7, 1844, shows the position of the two departments

of the Bank as provided for by the Act of 1844. The form
remained practically unchanged until November 28, 1928,
when the statement disclosed additional information of
particular interest to the money market. The changes are
shown in the two accompanying statements (see Tables 24
and 25).

TABLE 24

I. THE FIRST BANK RETURN AFTER THE
BANK CHARTER ACT, 1844

(Weekly Return of the Bank of England, Week Ending September 7, 1844)

Liabilities		*Assets*	
	ISSUE DEPARTMENT		
Notes issued	£28,351,295	Government debt	£11,015,100
		Other securities	2,984,900
		Gold coin and bullion.	12,657,208
		Silver bullion	1,694,087
	£28,351,295		£28,351,295
	BANKING DEPARTMENT		
Proprietors' capital ...	£14,553,000	Government securities.	£14,554,834
Rest	3,564,729	Other securities	7,835,616
Public deposits	3,630,809	Notes	8,175,025
Other deposits	8,644,348	Gold and silver coin...	857,765
Seven-day and other bills	1,030,354		
	£31,423,240		£31,423,240

The following is a brief description of the individual
items which appear in the weekly return of the Bank:

A. Issue department. *Notes in circulation* consist of
notes in the hands of the public and in the vaults of the
banks, and of notes held as cover for the excess note issue
of the banks in Scotland and Northern Ireland over and
above fiduciary limits as prescribed by Parliament. Notes
held by the Banking Department are not in circulation;
they represent the difference between the total amount of
notes issued and the amount in actual circulation. The
assets held as cover against notes are divided into two
parts: (1) the fiduciary portion, and (2) gold. The fiduciary portion of the note issue is backed chiefly by govern-

TABLE 25

II. THE FIRST BANK RETURN UNDER THE CURRENCY AND
BANK NOTES ACT, 1928

(Return for the week ended Wednesday, November 28, 1928)

ISSUE DEPARTMENT

Liabilities		Assets	
Notes issued:		Government debt	£ 11,015,100
In circulation	£367,001,148	Other government se-	
In banking depart-		curities	233,568,550
ment	52,087,797	Other securities	10,176,193
		Silver coin	5,240,157
		Amount of fiduciary	
		issue	£260,000,000
		Gold coin and bullion	159,088,945
	£419,088,945		£419,088,945

BANKING DEPARTMENT

Liabilities		Assets	
Proprietors' capital ..	£ 14,553,000	Government securities	£ 52,180,327
Rest	3,254,001	Other securities:	
Public deposits*	21,452,051	Discts. &	
Other deposits:†		advs. £13,586,293	
Bankers. £62,379,409		Securities 20,214,855	33,801,148
Other ac-			
counts . 37,185,203	99,564,612	Notes	52,087,797
		Gold and silver coin..	757,041
Seven-day and other			
bills**	2,649		
	£138,826,313		£138,826,313

* Including Exchequer, Savings Banks, Commissioners of National Debt, and
Dividend Accounts
† The division in "Bankers" and "Other accounts" is a re-adoption of the
Bank Return form used many years ago.
** Discontinued Sept. 1, 1934.

ment securities and by an amount of silver coin, which may
not exceed £5,500,000. The type of securities held by the
Issue Department is left to the discretion of the Bank.
The income derived from these securities is applied to meet
the expenses of printing, issuing, and cancelling notes, and
the balance is turned over to the Treasury as public revenue. *Government debt* represents the aggregate of loans
made directly by the Bank to the government.

Other government securities consist of government bonds,
Treasury bills, etc., while *Other securities* include commercial bills, bonds, stocks, and foreign exchange. Both classes

of securities are bought and sold in accordance with the
Bank's policy, but while each of them is subject to changes
from week to week, the total remains practically unchanged,
except when the fiduciary limit is altered.   While it is impossible to state with any degree of accuracy the amount
of foreign securities and bills of exchange held by the Issue
Department, it is a known fact that this item contains such
assets and that they have increased or decreased in accordance with the policy of the Bank concerning the pound
sterling.   *Gold coin and bullion* represents the monetary
stock of gold of the Bank of England and constitutes the
100 per cent cover which must be maintained against notes
issued in excess of the fiduciary issue.

    B.   Banking department.   The Banking Department is
the operating division of the Bank and functions in many respects as a commercial bank.   It acts as fiscal agent for the
British Government, receives as *Public deposits* the revenues collected all over the country, manages the accounts
of the national debt, issues Treasury bills for the government, and makes advances to the government on "Ways
and Means" when expenditure temporarily exceeds revenue.

    Bankers' deposits represent exclusively the balances of
British banks whose main business is conducted in Great
Britain.   These balances constitute a part of the cash reserves of the banks, and their importance in the credit
structure of the country is similar to that of the balances
of the member banks with the Federal Reserve banks in
the United States.   Although no legally fixed reserve requirements exist, the banks maintain balances with the
Bank of England equivalent, on the average, to about 5
per cent of their deposits, and any change in the money
market is reflected in this item.   An increased demand for
funds results in a decrease in bankers' deposits, which in
turn forces the joint stock banks to call loans from the
market.

    Other accounts include the balances of British banks op-
erating chiefly in the Dominions (including the Bank of

Ireland) and in foreign countries; the balances of foreign central banks, colonial banks, merchant bankers, and other financial houses; and the deposits of the Indian and Colonial governments, of British municipalities, and of private citizens.   The Bank pays no interest on deposits.

The *Seven-day and other bills,* also called *post bills,* are promissory notes issued by the Bank of England in amounts from £10 to £1,000, payable at seven days' sight to a specified payee or to order.   They are a relic of early years and were devised by the Bank of England "so that in case of the mails being robbed, the proprietor might have time to give notice thereof."

Government securities consist of direct obligations of the British Government (Consols, war loans, etc.), Ways and Means Advances to the Treasury, and Treasury bills acquired by the Bank on its own initiative and not offered to it for discount.   This item is comparable to the item "U. S. Government Securities" in the weekly statement of the Federal Reserve banks.   Through the purchase and sale of government securities the Bank of England carries on its open market operations.   An increase in government security holdings is intended either to offset an outflow of gold from London or to ease the money market.   Thus, to mention a single case, when London began to lose large amounts of gold to the Continent in the middle of July 1931, the Bank partially offset this outflow, as far as the money market was concerned, through the purchase of government securities.   Holdings of these securities increased from £30,021,000 on July 15 to £68,976,000 on September 30.   Through these purchases, the Bank prevented a decline in bankers' deposits and the calling of loans from the market by the joint stock banks.

Discounts and advances represent Treasury bills and bills of exchange discounted at the bank at the initiative of its customers, and loans made by the Bank to the bill brokers and private customers.   An amount of about £10,000,000 is considered to be the normal accommodation to the Bank's private customers. Whenever this item rises considerably above £10,000,000, it may be reasonably assumed that the joint stock banks have called part of their outstanding loans and that the bill brokers have been forced into the Bank. A simultaneous increase in "discounts and advances" and "bankers' deposits" is an indication that the banks are strengthening their cash position by calling funds from the bill market, possibly in preparation for dividend disbursements or as a precautionary measure in periods of financial stress. Such a situation arose shortly after England abandoned the gold standard, in September 1931, and when London was confronted with a large outflow of funds.

Securities comprise miscellaneous securities and commercial bills, domestic and foreign, bought by the Bank on its own initiative. They also include deposits kept with foreign central banks and the Bank for International Settlements, and advances made to foreign banks of issue.

Notes represent the Bank's own notes, which together with *Gold and silver coin*, consisting almost entirely of silver coin, constitute the cash on hand of the Banking Department. These two items constitute the "reserve." The "reserve" represents merely cash on hand maintained to meet any increased demand for currency, and does not refer at all to the convertibility of the notes. Prior to the Act of 1928 there were no legal provisions stipulating a definite procedure whenever a sudden demand for currency arose. The Issue Department could lawfully issue notes only against gold, but it is obvious that gold cannot be imported as fast as the demand for notes may arise. Hence, while this inelastic currency system functioned satisfactorily under normal economic and financial conditions, in a crisis there would be an increased demand for legal tender money which could be met only through increasing the fiduciary issue. On four occasions after the passage of the Bank Act of 1844—in 1847, 1857, 1866, and 1914—the Bank of England was confronted with a demand for notes exceeding the Bank's gold holdings and fiduciary limit.

The situation was met in each case by "suspension" of the Bank Act; *i.e.*, the government granted the Bank power to issue notes in excess of the fiduciary maximum, without interfering with the principle of convertibility. This lack of elasticity has been remedied by the Act of 1928, which permits an increase in the fiduciary issue with the permission of the Treasury.

The reserve is the basis for the expansion of credit by the Bank, and under normal conditions it is the key to the Bank rate. The amount of notes held by the Banking Department is the only stock of currency upon which the banks can rely to meet cash withdrawals. It also represents the maximum amount of gold that the Bank can part with short of a reduction in the volume of notes in circulation or an expansion of the fiduciary issue. The reserve is therefore carefully watched by the money market and, under normal conditions, the status of the reserve may determine the discount and open market policy of the Bank.

Under abnormal conditions, and particularly since the abandonment of the gold standard, the reserve position of the Bank has ceased to be a major factor in determining the discount policy. This fact was clearly demonstrated on December 15, 1932, when the payment in gold by the British Government of its war debt annuity to the United States resulted in a sharp decline in the reserve without a change in the discount rate of 2 per cent. The amount of gold held by the Issue Department dropped from £139,-422,097 on December 14, 1932, to £119,788,284 on December 21, 1932.

The ratio of notes and gold and silver coin held by the Banking Department, or the "reserve," to its deposit liabilities (public and other deposits and seven-day bills) is called the "proportion." It is analagous to the cash ratio of any commercial bank, but in so far as the country's credit system depends on the liquidity of the Banking Department, the "proportion" is a considerably higher percentage than the customary bank ratio. The "proportion" is not prescribed by law, but under more or less normal conditions it is not permitted to fall below 30 per cent. As a matter of fact, up to 1914 the average was around 43 per cent. From 1914 to 1927 the average proportion ranged from 14 per cent to 34 per cent. From 1927 the proportion kept increasing, and in the last week of February 1930 it reached 65 13/16 per cent, the highest point since 1896.

The Joint Stock Banks

Early developments. Next to the Bank of England, the joint stock banks are the most important institutional element in the London money market. In contrast to the United States, England has not enacted special legislation regulating the organization and management of banks. The latter are incorporated under the Companies (consolidation) Act of 1908 (amended in 1929) or, in exceptional cases (as of the Bank of England), under a Royal Charter and an Act of Parliament. Up to 1826 the Bank of England was the only joint stock bank, since no partnership of more than six persons was permitted to be organized for conducting a banking business. The panic of 1825, with its disastrous effects on the private banks, caused the passage of a law in 1826 that allowed the formation of banks with more than six partners but prohibited the establishment of joint stock banks within a radius of 65 miles of London. This restriction was abolished in 1833, but the note-issue privilege in London and within the 65-mile radius around London remained a monopoly of the Bank of England. These laws gave considerable impetus to the development of the joint stock banks. In 1834 the London and Westminster Bank (now the Westminster Bank, Ltd.) was organized as the first joint stock bank in London. It was followed by the formation of a number of other joint stock banks which grew rapidly and became keen competitors of the private bankers. The latter adopted a hostile attitude towards the joint stock banks and refused to admit them to the Clearing House until 1854, when a few of the joint stock banks were accepted as members. When the Companies Act permitted banks to incorporate with limited liability, almost all joint stock banks became limited liability companies and included the word "Limited" at the end of their names in accordance with the provisions of the Act.

Merger movement. The fact that the joint stock banks located in London and its vicinity were deprived of the note-issue power was chiefly responsible for the rapid development and growth of the deposit and checking business of these banks. From the early years of their existence the joint stock banks embarked on a program of expansion through amalgamations and absorptions of the numerous private and country banks, economic conditions being favorable for this development. The rapid economic growth of the British Empire during the nineteenth century required the service of large financial units, for which the joint stock banks were preëminently fitted because their corporate form of organization enabled them to increase their capital through the issue of new stock. Furthermore, while the confidence of the public in the private banks was undermined by the failure of such bankers as Overend and Gurney in 1866, Collie and Co. in 1873, and Barings in 1890, the joint stock banks successfully weathered the financial crises. At the same time the check was gradually replacing the country bank note, and with the organization of the "country check clearing" in 1858 the branch banking system spread rapidly. Branch banking not only permits great economies in the operation of a bank, but also makes possible the rapid mobilization and shifting of funds to take advantage of higher interest rates prevailing in different parts of the country or to meet a sudden emergency. The absorption and merger process progressed rapidly, for the larger the joint stock banks grew, the less the private banks were able to compete, and hence the latter were forced to surrender their independence. In 1890 England and Wales had 104 joint stock banks operating 2,203 branches, while at the end of 1913 there were only 43 banks with 5,797 branches.

The war caused a temporary halt in the amalgamation movement. When the movement was resumed in 1917, it assumed a different character—that of mergers between the great joint stock banks. It was perhaps an instinctive movement to strengthen the structure of the organizations in anticipation of the post-war financial convulsions. However, public opinion was opposed to further concentration of banking which might culminate in a "money trust" and the establishment of a virtual monopoly over the money market for the benefit of the banks' shareholders. In March 1918 a committee of the Treasury was appointed "to consider and report . . . whether it is desirable that legislation should be introduced to prohibit such amalgamations or to provide safeguards under which they might continue to be permitted." Although the legislation recommended by the committee was not enacted, a tacit agreement was reached that, prior to any merger, the banks involved should obtain the consent of the Treasury. To a parliamentary interpellation in February 1924, as to the policy of the government in a proposed merger between any of the "Big Five" joint stock banks, the Chancellor of the Exchequer replied: "Further amalgamation of the larger banks would not be likely to be viewed with favor." Since the end of the war the number of joint stock banks has decreased, and since 1928 their number has remained stationary at sixteen. These sixteen institutions (excluding the Bank of England) maintained 10,060 branches at the end of 1933 in England and Wales. While the 104 joint stock banks had, in 1890, £67,826,000 of capital and reserves and £368,663,000 in deposits, at the end of 1933 the 16 banks had £135,352,136 in capital and reserves, and deposits amounted to £2,025,230,732.

The bulk of the banking resources of Great Britain are concentrated in five banks, known as the "Big Five," as

shown in Table 26.   The importance of these five banks in
the banking structure of England becomes still clearer when
one compares their resources with those of the other eleven
joint stock banks and those of the private banks. (See
Table 27.)

TABLE 26

THE "BIG FIVE" AS OF DECEMBER 31, 1933

Institutions	Number of Branches	Paid-up Capital and Reserves	Deposits
Midland Bank, Ltd.	2,105	£ 25,748,012	£ 413,752,673
Barclays Bank, Ltd.	2,080	26,108,217	378,759,772
Lloyds Bank, Ltd.	1,915	23,810,252	364,553,939
National Provincial Bank, Ltd.	1,361	17,479,416	288,397,118
Westminster Bank, Ltd.	1,072	16,820,157	294,739,761
Total	8,533	£109,966,054	£1,740,203,263

TABLE 27

RESOURCES OF "BIG FIVE" AS COMPARED WITH RESOURCES
OF OTHER ELEVEN JOINT STOCK BANKS AND OF
PRIVATE BANKS

At End of 1933	Paid-up Capital and Reserves	Deposits	Total Resources
"Big Five"	£109,966,054	£1,740,203,263	£1,958,900,265
11 Other joint stock banks	25,386,082	285,027,469	330,036,627
4 Private banks*	2,425,000	16,451,840	21,757,792
Total	£137,777,136	£2,041,682,572	£2,310,694,684

* Figures for 2 banks as of December 31, 1933, 1 bank as of July 5, 1933,
and 1 bank as of September 30, 1933.

Thus, at the end of 1933, 85.2 per cent of the total bank
deposits in England and Wales were concentrated in the
hands of the "Big Five."   In addition to the sixteen joint
stock banks there are eight Scottish joint stock banks, with,
at the end of 1933, paid-up capital and reserves of £30,917,-
118 and deposits in the amount of £281,678,416; and three
Northern Irish joint stock banks, with £4,650,000 in paid-up
capital and reserves and £51,160,144 in deposits.

Deposits.   In contrast to many of the Continental European banks, the British joint stock banks are typical de-

posit banks. Their deposits are of two types: (1) balances on "current account," subject to withdrawal on demand and similar to demand deposits in the United States, and (2) balances on "deposit account," which cannot be withdrawn, as a rule, on less than seven days' notice. In London, except by a special arrangement, no interest is allowed on current accounts. Outside of London, on the other hand, current accounts sometimes receive a rate of interest as high as the rate allowed in London on "deposit accounts." The clearing banks in the London district usually pay on "deposit accounts" a rate 2 per cent below the Bank of England's discount rate. However, when the Bank rate was reduced on June 30, 1932, from $2\frac{1}{2}$ to 2 per cent, the rate on "deposit accounts" remained unchanged at $\frac{1}{2}$ per cent. "Fixed deposits," *i.e.*, large sums left on deposit for definite periods of several months, command a higher interest rate and are subject to special agreements. In recent years the volume of current accounts has decreased, while the amount of deposit accounts has increased (see Table 28).

TABLE 28

THE LONDON CLEARING BANKS
(Monthly averages)

Year	Current Accounts (per cent)	Deposit Accounts (per cent)
1919	67.2	32.8
1924	58.8	41.2
1925	57.6	42.4
1926	57.3	42.7
1927	56.2	43.8
1928	55.8	44.2
1929	54.1	45.9
1930	52.9	47.1
1931	52.7	47.3
1932	49.5	50.5
1933	51.3	48.7
1934 November	52.0	48.0

Division of assets. Although the operations of the joint stock banks are not regulated by law, during the course of years they have developed certain well-defined rules concerning the employment of their deposits. The usual approximate percentage of the London clearing banks' assets to their deposit liabilities is shown below in order of their liquidity:

Cash on hand.............................	6 per cent
Balance at Bank of England..............	5 per cent
Balances with other banks and items in process of collection.....................	3 per cent
Money at short notice and call............	8 per cent
Treasury bills and bills of exchange........	14 per cent
Investments (mainly a mixture of long- and short-dated British government securities..	16 per cent
Discounts, loans, and advances............	48 per cent

The last item, representing loans to customers, has increased from 38 per cent in 1919 to about 55 per cent in 1931, chiefly owing to the shrinkage of deposits and the inability or unwillingness of the banks to call the loans of their customers. As soon as conditions permitted, however, the banks restored the customary ratio, and at the end of 1933 discounts, loans, and advances amounted to 47.9 per cent of total liabilities. Though not so required by law, as is the case in the United States, the joint stock banks adhere by custom and tradition to the practice of maintaining a cash reserve of from 10 to 11 per cent against their deposits. Using this reserve ratio as a working basis, the banks as a rule refrain from granting new credits whenever the ratio of cash falls below 10 per cent of their deposits. Since the Bank of England has a monopoly of the note issue, it can through contraction or expansion of the cash holdings of the joint stock banks exercise a considerable influence over their credit policies. The self-imposed rule of maintaining a reserve in cash of 10 to 11 per cent of their deposits thus has the same effect as the legal reserve requirements of the Reserve banks in the United States.

Aside from the joint stock banks' practice of maintaining about one-half of their cash reserves in the form of deposits with the Bank of England, there is no direct con-

tact between them and the central bank. The aloofness of
the Big Five toward the Bank of England is traditional,
and possibly has its origin in the Bank's policy of not elect-
ing to its court of directors a director or official of the large
joint stock banks. It is a characteristic feature of the
London money market, which again is in sharp contrast to
the practice prevailing in the United States, that under
normal conditions the joint stock banks do not borrow from
the Bank of England. Whenever a bank finds its cash reserve below the customary percentage, it calls its loans from
the money market in which a part of its surplus funds is
kept. If the debtors cannot borrow funds from other banks
or financial institutions, they are forced into the Bank of
England. By borrowing from the central bank, the market
is enabled to repay its loans to the joint stock banks, and
the latter in turn to strengthen their cash position.

Analysis of earning assets. The earning assets of the
joint stock banks may be divided into two classes on the
basis of the degree of liquidity. The class of assets outside of the actual cash reserve, in which emphasis is placed
on liquidity rather than earnings, consists of "Money at call
and short notice" and "Bills discounted"; the second group
comprises "Investments" and "Loans and advances to customers."

Money at call and short notice constitutes a secondary
reserve, since it can easily be converted into cash. It represents loans to bill brokers and stock exchange firms secured
by bills of exchange and stock exchange collateral of the
highest type. The loans range for periods of from one day
to one week in the case of bill brokers, and to a fortnight
or a maximum of three weeks in the case of loans for stock
exchange transactions. The latter are known as "Fortnightly loans to the Stock Exchange." The rate of interest
charged on call money is usually above that paid in London on deposit accounts, and about one per cent below the
Bank rate. The banks also make overnight loans at a
lower rate in order to employ the surplus funds which they

may have at the close of business as a result of day-to-day changes in their balance sheets.   The rate on call and short notice money is extremely sensitive to the money market conditions, since some loans mature every day and the banks, in order to strengthen their cash position, may refuse to renew them.

Bills discounted consist of Treasury bills and approved bills of exchange discounted for private customers or bought from bill brokers in the open market.   In the post-war years the former have constituted the largest proportion of the bill portfolio.   Both commercial bills and Treasury bills usually run for a period of not more than three months, but their maturities are so arranged that a portion falls due daily in the case of commercial bills, and weekly in the case of Treasury bills.   The yield on Treasury bills is determined by competitive bidding on the part of the buyers for the weekly offering, and as a rule it is lower than the rate on commercial bills.

The *Investments* of the banks consist mainly of British Government securities.   At the end of 1933 the investments of the sixteen joint stock banks of England and Wales amounted to £612,298,669, of which £544,050,683, or 88.9 per cent, were British Government securities and £68,247,-986, or 11.1 per cent, other investments of the gilt-edge type. The investments of the banks fluctuate with the conditions prevailing in trade and industry.   During periods of great activity the increased demand for accommodation at the banks results in a decrease of investments and, vice versa, in periods of business stagnation investments increase.

Discounts, loans, and advances represent loans to customers, either in the form of overdrafts on current account, or by debits on loan account and credits on current account. These loans to trade and industry may be secured by stock exchange collateral or by documents conveying title to property or chattels, or they may be unsecured.   They are usually made to supply working capital for brief periods. As a rule, however, the banks place greater emphasis on the

246 The International Money Markets

purpose of the loan and on the credit standing of the borrower, rather than on the collateral. The rate of interest charged is ½ of 1 per cent above the Bank rate, with an agreed minimum of, usually, 4 to 5 per cent.

In contrast to the United States, and particularly New York, where the structure of earning assets of the banks changes greatly with variations in economic conditions, the composition of assets of the joint stock banks remains relatively stable, as may be seen from Table 29.

TABLE 29

COMPOSITION OF ASSETS OF 11 JOINT STOCK BANKS OF
ENGLAND AND WALES*
(In percentages of total assets;** end of June)

	1928	1929	1930	1931	1932	1933	1934
Cash in hand and at Bank of England	13.9	13.0	13.3	13.0	13.1	12.6	11.9
Money at call and short notice	7.0	6.7	6.7	6.4	6.0	4.7	6.8
Discounts	11.3	10.2	12.4	12.6	13.3	14.7	10.4
Investments	12.9	13.1	13.0	15.4	18.6	26.1	27.2
Advances	46.1	48.8	46.6	44.6	42.1	35.0	35.8

* Includes the Big Five.
** Buildings and sundry assets are excluded.

The joint stock banks and industry. As a result of the difficult position in which a number of British industrial establishments have found themselves in post-war years, it has often been stated that the City is better prepared to supply capital to foreign countries than to British industry and that, in contrast to the close relations existing between the American and German financial institutions and industry in their respective countries, the British banks maintain an attitude of aloofness toward British industrial establishments. This situation, however, is not the result of a definite policy adopted either by the banks or by industry, but is rather the natural outcome of historical developments and traditions in the banking and industrial system of the country.

Owing to the fact that commerce not only preceded industry but also played a greater rôle in Great Britain than in any other country, London has developed a financial organization to serve primarily the needs of domestic and international trade. Industrial establishments, on the other hand, did not require the banking facilities of the City, since they were originally composed of relatively small units owned and controlled on a family basis. They financed their growth during the nineteenth century out of their own profits, or through the resources of the families who owned the establishments, and hence only rarely resorted to the London capital market. To the extent that banking services were needed, industry availed itself of the independent or private banks operating in the localities where the plants were located. The independent industrialists considered it beneath their dignity to seek the assistance of the joint stock banks in obtaining capital, for this would involve interference by the banks in the management of their businesses. The industrial establishments jealously guarded their financial independence and were not willing to share control with bankers and financiers for fear that the latter might eventually gain full control.

This attitude on the part of a number of industrial leaders militated against close coöperation between them and the joint stock banks, and in addition, the established practices and traditions of the banks did not encourage close coöperation. The joint stock banks have endeavored to remain strictly deposit banks whose foremost duty is to preserve the funds of the depositors. Since liquidity is of prime importance, the banks have limited their relations with industry mainly to the financing of self-liquidating transactions or to the furnishing of temporary working capital. In spite of this policy, the large joint stock banks are and have been generous, possibly even too generous—as shown by the high percentage of loans and advances—in providing short-term credits to industry, but they have been and still are unwilling to furnish funds required for capital purposes. Since the bulk of their resources consist of current and short-term deposits, the joint stock banks take the position that medium- and long-term loans are outside the scope of their activities.

The joint stock banks seldom act as underwriters of corporate securities, since they prefer to adhere closely to the functions of commercial banks. However, loans made by the joint stock banks to industrial establishments may at times become frozen, particularly during periods of depression. Thus, for example, in spite of the great decrease in business activity in England during 1930 and 1931, the volume of discounts and advances actually increased in 1930, while the decrease in 1931 was substantially smaller than that of deposits.

In spite of the aloofness on the part of the joint stock banks to industrial loans, the need of closer coöperation between the financial institutions and industry has long been recognized by the City. The first step in that direction was taken on November 20, 1929, when the Securities Management Trust, Ltd., was formed under the auspices of the Bank of England. The purpose of the company is to "investigate and advise on financial, industrial and economic questions and to aid in formulation and execution of schemes of arrangement for financing, development, amalgamation or reconstruction of companies." The paid-up capital amounts to £1,000, and the borrowing powers are not limited. The company is, in fact, a subsidiary of the Bank of England, and Mr. Montagu C. Norman, Governor of the Bank, is chairman of the board of directors. In 1930 the company participated in the organization of the Lancashire Steel Corporation, Ltd., with an investment of £500,000.

The next step was taken on April 15, 1930, when the Bankers' Industrial Development Company, Ltd., was formed. The company was organized for five years, subject to extension, for the purpose of examining schemes of rationalization submitted by basic industries of the country. The company was not to deal with individual concerns but with industries as a whole or with regional divisions of industries. No direct financing by the company was intended, its purpose being to assist industries in obtaining the necessary capital for approved schemes through existing agencies. The company is capitalized at £6,000,000, which is divided into 45 "A" shares and 15 "B" shares of £100,000 each. The "A" shares, having one vote each, have been subscribed by the principal British banking and financial institutions, and the "B" shares by the Securities Management Trust, Ltd. Since each "B" share has three votes, the Bank of England controls 50 per cent of the total votes. The Governor of the Bank of England was elected chairman of the board of directors. Only 10 per cent of the capital was paid up. The company is not intended to be a profit-making institution, and the directors serve without fees.

These companies have not solved the problem of financing British industry. The Committee on Finance and Industry, headed by Lord MacMillan, commenting upon the relationship of the City to industry, said in its report:

> We understand that the creation of the Bankers' Industrial Development Company was due originally to the belief that help . . . might be given to industry by the City, which was not being given. We have been told, however, that the authorities of the Bank of England consider as we do, that these are not proper permanent functions for a subsidiary of a Central Bank. It would seem desirable, therefore, that the Bankers' Industrial Development Company should at a convenient stage be definitely separated from the Bank of England, have an independent existence, and rely upon its profit-making capacity as a private institution.

The report continues:

> It has been represented to us that great difficulty is experienced by the smaller and medium-sized businesses in raising the capital which they may from time to time require, even when the security offered is perfectly sound. To provide adequate machinery for raising long-dated capital in amounts not sufficiently large for a public issue, i.e., amounts ranging from small sums up to, say, £200,000 or more, always presents difficulties. The expense of a public issue is too great in proportion to the capital raised, and therefore it is difficult to interest

the ordinary investor by the usual method; . . . the only other
alternative would be to form a company to devote itself particularly to these smaller industrial and commercial issues. . . .
We see no reason why with proper management, and provided
British industry in general is profitable, such a concern should
not succeed.

On March 22, 1934, the organization of a company to be
known as Credit for Industry, Ltd., was announced by the
United Dominions Trust, Ltd., in which the Bank of England had acquired a controlling interest in February 1930.
According to the announcement, the company will have an
initial capital of £250,000, which will be increased from time
to time as required. The company will have the right to
issue debentures or short-term securities. It will specialize
in providing capital for plant and equipment and working
capital for small and medium-sized concerns unable to procure capital through the issue of securities. Individual
loans will be limited to £50,000 and will run for periods of
from two to twenty or more years.

CHAPTER X

London—Other Institutions of the Market

Private banks. Of the numerous private banks which once operated throughout England very few are still in existence. Most of them have either been absorbed by the joint stock banks or were liquidated. Of the few still in existence, some can trace their origin to the seventeenth century, and their continued existence is due to excellent business conduct. The decline in importance of the private banks can best be seen from the figures in Table 30.

TABLE 30

SURVEY OF PRIVATE BANKS IN ENGLAND, 1895–1933

End of	No. of Banks	Capital and Reserves	Deposits	Total Assets
1895	38	£11,834,400	£70,372,000	£85,483,700
1900	19	6,192,800	40,420,500	48,029,200
1905	12	4,393,900	27,775,000	33,270,400
1910	9	5,535,100	26,808,000	30,369,900
1915	7	3,180,707	32,890,739	37,158,216
1920	5	3,123,008	50,864,631	61,124,571
1925	4	2,625,000	27,780,929	36,157,277
1930	4	3,475,000	26,790,315	39,710,476
1931	4	3,175,000	22,246,034	36,680,061
1932	4	2,425,000	14,907,214	20,745,893
1933	4	2,425,000	16,451,840	21,757,792

These banks not only supply funds to the money market and make loans and advances to industry and trade, but also frequently participate in the underwriting of domestic and foreign capital issues. The ratio of their discounts and advances to total liabilities is larger than that of the joint stock banks, while the proportion of investments to total liabilities is smaller.

251

Dominion and Colonial banks. These institutions transact most of their business in the Dominions and Colonies, but maintain offices in London in order to facilitate the foreign trade and the international financial transactions of their respective countries. Besides financing transactions arising out of foreign trade, they also often act as issue houses and financial and fiscal agents for the loans contracted by their respective countries in the London market. These banks are important members of the London money market, for they not only originate bills of exchange but also appear as buyers of bills and thereby contribute greatly to the market's international character. Prior to the war these institutions, together with the London branches of foreign banks, were the principal factors in the foreign exchange market, since the foreign departments of the British banks were developed largely during the war and shortly thereafter. In the post-war period the London clearing banks have greatly enlarged their foreign activities and have built up their foreign acceptance business.

Foreign banks. In contrast to the restrictions imposed upon the establishment of branches of foreign banks by the State of New York and other states of the United States, Great Britain has no special laws relating to foreign banks, and the latter may establish branches in England and conduct their business under the same conditions as the British institutions. Like the Dominion and Colonial banks, the branches of foreign banks supply bills of exchange to the market, transact foreign exchange business, and place their surplus funds at the disposal of the money market. The branches of foreign banks in London bring a considerable amount of business to the City because, through them, a considerable portion of the foreign trade of the respective countries is financed. Since some of the branches act as fiscal agents for loans outstanding in London, they are at times in a position to place substantial amounts in the market. The branches of foreign banks were and still are the principal dealers in foreign exchange of the countries which they represent. During the war the branches of the German and Austrian banks were closed and have been liquidated since. The branches of the German banks were influential in the promotion and financing of Germany's foreign trade.

Overseas banks. The British joint stock banks have opened only a few branches abroad. They conduct their foreign business through correspondents, affiliated institutions abroad, and specially organized overseas banks. The latter usually maintain their head offices in London, although one of the most important, the Hongkong and Shanghai Banking Corporation, has its head office in Hongkong. The more important British overseas banks are:

1. Barclays Bank (Dominion, Colonial and Overseas).
2. Lloyds and National Provincial Foreign Bank, Ltd.
3. Hongkong and Shanghai Banking Corporation.
4. The Anglo-South American Bank, Ltd.
5. Bank of London and South America, Ltd.
6. The British Overseas Bank, Ltd.

These institutions engage primarily in international financial transactions, and their position in the money market is similar to that of the dominant Colonial banks. They also engage in the financing of domestic transactions in the countries where their branches are located. The world-wide activities of British banking institutions centering in London are to a large extent responsible for the universal demand and supply of sterling bills. All these institutions act as feeders to the London market, bringing to it the surplus funds of the world. At the same time they act as channels through which the funds in London are used to finance a considerable part of the world's trade.

Investment houses. In addition to the above described banking institutions, which concern themselves primarily with commercial banking and the placing of funds in the market, or in the creation of acceptances, there are a number of investment houses primarily engaged in the flotation of long-term loans, domestic and foreign. In contrast to the

large number of investment houses in the United States
prior to 1930, the number of investment houses engaged in
the underwriting of foreign securities is small, and the business is concentrated in the hands of a few internationally
known institutions which have been important factors in
the exportation of capital from Great Britain for many
decades. Furthermore, their field of operation is more or
less well divided, and one house does not often compete
for business that is considered the field of operation of another institution. Some of these investment houses also
engage in the creation of acceptances and in the financing
of short-term transactions, and at times place large funds at
the disposal of the money market.

In spite of the lack of legislation, and although the Bank
of England has no legal power to control the flow of long-
term capital, the Bank is always consulted before any foreign issue is offered. In times of national emergency it has
full control even over domestic issues, this being particularly
true in times when government operations of larger magnitude are pending.

Accepting houses. This type of institution is deeply
rooted in the economic history of England and has contributed greatly to the growth of the London money market. When domestic banking was still in its infancy, some
of the London merchants were carrying on a world-wide
trade. Merchants of smaller means who encountered difficulties in establishing a credit standing in foreign markets
conceived the idea of substituting for their own credit that
of a world-renowned house with which they had business
relations. The wealthy London merchants who, through
their business connections in various countries, were in a
position to obtain reliable credit information, were willing
for a commission to lend their name, *i.e.*, "accept" the bills
of the smaller merchants. As time went on, the commissions accruing from the acceptance business overshadowed
the profits derived from trade, and the latter was gradually
abandoned in favor of the acceptance business. The mer-

chants became bankers; hence the name "merchant bankers," which is still applied to the accepting houses.

The function of the accepting houses consists in accepting bills of exchange, thereby guaranteeing their payment on maturity. The signature of a London acceptance house makes possible instant conversion of international bills into cash, and since the bills are sold in the market, the burden of financing the underlying transactions is shifted from the buyer or seller to the discount market. The acceptance houses usually charge a commission varying from ¼ to ½ per cent on a three-month bill, the commission depending upon the credit standing of the drawer and nature of the risk involved. The drawer or originator of the bill, as a rule, places funds with the acceptance houses in time to meet the bills. The acceptor, however, must be prepared to take up the bills regardless of whether or not the funds have been provided. Usually balances are maintained by the drawers with the acceptance houses, and these balances are made available by the acceptance houses to the money market.

The discount facilities offered by the London market, the low interest rate policy usually followed by the Bank of England, and the number of highly specialized firms willing to assume foreign risks, attracted business to London from all over the world and made the sterling bill an international currency—used not only for transactions between Great Britain and foreign countries but also in trade between other countries. This elaborate machinery and the financial knowledge of those who operate it are responsible for the fact that more than half of the world's trade has been financed through London. In fact, the receipts from banking commissions and all other kinds of financial services contributed annually from £50,000,000 to £60,000,-000 to the British balance of payments. Although the joint stock banks, appreciative of the profitability of the acceptance business, have entered this field on a growing scale in the last twenty years, the bulk of the acceptance business is still done by the acceptance houses, as the figures given in the *MacMillan Report* show (see Table 31).

TABLE 31

STERLING BILLS ACCEPTED ON FOREIGN ACCOUNT*
(In millions of pounds)

	Dec. 31, 1927	Dec. 31, 1928	Dec. 31, 1929	Dec. 31, 1930	Mar. 31, 1931
By clearing banks and Scottish banks	31.7	51.3	40.0	35.7	32.3
By accepting houses, etc.	108.0	149.2	135.7	125.3	120.6
Total	139.7	200.5	175.7	161.0	152.9

* *MacMillan Report*, page 43.

The larger acceptance houses also receive deposits on current account, buy bills, participate in the underwriting of foreign loans of both governments and corporations, and act as fiscal agents for the latter. Some of the acceptance houses also deal in bullion. Although the acceptance houses also appear as buyers of bills, their main function is to accept. Long years of business experience have given them a priceless and indeed almost exclusive knowledge of the credit standing of the drawers of bills and of the underlying transactions, and this knowledge has enabled them to carry out their extensive business with practically no loss. It is only in times of great crisis, such as the outbreak of the war or the introduction of "standstill" agreements or other restrictions to the free movement of funds, that the acceptance houses suffer considerable losses. In such cases they usually rely upon and receive fully the assistance of the Bank of England.

The stagnation of international trade, the foreign exchange restrictions in existence in a number of countries, and the standstill in the international movement of capital have had an adverse effect on the accepting houses, which are the backbone of the London money market. While the bill brokers and discount houses found in the Treasury bill a suitable substitute for the commercial bills of exchange, the lack of new acceptance business and the great risk involved in the creation of new bills have greatly reduced the activities of London accepting houses. In order to maintain their organizations, some of them have endeavored to branch out into new activities. Some have undertaken to act as underwriters of domestic securities, but it is obvious that they lack the necessary experience for this type of work. Others have endeavored to develop their banking business and are now engaged in making short-term loans to industry and trade. This field of activity also is not considered as appropriate for accepting houses. In the first place, the latter come into competition with the joint stock banks, which have difficulties in finding a sound outlet for the huge volume of short-term funds; and second, the granting of loans may adversely affect the credit standing of some of the accepting houses.

The importance of the accepting houses to the London market is fully recognized, and in order to maintain them it has been suggested that they develop the domestic trade bill. Through the wider use of this credit instrument, it is argued, not only could the financing of domestic transactions be made cheaper, but also a new short-term bill could be furnished to the market to take the place of the gradually decreasing foreign bills.

The growth of the accepting houses has been based on the financing of foreign trade through the London market. It is obvious that if the policy of economic self-sufficiency adopted by so many countries is to continue, the accepting houses either will gradually disappear or will have to change their field of activity.

The bill brokers. A characteristic feature of the London money market is the existence of a buffer between the joint stock banks and the Bank of England; this is in the form of intermediaries whose exclusive function is to discount or purchase bills offered in the market. These intermediaries are either individuals or firms specializing in this field, and their knowledge of the credit standing of the acceptors makes them a valuable, integral part of the money market machinery. The bill brokers are the connecting link between the various members of the money market, and their mode of operation gives the market a great degree of liquidity. Their business consists of borrowing money from the clearing banks and other institutions from day to day and for periods of one week, and employing the funds in the discounting of bills at a higher rate; the difference in the rate constitutes their profit. The bills are commercial bills (domestic trade bills); foreign bills of exchange (international trade bills); and Treasury bills. They mature in from one to six months, most of them maturing within three months. The sellers of bills are merchants who draw bills under London acceptance credits; foreign and Colonial banks which receive bills from their offices and customers abroad for discount in the London market; and the British Government, which invites weekly tenders for Treasury bills.

Classification of bill brokers. There are three classes of bill brokers: (1) "running brokers," (2) private firms, and (3) public and private discount companies called "discount houses." There are eight running brokers who act as intermediaries between buyer and seller; they never act as principals in the transactions. The running broker works on a commission basis and consequently needs very little capital of his own. His specialized knowledge of the sources of supply and demand for bills of certain names and maturities, and likewise of the commitments of the individual acceptance houses, makes him a useful member of the money market. His opinion about the trend of money rates is sought by all interested parties, and his advice is usually accepted in the fixing of the rate when a substantial supply of bills is disposed of. The banks wishing to buy bills often avail themselves of the services of the running broker, who for the sake of his reputation will pass only on bills which he considers a first-class risk.

There are seventeen private firms, with an aggregate capital of about £8,000,000, who buy and sell bills for their own account. Almost their entire capital is invested in securities, which are pledged as collateral for loans obtained from banks and other lenders of short-term funds. They transact their business with borrowed funds and thus appear in the market in a dual capacity—as dealers in bills and as borrowers of short-term funds.

There are three big public and four private discount companies. The three public companies are Alexander's Discount Company, Ltd., National Discount Company, Ltd., and Union Discount Company of London, Ltd., with combined capital and reserves of £7,000,000, "bills discounted" in the amount of £111,515,701, and total resources of £144,433,557 (as of December 31, 1933). The four private companies have a capital of £1,625,000. In contrast to the clearing banks, which never sell bills or borrow money, the discount houses sell bills in case of need or when there is a chance of making a profit, and they borrow in the open market for a day or a week. The public companies also accept deposits at call or notice from the public (preferably from leading traders and merchants) on which they generally allow interest at ¼ to ½ per cent above the rates paid on deposits by the joint stock banks.

Since the funds employed in the discount market represent the bulk of the surplus short-term funds, this is the most sensitive market; it reflects immediately any change in demand and supply. If a contraction of credit takes place, this market is the first to feel it. A safety valve, however, is provided in the readiness of the Bank of England to discount bills at the Bank rate, which is usually one per cent above the lending rate of the clearing banks, or to make advances for not less than a week at a rate which is practically always ½ per cent over the Bank rate. The one per cent difference between the Bank rate and the standard lending rate of the clearing banks to the bill market constitutes theoretically the extreme range of the rate for bills. It is this narrow margin which, by a misinterpretation of conditions or a lack of knowledge of certain facts influencing the trend of money rates, may turn the bill broker's profit into a loss.   It therefore makes him the most alert student of financial conditions at home and abroad.

Although the funds employed in the London money market reach enormous proportions, the self-liquidating nature of the majority of transactions and the close relationship between the market and the Bank of England insure the smooth functioning of the money market machinery.   In fact, so well balanced and adjusted is the London market under normal conditions that only a comparatively small amount of gold was necessary to support all these transactions.

London Bankers' Clearing House.   The history of the London Bankers' Clearing House, the pioneer of clearing institutions of the world, dates back to the last quarter of the eighteenth century.   Up to the middle of the nineteenth century, private bankers were the only members of the clearing house, and they were reluctant to share this privilege with the growing joint stock banks.   In 1854, four of the joint stock banks were admitted, and in 1864 the Bank of England became a member.   Membership in the London Bankers' Clearing House is at present limited to the following eleven banks:

Bank of England	Martins Bank, Ltd.
Midland Bank, Ltd.	Williams Deacon's Bank, Ltd.
Barclays Bank, Ltd.	National Bank, Ltd.
Lloyds Bank, Ltd.	Glyn Mills and Co.
National Provincial Bank, Ltd.	Coutts and Co.[1]
Westminster Bank, Ltd.	

The Clearing House is governed by a committee consisting of one or more representatives from each member bank and of the Governor and Deputy-Governor of the Bank of England, who are ex-officio members.   The members practically have a monopoly of the London clearing facilities,

---

[1] The capital stock of Coutts and Company was acquired by the National Provincial Bank, Ltd., in 1919, the former retaining its corporate existence and name.

which are indispensable to all other banks operating in Great Britain. There are, in addition, twelve provincial clearing houses located in the most important cities of England and Wales, but their activities are limited to the banks in each clearing city and its immediate vicinity, and their total turnover is small as compared with that of the London Clearing House. The latter, owing to the fact that all important banks throughout the country maintain offices or correspondent relationships in London, is therefore the only central organization where checks can be cleared, no matter on what locality of the country they are drawn. The balances kept for clearing purposes with the members of the London Clearing House augment the deposits of the clearing banks, and thereby augment the funds available for the London money market.

The main object of a clearing system is the efficient collection of checks. This obviously results in a great economy in currency. Prior to the admittance of the Bank of England to the Clearing House, the final balances between each bank in the Clearing House and all the others were settled in currency. At present, the daily settlements are carried out in the same manner as in the United States—by debit and credit entries on the books of the Bank of England, with which each clearing bank must maintain an account.

The London Clearing House operates in three sections: the "Town Clearing" comprises the old City limits; the "Metropolitan Clearing" includes the rest of London and its suburbs; and the "Country cheque Clearing" serves all England and Wales. "Town Clearing" clears both bills and cheques within the same day. "Metropolitan Clearing" pays the day following presentation; it, too, clears both bills and cheques. The "Country cheque Clearing," as its name implies, clears only cheques, and its settlements are deferred for two days.

The "Town Clearing" figures, amounting in 1933 to 86.2 per cent of the total turnover, cannot be considered as an

TABLE 32

LONDON BANKERS' CLEARING HOUSE FIGURES

(In millions of pounds)

	1928	1929	1930	1931	1932	1933
Town Clearing	39,311	39,936	38,783	31,816	27,834	27,714
Metropolitan Clearing	1,854	1,882	1,812	1,668	1,610	1,657
Country cheque Clearing...	3,039	3,079	2,963	2,752	2,668	2,767
Total	44,204	44,897	43,558	36,236	32,112	32,138

index of the country's trade, for they are affected to a very great extent by the huge transactions of the money market and the financial operations of the City. The "Metropolitan Clearing" items constitute 5.2 per cent of the total and represent the retail trade of London; while the "Country cheque Clearing," which accounts for 8.6 per cent of the turnover, may be considered as an indicator of the general business conditions of the country.

The London Stock Exchange

Historical survey. In contrast to the rigid governmental regulation and supervision of the Continental European bourses and the stock exchanges in the United States, the London Stock Exchange is an autonomous body free from governmental control. The huge volume of British investments in the Dominions, Colonies, and foreign countries made the London Stock Exchange an international market par excellence. It is the greatest market in the world as far as the number of securities dealt in is concerned, and its turnover is surpassed only by that of the New York Stock Exchange.

The origin of the London Stock Exchange may be traced back to the Royal Exchange, where, in the last decade of the seventeenth century, business in government securities began to be transacted. As early as 1697 the government attempted to regulate dealings in securities through an Act of Parliament "to check stock-jobbing and to stem the tide of speculation." . In 1733 John Barnard's Act was passed prohibiting speculative transactions by making time transactions illegal. Although the Act was not repealed until 1860, it was not operative in fact. In 1884 an "Act for the Relief of the Brokers of the City of London" freed the Stock Exchange from the last vestige of control exercised by the authorities of the City of London, which prior to the passage of this act licensed the brokers upon payment of an annual fee.

On July 31, 1914, the Stock Exchange was closed. It remained so until January 4, 1915, when it reopened under emergency regulations which stipulated that all transactions should be for immediate cash settlement. In 1922, when term settlements were resumed, this provision was abandoned, except as applied to transactions in British and Colonial Government and municipal securities, which remained on a cash basis—*i.e.*, upon which payment and delivery take place on the business day following that of the transaction. Saturday sessions, suspended on April 28, 1917, were reinstated after fourteen years on September 19, 1931, which event coincided ironically with Great Britain's last day on the gold standard. The Stock Exchange was closed on September 21 and 22, 1931, and when it reopened on the 23rd of September, dealings for "account," options, and carry-over transactions were prohibited for a short period.

Membership and administration. The London Stock Exchange is owned by a private corporation, which administers the building through a "Committee of Management" appointed by the stockholders, who are members of the Exchange. No person can be registered as owner of more than 200 shares. About 14 per cent of the stock is owned by non-members. The committee (nine trustees and managers) leases the Stock Exchange hall and offices to the Stock Exchange Committee; it levies and receives the fees payable by members and clerks, but has no connection whatsoever with the Stock Exchange business. Although membership of the Stock Exchange is not limited to any number, it remains more or less constant at about 4,000. Membership is granted to physical persons only and not to corporations. A member is not permitted to be a member of any other stock exchange, nor may he or his wife carry on any other business. Candidates for membership must be recommended by three members, who obligate themselves to provide £500 each if their candidate should fail within four years. The candidates must, in addition, purchase the nomination of a deceased or retiring member, which at the end of 1933 was valued at about £900. (Between 1928 and 1931 the price of nominations varied from £50 to £1,850.) They also must acquire and retain three shares—at about £250 each, as of the end of 1933—in the company owning the building and other assets of the Stock Exchange. The admission is (end of 1933) 600 guineas (about $3,065 at old par), and the annual fee is 100 guineas (about $511 at old par).

Candidates who have served for four years as clerks on the floor of the Exchange pay only 300 guineas as an entrance fee and 50 guineas as an annual fee; they need acquire and hold only one share and must get only two members who are willing to provide surety of £300 each. The membership is largely recruited from the ranks of the clerks, since they have had experience in the business. In addition, the Committee designates yearly a certain number of clerk-candidates for membership who may be admitted in that year without providing a nomination.

Annually, on March 20, the members elect the Stock Exchange Committee (Committee for General Purposes) by ballot. The Committee consists of 30 members who for at least five years immediately preceding the election have been members of the Exchange. The Committee has absolute control over all the business done on the floor, makes and enforces rules and regulations, decides disputes between members, and has authority to refuse to elect applicants or to reëlect members without stating its reasons. The decisions of the Committee are final, and no appeal can be taken from them. A member's non-compliance with, or violation of, any of the rules and regulations or of the Committee's decision may be punished by the Committee by suspension or expulsion. Disputes between members arising out of deals made in the House (on the floor) must be submitted to the Committee for decision and may not be brought before the courts of law.

All members are elected for one year only, and written applications for reëlection must be made each year. While the members are usually reëlected, the Committee nevertheless has autocratic powers to reject the application for reëlection of a member whose conduct is unsatisfactory. Foreigners are not eligible for membership. Naturalized citizens may in exceptional cases and in the discretion of the Committee be admitted to membership, provided they have resided in the British Dominions for ten years and have been naturalized within such Dominions for at least five years. The members are forbidden to advertise in any way. They may not solicit business or send circulars, except to their own clientele. The Committee continuously advertises the fact that individual members are not permitted to advertise or circularize the general public, and that brokerage firms which do advertise are not members of the Stock Exchange. A list of all members is made available by the secretary of the Committee to anybody who may ask for it; the secretary, however, will refrain from suggesting any individual broker as one to perform a service.

The Stock Exchange issues two daily official publications —*The Stock Exchange Daily List of Officially Quoted Securities* and *The Stock Exchange Daily Supplementary List of Securities Not Officially Quoted*. The quotations on the "Official" and the nominal quotations on the "Supplementary" lists are fixed by the jobbers in the various markets. The supplementary list contains securities of lesser importance and activity, as well as new issues preparatory to their admission to the official list.

Brokers and jobbers. The members of the Exchange are divided into two classes: jobbers or dealers, and brokers. An applicant for membership in the Exchange must choose which of the two classes he will be identified with. These two groups, although complementing each other, are quite independent. They cannot be partners, and their business dealings with one another are carefully defined by the "Committee" on the assumption that the interests of the public are better served by having one class of members, the brokers, acting strictly as agents for the public and executing the latter's orders through the jobbers. The broker acts merely as an agent for those who wish to buy and sell securities. He may also execute orders on his own account, but he must disclose to his customer that he is acting as a principal, and in such case the transactions are usually put through a jobber's book as evidence that the deal has been consummated at the proper market price. For the same reason, offsetting transactions (matching orders) are passed through the books of jobbers. Direct trading between brokers is prohibited; all dealings must go through jobbers.

The brokers' remuneration consists exclusively of commissions allowed by the rules of the Stock Exchange. The commission is a service charge, as the broker has no direct interest in the transaction and incurs no risk except as regards the solvency of his client. Secret profits made on the price to the clients make the broker liable to punishment by expulsion. The brokers may not share either the risks or the profits or losses of the jobber, nor split the commission with a jobber. Partnerships with non-members are prohibited. Brokers may not maintain branch offices.

The jobber deals as a principal, and specializes ("runs a book") in only one "market" and in a limited number of securities. The jobbers who constitute the majority of the members of the Stock Exchange deal with each other and with the brokers, but are prohibited from dealing directly with the public. They may, however, by special permission transact arbitrage business abroad with non-members. Since the jobbers are always buying and selling for their own account, a market for securities is created irrespective of the existence of orders from the public. The jobber, when making a quotation to a broker, must quote a selling and a buying price without having any knowledge as to the broker's intentions or orders, and he is compelled to take or to give at the quoted price. If no number of shares or amount of bonds has been mentioned, the quantity is that covered by common practice in that particular market. The difference between the quoted selling price and the buying price is the jobber's profit or "turn." The "turn" is kept down by competition among the jobbers and varies with the degree of activity of the security. A broker asking for a quotation does not disclose to the jobber whether he is a buyer or seller, but he may state the quantity he wishes to deal in.

Settlement. The bulk of transactions on the London Stock Exchange are settled twenty-four times a year, of which twenty cover a period of two weeks each and four cover three weeks each. The settlements are fixed for the alternate Thursdays, at about the middle and end of each month, and the dates are announced by the Committee. The settlement takes four days. Business transacted after the Saturday, and during periods when the Exchange is not open on Saturdays, after the Friday preceding the Thursday settlement day, goes for the next "account." The first day—the Monday preceding the settlement day—Contango Day, is devoted to making up the accounts and arranging for carry-overs to the next Contango. Contango Day reveals the technical position of the market; it shows whether the "long" or "short" interests prevail. The Contango rate (carry-over rate) is the rate of interest charged to purchasers who wish to postpone the taking up of the security to the next settlement, and it is determined by the rate for money at short notice and the amount of funds required to carry the securities purchased to the next settlement date.   Interest rates on individual securities may vary in accordance with special circumstances affecting their status at the time.   However, during a "bear" market, when a large volume of securities has been sold short and the short sellers' demand for securities with which to make delivery is great, the buyers will be able to carry over their purchases free of interest or even receive a premium ("back" or "backwardation") for lending to the short sellers the purchased securities against the amount they have to pay. When concerted buying of a security sharply drives up its price, causing Contango difficulties, forced liquidation takes place and the weak accounts are "shaken out."

The next day—"name day," or "ticket day"—is devoted to the handing over of tickets to the sellers by the purchasers, who demand delivery of the securities bought. The tickets bear the names of the transferees of the securities, the price, and the amount ("consideration"), together with the names of the members who pay for them.   The tickets pass among the Stock Exchange members as the equivalent of cash.   The Stock Exchange Settlement Department, generally referred to as the Stock Exchange Clearing House, is of great assistance in the work of passing tickets.   If a ticket is not passed in time, the member who has to receive the "name" can order the Buying-In and Selling-Out Department to "sell out."   Such an order is executed by an official of the Exchange for cash at the best price, and the delinquent member must pay the department's charges and cover any loss that may result from the difference between the selling-out and the bargained price.   On the third day, "Intermediate-day," tickets for securities subject to the Settlement Department are passed. The fourth day, Thursday, is "pay day" (account day), on which the brokers and jobbers exchange checks on Town Clearing banks or the Bank of England in payment for purchased securities, for settlement of balances resulting from the deals during the "account," and for "differences" resulting from variation of the "making-up" prices from one

Contango to another.   No grace days are allowed for payment of the differences.   A member unable to meet his engagements is declared to be in default, and a notice to this effect is given to the press for publication.   The securities are delivered either on "pay day" or within ten days. If no delivery is made on the tenth day, the buying broker has the right to have the securities bought in by the Buying-In and Selling-Out Department at the cost and risk of the delinquent member.   This "account" system makes possible dealings within the settlement period without transfers of either securities or cash.

Brokers usually require from new customers a payment on account or a confirmation by a bank that a remittance, or the securities (in case of sale), will be forwarded upon receipt of the contract note.   If a bank has confirmed for a customer that "completion" (payment or delivery of securities) will take place at the next settlement, no "credit payment" (margin) need be made on account of purchases, nor, in the case of sales, must the securities be sent in advance.   Carry-over accounts are required to maintain margins ranging from 10 per cent to 50 per cent of the current market value of the securities.   Old customers usually deal for settlement without any margin at all.

Financing of stock exchange transactions.   The funds needed for Stock Exchange transactions fluctuate with the volume and price of the securities dealt in.   The stock market represents an additional bidding for "Money at Call and Short Notice" and thus comes into active competition with the bill market.   However, the term settlements of the London Stock Exchange, which create demand for money only twenty-four times yearly and on days that are designated and made public months in advance, enable the parties interested in short-term funds to anticipate the trend and to make proper arrangements.   The fortnightly settlement system, when contrasted with the daily settlement of the New York Stock Exchange, means an economy in the amount and turnover of funds.   The New York

Stock Exchange bids daily for funds on the "Call Money Market," while the London Exchange is in the money market only once in approximately two weeks, and the operations in the interim, with the exception of securities dealt in on a cash basis, are transacted on credit. London Stock Exchange loans are a liquid and profitable form of investment for short-term funds, the rate of interest usually ranging from ½ per cent below the bank rate when the collateral consists of British Government securities, to around 2 per cent above the bank rate when the security is of a speculative nature.

Money for the "account," i.e., funds to carry securities, comes from jobbers and brokers, banks, and other financial institutions. When money is dear, however, outside money flows to the market from independent sources which seek to profit temporarily by the higher rate.

CHAPTER XI

London—Instruments and Operation of the Market

Instruments of the Market

BILLS handled in the London money market may be divided into three types: the trade bill, the bank bill, and the Treasury bill. From the standpoint of safety the Treasury bill ranks first, the bank bill second, and the commercial bill third. The dealings in these bills require a certain degree of technique and a thorough knowledge of the market.

The trade bill. The trade bill, also called "fine trade paper," is a bill drawn by one well-known merchant on another. A bill bearing on its face evidence that it was drawn against a shipment of commodities is called, after the shipping documents have been detached, a "clean" bill. Such a bill is acceptable to the Bank of England for discount and as security for advances, provided it bears two English names, one of which must be that of the acceptor. Fine trade paper is normally dealt in at a rate slightly higher than that for bank bills. In the main, the trade bill arises out of purely domestic transactions. Trade bills arising out of foreign trade are rare and sell at a higher discount than fine trade paper.

The development of large scale organizations (cartels, combines, and firms with branches in several countries) has led to the development of a special kind of trade bill called "house paper." It is a bill drawn on a London firm by its foreign branch, or drawn by one branch of a firm and accepted by another, within the country. Bills drawn by a branch abroad on the main office in England are usually sold in the country where the branch is located and are forwarded to London, where, upon endorsement by a bank, they are traded as bankers' bills in the market. Bills drawn and accepted by domestic branches of a firm of large resources can be discounted at a rate only slightly above the rate on bankers' bills, although the paper bears actually one name. The market exercises wide discretion in dealing in "house paper," as the latter lends itself readily to abuses. The legitimate purpose of such a bill is to reimburse the producing branch of the firm while the goods are in transit to the selling branch. It might, however, also be used for obtaining working capital at market rates and thus make it unnecessary to borrow from the banks at the higher loan rate.

The bank bill. The bank bill is a draft accepted or endorsed by a London bank or accepting house, or by the London office of one of the large Indian and/or Colonial banks. It makes no difference in the marketability of the bill whether it originates abroad or in England. The "finest" bank bills are those which arise out of commercial self-liquidating transactions, which are evidenced on the bills themselves. Such bills as a rule command the lowest rate. There are various types of bank bills which may or may not be considered as "prime" bankers' bills.

The *finance bill*—vernacularly called "kite"—is used either to shift funds or to borrow money at advantageous rates of interest. It is usually drawn in round amounts, and the instrument itself does not indicate the underlying transaction. Finance bills accepted by London banks formerly were taken readily at the lowest rate, for the risk element was reduced to a minimum. When the Treasury was compelled both during and after the war to sell its bills in the discount market in ever-increasing amounts, the banks and accepting houses agreed to cease creating finance bills. The almost complete disappearance of such bills is one of the reasons for the post-war reduction in the total volume of sterling acceptances.

Foreign agency bills are bills accepted by the London branches and agencies of foreign banks. These bills do not comply with the requirements of the Bank of England that the acceptor must be an English name, and consequently cannot be discounted at the Bank of England. This discrimination is due to the fact that the bulk of the assets of the acceptor, who is primarily liable on the bill, are abroad and thus are not readily available (or are entirely out of reach, in case of war) in the event of non-payment of the bill at maturity. In normal times, the joint stock banks are willing to acquire, at the prevailing rate for prime bankers' bills, a limited amount of foreign agency bills as part of a parcel of bills offered to them for discount. In practice, however, London banks refuse to discount parcels of bills which contain more than 10 per cent of foreign agency bills. When foreign agency bills alone are offered in large amounts, the rate quoted is usually 1/16 to 1/8 per cent higher than that for prime British bills.

Foreign domicile bills are bills of exchange drawn and accepted abroad but made payable in sterling at a London bank. The purpose of such a bill is twofold: first, to eliminate the risk of currency depreciation in internal transactions between nationals of a country with a fluctuating currency or between nationals of different countries; and second, to partake of the discount facilities and the usually low interest rates prevailing in London. "Foreign domiciles" are excluded from the Bank of England and are not looked upon with favor by the London market. They constitute a very small portion of the total amount of bills dealt in and are discounted only at rates substantially above the market rate for prime bank bills. In contrast to Continental banks the English joint stock banks, as well as the discount houses, do not invest liberally in foreign bills— *i.e.,* bills stated in any currency other than pounds sterling.

The volume of bills outstanding in the London market is a good indication of the volume of international trade. It should, however, be noted that under normal conditions the volume of acceptances also depends upon the prevailing rates of interest in the leading financial centers, notably New York.

The Treasury bill. The origin of the Treasury bill dates back to 1877, when the Chancellor of the Exchequer, in need of funds and reluctant to increase the funded debt, and on the suggestion of Walter Bagehot, then editor of *The Economist,* devised a short-term government security similar to a commercial bill of exchange: the Treasury bill. The phraseology of the instrument is as follows: "This Treasury Bill entitles . . . or order to payment of . . . pounds at the Bank of England out of the Consolidated Fund of the United Kingdom on the . . ." It is signed by the Chancellor of the Exchequer. Through it the government is able to tap the floating supply of funds in the London market for its needs, and at the same time create an outlet for the surplus funds of the market. The bulk of the floating debt of Great Britain at present is in the form of Treasury bills.

During the war, the Treasury bill advanced from a comparatively unimportant position to that of a controlling factor in the money market. The absolute cessation of trade intercourse between Great Britain and a large part of Europe, the restrictions imposed on international trade, and the change in methods of financing domestic trade from a "time" to a "cash" or "sight" basis, with a resultant substitution of bank loans for bills of exchange, greatly reduced the volume of commercial bills. These were gradually replaced by the bills of the Treasury.

Treasury bills are issued by and are payable at the Bank of England, and have a maturity of three, six, nine, and twelve months, with three-month bills predominating. The bills are offered weekly in the market in amounts of about forty million pounds and are sold to the highest bidders.   On Friday of each week the government, through an advertisement in the *London Gazette,* calls for tenders for Friday of the following week and announces that at that time it will offer a certain amount of bills to the public. Those who are interested make application to the Bank of England, stating the amount desired and the price which they are willing to pay.   Applications must be in by 1:00 p.m. Friday.   A tender may not be for less than £50,000 and must be made through a London banker, discount house, or broker.   Such tenders as are made need not be accepted, and the Bank of England, acting for the government, may withdraw the offer in whole or in part.   In tendering for a share of the issue, the applicant may request that his allotment be issued to him on a particular day of the week, but separate tenders must be made for each date. Allotments are paid for in cash or by drafts on the Bank of England.   Thereafter a public announcement is made by the Bank of England, stating the price at which the bills were sold and the rate of discount, on a quarterly and on a yearly basis.

From 1915 to 1921 Treasury bills were not offered by tender, but at a fixed rate.   It was at this time that the market was entirely under the control of the government. The sale at advertised, fixed rates made it convenient for the general public to buy Treasury bills, which before the war had been almost exclusively held by banks and discount houses.   Occasionally issues are still offered to the public apart from the issues by tender.   These are known as "additional" Treasury bills issued at a fixed rate ("tap" rate) which is slightly below the average "tender" rate for the preceding Friday.   Nevertheless, such additional issues have become rare.

Government departments, however, such as the Post Office Savings Bank, the Road Fund, the Public Trustee, the Paymaster General, and the Courts of Justice, invest a large proportion of their surplus funds in Treasury bills obtained "through the tap."   It is not known to what extent the Bank of England acquires Treasury bills by tender or through "tap." The lower yield of "tap" bills is of no concern to the Bank of England, since the bills are held by the Issue Department and the latter's profits accrue to the Treasury. Lastly, the Exchange Equalization Account, probably the largest single holder of Treasury bills, obtains the bills through the tap.

The Bank of England and the Treasury endeavor as far as possible to balance the supply of bills with the demand. The supply must always be absorbed, for the sake of the prestige of the government and in order to maintain equilibrium among the different market rates. An oversupply of bills causes the open market rates to rise; money becomes tighter, and less credit is available for business. On the other hand, an undersupply means lower market rates and an increase in the amount of idle money. Nevertheless, there is a limit to the capacity of the market either to absorb bills offered for sale or to find employment for the proceeds obtained from redemptions of bills. Whenever the amount of Treasury bills redeemed is very large, as was the case in the spring of 1930, the supply of liquid funds increases and money rates decline sharply.

Day-to-day fluctuations in the volume of Treasury bills outstanding are caused by the uneven distribution of tender applications; *i.e.*, there may be more requests for bills running from the following Tuesday than from the following Wednesday. The market, therefore, must then find more money on Tuesday than on the following day. Similarly, bills maturing on Sunday or on a holiday somewhat disrupt the smooth operation of the market. There is also always some gap caused by an excess of redemptions over new issues and vice versa, or by the fact that redemptions are at times paid in part to an "outsider"—which means that the market will not have the full proceeds available to take up the new subscription.

Seasonal fluctuations also tend to disturb the equilibrium. They are greatest at the end of the financial year, when tax payments are being made to the government. The Treasury, in order not to disturb the money market, arranges its accounts in such a manner that there is a large excess of redemptions of outstanding Treasury bills over new issues. In spite of this precaution, there is usually a temporary scarcity of funds, partly owing to the fact that some bills are held outside the British banking system (for foreign account) and, thus, the proceeds from the redemption of Treasury bills are not immediately placed at the disposal of the market. Apart from seasonal factors, failure to balance the British budget, which necessitates increased borrowing, and the redemption of maturing loans or conversion operations on a large scale, exercise an influence on the bill market. These daily and seasonal fluctuations, however, are easily smoothed out by the open market operations of the Bank of England.

Prior to the return to the gold standard in 1925, the British Government made great strides in reducing the floating debt. The volume of Treasury bills was reduced from its peak of £1,120,000,000, in 1921, to approximately one-half of that amount in March 1931. (See Table 33.)

TABLE 33

TREASURY BILLS OUTSTANDING ON MARCH 31 OF EACH YEAR
(In millions of pounds sterling)

Year	Amount	Year	Amount
1917	463.7	1926	564.9
1918	973.5	1927	599.2
1919	957.2	1928	526.9
1920	1,107.3	1929	700.3
1921	1,120.8	1930	588.9
1922	877.2	1931	569.8
1923	616.0	1932	604.4
1924	588.3	1933	775.9
1925	576.6	1934	799.8

The reduction was carried out through conversions into long-term debts. However, Treasury bills outstanding on September 30, 1932, reached the amount of £866,180,000, bringing back the floating debt to its last high mark in 1922.

This amount included £150,000,000 issued for the establishment of the Exchange Equalization Account.

The principal demand for Treasury bills comes from banks, discount houses, other financial institutions, and large commercial and industrial enterprises. All these organizations are constantly in need of a highly liquid and safe type of investment for a part of their assets and/or surplus funds, and the Treasury bill offers a perfect instrument for this purpose.

The Bank of England is also a buyer of Treasury bills, which constitute a considerable portion of the securities held by the Issue Department against the fiduciary currency. The adoption of the gold exchange standard by many countries created an additional demand for Treasury bills, as the banks of issue of several of the gold exchange standard countries could include British Treasury bills as part of their monetary stock of gold. However, the suspension of the gold standard by Great Britain and the general trend toward the abandonment of the gold exchange standard have brought to a halt the demand for Treasury bills from this source.

The future of the bill market. As already pointed out, the volume of commercial bills arising out of foreign trade transactions has greatly decreased, and their importance has been surpassed by the Treasury bill. Although the creation of the Exchange Equalization Fund has increased the volume of Treasury bills, it has been the policy of the British Treasury to withdraw them from circulation as fast as possible. The gradual reduction in the volume of Treasury bills has raised the question as to what will take their place as an outlet for short-term funds. In fact, during the latter part of 1933 and the first part of 1934 the supply of funds outstripped the demand from the market, with the result that interest rates were extremely low.

Particularly because of the unsettled conditions in a number of foreign countries, which make the revival of the bankers' bill difficult if not impossible, the lack of suitable short-term credit instruments will place a serious problem before the London market when the amount of Treasury bills has shown a substantial decline. It is obvious that, while the domestic trade bill may increase in importance, it cannot take the place of the Treasury bill or of the foreign bill. Those who concern themselves with this problem believe that London will further cultivate its relationship with the Dominions, and that the newly created and proposed central banks in the various Dominions will further strengthen the financial ties of London with the Dominions and Colonies. It is also expected that New York will not be able to recover the position it enjoyed up to the end of 1932, and that a considerable part of the foreign business which was previously handled by New York will come to London. Whether or not these developments will take place is difficult to state at the moment.

Money Rates

Bank rate. The condition of the market as affected by national and international conditions is reflected in the various rates of interest, of which the discount rate of the Bank of England is the most important. The Bank of England rate, generally called the "Bank rate," is the rate at which the Bank of England will discount certain types of "approved" bills for its customers. Up to 1878 the Bank rate was the rate at which the Bank of England was willing to discount approved bills of exchange and made advances on approved collateral (mercantile securities) for short periods. In that year the Bank of England adopted the practice of differentiating between customers and non-customers and began to discount for the former at lower rates, known as market rates. This practice has been adhered to since. The Bank of England, when buying or selling bills on its own initiative, does not apply the bank rate, but carries out these transactions at rates agreed upon between itself and the buyer.

Although there is no law or statute defining the term "approved bills," and it is entirely within the discretion of the Bank of England to take or exclude certain bills, it has been a consistent policy of the Bank to require that, in order to be eligible for discount, bills should bear at least two good British names, one of which must be the acceptor. This rule makes it impossible for the Bank of England to acquire bills created by foreign banks, and thus the rule protects the Bank from complications that may arise in case of war or in case of transfer moratoria or standstill agreements.

Although little or no business may be transacted at this rate, the Bank rate is the pivotal rate of the money market, for upon it depends to a considerable extent all other rates. The Bank rate represents the cost which the market must pay in order to have access to the Bank of England. It is, therefore, the rate for the marginal amounts which cannot be supplied by the market; it is the rate at which the Bank of England, as "lender of last resort," is willing to lend, and is generally higher than the market rate. It is consequently a punitive rate, having been conceived as such in order that it might be an efficient instrument for the control of the money market. Furthermore, because of the practice of the banks in basing their deposit and loan rates on the Bank rate, the fluctuations of the latter determine the movement of the other rates. For instance, the rate of interest paid by the clearing banks in London on "Deposit accounts" is usually 2 per cent below the Bank rate, while the normal minimum rate charged by the banks on loans to the market is usually one per cent below the Bank rate. Each rate varies within a certain range, and ordinarily the level of each rate moves with the Bank rate. Table 34 shows the movement of the more important rates during the past seven years.

In order to insure the economic and financial stability of the country, the Bank traditionally endeavors to maintain a stable and, if possible, a low discount rate. The movement of the discount rate under normal conditions is determined by numerous factors, both domestic and foreign, and especially by the condition of the bank reserve—*i.e.,*

TABLE 34

LONDON RATES

(Annual averages*)

	1927	1928	1929	1930	1931	1932	1933
Bank rate	4.65	4.50	5.50	3.43	3.95	3.01	2.00
Bankers' acceptances, 3 months	4.24	4.16	5.26	2.57	3.60	1.87	0.68
Treasury bills, 3 months	4.26	4.13	5.25	2.53	3.49	1.64	0.59
Day-to-day money ..	3.65	3.51	4.47	2.27	2.93	1.58	0.67
Bankers' allowances on deposits	2.67	2.50	3.48	1.44	2.12	1.27	0.50

* Computed from the monthly averages of the *Federal Reserve Bulletin.*

the amount of cash held by the Banking Department—and
by the fluctuation of the pound and the movement of gold.
In times when specie payment is suspended, however, these
factors are of less importance, and the discount policy is
determined entirely by domestic considerations. Increases
in the Bank rate are usually made in stages of one per cent,
and decreases in stages of ½ per cent. Besides using the
Bank rate, the Bank of England employs the so-called lombard rate for secured loans. The lombard rate is usually
½ per cent above the discount rate.

Bill rate. Next in importance to the Bank rate is the
bill rate, generally referred to as the "market rate." This
may be defined as the rate commanded by three-month
prime bank bills, *i.e.*, bills accepted or endorsed by a London bank or accepting house. It moves within a certain
range—usually between the Bank rate, which constitutes
the upper limit, and the loan rate of the clearing banks to
the bill brokers, which constitutes the lower limit. The
upper limit is more or less fixed by the fact that the Bank
of England stands ready to discount bills offered to it at
the Bank rate and that, if the market rate should go above
the Bank rate, sellers of bills would naturally offer their
bills to the Bank of England. The lower limit is more or
less fixed by the loan rate, for it is at that rate that the bill
brokers obtain funds with which to operate. Should the

bill rate drop below the rate at which bill brokers borrow in the open market, the latter obviously would be operating at a loss, paying more for their money than they receive on their bills. When money is tight or when confidence is impaired, and there is little demand for bills, the market rate moves up toward the Bank rate. The Bank rate is then said to be "effective," and the Bank of England is in control of the market. On the other hand, when money becomes plentiful and bills scarce, competition drives the market rate down at times to a point even below the loan rate. On these occasions, the Bank rate is said to be "ineffective": the Bank of England has lost control of the market.

Since the Bank of England has the coöperation of the London clearing banks, it is able to effect a change in the market rate without resorting to changes in the Bank rate. In the beginning of 1931, for example, when the Bank of England was reluctant to check the French withdrawals of gold by raising the Bank rate during a period of business stagnation, the bill rate was raised to 2½ per cent, while the Bank rate remained unaltered at 3 per cent. In this way a more attractive rate was offered for foreign funds without affecting the loan and deposit rates, which if affected would have placed an additional burden on business in Great Britain.

Apart from these general limits, rates on bills vary chiefly with regard to the financial standing of the acceptor. A fine trade bill, i.e., a bill bearing prime commercial names, will sell at a higher rate of interest, or at a lower price, than prime bankers' bills. Of course "hot" treasury bills, i.e., bills dealt in during the week in which they are redeemed, command the lowest rate of interest.

The bill rate is always influenced by two factors; namely, the demand for and supply of short-term funds and the demand for and supply of bills. Normally these forces adjust themselves and equilibrium is established without recourse to changes in the discount rate. Since, however,

under normal conditions, the bill rate depends to a large
extent upon the Bank rate, the level of the latter affects the
volume of bills drawn on London. A low Bank rate generally means a low bill rate, and normally leads to an increase in the volume of bills drawn on and discounted in
the London market. On the other hand, high money rates
under normal conditions will drive the acceptance business
to other financial markets. During the post-war period,
when the foreign short-term funds became an important
factor in the various international money centers, the policy of maintaining a low Bank rate favorable to trade
and industry and to the attraction of foreign acceptance
business often clashed with the desire, and sometimes even
with the necessity, for maintaining a higher rate in order
to prevent an outflow of the foreign short-term funds.
Throughout the greater part of the post-war period, England was confronted with this dilemma. A high rate of
interest resulted in an inflow of foreign short-term funds
but tended to decrease the volume of sterling acceptances,
while a low rate of interest resulted in an increase in the
volume of acceptances but also caused an outflow of funds.
If the Bank followed a high-rate policy, it created a large
volume of surplus funds without an adequate means of
investing them; on the other hand, a low-rate policy resulted in an increased supply of bills and outflow of funds,
thereby affecting adversely the pound sterling.

The day-to-day rate. This rate applies to loans made
by joint-stock banks for one day, and corresponds to the
call rate in the United States. Such loans are usually made
to bill brokers and are secured by acceptances, Treasury
bills, and short-term government bonds. They are also
used to finance spot delivery transactions in gilt-edged securities. The rate on day-to-day money is not fixed in the
open market, usually being determined by the individual
banks on the following day. The borrowers do not know
until the following day the rate of interest which they will
pay on loans contracted on the previous day. It is also

not uncommon for one borrower to pay a higher rate than
another. In most cases, however, the rate is more or less
uniform, since each lender fixes the rate only after "feeling
out" the market. The rate is usually low, since the surplus
funds, if not placed on the market, would be left with the
Bank of England, which pays no interest.

Loans on short notice. Closely connected with the
money on call are loans on short notice, which as a rule
mature within seven days. They are used for almost the
same purpose as day-to-day loans, and the rate charged is
practically the same. The various rates fluctuate almost
daily, depending upon the demand and supply of short-
term funds as well as upon the supply of bills. The fluctuation, however, is uniform and the rates move in unison.
Usually the rate of interest paid by the banks on deposits
is the lowest. The day-to-day rate, the Treasury bill rate,
the rate on prime bankers' bills, the prime commercial bill
rate, and finally the Bank rate and the lombard rate of
the Bank of England, are progressively higher. The only
rate which is higher than the Bank rate is the banker's
advance rate. The latter rate, however, is not uniform and
is not published.

Operation of the Money Market

The term "money market" is an abstract concept which
can be defined only by a description of its attributes. The
money market has no physical boundaries, no recognized
place for transacting business, no codified rules and regulations. Its smooth functioning is based not upon law but,
primarily, upon tradition and upon the mutual confidence
between buyer and seller (borrower and lender). The commodity dealt in consists of short-term credits, and the price
is quoted in rates of interest. The funds available in the
market are supplied mainly by the joint-stock banks, the
London offices of the Colonial, Dominion, and foreign
banks, and the big insurance companies. At the end of
1933, the sixteen British joint-stock banks reported £145,-

250,341 "at call and short notice" and £292,811,181 in "discounts," and the eight Scottish banks showed, under the same headings, £25,719,713 and £21,968,532, respectively. H. W. Greengrass, in his book *The Discount Market in London,* estimates the amount of money employed by all banks in the money market (bill and stock exchange markets) at about £900,000,000. The fact that at least one-third of this amount is due within the period of from one to fourteen days, and that almost the entire balance matures in three months, is eloquent testimony of the liquidity of the London market. This liquidity is not merely theoretical, as is the case in the New York call market, where the liquidity of the call loans depends on the marketability of the securities; rather, it is to a large extent an actual liquidity, for the underlying collateral consists to a considerable degree of self-liquidating commercial bills of best names, and most of the instruments traded in the market can be discounted with or used as collateral for advances from the Bank of England.

The money offered in the market, the general loan fund of the country, consists of the surplus funds of Great Britain and, in normal times, of a considerable portion of the liquid funds of other nations. There is always a supply of "old" money seeking reëmployment, as well as a supply of "new" money representing the current savings of the nation or a fresh inflow of funds from abroad. These additional funds reach the money market through the banks, and their inflow and outflow are primarily responsible for the fluctuations of the market. The equilibrium between supply and demand is from time to time further disturbed by temporary causes, such as dividend and interest payments; by more fundamental causes, such as stagnation of industry and trade, which usually releases a large volume of funds previously employed; or by a large influx of foreign funds caused by economic and political disturbances abroad. The margin of idle money is usually reflected in the increase of "other deposits—bankers" with the Bank of England and is ordinarily accompanied by a decline in interest rates. The disturbances in the money market caused by an oversupply of funds are usually due to an influx of "new" money, because the volume of funds supplied by the chief lenders, the clearing banks, is relatively stationary. Thus, the volume of cash in hand and money at call and short notice of the joint-stock banks in England and Wales fluctuated between about £415,000,000 and £494,000,000 during the period 1925–32 in spite of the great change in business activity.

The determining factor in the money market is, in most cases, the demand for funds. It changes with the volume of domestic and foreign trade and is to a considerable extent influenced by the status of the Treasury and of the capital and speculative markets.

Influence of the Bank of England

The conditions of the money market depend not only upon the factors of demand and supply but also upon the policy of the Bank of England. The Bank's control of the money market is exercised by means of the Bank rate and/or open market operations and through the interchange of opinion and the coöperation between the Bank of England and the members of the money market. Furthermore, since the Treasury bill became a dominant factor in the money market the Bank of England, in coöperation with the Treasury, has been able to reduce or increase the supply of funds in the market by increasing or decreasing the amount of Treasury bills offered each week. However, the range of control through this measure is limited by the fact that the Treasury must borrow a certain amount to cover the discrepancy between current revenues and current expenditures, and that an offering of bills in too large an amount would result in higher open market rates.

It is obvious that an important international financial center such as London should be greatly influenced by monetary conditions prevailing abroad. Under normal

conditions any increase in interest rates in another important financial center, notably New York, is bound to draw
funds and gold from London, and thereby reduce the funds
employed in the market and cause a rise in interest rates.
It may be said that the high rates of interest which prevailed in London during 1929 and caused the Bank of England to raise its rate to 6½ per cent, one of the highest rates
in peace time, were chiefly due to the influence exercised
by New York.

Discount policy. The Bank rate was the classical instrument of control during the pre-war period. A rise of the
Bank rate tended to curtail the volume of new foreign
acceptances offered in the market and, at the same time,
caused an inflow, from abroad, of funds and of gold intended
to take advantage of the higher rate. Conversely, a lowering of the rate increased the volume of foreign bills, which,

TABLE 35

BANK RATE SINCE 1910

Year	No. of Changes	Highest	Lowest	Year	No. of Changes	Highest	Lowest
1910	9	5	3	1923	1	4	3
1911	4	4½	3	1924	None	4	4
1912	4	5	3	1925	4	5	4
1913	2	5	4½	1926	None	5	5
1914	8	10	3	1927	1	5	4½
1915	None	5	5	1928	None	4½	4½
1916	1	6	5	1929	5	6½	4½
1917	2	6	5	1930	4	5	3
1918	None	5	5	1931	4	6	2½
1919	1	6	5	1932	6	6	2
1920	1	7	6	1933	None	2	2
1921	4	7	5	1934	None	2	2
1922	4	5	3				

in addition to starting an outflow of funds, absorbed the
idle funds.

Although London, perhaps more than any other financial
center, is subject to international influences, the Bank of
England has endeavored as far as possible to keep an even
and low bank rate, as may be seen from Table 35. But

since the London market is more sensitive to international monetary conditions than any other important financial center, the changes in the discount rate of the Bank of England obviously are more numerous than those of the Bank of France, the Reichsbank, or even the Federal Reserve Bank of New York. A rise in the Bank rate, however, is effective only when "other deposits" with the Bank of England are low—an indication that the joint-stock banks will be forced to call loans from the market. If, on the other hand, the Bank rate is raised primarily for the purpose of protecting the reserves against a drain of gold from abroad while, at the same time, "other deposits" are high, the market rate, under the pressure of idle money, will not follow the official rate. The Bank of England under such circumstances loses contact with the market, unless it draws funds from the market through the sale of government securities. The efficacy of the Bank rate to arrest an outflow of gold stands in inverse relation to the margin of idle funds, being smallest when "other deposits" are at a high figure.

International aspect. In post-war years the flight of capital from countries with depreciating currencies, together with the widely adopted gold exchange standard, created a large volume of short-term funds which became an important factor on the London market. While London's short-term position with respect to the rest of the world before the war was more or less in equilibrium, during the post-war period London was a debtor on the short-term money market—*i.e.*, her gross liabilities for foreign short-term bills and deposits largely exceeded her claims on acceptances on behalf of foreign obligors. In the post-war period London not only was doing an international acceptance business but was also carrying on large-scale international deposit banking without being able to increase and correspondingly maintain its international cash assets.

The *MacMillan Report*, page 301, gives the figures (see Table 36) for London's international position. Although

TABLE 36

DEPOSITS AND STERLING BILLS HELD IN LONDON ON
FOREIGN ACCOUNT, AND STERLING BILLS ACCEPTED
ON FOREIGN ACCOUNT
(In millions of pounds)

	Dec. 31, 1927	Dec. 31, 1928	Dec. 31, 1929	Dec. 31, 1930	Mar. 31, 1931
Deposits with Bank of England, clearing banks, and Scottish banks	117	139	118	165	146
Accepting houses	89	104	79	82	81
Sterling bills held through Bank of England, clearing banks and Scottish banks	162	195	200	145	137
Accepting houses	13	17	20	8	7
Advances to Discount Market by branches of foreign banks and other foreigners	38	47	34	35	36
Total deposits, bills and advances	419	502	451	435	407
Acceptances on Foreign Account by clearing banks and Scottish banks	32	51	40	36	32
Accepting houses	108	149	136	125	121
Net liability of London	279	302	275	274	254

a gradual decline in foreign funds employed in London
has taken place since 1928, deposits and sterling bills held
in London on foreign account (exclusive of sterling bills
held by foreign banks in their own custody) amounted in
March 1931 to £407,000,000, of which amount £153,000,000
represented bills accepted for foreign account, London thus
being left a debtor to the extent of £254,000,000. The
figures showing the total amount of British short-term
claims abroad as of that date are not available. While it
may be assumed that these balances were quite substantial,
a considerable part of them was frozen in Germany and in
other European countries. Consequently they could not
be called to meet the rapid withdrawal of foreign funds
which set in after the collapse of the German banking structure. The fact that Great Britain had long-term investments abroad to the extent of about $20,000,000,000 was of
no avail, since these could not be liquidated.

While an international financial center derives, under normal conditions, great profits from the administration of a large portion of the floating surplus funds of the world, in abnormal times the foreign short-term balances constitute a grave danger to the currency of the country. Even in more normal times a financial center in which a portion of the floating short-term funds of the world is maintained is exposed to the loss of part of them because of monetary and credit conditions prevailing in other countries. For the sake of retaining foreign balances, the withdrawal of which might become embarrassing, such a money center may at times be compelled to maintain a discount rate unsuitable or even detrimental to domestic business conditions.

As a rule, however, a change of the Bank rate is justifiable when a contraction or expansion of credit at home is desired, but a rise in the rate for the sole purpose of attracting or retaining foreign funds, except for transitory adjustments of the balance of international payments, is not warranted. In post-war years, however, owing to the influence exercised by New York and in order to avoid an outflow of gold to that center, it was often necessary for the Bank of England to maintain a higher discount rate than was warranted by business conditions at home. The Bank was therefore often forced to engage in open market operations in order to maintain easy money market conditions.

Open market operations. The second instrument used in the control of the money market, in conjunction with the Bank rate or, in the case of minor day-to-day movements, independently of it, is that of open market operations. These consist of the buying and selling of securities, acceptances, and foreign exchange, and they affect the volume and the quality of credit outstanding by increasing or decreasing the amount of bankers' deposits with the Bank of England. The quality of credit may, without changing its quantity, be altered by an exchange of the assets of the Bank. Thus, gold movements may be offset by the purchase and sale of government securities, or long-term securities ('consols) may be exchanged against short-term securities (Treasury bills).

The sale of securities or acceptances by the Bank of England results in a contraction of credit, because it leads to a reduction of bankers' deposits with the Bank of England, and these deposits constitute the basis for credit. A reduction in bankers' deposits may also take place when the Bank of England adopts a policy of non-interference with the money market or deliberately refrains from open market operations at a time when the demand for funds increases. Thus, for example, during the transfer of dividend payments from the companies to the stockholders, or when tax payments or subscriptions to new government loans are made to the British Government by checks drawn on British banks, a temporary demand for funds sets in which, if not counteracted by open market purchases of the Bank, results in a decrease in the volume of bankers' deposits. A similar situation arises when currency is withdrawn by the public for holiday periods or hoarding. Any payments made by banks or depositors of banks to the Bank of England, or to any customer of the Bank of England other than a bank, reduce bankers' deposits and consequently narrow the cash position of the banking system. Conversely, the cash position of the banks is broadened whenever the Bank of England or one of its customers other than a bank makes payments. All payments made by the British Government increase bankers' deposits with the Bank of England because, whether these payments represent wages and salaries of government employees or interest on government bonds, they will find their way to the banks. The movement of funds from and to the Bank of England is counteracted by the daily open market operations of the Bank, which by such action keeps the money market on an even keel.

The bills and securities sold by the Bank of England are paid for with checks which, being drawn on the banks, reduce the latters' reserve balances with the Bank of England. The banks replenish their reserves, not by borrowing from the central bank, as is the case in the United States, but by calling loans from the bill brokers or by not reinvesting the funds obtained from the daily maturing acceptances. Whenever this action takes place the bill brokers are forced to discount their bills with the Bank of England at the Bank rate or to borrow at the lombard rate. Since these rates are above the market rate, the bill brokers are penalized, and in order to avoid future losses they must raise their rates on acceptances. However, the loans made by the Bank of England to the bill brokers increase the bankers' deposits with the Bank, and thereby tend to make money more plentiful and thus bring about a lowering of interest rates.

Coöperation of the money market with the Bank of England. Aside from the influence of its discount rate and open market operations, the Bank of England exercises an influence over the various elements of the money market through the coöperation of the various institutions. In the evidence given before the Committee on Finance and Industry (*MacMillan Report*), Sir Ernest M. Harvey, Deputy Governor of the Bank of England, said:

> The relations between the Bank and the discount market are exceedingly intimate. Seeing the sort of obligation that the Bank accepts towards the discount market, we claim the right to be kept fully informed regarding their position, if need be, to see their balance sheets, and the right—of course in the strictest confidence—to the fullest information.

On this point the *MacMillan Report* states as follows (page 155):

> The practice of frequent meetings between representatives of the Bank and the leading bill brokers by which the wishes and intentions of the Bank are confidentially communicated to the latter needs no improvement. The contact between the Bank and the leading issuing houses is also intimate. We understand that important foreign issues made by these houses are seldom underwritten in London unless the Governor of the

Bank of England has been first consulted and that any opinion he may offer will carry great weight.

As to the relationship between the powerful clearing banks and the Bank of England, the *Report* states that

> these relations might with advantage be somewhat closer than they now are. It is a result of causes originating in the now distant past that there is still a degree of aloofness and remoteness in the daily relations between the Bank of England and the clearing banks. . . . It is desirable that the clearing banks should be made aware in the plainest possible manner whether the general tendency of the policy of the Bank of England at any time is towards a relaxation or towards a contraction of the conditions of domestic credit.

It is this close coöperation between the Bank of England and the various members of the money market which has made possible the smooth and efficient workings of the latter without government interference or regulation. In this respect the London market is unique and differs from all other centers.

The Exchange Equalization Account [1]

The suspension of the gold standard in September 1931 not only left the pound sterling unprotected against the inevitable fluctuations resulting from temporary maladjustments of the balance of payments, but also exposed it to the danger of speculative operations. It is obvious that wide fluctuations of the monetary unit are detrimental to the national economy of a country; therefore, means had to be devised to control such movements. The only method of intervention is the official buying and selling of pounds against foreign currencies and gold. At the beginning, the Issue Department of the Bank of England undertook these operations, and for a time a substantial amount of the cover against the fiduciary issue consisted of foreign bills of exchange.

After several months, however, it became evident that the resources which the Bank could legitimately employ in

---

[1] Also called the "Exchange Equalisation Fund."

foreign exchange transactions were inadequate for "ironing out" sterling fluctuations, and that the Bank could not be expected to assume the risk inherent in such operations. It was felt that interventions in the foreign exchange market undertaken in the public interest should be executed with public funds. Consequently a special machinery, the "Exchange Equalization Account," was set up to check the fluctuations of the pound.

On April 19, 1932, the Chancellor of the Exchequer, announcing the plan for the Exchange Equalization Account in the House of Commons, said: "It is essential for us to hold adequate reserves of gold and foreign exchanges, in order that we may meet any sudden movement of short-dated capital and check and repel the speculative movements." On April 25, 1932, the day the Exchange Equalization Account was voted, the Financial Secretary to the Treasury explained in the House of Commons the reasons for creating the Exchange Equalization Account, and stated: "The speculators of the world who have looted and plundered so many great currencies know well, as did Blucher, what a city to loot was London. There are other financial Bluchers, with greater power to loot than Blucher himself, watching that city."

The Exchange Equalization Account came into official existence on June 24, 1932. It was originally limited to £150,000,000 plus the balance of the old Dollar Exchange Reserve, amounting to £25,000,000. Although the method and volume of operations of the Account have never been disclosed, certain conclusions as to its operations can be drawn from official utterances and from a careful analysis and interpretation of developments in the money market.

When asking Parliament to authorize the establishment of the Exchange Equalization Account, the Chancellor of the Exchequer said:

> The details of assets in the Account will not be published, but they may take various forms, either gold, or sterling securities or foreign exchange. That will give us a very large, ex-

tended power of purchasing exchange. The new powers, combined with the powers already possessed by the Bank—on which, of course, the main responsibility for the management must continue to rest—will enable us to deal far more effectively than we have done hitherto either with an unwanted inflow of capital or, if the alternative should again arise, with an outflow of capital from this country.

From this comment one may conclude that the Exchange Equalization Account consists of gold, foreign exchange, and sterling assets (most probably Treasury bills) in unrevealed proportions. These holdings may be exchanged from one asset into another as deemed expedient to the Bank of England, which is intrusted with the management of the Account. Initially, the assets of the Account consisted of Treasury bills. Since the entire amount was not immediately needed, a part was left with the Treasury in the form of an advance which could be drawn by the Account any time it needed additional assets. One may assume that the Account, in accord with the usual practice of the Treasury, does not maintain idle cash balances with the Bank of England, and that such balances are either invested in Treasury bills or lent to the Treasury as an "advance" from a public department.

The Account commenced its operations with the acquisition, from the Bank of England, of the latter's foreign exchange holdings, paying for them with government securities—probably Treasury bills. This transaction accomplished two things: it relieved the Bank of England of the risk involved in holding a fluctuating asset and gave the Account a substantial foreign exchange reserve. The Account also indemnified the Bank of England for an actual loss of about £8,000,000 incurred in connection with the repayment of credits obtained from the Bank of France and the Federal Reserve banks in 1931, prior to the suspension of the gold standard. Another loss—of about £22,000,000—on the repayment of the £80,000,000 credits obtained August 28, 1931, in the United States and France was also charged to the Account.

The Account intervened in the foreign exchange market mainly by buying dollars and francs and converting such balances into gold from time to time. The operations were successful in smoothing out minor fluctuations of the pound and deterring speculators. The Account apparently made no attempt to control major movements of the pound.

On December 15, 1932, the Account realized a profit of £10,000,000 by receiving from the government £29,500,000 in currency, and then buying £19,500,000 in gold at par from the Bank of England for the payment of war debts to the United States.

In reply to questions in the House of Commons about the operations of the Exchange Equalization Fund on February 23, 1933, the Chancellor of the Exchequer stated:

> For various reasons large sums of foreign money which have been coming here recently are bad money in the sense that we cannot rely on retaining them. If no precautions were taken these capital movements would result in a sharp rise of sterling to be followed later by a sharp fall. Such fluctuations, which are harmful to trade, should be limited as far as possible, but it is not in the general interest to state what particular methods may be adopted to check them.

This statement explained the large accumulation of gold, which was obtained through the selling of pounds by the Account. In this manner the Account was able not only to prevent a sharp rise of the pound but later, through the sale of gold and/or foreign exchange, to prevent its decline.

When the United States imposed an embargo on gold exports in April 1933, the Account ceased to sell pounds against dollars. The Account had apparently converted its dollar balances into gold prior to the embargo, for the Chancellor of the Exchequer assured the House of Commons that auditors had examined the Account and reported that if it had been liquidated on March 31, 1933, "there would have been no loss."

On May 4, 1933, the Chancellor of the Exchequer asked the House of Commons for an additional £200,000,000 for the Account, explaining that the original amount would have sufficed were it not for a "new phenomenon . . . refugee capital . . . capital which came to London because the owners got alarmed about conditions in their own countries and thought the capital was temporarily safer in London than anywhere else." The House of Commons voted the proposed amount, and thus brought up the total of the Account to £375,000,000.

On the whole the Account has proved to be an effective means of managing the pound with the object of affording British trade a certain degree of stability of the currency. In terms of French francs, the pound fluctuated between 92 and 80 francs in 1932, between 90 and 78 in 1933, and between 84 and 74 in 1934.

While the establishment of the Account led immediately to an increase of £150,000,000 in the floating debt, this increase had no immediate effect on the money market. It was only when the Account began to pay with Treasury bills for foreign exchange that the increase in the floating debt became noticeable in the money market. Consequently the influence of the Exchange Equalization Account on the money market at any given moment depends upon the amount of Treasury bills which the Account has placed in the market.

Although the Account is legally limited at present to £375,000,000, it can to a certain extent increase its activities beyond that limit by converting foreign exchange into gold and, by selling the gold to the Bank of England, obtain pounds for further purchases of foreign exchange. Theoretically this process could be repeated indefinitely, were it not for the fact that the Bank of England is obliged to carry gold held by the Issue Department at the statutory par value. Thus a 35 per cent depreciation of the exchange value of the pound means that, when the Account sells to the Bank of England a quantity of gold for which it had paid £1,000,000, it receives only £650,000. While this is merely a temporary bookkeeping loss which will eventually be wiped out either by the sale of the gold at the market price or by a revaluation of the Bank of England's gold reserve, it nevertheless reduces the amount of pounds available to the Account for the further purchases of foreign exchange and gold, and this reduction sets a definite limit to the ability of the Exchange Equalization Account to act as a medium for the importation of gold.

Owing to the operation of the Exchange Equalization Account, on December 27, 1933, the gold holdings of the Bank of England reached the amount of £190,725,833, a record level in the history of the Bank. This figure represents a net addition of £70,937,549 to the gold stock of the Bank of England during the year 1933. Since the Bank acquired the gold only during the first seven months of the year, it may be assumed that gold subsequently purchased was retained by the Account. It is believed that at the beginning of 1934 the Account held between £20,000,000 and £30,000,000 in gold in its own possession, since the outlook for the gold currencies did not warrant the investment of substantial amounts in these currencies.

Should the Account be forced to sell gold in order to prevent a depreciation of the pound, it could sell gold out of its own holdings without disclosing the fact, while sales of gold by the Bank of England would immediately be reflected in the weekly statement. London thus possesses at present two reserves of gold and foreign exchange: that of the Bank of England, which affects domestic credit conditions, and that of the Exchange Equalization Account, which fluctuates according to the inflow and outflow of foreign funds without having any influence on domestic credit conditions.

The Account must at present show a loss, since the Bank of England buys gold from it at the statutory par and the difference is borne by the Account. The loss must be considerable, since the statutory price is 77/9 shillings per standard ounce against a market price, in December 1934, of about 141 shillings per fine ounce. However, one may expect that when the pound is eventually revalued at a lower rate which corresponds to the current market price of gold in paper pounds, the value of the £192,000,000 gold (in round figures) held by the Bank will automatically increase to about £321,000,000, which difference may not only wipe out the loss of the Account but also result in a profit in favor of the Treasury.

CHAPTER XII

Paris—The French Banking System

Pre-war period. For a number of years before the World War most of the industrial establishments in France were comparatively small, and their demand for capital was limited. French industrial and trading enterprises were operated conservatively and were financed largely from the private resources of the owners. On the other hand, owing to the habit of saving and the desire to create an independent income—traits deeply ingrained in the French people—the domestic supply of capital grew steadily. The resulting accumulation of capital in larger amounts than could be profitably employed at home has had a decided influence on the development of the Paris money market.

From the latter part of the nineteenth century until 1914, the Paris money market was characterized by low and stable interest rates. During the fifteen years from 1898 to 1913, the discount rate of the Bank of France not only was lower on the average than the discount rates of other leading European central banks, but was changed only fourteen times, as contrasted with fifty-eight changes in the discount rate of the central bank of Switzerland, sixty-two in Germany, and seventy-nine in Great Britain. This comparison is shown more fully in Table 37.

In spite of its low interest rates, Paris was not an important international financial center before the war. There are several reasons why the volume of foreign short-term funds employed in the Paris money market remained comparatively small. In the first place, there was little economic basis for an international money market. Unlike London, Paris was not an important center for international trading in commodities or securities.   France is not a great trading nation, as is England, and the French financial institutions devoted themselves almost exclusively to financing the foreign trade of their own country.   Furthermore, there was almost a complete absence of financial transactions arising out of French shipping and insurance services to other countries.

TABLE 37

DISCOUNT RATES OF LEADING EUROPEAN CENTRAL BANKS, 1898–1913

	Bank of France	Reichs- bank	Bank of England
Number of changes	14	62	79
Maximum rate	4½%	7½%	7%
Minimum rate	2%	3%	2½%
Average rate	3.09%	4.59%	3.69%

	Austro- Hungarian Bank	National Bank of Belgium	Nederlandsche Bank
Number of changes	25	39	31
Maximum rate	6%	6%	6%
Minimum rate	3½%	3%	2½%
Average rate	4.33%	3.74%	3.59%

In the second place, the French currency system constituted a technical obstacle to the development of an international money market.   Before the war France was on the so-called "limping" standard.   Although the currency was based on gold, the Bank of France was permitted to redeem its notes in silver five-franc pieces rather than in gold if it elected to do so.   Thus, foreigners had no assurance that short-term funds employed at Paris could be freely withdrawn in gold.

Finally, Paris never developed facilities for the employment of a very large volume of funds in the money market. This lack of facilities was due chiefly to the predominance of the small family type of business enterprise and to long-established French financial tradition.   As a rule, French companies in need of temporary financial accommodation preferred to deal directly with their banks rather than to borrow in the open market. The French bankers, on their part, preferred to extend credit on the basis of close, confidential relationships with their clients rather than on the impersonal basis of the open money market. The bankers' aversion to financing transactions over which they could not exercise a close personal supervision is another important reason why they did not attempt to develop an international acceptance business. Finally, the freely available discount facilities of the Bank of France greatly minimized the need of an open money market.

Although the French banks were accustomed to invest a considerable amount of short-term funds in neighboring countries, particularly in Germany, the surplus capital accumulated in France found its chief outlet in long-term foreign loans. For many years before the war, France was one of the leading capital-lending countries of the world. The total nominal value of its foreign long-term investments in 1914 is estimated to have been 45,000,-000,000 gold francs.[1]

To summarize, then, during the pre-war period no effort was made to develop Paris as a money market, and with the exception of certain funds loaned abroad, Paris did not play an important rôle in the international short-term money market. The chief function of Paris as an international financial center was the accumulation of domestic savings and the investment of these funds in foreign long-term securities.

The war and inflation period, 1914–28. With the outbreak of the war and with the suspension of the gold standard, the French money market assumed an entirely different aspect. The heavy cost of the war forced the government to borrow huge amounts, and the capital market was virtually closed to foreign capital issues. During the entire war period, therefore, one of the chief functions of the

---

[1] Herbert Feis, *Europe, the World's Banker, 1870–1914*, Yale University Press, New Haven, 1930, p. 51.

French banks was the collection, throughout the country, of funds to be placed at the disposal of the government. With the end of the war, the restoration of the devastated areas created a new need for funds. In the post-war years, however, the French Government encountered keen competition in the capital market from domestic industrial establishments, which were reorganizing and increasing their plant equipment. The acquisition of the industrialized provinces of Alsace and Lorraine was also an important factor in this new demand for funds.

The post-war period, up to the end of 1926, was also marked by two significant developments which had a decided influence on the money market, namely: (1) the depreciation of the currency; and (2) the flight from the franc. During the war the French currency was pegged, partly with British and American financial assistance. But when the pegging of the exchange ceased, the franc began to decline and there was a general movement on the part of the French people to place their funds in countries whose currencies were more stable. Although as early as 1916 a law was passed prohibiting the free exportation of capital, a large amount of French capital left the country and huge short-term balances were accumulated abroad.

Towards the end of 1926 the French franc was *de facto* stabilized at about 3.92 cents in United States currency. With the stabilization of the franc, confidence in the currency returned and a repatriation of French capital set in on a large scale. The return flow of funds greatly eased the situation in the Paris market and facilitated the rehabilitation of the French public finances. The Treasury took advantage of the favorable conditions to refund a substantial amount of short-term obligations, which had previously constituted a serious threat to financial stability, into securities of longer maturity. The return of French capital on a large scale also enabled the Bank of France to increase substantially its monetary stock of gold both through gold imports and through the purchase of gold released from hoarding. At the same time it greatly increased its foreign exchange holdings, and at the end of June 1928 its position was so strong that no foreign credits were required to assist in the legal stabilization of the currency.

Development since legal stabilization, 1928–34. With the legal stabilization of the currency on June 25, 1928, and with the refunding of the short-term debts of the government, the Paris money market entered into a new phase, which resembled in certain respects the pre-war situation. Business prosperity and a favorable balance of international payments combined to produce an accumulation of capital in larger amounts than could be profitably employed at home. However, France did not revert to the pre-war policy of investing this surplus in foreign long-term securities. It is true that some loans were floated for countries politically allied with France and that portions of the Dawes and Young loans to the German Government were taken by French investors, but foreign long-term lending remained far below the level of the pre-war period.

The stagnation of the French market for foreign capital issues was attributable to several factors. In the first place, French investors had suffered severe losses on their pre-war commitments in Russia and in central and southern Europe. It is estimated that losses on the repudiated Russian bonds alone amounted to about 11,000,000,000 gold francs of the old parity. As a result of this bitter experience, French financial circles were not receptive to new foreign loans unless there was some special inducement offered in the way of political advantage. Secondly, the government was opposed to the flotation of a large volume of foreign issues, because it wished to obtain the most favorable conditions for the refunding of the public debt at lower rates of interest. For this reason the war-time prohibition of the listing of new foreign capital issues on French stock exchanges continued after the war. Furthermore, the government continued to impose a high income tax on foreign securities and, although the rate has been reduced several times since 1926, it is still considerably higher than before the war. Finally, the French continued to seek political advantages through foreign loans which other countries were often reluctant to grant.

In the absence of active foreign lending, the favorable balance of payments of France resulted in the accumulation of large short-term balances abroad. It is estimated that, at the end of 1930, the amount of French funds temporarily invested in other countries totaled $1,500,000,000, of which $1,026,000,000 represented funds of the Bank of France, the rest belonging to the Treasury and to the various banking institutions. It was generally assumed that the Bank of France and the French Treasury kept their funds almost exclusively in London and New York, while the commercial banks placed their funds in a number of different countries where the rate of interest was more attractive. While it is difficult to state with any degree of accuracy the amounts kept in the two principal financial centers, it has been conservatively estimated that the French balances in London at the end of 1930 amounted to between $500,000,000 and $600,000,000. No reliable estimates have been published as to the New York balances, but it is known that they were very large. From 1928 up to the fall of 1930 the French banks resumed their practice of placing short-term loans in Germany, but they did not place them in the same volume as before the war. Formerly, between 800,000,000 and 1,000,000,000 gold francs, or $160,000,000 to $200,000,000 of short-term funds, were invested in Germany at short-term, but at their peak in the summer of 1930 it is estimated that the French balances in Germany totaled not more than three billions in paper francs, or $120,000,000.

The existence of this huge volume of French funds in the international money markets was a source of considerable instability for some years after the stabilization of the franc. The French bankers are extremely sensitive to political developments in the countries where their funds are invested, and in addition, it is generally believed that they are not unresponsive to the interests of the French Foreign Office. At any rate, there was a large withdrawal of French funds from Germany following the substantial gains made by the Nazi party at the election in the fall of 1930, and after the proposal of an Austro-German customs union in the early part of 1931, there was a further withdrawal of French funds from Germany, Austria, and Central Europe. To what extent these developments contributed to the international financial panic which started in Austria in May 1931, spread to Germany, and finally resulted in the abandonment of the gold standard by England and many other countries, remains a matter of conjecture. The collapse in 1931 put an end to the efforts to develop Paris as an international financial center, and thereafter the policy of the French banks, including the Bank of France, was to repatriate their foreign balances as rapidly as possible even though such balances had to be held in the form of unproductive gold.

The Bank of France

The Bank of France is predominant in the French financial system, and its influence on credit conditions is perhaps greater than that of the Bank of England and the Federal Reserve banks. The dominance of the Bank of France is due chiefly to the fact that it not only performs the ordinary functions of a central bank but, in addition, is the largest commercial bank in France. It is not exclusively a bankers' bank, as are the Federal Reserve banks in this country, nor does it deal chiefly with banks, as does the Bank of England. On the contrary, a great part of the business of the Bank of France is done directly with individuals and business concerns. In order to carry on its general banking business, the French central bank operates a nation-wide system of 660 branch offices and agencies. Anyone who is properly introduced and identified may open an account with the Bank of France and submit bills for discount; in fact, the Bank carried on its books 388,024 accounts at the end of 1933. Nevertheless, there is a close relationship between the commercial banks and the central bank. While not required by law to carry reserves with the Bank of France, the commercial banks customarily maintain substantial balances on deposit and make full use of the central bank's facilities for discounting and collecting commercial paper.

Thus the Bank of France is able to influence credit conditions and money rates directly through its own relations with commerce and industry, as well as through dealings with the commercial banks and other financial institutions, as is the case in certain other countries. Any change in its discount rate immediately affects the cost of credit in France. The influence of the Bank of France is further strengthened by the fact that, in the absence of a well-developed checking system, its banknotes are the most important medium of exchange in the country. The French banks are thus more dependent upon the central bank as the sole source of currency than are the banks of England and the United States, where most business transactions are settled by check.

Organization and administration. The Bank of France was established in 1800 by Napoleon, as First Consul of the French Republic, and during the course of the past 134 years its statutes have been frequently changed. But, like most European central banks, it has remained a privately owned institution operating under the close supervision of the government. Its capital stock, now amounting to 182,500,000 francs, is privately held and is actively traded on the bourse.

The management of the Bank of France is vested in a general council, consisting of a governor and two deputy governors, fifteen regents, and three *censeurs* or auditors. The governor and the deputy governors are appointed by the French Government and are the chief executive officers of the bank.   The regents and auditors are elected by the general assembly of stockholders, consisting of the 200 largest stockholders of the Bank, all of whom must be French citizens.   Five of the regents and the three auditors must be representatives of industry and commerce; one regent represents agriculture, and three must be Treasury officials. All must be stockholders.   The regents, who correspond to corporate directors in Anglo-Saxon countries, are responsible for the general administration of the Bank.   They are organized into several committees, each devoted to some particular phase of operation, such as the discount committee, committee on banknotes, committee on books and portfolios, etc.   The primary function of the auditors is to see that all the affairs of the Bank are conducted in accordance with its statutes, and they are required to submit a report annually to the general assembly of stockholders.   They have no voting power, but at least one must be present at all meetings of the general council.   In addition, there is a discount council consisting of twelve stockholders, engaged in business in Paris, who are appointed by the auditors from a list of thirty-six nominees submitted by the regents. The members of the discount council assist the discount committee of regents in an advisory capacity.

Discounts and advances.   As a result of the extensive use in French commerce of the domestic bill of exchange, or trade acceptance, the discounting of this type of commercial paper is one of the principal activities of the Bank of France.   The Bank's statutes and regulations governing discounts are comparatively simple.   The essential requirements are that bills be drawn to order, have a fixed maturity of not more than three months, and bear the signatures of three persons or firms known to be solvent.   No distinction is made between trade acceptances and bankers' acceptances.   Paper bearing only two signatures may be discounted provided it is collateraled by stock of the Bank of France or by any other securities on which the Bank is authorized to make advances.

Unlike the Bank of England, the French central bank does not discriminate against foreign bills; it discounts paper accepted or offered by foreign banks on the same basis as domestic paper offered by French institutions or individuals. In time of need, foreign banks have not hesitated to take advantage of this privilege. The Bank of France also discounts, under conditions determined by the general council, bills payable in the French colonies and in foreign countries.

In order to be in position to appraise accurately the paper offered to it for discount, the Bank of France maintains extensive files of credit data and keeps in close touch with local business conditions throughout the country. It also has well-developed facilities for the collection of bills, and it is customary for the French banks and business concerns to discount bills about eight days before maturity in order to avoid the costs of collection.

Like other European central banks, the Bank of France makes credit available by advances on securities, or lombard loans, in addition to discounting bills. Originally such loans could be made only on French Government securities of fixed maturities, but in 1834 the privilege was extended to all government securities and a royal ordinance was issued governing these lending operations. The ordinance provides that advances may not exceed four-fifths of the current market value of the securities pledged, that the maturity may not exceed three months, and that, in case the market value declines by 10 per cent, additional margin must be provided. Subsequent laws enlarged the group of securities eligible as collateral for lombard loans to include bonds and stocks of the French railways and securities of French cities and departments, of French colonies and protectorates, and of the Crédit Foncier and the Société Générale Algérienne. However, bonds of the cities, departments, colonies, and protectorates must be approved by the general council of the Bank in order to be eligible for advances. Besides advances on securities, the Bank may make loans against the deposit of gold bullion or foreign gold coins.

In spite of the gradual liberalization of the regulations governing advances on securities, the Bank of France has remained primarily a discounting institution. The volume of discounted bills held by the Bank is normally about two to three times as large as the volume of advances on securities, or lombard loans. Advances on gold and gold coin have attained appreciable volume only in the last few years, but have averaged an amount only about one-half as large as advances on securities. The interest rate on lombard loans is usually 1½ to 2 per cent higher than the discount rate, and the rate on advances on gold is normally ½ to 1 per cent higher.

Credit control by the Bank of France. In contrast to its broad powers to discount bills and make advances, the Bank of France has very limited authority to engage in open market operations. Its statutes permit three types of open market operations, namely: (1) dealings in bonds of the Caisse Autonome d'Amortissement; (2) the purchase of bills and short-term securities for the account of foreign central banks; and (3) dealings in foreign exchange.

In accordance with the convention of June 23, 1928, there were issued to the Bank of France 5,930,000,000 francs of bonds of the Caisse Autonome d'Amortissement (an autonomous bureau for the amortization of the public debt) in settlement of certain advances made by the Bank to the government during the war. In December 1931 an additional 2,342,000,000 francs of Caisse Autonome d'Amortissement bonds were delivered to the Bank to cover losses on its holdings of sterling bills consequent upon the abandonment of the gold standard by Great Britain. The convention of June 23, 1928, authorized the Bank of France to sell these bonds in the open market "if it seems expedient, in order to influence the volume of credit" and, likewise, to repurchase them. This privilege opened the way for the Bank of France to develop a new instrument of credit control.

By gradually disposing of these securities it could have created an open market in which it could, like the Bank of England or the Federal Reserve banks, buy or sell bonds. However, none of the bonds have ever been sold, and the Bank has never attempted to develop open market operations in securities. Regular amortization gradually reduced the amount of these bonds to—in the middle of 1934—5,950,000,000 francs.

Although the Bank of France has no authority to deal in the open market in bills and securities for its own account, other than in bonds of the Caisse Autonome d'Amortissement, it is permitted to engage in such operations for the account of foreign central banks. The convention of June 23, 1928, between the government and the Bank provided that: "the Bank of France shall have authority to purchase bills and short-term securities for the account of such foreign central banks as shall have opened current accounts on its books." The Bank may guarantee such bills and securities and may also rediscount them at the request of foreign central banks. Such open market operations, if conducted on a sufficiently large scale, would have an appreciable effect on credit conditions in France. However, they are of little significance as a means of credit control, since the initiative must come from foreign central banks rather than from the Bank of France. Ordinarily they serve merely to facilitate the maintenance of working balances in Paris by foreign central banks, but in times of financial crisis they would permit foreign institutions to assist the Bank of France by placing additional funds at the disposal of the money market.

The only effective method available to the Bank of France for influencing credit conditions by open market operations is dealings in foreign exchange. The Bank has full authority to buy and sell foreign bills of exchange and employ balances abroad. The purchase or sale of foreign bills in France has the same effect on the money market as dealings in securities. The purchase of foreign bills from

French owners places funds at the disposal of the money market, while the sale of bills withdraws funds. However, such operations affect not only the money market but also exchange rates. Active bidding by the Bank of France for, let us say, sterling bills would tend to raise the exchange rate on London and might possibly lead to gold exports. Conversely, the sale of sterling bills in large volume would depress the sterling rate and might cause a movement of gold from London to Paris. For this reason the power of the Bank of France to use open market operations in foreign exchange as a method of credit control is rather limited, and there is little evidence that it has ever been used primarily for this purpose.

Under these circumstances the Bank of France, to influence credit conditions, has to rely chiefly on its control of discounts. Owing to the structure of the French financial system, this instrument has proved effective. The discount rate is not only the rate at which the commercial banks borrow from the central bank, but also the rate at which the money market and, to some extent, business in general borrow. Any change in the rate is directly and immediately effective. Furthermore, the amount of bills discounted, as well as the volume of advances, is subject entirely to the discretion of the general council of the Bank, and thus close regulation of the amount of credit available to business and the money market is permitted. Finally, the French banks, like the British banks, are generally receptive to suggestions as to credit policies emanating from the central bank.

Note issue. The principal function of the Bank of France which distinguishes it as a central bank, in spite of its extensive commercial banking activities, is the issuance of bank notes. Originally it was, without exclusive privileges, merely authorized to issue notes, but since 1848 it has been the sole bank of issue in France. Prior to June 28, 1928, the amount of notes which the Bank might issue was limited by law, and the amount was frequently changed.

However, the amount and nature of the reserves to be held against notes in circulation was not defined by law, but left entirely to the management of the Bank. Bank of France notes were legal tender, and the Bank was required to redeem them on demand in gold or in silver five-franc pieces at its option.

At the time the war broke out in 1914, the maximum note issue of the Bank of France was fixed at 6,800,000,000 francs. On August 5, 1914, the limit was raised to 12,000,-000,000 francs, and the obligation of the Bank to redeem its notes in specie was suspended. Subsequent laws gradually raised the limit of the note issue to a maximum of 58,500,000,000 francs (December 4, 1925). During the war, the franc was under heavy pressure in the exchange markets as a result of the huge purchases of war materials abroad, but was pegged with British and, later, with American financial assistance at between $0.17 and $0.18 to the franc. When the pegging operations ceased in the early part of 1919, the franc began to depreciate rapidly. By the middle of 1926, when the situation of the French Treasury became extremely critical, the franc had depreciated from its pre-war parity of $0.193 to less than $0.02.

On July 24, 1926, a National Union Ministry under Premier Poincaré assumed office and immediately formulated a decisive program for rehabilitating the French public finances. This program included a heavy increase in taxation and the creation of the Caisse Autonome d'Amortissement, which was charged with servicing and amortizing the National Defense bonds and certain other short-term Treasury obligations. On August 7, 1926, the Bank of France was authorized to issue notes in excess of the fixed maximum for the purchase of gold, silver, and foreign exchange in the open market at attractive rates.

These measures brought about an immediate revival of confidence in the franc. Hoarded gold and silver began to flow back to the Bank of France, and French capital began to be repatriated in large volume. The position of the franc was suddenly reversed, and the problem of the French financial authorities became one of preventing the franc from rising too rapidly. The franc was stabilized *de facto* at about $0.0392 toward the end of 1926, and legal stabilization was effected by the end of June 1928.

The monetary law of June 25, 1928, fixed the gold content of the franc at 65.5 milligrams of gold 0.900 fine, and thus gave it a par value of $0.0392 in terms of the dollar. However, the law provides that "the present definition is not applicable to international payments which, prior to promulgation of the present law, have been validly stipulated in gold francs." In other words, the new value of the franc applied only to internal debts and not to existing international gold obligations. The latter provision was designed to protect French investments in foreign bonds, most of which provided for payment in gold francs.

The new law placed France on a gold bullion standard. The central bank's option of redeeming its notes in gold or silver was eliminated, and the Bank of France is now required to redeem its notes in gold on demand, although only at its central office and only in "such minimum amounts as shall be fixed by agreement between the Minister of Finance and the Bank of France." This minimum was fixed at 215,000 francs. The former system of a fixed maximum note issue was abandoned, and the Bank is now required to maintain gold reserves equivalent to not less than 35 per cent of the amount of notes in circulation plus other demand liabilities.

Operation of the gold standard. With the legal stabilization of the franc, the Bank of France assumed a new rôle in international finance. Its position rapidly changed from that of a distressed institution struggling to prevent the collapse of the French currency to that of one of the strongest and most influential central banks in the world. The balance of payments of the country was very favorable as a result of reparation receipts from Germany, large tourist expenditures, and the repatriation of French capital from abroad, while capital exports remained at a low level.   As a result, the Bank of France was able to increase its gold reserves steadily and, at the same time, maintain large short-term balances in foreign money markets.

In view of the widespread criticism of the policies of the Bank of France during the last few years, it is pertinent to examine the development of its gold and foreign exchange holdings since the stabilization of the currency. During the last six months of 1928, foreign exchange continued to flow into the Bank of France as French capital returned home, and the total holdings of foreign exchange increased from 26,529,000,000 francs on June 25, 1928, to 32,760,000,000 francs at the end of the year.   During the same period the Bank's gold holdings increased by about 2,900,000,000 francs.   However, contrary to its policy during the first half of the year, the Bank made little effort to build up its gold reserves, and most of the increase represented domestic purchases of gold previously hoarded. In other words, the Bank of France adopted a *laissez-faire* policy toward international gold movements.

Bank operations during 1929.   The *laissez-faire* policy was temporarily suspended during the first half of 1929. High interest rates abroad, particularly in New York, caused an outward movement of French funds and, for the time being, offset the effects of the favorable balance of payments.   As a matter of fact, the total gold and foreign exchange holdings declined by 2,260,000,000 francs during the first six months of the year.   Under these circumstances the management of the Bank of France apparently deemed it advisable to build up its gold reserve, which at the end of 1928 amounted to only 38.5 per cent of notes in circulation and other demand liabilities.   This end was accomplished partly by domestic purchases of gold but chiefly by the conversion of foreign bills into gold.   Thus, during the first half of the year, the gold reserve increased by 4,648,000,000 francs and the reserve ratio rose to 44.1 per cent, while foreign exchange holdings decreased by 6,909,000,000 francs.

In June 1929, however, the *laissez-faire* policy was resumed and, according to the Bank's annual report for 1929,

> From June to December we never took the initiative in acquiring gold by means of foreign bills. We were obliged, in fulfillment of our obligation to regulate the currency, to accept all gold of foreign origin which was offered to us over the counter for francs, but we did not at any time intervene in the exchange market to accelerate the pace of these gold imports.

Nevertheless, gold continued to flow into the Bank of France, and the rapidly mounting gold stocks, which afforded a reserve ratio far in excess of the minimum required by law, were the subject of no little adverse comment in foreign financial circles. In answer to this criticism the annual report for 1929 declared:

> The bank has opposed no obstacle whatever to the free play of the money market under the gold standard. It will not depart from this attitude, whatever may be the direction of capital movements. Whenever, under the influence of an advance in foreign exchange rates, gold shall be demanded over our counters instead of being offered, the bank will permit gold to flow out in execution of the monetary law just as freely as it permitted it to flow in.

Period from 1929 to 1931. For the next two years—that is, from the middle of 1929 to the middle of 1931—the Bank of France adhered rigidly to this policy, even to the extent of maintaining its foreign bills and balances at approximately the same level. Meanwhile, the favorable balance of payments was further accentuated by the withdrawal of French capital from foreign money markets and the tendency for nervous foreign capital to take refuge in France. As a result, the gold reserves of the Bank increased steadily from 36,625,000,000 francs at the end of June 1929, to 58,407,000,000 francs at the end of July 1931.

The international financial panic of 1931 changed the situation entirely. Although the French commercial banks and financial institutions undoubtedly contributed to the panic by hasty withdrawals of balances from Austria and Germany, and later from England, there is every reason to believe that the Bank of France coöperated fully with other central banks to prevent a breakdown of the gold standard. In June 1931 it participated to the extent of $25,000,000 in a $100,000,000 credit to the Reichsbank which was granted by a group of foreign central banks. On August 1 it extended a credit of $121,520,000 to the Bank of England; one-half was taken up by the Paris banks. A similar amount was advanced by the New York Reserve Bank. Again, on August 28, the Bank of France arranged for a second credit, of $196,000,000, to the Bank of England by the sale of British Treasury bills to the French banks.

The Bank of France apparently made no effort to withdraw its balances from London until the last hope of maintaining the stability of the pound sterling was abandoned. The total of its foreign bills and balances was reported at 26,416,000,000 francs on September 11, 1931, as compared with 26,162,000,000 at the end of July. During the week ended September 18, this total declined to 25,120,000,000. The sudden increase in the Bank's "foreign bills discounted" from 79,000,000 francs on August 7 to 2,488,000,000 on September 25 seems to indicate that it was endeavoring to relieve the strain on sterling by freely discounting sterling bills.

After the abandonment of the gold standard by Great Britain on September 21, followed by similar action on the part of a number of other countries, the authorities of the Bank of France determined to liquidate the greater part of their foreign bills and balances. From the end of October 1931 to the end of October 1932, the total foreign exchange holdings declined rapidly—from 25,109,000,000 francs to 4,721,000,000. Thereafter liquidation was more gradual, but by the end of 1934 the total had been reduced to only about 963,000,000 francs. In commenting on these operations, the Bank in its annual report for 1932 stated that they had been conducted in complete agreement with foreign central banks and that "the bank in all circumstances made use of such technical procedure as was best suited to carry through the program outlined. It consistently abstained from intervention during periods when the exchange markets exhibited signs of nervousness." The report further stated that "the bank refrained from disposing of its dollar balances during the autumn of 1931, when the United States was forced to meet large withdrawals of foreign funds."

The liquidation of such a large volume of foreign bills and balances naturally resulted in a tremendous increase in the Bank's gold holdings. Between the end of September 1931 and the end of November 1932, the gold reserve increased from 59,346,000,000 francs to 83,342,000,000 francs. However, early in 1932 the adverse development of the French balance of international payments became apparent. This was the result of a combination of factors, including the suspension of reparation payments, the decline in tourists' expenditures, and the unfavorable trade balance. Although the Bank's gold reserves continued to rise during 1932, the increase was less than the reduction in its foreign exchange holdings, and at the end of the year the total of gold and foreign exchange was about 1,800,000,000 francs less than at the end of 1931.

Operations during 1933 and 1934. During 1933 the position of the Bank of France became more strained than it had been at any time since the stabilization of the currency. The abandonment of the gold standard by the United States and the subsequent depreciation of the dollar, uncertainty as to the currency policies of the United States and Great Britain, the large deficit in the French budget, and a considerable degree of domestic political unrest—all combined to cause a widespread loss of confidence in the French currency. In international financial circles there developed a strong feeling that France would be forced to abandon the gold standard. However, the authorities of the Bank of France and the French Government repeatedly avowed their determination to maintain the stability of the franc. The central bank met all demands for gold; and during the year its metallic reserve was reduced from 83,017,000,000 to 77,098,000,000 francs, a part of the loss representing exports and a part withdrawals for domestic hoarding. The annual report of the Bank for 1933 states that it "offered no objection to withdrawals from its gold reserve, just as it had not sought in the past to accentuate or moderate the flow of the metal to France. It acted in scrupulous conformity with the principles which it has always defended."

The most serious test of the strength of the French franc did not come, however, until February 1934. When President Roosevelt legally devalued the dollar on January 31, 1934, there was an immediate rush to repatriate American capital which had taken refuge in the gold standard countries during and prior to the period of dollar depreciation. To this repatriated capital was added a substantial amount of foreign funds whose owners regarded the devalued dollar as a safer currency than the currencies of the European gold bloc. At this time confidence in the French franc was at a low ebb. The French budget showed a large deficit, and Parliament appeared unable to agree on means to balance it. Political unrest began to manifest itself in street rioting in Paris.

Under these circumstances the extraordinary demand for the dollar in the foreign exchange markets raised the dollar to such a premium over the new parity with foreign gold currencies as to make large gold shipments profitable. During the month of February, gold imports to the United States totaled $452,600,000, the largest amount ever imported in any one month. From January 26 to March 2, 1934, the Bank of France suffered a reduction in its gold holdings of 3,127,000,000 francs, or $207,430,000 at the new par of exchange. Although the Bank raised its discount rate from 2½ to 3 per cent on February 9, 1934, it placed no obstacle in the way of the outflow of gold. Finally, as the rush of funds to the United States subsided and as the Doumergue government in France gave evidence of restor-

ing political and financial stability, confidence in the franc
revived and, during the next few months, there was a steady
increase in the gold holdings of the Bank of France.

This survey of developments since the stabilization of the
franc indicates that the Bank of France has adhered closely
to the rules of the international gold standard. From the
end of June 1928 until September 1931 the Bank deliberately refrained from liquidating its large balances in foreign
currencies, except for a slight reduction in the early part
of 1929 which was motivated by the need of maintaining
an adequate gold reserve against increasing demand liabilities. During this period the Bank pursued a *laissez-faire*
policy regarding gold movements, permitting the country's
favorable balance of payments to have its normal effects
on its gold reserves. In view of the general currency instability that developed after England abandoned the gold
standard, the Bank of France can hardly be blamed for
attempting to minimize its losses by converting its foreign
balances into gold. Even then it conducted the conversion operations with due regard to the interests of foreign
financial centers, although this regard involved considerable
financial risk. Finally, when gold began to flow out of
France, the Bank consistently adhered to its *laissez-faire*
policy and permitted the free withdrawal of gold.

The Commercial Banks

The French commercial banking system, which has
gradually developed over a long period with comparatively
little government regulation or supervision, comprises a
variety of types of banking institutions. The French
banks may be roughly classified into four main groups: (1)
the credit banks—*banques de depots;* (2) investment banks
—*banques d'affaires;* (3) local and regional banks; and
(4) private banks—*hautes banques.* There are, in addition, a number of foreign banks with offices in France, as
well as savings banks and agricultural credit and coöperative
banks.

Credit banks. As far as the money market is concerned, the credit banks are the most important. In financing industry and trade by making short-term loans and discounting trade bills, they operate along the same lines as the commercial banks in the United States and the large joint-stock banks in England. Although the large credit banks engage to some extent in the distribution of securities they do not provide permanent capital to business enterprises and are not closely associated with individual business concerns, as are the *banques d'affaires.*

The number of credit banks in France is comparatively large, but the following six are the most important: (1) Crédit Lyonnais, (2) Comptoir National d'Escompte de Paris, (3) Société Générale, (4) Crédit Commercial de France, (5) Crédit Industriel d'Alsace et de Lorraine, and (6) Banque Nationale pour le Commerce et l'Industrie.

Branches and affiliates. In order to be in a position to accumulate deposits and finance local business enterprises, the credit banks have established an extensive system of branches and agencies covering the entire country. The larger institutions—namely, the Société Générale and the Crédit Lyonnais—have more than a thousand such offices. However, one of the large credit banks, the Crédit Industriel d'Alsace et de Lorraine, has adopted a system similar to what is known in the United States as chain banking. Instead of establishing a large number of branch offices, it has acquired interests in a number of small local banks. The essential difference between the method of operation of the Crédit Industriel and that of the other large credit banks is that the former utilizes local capital and is more closely allied with local business interests.

The branch banking system was extended rapidly during the post-war period and even through the first two years of the economic depression, but in 1932 the decline in banking activity forced the banks to discontinue some of their branches and agencies. The total number operated by the six large institutions was reduced from 4,355 at the end of

1931, to 3,716 at the end of 1932. About one-half of this number are permanent offices, and the others are open for business only at certain seasons of the year or on certain days of the week, usually on market days. Table 38 shows the number of permanent and periodic or seasonal branches and agencies of the six large credit banks at intervals during recent years.

TABLE 38

BRANCHES AND AGENCIES OF THE LARGE CREDIT BANKS

End of	Permanent	Periodic or Seasonal	Total
1925	1,803	1,317	3,120
1929	2,069	1,957	4,026
1930	2,166	2,117	4,283
1931	2,202	2,153	4,355
1932	1,857	1,859	3,716

The large French credit banks have opened, in addition to branches and agencies at home, a number of branches in its colonies and protectorates, as well as in foreign countries. Furthermore, some of the larger banking institutions have also established some affiliated institutions in foreign countries. Thus, for example, the Crédit Lyonnais has 19 agencies in the French colonies and protectorates, 17 branches in foreign countries, and a foreign affiliate—the Crédit Franco-Portugais. Similarly, the Société Générale has 13 agencies in the colonies and protectorates, as well as offices in London and a number of foreign affiliates, of which the most important are the Société Générale de Banque pour l'Etranger et les Colonies (Spain), the Société Française de Banque et de Depots (Belgium), the Banque Française de Syrie, and the Société Générale Alsacienne de Banque, which has branches in Germany, Switzerland, and the Saar. The Comptoir National d'Escompte has 29 offices in the French colonies and in foreign countries and a part interest in the French-American Banking Corporation.

Capital resources. The large French credit banks resemble the joint-stock banks of England in that the ratio of capital resources to deposits is comparatively low. This low ratio is primarily the result of the depreciation of the currency, which resulted in a more rapid increase in deposit liabilities than in capital funds. At the end of 1931 the ratio of capital to deposits for the four large French credit

TABLE 39

PERCENTAGE RATIO OF BANKS' OWN RESOURCES TO PUBLIC LIABILITIES
(Excluding acceptances and sundry accounts;
Amounts in millions of francs)

End of Year	1913	1930	1931	1932	1933
Crédit Lyonnais:					
Capital funds	425	1,208	1,208	1,208	1,208
Deposits	2,221	13,460	15,235	14,924	12,692
Percentage ratio	19.1	9.0	7.9	8.1	9.5
Société Générale:					
Capital funds	377	707	711	711	712
Deposits	1,791	12,821	11,912	11,752	10,539
Percentage ratio	21.0	5.5	6.0	6.1	6.8
Comptoir National d'Escompte de Paris:					
Capital funds	239	834	836	838	840
Deposits	1,415	9,211	9,507	9,104	7,871
Percentage ratio	16.9	9.1	8.8	9.2	10.7
Crédit Commercial de France:					
Capital funds	53	403	412	418	420
Deposits	153	3,262	2,731	2,706	2,638
Percentage ratio	34.6	12.4	15.1	15.4	15.9
Aggregate (four banks):					
Capital funds	1,094	3,152	3,167	3,175	3,180
Deposits	5,580	38,754	39,385	38,486	33,740
Percentage ratio	19.6	8.1	8.0	8.2	9.4

banks was 8.0 per cent, as compared with 19.6 per cent at the end of 1913. Contraction of deposits during the past few years of business depression has resulted in an increase in the ratio to 9.4 per cent (at the end of 1933), which is somewhat higher than the ratio of 6.3 per cent for the "Big Five" British banks on the same date. Table 39 shows the capital funds, deposits, and percentage ratio for each of the large credit banks.

Discounts and advances. The chief function of the French credit banks is to provide short-term financial accommodation to business. Contrary to the general practice in the United States, this credit is extended principally by discounting trade bills or trade acceptances. In trade financing in France usually the seller of merchandise draws a draft on the buyer, and thereby creates a trade bill which is a two-name paper. The maturity of trade bills varies from 30 days to three months or more. In case the seller desires to obtain cash, the trade bill can be discounted with a bank. Such paper is considered one of the safest and most liquid forms of investment, and provided it meets the eligibility requirements, it can be discounted with the Bank of France.

Bills discounted constitute the principal asset item in the balance sheets of the large credit banks and ordinarily represent about one-half of their total assets. However, this item includes National Defense (Treasury) bonds, which the banks hold as liquid reserves. At the end of 1932 the total bills discounted of the four large credit banks which issue monthly statements amounted to 21,932,000,000 francs. Of this amount, it is estimated, about 13,000,000,-000 francs represented Treasury bonds. The proportion on that date was probably unusually high, on account of the low demand for commercial credit and the banks' policy of maintaining a highly liquid position.

The credit banks also provide financial accommodation to their customers by advances on current account. These are unsecured loans which take the form of over-drafts on the customers' accounts. Such loans usually represent about 20 to 25 per cent of the total resources of the larger banks. Contrary to the situation in the United States, the French banks employ a comparatively small proportion of their funds in secured loans. Secured loans consist partly of "report loans" on stock exchange collateral made to finance trading in securities, but chiefly of advances secured by warehouse receipts or other documents evidencing title to commodities. Loans and advances, other than on current account, constitute only in the neighborhood of 3 to 4 per cent of the aggregate resources of the credit banks.

Deposits. The credit banks accept three chief types of deposits: deposits on current account which are subject to check; sight deposits payable on demand; and time, or fixed, deposits which are made for a stipulated period or are payable only after due notice in advance. Deposits on current account constitute 50 to 60 per cent of the total deposits of the large credit banks and sight deposits average around 40 per cent, while time and fixed deposits are comparatively small.

The rate of interest paid by the various French banks on deposits maturing within less than thirty days is fixed by the syndicate of banks which, while similar to the American Bankers' Association, has greater powers over its members. This organization includes not only the commercial banks but also the *banques d'affaires* and the private banking institutions. Members of the bankers' syndicate are divided into three groups: (1) prime banks, which pay the lowest rate of interest; (2) middle-class banks, which pay a slightly higher rate; and (3) third-class banks, which pay the highest rate. Banks that endeavor to increase their deposits through the payment of a higher rate of interest find it desirable to be put in a lower class in order to be able to pay higher rates of interest. Thus, for example, the Banque de Paris et des Pays-Bas, although one of the largest French banking institutions, for a long time belonged to the second class. In order, however, to avoid unfair competition, the other banks insisted that the bank be placed among the prime banks and therefore be forced to pay the same rate of interest as the other large banks. The rate of interest paid on time deposits is determined by the individual banks.

Distribution of securities. The fact that the large credit banks have an extensive system of branches and agencies all over the country which enables them to accumulate the surplus funds of the nation makes them excellent vehicles for the distribution of securities. Before the war, the credit

banks took a very prominent part in the distribution of
foreign securities which were offered in the French market.
After the outbreak of the war they played a leading rôle
in distributing government securities, and after the government ceased to be a large borrower in the open market,
these French banking institutions turned to the distribution of securities of the industrial and commercial côrpora-
tions.   The banks usually obtain a substantial commission
on the sale of securities, and this activity constitutes a re-
munerative part of their business.   While the banks cannot deal directly on the stock exchanges but must employ
brokers, the principal institutions have their own counters
inside the bourse premises and are in closer contact with
the security markets than are banks in most other countries.

Unlike the German banks, the French commercial banks
do not take participations in business enterprises, but merely
act as distributors of their securities.   Furthermore, the
credit banks do not make loans for long periods to corporations.   In order, however, to provide French industry
with longer-term credits, particularly in times when the
market is not favorable for the flotation of new securities,
the French credit banks have founded a number of subsidiaries.   Through this method they can shift longer-term
credits to their subsidiaries and thus preserve their own
liquidity.   The purpose of these subsidiaries is to provide
medium-term credit to the various French industries and
to carry them until their securities can be sold to the public.

Another purpose of the subsidiaries is to grant longer-
term credits for the financing of foreign trade.   Shortly
after the war, the more important credit banks combined
for the purpose of creating such institutions.   In 1919 the
Crédit Lyonnais and the Comptoir National d'Escompte de
Paris organized the Union pour le Crédit à l'Industrie
Nationale, generally known as the U. C. I. N. A., with a
capital of 25,000,000 francs which was later increased to
50,000,000.   In 1929 the U. C. I. N. A. and the two above-

mentioned institutions formed a new subsidiary bank, l'Omnium Financier pour l'Industrie Nationale, known as the O. F. I. N. A., with a capital of 50,000,000 francs. The purpose of both of these institutions is to finance industries and to grant them longer-term credits. Similarly, in 1928 the Société Générale, with the collaboration of other banks, organized the Société Anonyme de Crédit à l'Industrie Française (C. A. L. I. F.), with a capital originally of 50,-000,000 francs, later increased to 100,000,000 francs.

In 1929 the Crédit Industriel et Commerciel, in coöperation with several other institutions, organized the Union des Banques Régionales pour le Crédit Industriel, with a capital of 40,000,000 francs. Some of these institutions, besides granting credit to industrial establishments, furnish credit for the financing of foreign trade. The most important institution organized for the purpose of financing foreign trade is the Banque Nationale Française du Commerce Extérieur, which specializes in acceptance credits.

Banques d'affaires. The investment banks, also known as *crédit mobilier banques* or *sociétés financières,* are engaged chiefly in providing long-term capital for business enterprises. Their ordinary commercial banking business is conducted only as a side-line. Their principal functions are the promotion and financing of new enterprises, the provision of new capital for existing companies, and the arrangement of business combinations. The services of the *banques d'affaires* usually consist of the organizing of syndicates for the underwriting and distributing of new issues of securities, but in case circumstances do not warrant a public issue, these banks sometimes arrange syndicates to take up and hold securities pending distribution to investors. At times, they make temporary advances to business concerns to be funded by the subsequent sale of securities. The very nature of their business limits the *banques d'affaires* to a comparatively few important clients, with which they have a close relationship and in which they often have a direct financial interest. Frequently the managers or some directors of the investment banks are appointed as directors of client companies, but it is usually considered more advisable to exercise control and supervision by more indirect means.

The most important institutions of this group of banks are the Banque de Paris et des Pays-Bas, founded in 1872; the Banque de l'Union Parisienne, established in 1904; and the Banque Française pour le Commerce et Industrie, established in 1901. Although these three institutions are of the same general type, their operations differ in many respects. Thus the Banque de Paris et des Pays-Bas is primarily engaged in investment banking, and therefore does not endeavor to deal directly with the public. It was instrumental in the development of a number of industrial establishments both in France and abroad, and before the war was one of the chief mediums through which foreign issues were placed in the French market. The Banque de l'Union Parisienne, on the other hand, even before the war, engaged in the discounting of bills and in a general banking business in addition to its investment banking function. In May 1932 this institution was absorbed by the Crédit Mobilier Français.

To a large extent the *banques d'affaires* operate with their own capital and with the funds of capitalists who keep large deposits with them. In recent years, their capital and reserves have amounted to from one-fifth to one-third of their total deposits, one institution now having a ratio of about 40 per cent. In contrast to the deposits of the credit banks, about one-third of the investment banks' deposits are time deposits. Hence investment banks do not maintain as high a degree of liquidity as the credit banks. Direct participations and investments in securities of private enterprises are usually about equivalent to the amount of the banks' own capital. In addition, the banks hold substantial amounts of government securities as well as commercial loans and discounts.

The various *banques d'affaires* have not developed a system of branches at home, but they have established a number of branches and subsidiaries in foreign countries through which they do their foreign business. After the stabilization of the currency and with the decrease in the volume of domestic issues, the *banques d'affaires* began more and more to engage in commercial banking business. Not having branches through which to accumulate the necessary funds, these institutions have entered into a close relationship with a large number of smaller banks located in the provinces. The latter prefer to deal with the *banques d'affaires* because, not having branches in the provinces, they do not compete with the local banks. On the other hand, the *banques d'affaires* offer the local banks all the facilities of their main offices in Paris. At present the *banques d'affaires*, therefore, represent a mixture of investment and commercial banking.

Local and regional banks. While the large credit banks with their elaborate system of branches do the bulk of the banking business in France, the local and regional banks located in Paris and in the provinces are an important element in the French banking system. There are about a dozen large regional banks as well as several hundred small local banks. Since the war the number of these institutions has been reduced as a result of the competition of the big credit banks. For the most part the credit banks have expanded by opening new branch offices in competition with the local banks rather than by absorbing the latter. To some extent the local banks have met the competition of the big Paris banks by combining with other institutions in the same locality and forming regional banks which are able to offer their customers more complete banking facilities. Furthermore, the local banks have the advantage of an intimate knowledge of their localities and long-established connections which have helped them to hold their own, although many of the weaker ones have failed during the past few years of business depression.

The operations of the local and regional banks vary widely. Some are so closely connected with industrial enterprises and business concerns in their localities that they

have somewhat the same characteristics as the *banques
d'affaires,* while others restrict themselves more closely to
ordinary commercial banking. In general, they do not
maintain as liquid a position as the big credit banks usually
maintain.

Private banks. The private banks consist of some six
or seven large and influential firms located in Paris and
known as *les hautes banques,* as well as a much larger
number of private banking houses in both Paris and the
chief provincial cities. The *hautes banques* are for the
most part old, established family concerns with a long
record of conservative banking practice. Their activities
are quite varied. Some of them engage principally in
managing family fortunes and the estates of wealthy
clients. Others have played an important rôle in the distribution of securities and have substantial interests in industrial enterprises, including representation on their boards
of directors. The larger Paris institutions are dealers in
trade bills, acceptances, and foreign exchange; they also
make loans to selected clients, accept deposits, and create
acceptances. Although the large private banks still have
great prestige, they are today less important in the French
financial system than they were before the war.

The French Banks in the Depression

Although the French banking system has come through
the depression better than those of many other countries,
the strain of the past few years has had far-reaching effects.
The chief characteristics of French banking during these
years have been: (1) a moderate deflation of bank credit;
(2) a marked increase in the banks' liquidity; and (3) bank
failures and mergers resulting in a marked trend toward
banking concentration. Table 40, showing the principal
balance sheet items of the four large credit banks, derived
from the Service d'Etudes Economiques of the Bank of
France, reveals the recent changes in the position of the
banks.

TABLE 40

PRINCIPAL ITEMS OF THE FOUR LARGE CREDIT BANKS

(In millions of francs; end of year)

	1928	1929	1930	1931	1932	1933	February 1934
1. Cash in hand and with banks, etc.	2,735	2,827	3,957	12,599	9,945	6,514	5,448
2. Commercial portfolio and national defense bonds	21,220	21,064	20,224	18,269	21,932	19,698	18,073
3. Advances and report loans	2,347	1,935	1,577	1,100	1,044	1,250	1,360
4. Correspondents and debtors on current account	11,388	12,589	14,761	9,803	8,011	7,381	7,977
5. Securities and participations	182	196	212	233	233	234	234
6. Sight deposits	12,974	13,554	14,837	14,672	15,313	13,827	13,048
7. Current accounts	21,502	19,437	20,447	22,351	21,178	17,946	16,843
8. Time deposits	896	1,074	1,397	1,222	1,268	862	845
9. Total deposits	35,372	34,065	36,681	38,245	37,759	32,635	30,736
10. Acceptances	884	1,275	921	576	295	273	334
11. Capital and reserves	1,316	2,774	2,852	2,863	2,877	2,879	2,879

The general business depression was not felt seriously in
France until after it became acute in most other countries,
and it was not until 1931 that there began to be a noticeable
contraction of bank credit. Because of the summary nature of the French bank statements, it is impossible to
measure exactly the extent to which bank loans and discounts have decreased, but the total deposits of the four
large credit banks, as shown in Table 40, have declined
from a peak of 38,245,000,000 francs at the end of 1931 to
32,635,000,000 francs at the end of 1933—a shrinkage of
about 15 per cent. This percentage of decrease is considerably less than that for the United States, Germany,
and several other countries during the same period.

The aggregate bill portfolio of the four credit banks declined gradually during 1929, 1930, and 1931, increased in
1932, and again declined in 1933. However, this is not an
accurate indication of the amount of credit extended to
business through discounts, since the bill portfolio includes
Treasury bonds as well as commercial bills. It is estimated
that the holdings of Treasury bonds of the four banks increased by some 5,000,000,000 francs in 1932, indicating an
actual decrease of about 1,300,000,000 francs in commercial bills discounted during that year.

Similarly, it is difficult to interpret the changes in the
item "correspondents and debtors on current account," since
it represents both loans to customers and balances held
abroad. The sharp decrease in this item from 14,761,000,-
000 francs at the end of 1930 to 7,381,000,000 francs at the
end of 1933 is attributable chiefly to a withdrawal of foreign balances induced by disturbed financial conditions
abroad, although there was undoubtedly a considerable decrease in loans on current account. There has also been a
substantial decline in the advances and report loans of the
credit banks.

One of the most marked changes in the position of the
large credit banks during the past few years has been
the great increase in their liquidity. This development

has been due partly to a desire to be in position to meet demands of nervous depositors, partly to the inability to find profitable opportunities for commercial loans and discounts, and partly to the large-scale repatriation of foreign balances.   Cash assets of the four credit banks, which include balances with the Bank of France, the French Treasury, and other banks, increased from 2,827,000,000 francs at the end of 1929 to 12,599,000,000 francs at the end of 1931.   The decrease in this item in 1932 and 1933 is attributed to the purchase by the banks of large amounts of Treasury bills, issued to finance budget deficits.   The latter development was reflected in the increase in the bill portfolio at a time when commercial discounts were decreasing.   It is estimated that, at the end of 1932, approximately one-half of the total resources of the credit banks consisted of cash assets and government securities.

Although most of the larger banks were able to weather the depression without difficulty, the same was not true of all the French banks.   A number of institutions proved to be so illiquid that they were forced to close their doors, merge with stronger banks, or seek government assistance. It is estimated that the French Treasury advanced a total of 3,200,000,000 francs in 1931 and 1932 to aid embarrassed banks.

The most serious breach in the French banking system was the failure of the Banque Nationale de Crédit, which ranked fourth in size among the large credit banks.   A run on this institution developed in September 1931, and it was immediately announced that the government had created a guarantee fund of 2,000,000,000 francs for the protection of depositors.   Shortly thereafter the bank went into liquidation, and its assets and liabilities were taken over by a new organization—the Banque Nationale pour le Commerce et l'Industrie.

The outstanding merger among the *banques d'affaires* was the one between the Banque de l'Union Parisienne and the Crédit Mobilier Français, effected in May 1932.   The former institution, second in size among the *banques d'affaires,* had suffered a large loss of deposits, while the latter was in a highly liquid condition. The reorganized institution is continuing as the Banque de l'Union Parisienne.

Among the regional and local banks, failures were numerous. As early as November 1930 a regional bank operating in Boulogne was forced to close its doors, and the difficulties of this institution led to runs on other provincial banks which caused several more failures. In the early part of 1931 the important Banque d'Alsace et Lorraine had to be assisted by the government and was finally taken over by the Crédit Industriel et Commerciel. The repercussions of the Banque Nationale de Crédit failure caused the closing of a number of local banks in the fall of 1931, and there were scattered bank failures in the provinces through 1932 and the early part of 1933. The result of these developments was a considerable reduction of the number of banks in operation in France and a concentration of the country's banking resources in the hands of fewer institutions.

CHAPTER XIII

Paris—Operation of the Money Market and the Bourse

IN spite of the great financial power and prestige of France, the Paris money market has never developed the breadth and flexibility of the London and New York money markets. The failure to develop more elaborate open-market facilities at Paris is partly due to legal and fiscal obstacles, but the basic reason is that there has been little economic need for them. French commerce is financed chiefly by direct loans from the banks and by trade bills which are discounted with the banks. The banks in turn rely on the Bank of France for financial accommodation and, unlike the joint stock banks of London, freely utilize the central bank's facilities for rediscounting their bills. Owing to the system of term settlements, only a comparatively small amount of funds is required to finance stock exchange operations and there is little demand for funds for trading in commodities.

Thus the Paris money market is primarily a market for short-term bank credit rather than an open market. Loans and discounts are generally regarded as individual transactions subject to private negotiations between the bank and the borrower, and are usually surrounded with great secrecy. Different interest rates are applied to similar transactions on the basis of the individual relations of the borrower with the bank, and hence the published money market rates are largely nominal. In New York, on the other hand, the call money rate applies to all brokers, regardless of the magnitude of the loan or the amount of

business done by the brokerage house.   In London the
rate for day-to-day loans applies, with very few exceptions,
to all borrowers.   In other words, in New York and London
credit is regarded as a more or less standard commodity and
is dealt in at practically the same price for all borrowers
of the same standing, while in Paris credit terms are not
well standardized and personal connections are influential.

Divisions of the Money Market

The principal divisions of the short-term money market
at Paris are: (1) the private discount market; (2) the
day-to-day money market; (3) the market for the *location,*
or lending, of bonds; and (4) the *report* money market.
The acceptance market is ordinarily regarded as a part of
the private discount market, but because of its special importance from an international standpoint it is discussed
separately in a subsequent section.

Private discount market.   The private discount market,
or *marché hors banque,* corresponds roughly to the bill
markets in New York and London, except that it is concerned chiefly with the discount of trade bills, or trade acceptances, rather than with bankers' acceptances.   The
trade bills are the common type of negotiable instruments
used to finance commercial transactions in France.   They
arise out of the sale of goods, mature in from 30 days to
six months, and are usually drawn in amounts of 10,000
francs or more.   Bankers' acceptances constitute a comparatively small part of the bills negotiated in this market
and are discounted on approximately the same basis as
trade bills.   There is also a small amount of trading in
finance bills.

The supply of bills is provided by the larger business enterprises and, in the case of bankers' acceptances, by import-
ing and exporting firms.   The principal buyers are the large
credit banks, the *banques d'affaires,* the private banks, the
branches of foreign banks, the insurance companies, railroads, and the larger industrial and commercial concerns.

In addition, the Bank of France buys and sells bills for the account of its foreign correspondents. The larger banks appear only on the buying side of the market, since the sale of bills from their own portfolio is contrary to the French traditions of financial conservatism.

The private discount rate on prime trade bills is usually slightly lower than the discount rate of the Bank of France, but in periods of credit stringency it may temporarily rise above the central bank's rate. There is little difference with regard to rates between prime trade bills and bankers' acceptances. The rate on finance bills is usually about one-half of one per cent higher than that on trade bills.

The private discount market lacks a strong system of middlemen. A holder of bills may arrange to discount the bills directly with a bank or other buyer, or may utilize the services of a *courtier*. The *courtier* is simply a commission broker who acts as an intermediary in arranging for the sale of bills. He does not endorse bills or buy and sell them for his own account. He merely acts as agent for the seller in finding a buyer and receives a commission of 1/32 to 1/16 of one per cent of the face amount of the bills sold. There are some five or six important *courtiers* at Paris and a number of smaller firms. With the exception of the Compagnie Parisienne de Réscompte, there are no middlemen at Paris comparable to the discount houses of London or the bill dealers of New York. The Compagnie Parisienne de Réscompte differs from the *courtiers* in that it does buy bills for the investment of its own capital funds; but the amount of its bill portfolio is comparatively small.

In the absence of a strong institutional organization, the Paris discount market compares unfavorably with the London and New York markets in two respects. In the first place, there is sometimes difficulty in placing a large amount of bills of a single acceptor. For the sake of diversification buyers prefer to distribute their bill holdings among a number of different credit risks, and it is often necessary for a *courtier* to contact a number of his customers in order to dispose of a large offering. In London or New York a large block of bills is readily absorbed by the discount houses or dealers and marketed in the ordinary course of business.

The second defect of the Paris discount market is its lack of uniform rates of discount. Rates are determined by what individual buyers are willing to pay, and rates on bills bearing the same name sometimes vary by as much as ¼ of one per cent.

Day-to-day money market. There does not exist at Paris a market for short-term loans on collateral such as is found in other financial centers. The development of such a market has been seriously hampered by both legal and fiscal obstacles. The chief legal difficulty is found in Article 93 of the Commercial Code, which requires that in the event of default on a collateral loan the creditor may not sell the security pledged until eight days after giving to the debtor notice of his intention to do so. This provision greatly impairs the liquidity of short-term collateral loans. Contrary to the view sometimes expressed, the provisions of the Civil Code which circumscribe mortgage loans with much more onerous legal technicalities do not apply to ordinary financial transactions between business concerns. The fiscal obstacle is the tax on the income from loans, which is still very high.

Although these difficulties have prevented the development of an active collateral loan market at Paris, the French banks have evolved several devices which enable them to arrange for short-term financial accommodation among themselves. One of the most common methods is the exchange of checks (*échange de virements*) in much the same manner as the Federal Reserve member banks loan "Federal funds." Thus one bank may accommodate another by issuing to it a cashier's check. The borrowing bank deposits the check with the Bank of France, or some other bank, and thereby increases its cash reserves. At the same time the borrowing bank issues its cashier's check for the same amount plus interest, but dated a day or two in advance, to the lending bank. When the second check is paid, the loan is liquidated. This transaction is thus the equivalent of a short-term unsecured loan accomplished without the lender's becoming subject to the tax on interest.

In many cases, however, it is desirable that such loans be secured, and a second device, known as a *pension* transaction, provides the lender with collateral. A *pension* transaction is simply a sale of bonds or bills under a repurchase agreement. The bank needing funds sells a block of securities, usually short-term National Defense bonds, Treasury bills, or trade bills, to another bank, receiving the latter's check in payment. After the lapse of the agreed period, the seller repurchases the securities at the same price plus interest. This operation not only permits the lender to avoid the tax on interest, but also avoids the eight-day restriction on the sale of pledged collateral.

Market for location of bonds. The *location* of bonds is a third type of money market transaction closely connected with *pension* operations. It consists merely of the lending of bonds by one institution to another institution, which uses the bonds as collateral for a loan from a third institution. Thus it resembles somewhat the American practice of lending securities to cover short sales. The lender of bonds obtains no security but is compensated for the use of the securities.

The large Paris banks consider it inconsistent with their prestige to engage in these various operations to obtain short-term financial accommodation, but often act as lenders in the short-term money market. The principal borrowers are the smaller French banks and the branches of foreign banks. *Pension* transactions were carried out on a comparatively large scale a few years ago, when the demand for credit was expanding and when there was outstanding a large volume of short-term National Defense bonds, which were commonly used for this purpose. However, with the contraction of credit since 1930 and the refunding of the short-term National Defense bonds into issues maturing in two years or more, there has been a marked decline in this type of lending operation.

Report money market. Speculative operations on the Paris stock exchange are financed chiefly through "report" loans. A report loan is similar to a *pension* transaction in that it is essentially a sale of securities under a repurchase agreement. By this arrangement a holder of a contract for the purchase of securities can carry over his position from one settlement period to another by accepting delivery of the securities and selling them under an agreement to repurchase at the next settlement date at the same price plus interest for the period.

On the *parquet,* the official brokers (*agents de change*) carry out the financing of the stock exchange transactions. The *agents de change* receive money offers directly from private individuals and firms, and then, in accordance with the demand for funds and the supply of money offers received, the brokers fix the carry-over rate, which is in force for the next two weeks. Since, however, at times the demand for funds is larger than the supply, the *agents de change* have to apply to the banks for the rest of the amount needed. For such marginal amounts as the brokers obtain from the banks they pay a higher rate of interest, and this rate then determines the carry-over rate for the next two weeks. This fact is primarily responsible for the wide fluctuations in the carry-over rate on the Paris market. Since the carry-over rate is determined by the rate of interest charged by the banks for the marginal demand for credit, this rate is not fully indicative of the actual situation of the money market.

The financing of security transactions on the *coulisse* is carried out directly by the banks, which fix the rate according to their own decisions. Since the carry-over rate on the *coulisse* is for one month and thereby ties up the funds of the lenders for a longer period than loans on the *parquet,* and since the *coulisse* stocks are of a more speculative character, the carry-over rate in this market is substantially higher than that of the *parquet*.

The Acceptance Market

Although the use of the bankers' acceptance in the financing of international trade was widely developed during the nineteenth century, the French banking system has been slow to avail itself of this type of instrument. It is estimated that the acceptance liabilities of French financial institutions in 1913 were only about 1,200,000,000 francs, or $240,000,000, of which approximately one-half represented acceptances created by the six large credit banks. These acceptances were drawn almost entirely to finance French trade; only a very small amount of acceptance credit was created to finance the trade of other countries.

With the outbreak of the war and the abandonment of specie payments, currency fluctuations made it impracticable to use the franc bill even in financing the foreign trade of France, and the volume of acceptances declined rapidly. By the end of 1918 the total amount of acceptance credit created by the six large French banks had declined to less than 100,000,000 francs, and the use of these credits was restricted to internal transactions. During the post-war period of currency instability the volume of acceptances stated in terms of francs gradually increased as the French currency depreciated, but in terms of gold standard currencies there was little change.

Conditions after currency stabilization. With the stabilization of the currency in 1928, however, conditions affecting the acceptance market were radically altered. The "limping" standard, which had constituted such a serious obstacle to the development of Paris as an international money market before the war, was eliminated by the adoption of an unqualified gold bullion standard. Furthermore, with the rapid increase in the gold and foreign exchange reserves of the Bank of France, the franc became one of the most stable currencies in the world.

Again, the rehabilitation of the public finances, the return of economic prosperity, and the repatriation of French funds from abroad all contributed to bringing about lower and more stable interest rates than those prevailing in other centers, notably London. Even after the stabilization of the pound sterling in 1925, interest rates in London remained comparatively high, and in this respect Paris enjoyed a substantial advantage.

The French banking system was, finally, in an excellent position to develop the international acceptance business. Most institutions had come through the period of financial chaos in good condition and with adequate capital resources to support a volume of acceptance credit at least as large, in terms of the stabilized franc, as before the war. The acceptance capacity of the French banks in 1928 may be conservatively estimated at 6,000,000,000 francs, and with the increase in capital resources during the next few years this figure rose, by 1930, to possibly 10,000,000,000 francs.

The foreign banking connections of France, furthermore, were even more extensive at the time the franc was stabilized than before the war. As previously indicated, the large credit banks maintain numerous agencies in the French colonies and protectorates as well as offices in foreign countries, while several have foreign affiliates. On the other hand, a number of foreign banks, particularly British and American institutions, operate branches or agencies at Paris. All these foreign banking connections afforded excellent opportunities for the financing of international trade.

Movement to develop the acceptance market. The favorable conditions for the development of an international money market at Paris after the stabilization of the franc were immediately recognized in French financial circles. It was believed that this development could best be accomplished by the expansion of the acceptance market, and to this end a movement was soon inaugurated which assumed the proportions of a national policy. The leadership was assumed by the Bank of France, which secured the coöperation not only of the other financial institutions but also of the government. The attitude of the Bank toward the development of the Paris money market is set forth in its annual report for 1929 as follows:

> A very large metallic reserve safeguarded by a large supply of foreign bills assures the French market of exceptionally favorable credit conditions and opens before it the prospect of security and growth. This favorable situation . . . should be utilized henceforth in the interests of the country itself and of the world economy. This situation affords the Paris market an excellent opportunity, and imposes upon it the obligation to participate more actively in the distribution of international credit in collaboration with the other great world markets.

The motives which inspired this program for expanding the Paris money market are to be found in the changed financial relationship of France to the rest of the world after the stabilization of the currency. During the period of currency depreciation the flight of capital from France resulted in the accumulation of a huge amount of short-term funds abroad. For the most part this money was invested in short-term loans, bankers' acceptances, and other short-term credit instruments outstanding in the principal foreign financial centers, particularly London and New York. In effect, the French simply placed their capital at the disposal of the foreign markets with little direct supervision or control over the particular transactions it was used to finance. This policy was of course at variance with the traditional French policy of exercising close supervision over all lending operations. But the development of the international acceptance business obviously offered a means of correcting the situation. It would mean that acceptance credits would be created by French financial institutions with full control over their utilization, while the acceptances so drawn would constitute a first-class medium of investment for short-term funds in the domestic market and obviate the necessity of seeking such investments in foreign financial centers. A further consideration, no doubt, was that the profit derived from the acceptance business would accrue to French financial institutions rather than to foreign money markets operating, to a considerable extent, with French funds.

A second motive was the desire to correct the maladjustment in the French balance of international payments. The maladjustment consisted of an excess of French claims on foreign countries over the claims of foreign countries on France—often a source of some embarrassment in that it caused a steady flow of gold to France. Even in 1929 there was bitter criticism in certain foreign financial circles of the rapid increase in the gold stocks of the Bank of France, and the French were accused of contributing to a further maldistribution of the world's monetary gold supply. In the absence of large-scale long-term foreign lending, short-term lending through the granting of acceptance credits appeared the logical alternative.

And, finally, considerations of national pride and prestige undoubtedly were a factor in the program to make Paris a great international financial center. Since the war France has been politically the most important country on the Continent of Europe. It was quite natural for the French to feel that their strong currency and banking system and their huge surplus of capital available for investment entitled their country to a more prominent place in the field of international finance.

Measures to develop the Paris money market. As the leader of the movement the Bank of France, in order to facilitate the development of the international acceptance business, immediately adopted such technical measures as lay within its power as a central bank. By virtue of the convention of June 23, 1928, it had already obtained authority to deal in bankers' acceptances for the account of its foreign correspondents, which dealings gave it a direct contact with the market; but in the absence of power to buy and sell acceptances for its own account, it was unable to play such a dominant rôle in fostering the acceptance market as the Federal Reserve banks have done in this country. Consequently the Bank of France concentrated its attention on steps to improve the financial basis for an acceptance market.

It was generally recognized that one of the basic defects of the Paris money market was its inflexibility. In the absence of an active call money or day-to-day money market, the banks could meet a sudden increase in the demand for credit only by rediscounting bills with the Bank of France or by resorting to the exchange of checks or to *pension* transactions. However, the regulations of the Bank of France required that bills for discount be submitted before noon each day for approval by the discount committee, which meets early in the afternoon. It was often difficult for the banks, particularly those with extensive systems of branches throughout the country, accurately to estimate in the morning the demands which would be made on them later in the day. Consequently, when there were sharp fluctuations in the demand for funds, such as those caused by the maturity of a large volume of commercial bills or by end-of-month settlements, temporary credit stringency often developed which affected interest rates and even foreign exchange rates.

In order to alleviate this situation the Bank of France modified its discount regulations toward the end of October 1929: it permitted the principal banking houses to submit bills for discount up to three o'clock in the afternoon. This provision enabled the banks to adjust their cash positions more readily, to avoid burdensome emergency loans, and to use their available funds more rationally. A second measure along the same lines was adopted on December 16, 1929, when the Bank of France extended to certain Paris institutions the privilege of discounting with it bankers' acceptances of commercial origin and repurchasing them after an interval of several days before their maturity. The usual period for such discounts under repurchase agreements is seven days, with the privilege of extension for an additional five days. The rate on these discounts is one-half of one per cent above the regular discount rate.

The management of the Bank of France said, in the Bank's annual report for 1929,

> We think that the combined effect of these two measures will help not only to facilitate and regulate the domestic movements of capital, but also to further the creation and growth in France of a large international acceptance market and thus to prepare Paris for the more extended rôle which henceforth it can and should assume.

The coöperation of the French Government with the program for the development of the Paris money market took tangible form in April 1930 in the reduction of taxation on acceptances. Prior to that time the tax on bills accepted or payable in France, regardless of the nationality of the parties thereto, was 0.15 per cent of the face amount. Since acceptances are most commonly drawn for a period of three months, this tax was equivalent to one of 0.60 per cent per annum. The serious handicap which this law imposed on the acceptance business in France is shown by the fact that the tax on acceptances in England, Holland, and Switzerland is only 0.20 per cent. The handicap was removed by the budget law of April 17, 1930, which reduced the tax on acceptances drawn by foreigners and payable in France, as well as on foreign bills circulating in France, to 50 centimes per 2,000 francs. This tax is equivalent to 0.025 per cent of the face amount, or to 0.10 per cent per annum for three-month bills. The rate of taxation on domestic acceptances was not changed. As a result of this legislation the acceptance business in France was given a distinct advantage, from the standpoint of taxation, over its competitors in London, Amsterdam, and Switzerland.

The third major point in the program was the development of specialized institutions to create and deal in acceptances. In this the large credit and investment banks, with the sponsorship of the Bank of France, played the leading part. There were already in existence several banks engaged chiefly in foreign trade financing, notably the Banque Nationale Française du Commerce Extérieur and the Banque Française et Italienne. In 1929 a group of banking houses coöperated to establish the Compagnie Parisienne de Réscompte with a capital of 12,000,000 francs, for the purpose of broadening the discount market. However, the most important step in the direction of creating specialized facilities for the acceptance business was the organization, in December 1929, of the Banque Française d'Acceptation. Its capital of 100,000,000 francs, of which one-fourth has been paid in, was subscribed by a consortium of banks which included four large credit banks, three *banques d'affaires,* one colonial bank, and two Belgian banks. The primary purpose of this institution is to create acceptances to finance trade between France and other countries; but in addition it was intended to exercise an important influence in fostering and promoting the general expansion of the use of acceptance credits in France. Its close connection with the leading French banks placed it in a particularly favorable position to do this task. Representatives of these banks constitute the Board of Directors of the acceptance bank, and the weekly meetings of the Board afford an opportunity for these men to exchange views and collaborate in the development of the acceptance business.

The acceptance market since 1928. During the years 1928 and 1929 the volume of acceptance credit granted by the French banks increased rapidly, and probably reached a peak by the early part of 1930. The acceptance liabilities of the six large credit banks rose from 442,000,000 francs at the end of 1927 to 1,742,000,000 francs at the end of 1929. At the same time the three large investment banks increased their acceptance liabilities from only 17,000,000 francs to 217,000,000 francs. If it may be assumed that the acceptances created by the large credit banks represented about one-half of the total acceptance liabilities of all the French banks, as was the case before the war, the total amount of acceptance credit outstanding in France at the end of 1929 may be estimated at approximately 3,500,000,000 francs.

Although sharp gains were made in these years, they fell far short of making up for the contraction caused by the war and post-war period of currency instability. In terms of pre-war gold francs, the total amount of acceptance credit outstanding at the end of 1929 amounted to only about 700,000,000 gold francs, as compared with 1,200,000,-000 gold francs in 1913. Nor did the total amount of acceptances created in France assume anything like the same proportions as the amount outstanding in England and the United States. The total in France at the end of 1929 was equivalent to about $137,000,000, as compared with $1,732,000,000 outstanding in the United States on the same date.

The expansion of acceptance credit which took place in France during 1928 and 1929 was due only to a very small extent, if at all, to the concerted movement to develop the Paris money market, since the principal measures involved in this program were not adopted until the latter part of 1929 and the early part of 1930. It was rather the result of the stabilization of the currency and the general increase in prices and in business activity. Although the steps taken by the Bank of France, the French Government, and the private financial institutions undoubtedly improved the facilities for creating and dealing in bankers' acceptances at Paris, the entire program was doomed to failure. Even as it was being launched, the first evidences of the greatest world economic depression in recent history were appearing, and in the next few years the entire international currency and credit structure so laboriously built up after the war was virtually wrecked in the currents of deflation and financial panic.

By the end of 1930 there was already some decline in the volume of acceptance credit in France. During the year there was a reduction, from 1,742,000,000 francs to 1,242,-000,000, in the acceptance liabilities of the six credit banks. If this is taken as representative of the trend for the other credit banks, a total decline of perhaps 900,000,000 francs is indicated. The decline was partially offset by the activity of the new Banque Française d'Acceptation, which reported acceptance liabilities of 565,000,000 francs at the end of 1930, after only a year of operation. But during the next three years the contraction was rapid. At the end of 1933 the outstanding acceptances of the six large credit banks amounted to only 325,000,000 francs, as compared with 442,000,000 in 1927, before the stabilization of the franc. The acceptance business of the investment banks was more stable, declining from 217,000,000 francs at the end of 1930 to 92,000,000 at the end of 1932, and rising at the close of 1933 to 147,000,000.[1] The high hopes entertained for the Banque Française d'Acceptation, however, were gradually dispelled as its acceptance liabilities dwindled steadily to only 101,000,000 francs (at the end of 1933).

TABLE 41

ACCEPTANCES OUTSTANDING
(In millions of francs)

End of	Six Credit Banks	Three Investment Banks	Banque Française d'Acceptation
1927	442	17	. . .
1928	1,223	125	. . .
1929	1,742	217	. . .
1930	1,242	217	565
1931	718	207	323
1932	357	92	178
1933	325	147	101

[1] This increase may be due merely to a change in the financial statement of the Banque de Paris et des Pays-Bas. Formerly this bank did not report acceptance liabilities as a separate item, although they may have been included with some other item. At the end of 1933 it reported acceptance liabilities of 87,000,000 francs.

Table 41 is indicative of the development of acceptance credit in France from the end of 1927 to the end of 1933.

Outlook for the Paris money market. The disintegration of the international financial structure during the last few years has necessarily put an end to French ambitions to expand the Paris money market, and there appears to be little likelihood that the project will be revived in the near future. Although the prestige of the French franc is now even greater than before, as a result of the depreciation of the pound sterling, the dollar, and other leading currencies, and although interest rates in France continue to compare favorably with those prevailing in other countries, the principal considerations which motivated the efforts to develop the international acceptance business are no longer of great importance. The French balances abroad have been almost completely repatriated and, consequently, the problem of efficiently employing them has disappeared. Furthermore, the unfavorable development of the French balance of payments has virtually eliminated the problem of finding an outlet for the surplus capital of the country. Finally, in the present chaotic state of the world's finances, there is little prestige attached to eminence in international finance.

Given a return to more normal conditions in the next few years, the volume of acceptances outstanding in France will undoubtedly increase along with expansion in other financial centers. However, there is little likelihood that Paris will rival London as an international money market in the next decade, for the reason that the country has neither an adequate financial system nor an adequate economic basis to support a large volume of international credit operations.

The capacity of the French banking system to create acceptances is limited by its comparatively small capital resources. At the end of 1933 the total capital and reserves of the six large credit banks totaled 3,372,000,000 francs, equivalent to £27,150,000 at par of exchange or to £40,500,000 at the then current exchange rate, compared with total capital funds of £109,965,000 reported by the "Big Five" banks of London. With the exception of the Banque Française d'Acceptation, Paris does not have the specialized institutions such as exist in other international financial centers.

A second weakness is the narrowness and inflexibility of the Paris money market, which makes it incapable of handling efficiently a large amount of bills. The chief defect is the lack of well-developed market middlemen such as the discount houses of London or the bill dealers of New York, who "make the market" by standing ready to accept all offers and meet all bids at their quoted rates. However, a requisite for the operation of such institutions is the existence of a collateral loan market through which they can finance the carrying of their bill portfolios. Legislation reducing the taxation on interest derived from short-term loans, and eliminating the prohibition on sale of pledged collateral in event of default until eight days after notice to the debtor, must be enacted before a day-to-day loan market can be developed in France.

Much more important than these weaknesses, which are susceptible to remedial measures, is the fact that the economic structure of France does not provide an adequate basis for a great international financial center. A money market is not an end in itself, but an auxiliary institution serving to finance trade and commerce. The strength of the London market is based not merely on the organization of the money market as such, or on its ability to absorb any amount of both short-term credit instruments and funds without disturbance, but on the fact that London is a great center of international trade and a world market for many staple commodities. If one further considers that England is a great creditor nation, receiving from debtor nations large sums for the payment of debt service, it is obvious that London's financial strength is not based merely on organization.

Paris does not enjoy all these advantages. International transactions in commodities at Paris are not important.

Unlike the British "merchant bankers" of the nineteenth century, who developed the acceptance business in response to a real demand for assistance in financing international trade, the French bankers attempted to develop an acceptance business merely to find employment for surplus funds. While there is undoubtedly considerable room for French participation in the financing of the world's commerce, there is little possibility, so long as international trade continues to move through its present channels, that Paris will threaten the supremacy of London.

The Paris Bourse

The Paris Bourse is the third largest stock exchange in the world. Listed on its various markets are some 3,500 different stocks and bonds. Stock exchanges exist in other cities of France such as Lyons, Bordeaux, Toulouse, and Nantes, but the volume of trading on these exchanges is comparatively small, and by far the larger number of French transactions in securities take place at Paris.

The Paris Bourse comprises three markets, closely related but functioning separately. These are (1) the official market, or *parquet*, which occupies the interior of the Bourse building; (2) the curb market, or *coulisse*, or *marché in banque;* and (3) the free market, or *marché libre*, or *marché hors côte*, which deals in securities not quoted on the *parquet* or *coulisse*.

The official market (parquet). The term "official market" is literally applicable to this market, which is the most important of the three. It is the only stock exchange in the world where the brokers are appointed by the government and given a legal monopoly of trading in a selected list of securities. The monopoly is a result of an amendment to the budget law of 1898 requiring that transactions in officially quoted securities, to be legally valid, must be supported by a bill of sale issued by an official stockbroker.

Brokers. The official stockbrokers, limited in number to seventy, are appointed by the President of France and have the status of public officials. This group comprises the Association of Official Stockbrokers of Paris (Compagnie des Agents de Change de Paris), which through its administrative body, the Syndical Chamber, governs the operations of the official market and publishes the official stock quotations. The Association of Official Stockbrokers is closely supervised by the French Government. A unique feature of this organization is that all of the members are jointly and severally responsible for the liabilities of each individual member. This feature, together with the monopoly privilege and the limited membership, has given the Association a high degree of solidarity and its members great financial and social prestige.

The requirements for membership are very strict, and the members are rigidly limited in their activities. Official stockbrokers must be French citizens at least twenty-five years of age, must have served a period of probation, and must have taken oath as public officials. They must put up a bond (*cautionnement*) of 250,000 francs with the government. With the permission of the Syndical Chamber and the Minister of Finance, stockbrokers may have silent partners who participate in all profits and who are subject to losses up to the amount of their capital investment. The stockbroker himself, however, must always own personally at least one fourth of the amount representing the price of his membership and of his bond. Together with his associates, the stockbroker forms a company bearing his name and subject to special regulations as to publicity and as to the resignation of partners. He has, however, the right of passing on his office to a successor under certain conditions.

Official stockbrokers are not permitted to engage in any business other than that of acting as intermediaries of investors on the official market. They cannot deal personally in securities or have any capital invested in outside business enterprises. They cannot advise investors to buy or to sell, nor can they recommend special securities; and they may not establish branch offices. Their action is limited solely to that of intermediaries in security transactions, and their compensation is fixed by regulations. The official pit is open only to the seventy members, or their designated deputies, and to a limited number of assistants.

Listing of securities. Securities are admitted to listing on the official market only after examination and approval by the Syndical Chamber. An exception is made, however, in the case of French state funds, which are automatically listed. The principal requirements for the listing of stocks are that a transfer agent and, in certain cases, an office must be maintained at Paris; that the purpose of the issue must be a proper economic one; and that the price of issue together with a list of subscribers be officially furnished to the Syndical Chamber.

As an emergency war-time measure a law was enacted in 1916 prohibiting the introduction of all foreign and private domestic issues on the French stock exchanges except with the permission of the Minister of Finance. This law was repealed in 1920 in so far as it applied to domestic issues but remained effective as to foreign issues. Permission has been given for the listing of a few foreign issues, but bankers and dealers are not permitted to engage in the distribution of such securities.

At present there are approximately 2,500 securities listed on the official market, as compared with only five in 1815. The listed securities are divided into two general classes: those traded in for cash and those traded in for future account. While less than a hundred securities are listed for future trading, operations of this type are the more important.

The curb market. Although the official market has a legal monopoly of trading in officially listed securities, there are no restrictions on trading in securities not listed on the *parquet.* Consequently there has developed an active market for such securities outside the official market. This market, corresponding to the American curb market and known colloquially as the *coulisse,* operates on the veranda and steps of the Palais de la Bourse.

The curb syndicates. For many years the curb market was unorganized, but in 1898 two curb syndicates were formed which adopted common rules and maintained professional discipline among the brokers belonging to them. The two syndicates corresponded to the cash market and the term market and were known as the Syndicate of Cash Bankers (Le Syndicate des Banquiers en Valeurs au Comptant) and the Syndicate of Credit Bankers (Le Syndicate des Banquiers in Valeurs à Terme). These syndicates have since been merged into one organization.

The organization of the curb syndicate is similar to that of the Association of Official Stockbrokers. A syndical chamber is elected which supervises the operations of its members and publishes the quotation sheets. However, the members do not have the joint liability for individual obligations, as in the case of the official stockbrokers; the requirements for membership are not so rigid, and members are not so closely restricted in the conduct of their business. Admission of new members is in the hands of the members themselves; the Government has no voice in the matter. Prospective members are required to have a certain minimum capital. In recent years the organization has taken steps to make its market more attractive by a more judicious selection of newcomers and by requesting their present members to increase their capital.

The curb brokers have much greater latitude in carrying on their stock exchange operations than their colleagues of the official market. While official brokers may act only as intermediaries between customers, the curb brokers may trade on their own account and may act as counter-party to a customer in executing an order. Curb brokers have the right to give information and advice to their customers but are bound by professional secrecy with respect to the business of customers. The commission rates charged clients are established by the syndicate and must be rigidly adhered to.

Listing. The admission of securities to trading on the curb market is dependent upon the decision of the syndicate organization. In general, the securities dealt in on the curb market include those which the Syndical Chamber of the official market has not deemed advisable to admit and those which have not fulfilled the prescribed conditions for listing on the official market. As on the official market, the securities listed on the curb are divided into those traded in for cash and those eligible for future trading.

The listing of foreign securities is subject to the approval of the Minister of Finance. Prior to the war the French Government did not oppose the listing on the curb market of foreign securities which it did not permit to be listed on the official market, and a substantial volume of trading in such issues developed. During and since the war, governmental restriction on the listing of foreign issues has considerably reduced trading in these securities.

The free market. The free, or *hors-côte* market is, in general, the market where securities are traded in during the period between their issuance and their listing on either the official or the curb market. It is also the market for dealing in stocks of small companies which are inactive and which cannot be quoted in either of the other two markets. Although the free market is largely in the hands of the curb brokers, it has enough distinct characteristics to warrant separate consideration.

Before the war, transactions in the free market were very few, but with the cessation of war conditions and with disturbances in the regular markets from 1919 to 1926, the volume of trading in the free market increased considerably. This market, however, was only very loosely organized. It operated at unusual hours and places, the execution of orders was not certain, and quotations lacked authenticity. In addition to the curb brokers who operated in the free market, there were many entirely uncontrolled operators, whose poor reputation threatened to prejudice the standing of the curb brokers.

The curb brokers, therefore, decided to organize a special group among themselves for trading in unlisted securities. The group, while not excluding outside operators, would give some organization to the free market and afford protection for the curb brokers and their clients. The first attempt at organization failed as a result of financial scandals involving stocks traded in on the free market. Finally, in January 1929, the Syndicate of Credit Bankers made an agreement with the Minister of Finance whereby certain regulations were established for trading in the free market by members of the Syndicate.

In general this agreement imposes on the members of the Syndicate of Credit Bankers the same regulations for trading in stocks in the free market as the regulations that apply to trading on the curb market. In addition, a special protective measure was adopted. Before an unlisted security is eligible for trading between members of the Syndicate, a portfolio (*dossier*) must be filed with the Syndical Chamber containing the statutes of the issuing company, the list of directors, the last balance sheet published, and clippings from the Bulletin of Compulsory Legal Announcements. A similar portfolio must be filed with the police commissioner at the stock exchange. This requirement may be waived by the Syndical Chamber in case of companies organized for more than two years, but it is strictly obligatory for companies in existence less than two years.

At the time this agreement went into effect, special space was allotted to the free market in the Bourse building and facilities were provided for recording transactions and posting quotations. The quotations thus posted are published once a week in a supplement to the daily quotation bulletin of the Syndicate of Credit Bankers. A survey of securities quoted and negotiated in the free market, compiled from *L'Information Financière* of March 13, 1930, shows that 132 securities are quoted in the bulletin of the curb brokers and that 79 securities were traded in by others than curb brokers. The companies represented are for the most part mining, automobile, construction, colonial, and real-estate companies.

Remisiers. An important part of the mechanism of the Paris Bourse is the group of middlemen known as *remisiers,* who act as intermediaries between brokers and individuals transacting business on the stock exchange. Their primary function is to collect orders and transmit them to brokers for execution. For this service they receive from the brokers a percentage of the broker's commission, called a *remise,* or rebate; hence the name *remisier.*

This type of middleman is found at all important stock exchanges, but the *remisiers* have flourished particularly at Paris, because of the rule prohibiting official stockbrokers from giving information or advice to their customers. The furnishing of information and advice is the principal means by which the *remisier* builds up his clientele. Some *remisiers* have established such reputations for financial sagacity that their clients maintain discretionary accounts with them, in which cases the *remisier* usually receives a share of the profit that he realizes in handling the account.

There are various grades of *remisiers,* ranging from the individual who brings in occasional small orders to those who have large suites of offices and who, by reason of their clientele and ability, stand high in the favor of the brokers. The curb brokers themselves have long acted as *remisiers* for the official brokers and bring them a large volume of business. Recently the large banks, in collecting thousands of orders from all over France and forwarding them to the brokers, have come to overshadow all others.

Settlements. The settlement of transactions on the Paris stock exchange is complicated by the use of future contracts. Cash transactions are settled, as in New York, simply by delivery of securities and payment of cash, but future contracts require a special system of settlement. All future contracts in both curb and official markets must be settled during the regular settlement periods and in accordance with the procedure established by the governing bodies of the two markets. In the official market there are two settlement periods each month, one beginning the fifteenth of the month and lasting four days and the other beginning at the end of the month and continuing for five days. There is only one settlement period per month on the curb market; it begins at the end of the month and lasts five days.

The procedure of settlement is similar in both markets. On the first day of the settlement period the Syndical Chamber fixes a price, called the compensation price, for each security, and it is at this price that all contracts must be settled. The compensation prices are usually based on the quotations for cash transactions on the first day of the period, but under special circumstances the prices may be fixed arbitrarily. Upon the announcement of the compensation prices, buyers or sellers must arrange with their brokers to liquidate their contracts or carry them over until the next settlement day. The second and third days— except at the mid-monthly settlement on the official market, when only the second day is required for this work—are devoted to bookkeeping and office work. On the fourth day customers who owe money or securities to brokers must settle their accounts; if they fail to do so their accounts may be liquidated by the brokers without further notice. The last day of the period is given over to the exchange of cash and securities among the brokers themselves. Both markets provide certain facilities for the clearing of settlements between brokers.

Carry-overs. The advent of the settlement period, however, does not mean that a customer must liquidate his commitments and take his profit or loss. If he wishes to maintain his position until the next settlement period, he may do so by the *operation du report,* or carry-over operation. This operation may best be made clear by an example:

A buyer has entered into a future contract for the purchase of securities. At the settlement date he has a profit on the transaction, but thinks that the price will continue to go up. So he accepts delivery of the securities at settlement and immediately sells them under an agreement to buy them back at the next settlement date at a slightly higher price. This transaction is really a loan against the securities up to their full market value, and the difference between the selling price and the repurchase price is the interest charged by the lender of the funds. The speculator, by this operation, has resumed his "bull" position; if the market price is higher at the next settlement period he will profit by obtaining delivery of the securities at the repurchase price.

The "bear" operator may maintain his position similarly by acting as the lender of funds or, in other words, as counter-party to the "bull" under the repurchase transaction. Thus, at the settlement date the "bear," who is always the seller on a future contract, makes delivery of the securities and receives cash in exchange. He immediately takes the cash and buys the same securities, under an agreement to resell them at the next settlement date at a slightly higher price. At the same time he sells for cash the securities he receives. Consequently, if the price goes down, as he anticipates, he will profit by obtaining the securities at the lower market price and delivering them under the repurchase agreement at the repurchase price.

CHAPTER XIV

Berlin—The Reichsbank and the Public Credit Institutions

Pre-war period. The Berlin money market became an important international money center shortly after the Franco-Prussian War, and its history therefore embraces a period of approximately sixty years. The Reichsbank was established in 1875, and about ten years later Berlin assumed an influential position as an international money market. One of the distinguishing characteristics of the Berlin and of the continental European banks in general, was the extent of their active participation in the development of industrial establishments which carried on their operations, to a large degree, with the aid and under the direction of the banks. The German banks were more closely connected with industry than the British, French, or American credit banks, but they were less involved in industrial enterprises than those of Austria and Hungary.

The close alliance of the German banks with industrial enterprises had an important influence on the operations of the banks, for they not only engaged in financing short-term transactions but also acted as investment bankers, and in this capacity they extended long-term loans to industrial establishments and issued securities of corporations. In order to maintain still closer contact with the individual enterprises, the German banking institutions often retained a portion of the capital stock of these enterprises which they carried on their books as "participations."

With the growth of the German national economy and with the accumulation of wealth, the German banks became important instruments in the financing of foreign governments as well as industrial enterprises and public utilities abroad. The German banks were therefore responsible to a considerable extent for the expansion of German investments abroad which, at the outbreak of the war, amounted to about five billion dollars. While there was a great demand for long-term capital within Germany, both the German Government and the large banks recognized that German political and economic influence could not penetrate to the far corners of the earth unless necessary financial aid was extended.

In spite of the rapid accumulation of wealth in Germany, the German banks operated to a considerable extent with the aid of foreign short-term credits. These funds were attracted to Germany by the higher rates that usually prevailed in Germany. Thus, during the pre-war period, Germany was a lender of long-term capital and a borrower of short-term funds. While exact figures as to the amount of short-term credits used by the German banks are not available, the total was estimated shortly before the war at about one billion marks.

The large German banks opened branches in Brussels, Paris, and London, and also established branches and overseas banks in other foreign countries, particularly in South America. The concentration of banking resources and the growth of certain individual banks were also characteristic of the pre-war period. In 1872 there were about 130 deposit banks in Germany, but by 1914 most of the liquid capital and credit resources of the country were in the hands of about a dozen banks. Four of these—the Deutsche Bank, the Disconto-Gesellschaft, the Dresdner Bank, and the Darmstaedter Bank (Bank fuer Handel und Industrie) (the so-called "D" banks) greatly surpassed all the others both in resources and volume of business.

War period and inflation up to November 1923. The outbreak of the war in 1914 had a disastrous effect on German banking. The foreign branches and agencies located in the allied countries were closed and, in many instances, their assets were confiscated. Germany was cut off from the western world after the United States entered the war, and the only international money markets open to her were those of Amsterdam, Zurich, and of the Scandinavian countries. Since Germany was not in a position to borrow abroad, and since she was called upon also to finance all of her allies, the main function of the banks during this period was that of assisting the government in financing the war through the issuance of war loans.

The treaty of peace and the period of inflation which followed had a more disastrous effect upon the German banks than the war. Under the Treaty of Versailles the greater part of Germany's overseas investments were expropriated, and thereby substantial losses were sustained by the German banks. The depreciation of the currency reduced considerably the value of a large part of their liquid assets, and the only way open to the German banks to salvage the remaining portion of their own funds was through the purchase of real estate or through the exportation of capital.

Stabilization of the currency. In November 1923 the German mark was *de facto* stabilized. It was only after that event that the great impoverishment caused by the war and by currency inflation became apparent. At the end of September 1923 the total volume of Reichsbank notes in circulation amounted to 1,520,511,000,000,000,000,-000 marks, the gold value of which was only $361,900,000, as compared with a total circulation including gold of about 6,000,000,000 marks, or $1,430,000,000, before the war. Whereas the per capita currency circulation in terms of gold amounted to about $21 before the war, it amounted to only about $6 in 1923.

The effect of the war and the currency depreciation on the German banks may be seen from Table 42, which shows the principal balance sheet items of the German credit banks before the outbreak of the war and at the beginning of 1924, when the balance sheets were drawn up on a gold basis for the first time since 1914. The capital and sur-

TABLE 42

SOME BALANCE SHEET ITEMS OF PRIVATE
INCORPORATED BANKS*
(In millions of reichsmarks)

ASSETS		Dec. 31, 1913		Jan. 1, 1924
Checks and bills.....................		3,743.2		227.9
Due from banks and bankers........		965.1		784.3
Securities		1,320.8		275.0
Loans in current accounts...........		10,209.3		1,360.5
Long-term loans		12,237.5		145.2
Total assets		31,176.3		4,044.6
Index		100.0		13.0
LIABILITIES				
Capital		4,158.3		1,131.8
Surplus		986.3		286.0
Creditors:				
Deposits of German banks	620.3		163.2	
Other creditors	10,088.6	10,708.9	2,045.0	2,208.2
Acceptances		2,637.4		8.0
Number of banks included..........		399		500

* *Statistisches Jahrbuch fuer das Deutsche Reich, 1929*, pp. 316–319.

plus of these institutions was reduced to about 28 per cent, and liabilities to creditors (mainly time and demand deposits) to 21 per cent, of the respective amounts at the end of 1913, while the acceptance business had almost completely disappeared. Although these figures do not represent exactly the actual situation of the various institutions because of the conservative way in which the first gold balance sheets were drawn up, they nevertheless indicate the great shrinkage in resources caused by the war and its aftermath.

In the fall of 1924 the Dawes Plan was adopted and the currency was legally stabilized. The restoration of confidence in Germany, together with high rates of interest prevailing in the German money market, brought an inflow of large amounts of foreign short-term funds. From that time up to the middle of 1931 the Berlin money market was almost entirely under the influence of the movement of foreign short-term funds.

Germany's dependence on foreign funds. The transition of Germany from the status of a creditor to that of a debtor nation had a profound effect on its banking practices. The impoverishment of Germany caused by the war and inflation, the payment of reparations, the very slow process of accumulation of capital within the country, and the need for a large volume of capital for the reorganization of industries, are the principal causes for Germany's dependence on foreign capital. This dependence is evidenced by the fact that at the end of 1930 about 30 per cent of the total deposits of the six large Berlin banks originated abroad. Since a large part of the foreign short-term funds was subject to repayment at the demand of the depositor, the German banks were forced not only to increase their liquidity in order to meet withdrawals of such funds, but also to keep a substantial portion of their total liquid assets in foreign currencies. The necessity of attracting and retaining foreign capital is evidenced by the relatively high interest rates prevailing in Berlin as compared with other financial centers. (See Table 43.)

TABLE 43

COMPARISON OF MONEY RATES IN GERMANY AND ABROAD

Period	Monthly Average Rate 3-Month Funds Germany	Abroad*	Spread Between Germany and Abroad	Spread Between Germany and New York
1925	9.13	3.74	5.39	5.49
1926	6.58	3.90	2.68	2.65
1927	6.67	3.49	3.18	2.90
1928	7.55	3.83	3.72	3.08
1929	8.08	4.79	3.29	2.62
1930	5.49	2.60	2.89	2.46
1931 June	6.84	1.45	5.39	5.31

* Simple arithmetic average of rates in New York, London, Paris, Amsterdam, and Zurich.

With the establishment of rigid foreign exchange restrictions within Germany and with the conclusion of the standstill agreement toward the end of 1931, the movement of foreign funds no longer had an influence on the German money market. Interest rates in Berlin on the whole have moved closely with those of other financial centers although, owing to political and other uncertainties, a substantial discrepancy has existed at times.

The German banking system. A classification of German banks according to their functions is impossible, because of the variety of activities which they carry on. A more feasible classification is that of public and private institutions. The former are classified as such either because they are government-owned or because their operations are more or less of a public character, and because they are very closely regulated and supervised by law. In many instances the government of the Reich or those of political subdivisions are represented in the management of the banks and exercise a considerable influence on their policy. The private banks consist of the incorporated credit banks and the private bankers. Since the banking crisis of 1931, however, most incorporated private credit banks have come under the control of the government through direct or indirect stock purchases by the latter.

A detailed classification of the German banks on this basis follows:

I. Public credit institutions:
    1. Reichsbank.
    2. Gold Discount Bank.
    3. Other banks of issue.
    4. State banks.
    5. Reichs-Kredit-Gesellschaft.
    6. Provincial and communal banks.
    7. Savings banks.
    8. Central clearing institutions.
    9. Public mortgage banks.

II. Private credit or commercial banks:
    1. Incorporated credit banks.
    2. Private banks.

The Reichsbank

The Reichsbank is the heart of the German banking and credit system. It is the central bank of the country, the custodian of the gold reserve, and the ultimate source of credit. The serious lack of capital in Germany, combined with the country's dependence on foreign short-term credits, has greatly enhanced the importance of the Reichsbank. Not only is it called upon for a greater amount of credit than before the war, but it also plays a much more important rôle in the foreign exchange market than it ever did before the war.

The history of the Reichsbank can be traced back to 1765, when Frederick the Great founded the Koenigliche Bank in Berlin as a state institution. In 1846 it was transformed into the Preussische Bank, which in turn was changed by the law of March 14, 1875, into the Reichsbank. The statutes of the Reichsbank have been amended from time to time, but the most drastic change was made in 1924, when the Bank was completely reorganized in accordance with stipulations contained in the Dawes Plan. The statutes were further modified when the Young Plan was placed in operation in 1930 and, again, in October 1933.

Up to 1875 the note-issue privilege was enjoyed by 33 private banks, which were allowed to retain this privilege in a greatly restricted form after the organization of the Reichsbank in 1875. The Reichsbank, on the other hand, was endowed with a fundamentally elastic system of note issue. The smaller banks of issue gradually relinquished their note-issue privileges, and in 1906 only four of the original 33 retained the privilege—namely, the Bayerische Notenbank, the Wuerttembergische Notenbank, the Saechsische Bank, and the Badische Bank. The aggregate amount of their notes outstanding is relatively unimportant and is fixed by the law of August 30, 1924, at a maximum of 194 million reichsmarks. These notes are not legal tender and may not be made such by a law of any state.

A decree of December 18, 1933, terminated the note-issue privilege of these banks as of December 31, 1935.

In accordance with recommendations of the Dawes Plan, the present Reichsbank was organized under the law which went into effect October 11, 1924, for the purpose of taking over the old Reichsbank. The Reichsbank is a public institution of a peculiar legal status. It is owned by private stockholders but is under the control of the Reich. By virtue of the 1924 Bank Law, the management of the bank was in the hands of a managing board and of a general council. Under this law the managing board was composed of 21 members appointed by the president of the Bank, subject to approval by the general council. The general council consisted of fourteen members, seven of whom were German citizens and seven foreigners. The general council, by a majority of nine members—six of whom were required to be Germans—elected the president of the Bank, subject to the approval of the President of the Republic. The general council also elected one of its foreign members to serve as currency commissioner.

The Banking Law of October 11, 1924, was considerably modified by amendments, which became effective on May 17, 1930, and December 1, 1930. These amendments provided for the removal of the foreign control of the Reichsbank and the reduction of the membership of the general council from fourteen to ten, all of whom must be Germans. Similarly, the commissioner of the currency, who up to that time was a foreigner, is now a German, in the person of the President of the Court of Accounting of the Reich. However, proposals to change the provisions of the Bank Law of 1924, as amended by the Hague Conference Agreement of January 1930, must be submitted by the German Government to the board of directors of the Bank for International Settlements for approval. This international agreement, prohibiting the Reich to alter unilaterally relevant stipulations of the Bank Law, will remain in force until the Lausanne Agreement of 1932 is ratified. The Bank for

International Settlements, has tacitly approved the October 27, 1933, amendments to the Bank Law. According to these amendments the President of the Reich will appoint the president of the Reichsbank for four years on the suggestion of the directors of the Bank. The Reich President will also nominate for a period of twelve years the directors of the Bank proposed by the Reichsbank president. Under certain conditions the Reich President may dismiss the president and directors of the Bank.

Functions of the Reichsbank. The Reichsbank is charged with the duty of regulating the supply of currency, providing clearing facilities, and controlling as far as possible the flow of credit. To this end, it is authorized to issue notes, to discount certain strictly defined types of commercial paper, to make loans secured by certain specified types of collateral, and to engage in open market transactions. The legal provisions with regard to discounts, loans, and open market transactions permit the Reichsbank to do the following:

1. To buy and sell gold, silver, and foreign exchange.
2. To discount, buy, and sell bills of exchange arising out of a bona fide commercial transaction with a maturity of not more than three months, carrying at least three signatures of parties known to be solvent.
3. To discount, buy, and sell Reich Treasury bills with a maturity of not more than three months which are endorsed by a third party known to be solvent.
4. To make loans collateralled by
   a. gold and silver,
   b. certain stipulated securities,
   c. bills of exchange,
   d. merchandise.

The Reichsbank is also authorized to discount bills arising out of commercial transactions with two signatures, provided additional collateral security is offered. The total amount of two-name paper discounted with the Reichsbank, however, may not exceed one-third of the total nominal amount of bills discounted with the Reichsbank. Bills

bearing three signatures, therefore, must always amount to
not less than two-thirds of the total discounts of the Reichsbank.

The limitation of two-name paper to one-third of the
total nominal amount of bills discounted represents a com-
promise between the Anglo-Saxon and the French principle
of central banking.   The Reichsbank deals with the banks
and bankers as well as with the general public, but by
requiring a third signature, which is usually supplied by a
bank, the Reichsbank interposes between itself and the
business of the country a buffer which protects its liquidity.

Bills presented to the Reichsbank for discount by banking institutions usually run from 20 to 35 days, while those
presented for discount by others than banks usually run
for between 52 and 56 days.   There is, however, an old and
established practice regularly followed by the Reichsbank—
that of granting two extensions on agricultural paper—
which means, in reality, the discounting of nine-month bills.
In the case of Russian trade acceptances the Reichsbank
has often extended the term up to eighteen months.[1]   The
discount rate of the Reichsbank applies to all bills which it
discounts.   Bills of an amount of 5,000 reichsmarks or more
are discounted usually for not less than five days, whereas
bills of an amount less than 5,000 reichsmarks must be discounted at least ten days before maturity.

The amount of Treasury bills which the Reichsbank may
acquire through discount or purchase, or hold as collateral
for loans, was limited by the Bank Act of 1924 to 400,000,-
000 marks at any given time.   The total amount of Treasury bills must be shown in the weekly statements; Treasury
bills could not be used as cover against notes in circulation.   This provision narrowed the scope of the Reichsbank's open market transactions, but those limitations
were surmounted by the open market operations of the
Golddiskontbank, a subsidiary of the Reichsbank.   The

---

[1] *Wirtschaftsfragen der Gegenwart,* Speech by the Reichsbank president,
Dr. Luther, on July 8, 1932. (*Kieler Vortraege,* # 38, page 68.)

1933 amendments to the Bank Act finally removed the restrictions.

Loans and advances (lombard operations). In addition to discounting eligible commercial paper, the Reichsbank may also make loans (lombard loans) against certain specified collateral for periods not exceeding three months and for as short a period as one or two days. However, the Reichsbank may call lombard loans at any time before their nominal maturity, and borrowers may repay the loans any time before maturity. The lombard rate is usually one to two per cent higher than the discount rate and applies to all classes of loans with the exception of those secured by gold, which may bear a lower rate than that on securities. Such loans, however, are very rare and only for small amounts. During the banking crisis of 1931 the spread between the discount and lombard rate was 5 per cent.

The securities on which the Reichsbank may make loans are as follows:

1. Fully paid shares, common and preferred, of the German Railway Company up to 75 per cent of the market value.

2. The bonds of German public land credit institutions and of German mortgage banks, up to 75 per cent of the market value.

3. Bearer bonds of the Reich, German states, and municipalities maturing within one year, but such loans may be made only to banks in good standing and up to three-fourths of the market value of the securities. (The amendment of December 1, 1930, to the Bank Act also enables the Reichsbank to make loans on government, state, and municipal securities, as well as on securities issued by public credit institutions having a maturity of more than one year.)

4. Interest-bearing bonds of foreign states or railroads, provided the latter are government-guaranteed, up to not more than 50 per cent of their market value.

Bills of exchange are eligible as collateral for lombard loans up to 95 per cent of their market value, provided the drawer and drawee are known to be solvent. Loans may also be made, up to two-thirds of the value of the merchandise, on merchandise stored in Germany. The Reichsbank is explicitly prohibited from accepting bills of exchange, from making loans collateralled by real estate, mining property, oil fields, or stocks (shares), and from acquiring real estate except for its own use.

Of the various classes of collateral which the Reichsbank may accept as security for loans, securities and commercial bills are by far the most important. Thus, at the end of 1933 the total amount of lombard loans made by the Reichsbank aggregated 183,278,900 reichsmarks. Of this total 150,870,300 reichsmarks represented loans against securities; 22,888,300 reichsmarks were secured by Treasury notes, 6,309,100 reichsmarks by commodities, and 3,157,200 reichsmarks by commercial bills; while only 54,000 reichsmarks were loans against gold and silver. Although the lombard rate is usually higher than the discount rate, banks prefer to borrow rather than to discount, because the loan may be obtained for one or two days, while a discount usually has to run for a longer period.

The Reichsbank may buy and sell bonds of the type which it may receive as collateral for loans; may act as collecting and paying agent for its customers; may receive deposits on which it pays no interest; may grant to the federal government loans running for not more than three months and not to exceed 100,000,000 reichsmarks. On July 15 of each year the Reich must not be indebted to the Reichsbank. It may also make loans to the post office up to an amount not exceeding 200,000,000 reichsmarks.

The October 27, 1933, amendment to Section 21 of the Bank Law permits the Reichsbank to buy and sell for its own account in the open market fixed-interest bearing securities, with the exception of industrial and foreign bonds. While these open market operations are not limited legally to any amount, they are in fact restricted to the amount of deposits maintained with the Reichsbank, unless the latter issues currency against the securities purchased in the open market. Since the banks are not bound by law to maintain reserves with the Reichsbank, and since their balances are usually small, the open market power is relatively limited.

The Reichsbank acts as fiscal agent for the government and the post office and deals not only with banks but also with private parties.   On August 7, 1928, 41,501 firms and individuals, as contrasted with 61,683 accredited concerns on November 15, 1912, were accredited to the Reichsbank and entitled to obtain credits.   However, the Reichsbank also discounts eligible paper for concerns which do not maintain accounts with it.   Table 44 shows the number of firms and individuals accredited at the Reichsbank, classified by groups and amounts of credit granted, on November 25, 1912, and on August 7, 1928.

Note issue.   The Reichsbank notes in circulation must, in accordance with the Bank Law of 1924, be secured by a minimum of 40 per cent in gold and foreign exchange. Since the amount of foreign exchange held as cover against notes in circulation may not exceed 25 per cent of the total cover, each note must be covered by at least 30 per cent in gold.   Foreign exchange eligible as cover for notes consists of bank notes of foreign banks of issue, foreign bills of exchange arising out of commercial transactions having a maturity of not more than fourteen days, and sight drafts drawn on banks of known standing in important financial centers.   The balance of the security above the legal reserve against notes in circulation consists of discounted domestic and foreign bills of exchange with a maturity not exceeding three months.   Under the Bank Act of 1924, whenever the cover fell below the legal minimum, the Reichsbank was required to pay to the government a graduated tax on the note issue in excess of the amount against which the reserve equaled 40 per cent, and at the same time had to raise the discount rate by at least one-third of the percentage of the tax payable, using as a basis a minimum discount rate of at least 5 per cent—which must be maintained whenever the reserve drops below 40 per cent.   Accordingly, when

TABLE 44

CREDIT GRANTED BY REICHSBANK

OCCUPATION	TOTAL NUMBER ENTITLED TO CREDIT		IN PER CENT OF TOTAL					
			UP TO 30,000 (REICHSMARKS)		OVER 30,000, UP TO 100,000 (REICHSMARKS)		OVER 100,000 (REICHSMARKS)	
	Nov. 15, 1912	Aug. 7, 1928	Nov. 15, 1912	Aug. 7, 1928	Nov. 15, 1912	Aug. 7, 1928	Nov. 15, 1912	Aug. 7, 1928
1. Merchants and trading companies......	22,137	10,423	74.4	69.3	19.5	23.9	6.0	6.8
2. Industrialists and industrial companies	19,671	14,983	55.6	46.5	27.4	32.6	17.0	20.9
3. Agriculturists and agricultural establishments	9,121	11,463	85.4	84.2	12.2	13.6	2.4	2.2
4. Banks and bankers.........	2,201	1,891	20.6	28.0	30.4	28.8	49.0	43.2
5. Public savings banks.........	......	725	......	80.1	......	16.3	......	3.6
6. Coöperatives	1,014	1,205	44.5	63.2	37.7	28.2	17.8	8.6
7. Others—craftsmen, etc.........	7,539	811	82.3	88.2	14.0	10.2	3.7	1.6

the legal reserve fell to 35.8 per cent on July 16, 1931, the Reichsbank raised its discount rate from 7 per cent to 10 per cent. The provision of the statute that the discount rate may not be reduced below 5 per cent so long as the note coverage is below 40 per cent was suspended until September 1934 by a presidential decree of September 19, 1932. This decree was issued only after the Bank for International Settlements had agreed not to avail itself of its right to object to this change in the Bank Act.

The provision for the graduated currency tax and the 5 per cent minimum discount rate in periods of deficient reserves was abrogated by the October 27, 1933, amendments. These amendments have also altered the reserve provisions of section 28 of the Bank Law, which makes securities acquired by the Reichsbank or held as collateral against daily maturing loans eligible for cover against notes in circulation. While the principle of maintaining a 40 per cent metallic reserve against notes in circulation was retained in the law, the amendments provide that a concurrent resolution of the central committee of the stockholders and of the directors of the Reichsbank can empower the latter to let the metallic reserve fall below the legal minimum.

(' Thus these amendments permit the Reichsbank in fact to issue currency covered by bonds of the government, states, municipalities, railroads, public credit institutions, and organizations controlled by the government, and by government-guaranteed bonds, regardless of the metallic reserve.'' In the *Deutsche Volkswirt* of November 24, 1933, Professor Prion stated:

> As it has also been laid down that the securities thus bought (by the Reichsbank in the open market) are to be equivalent to bills for the purposes of note cover, and as the gold and foreign exchange cover is practically of little importance, there are practically no longer any limits to the issue of notes. . . . Actually the Reichsbank is no longer a note-issuing bank in the old sense, but a bank to provide money for the State, *i.e.*, for the tasks which the new state has set itself in the new Reich.

Article 31 of the Law of 1924 required the Reichsbank to redeem its notes in gold coin or bars, or at the option of the Bank, in foreign exchange at the market value, in gold, of the foreign currency. The putting into effect of Article 31 required a joint resolution of the managing board and the general council of the Reichsbank. This concurrent resolution was adopted on April 15, 1930, when it was decided that Article 31 should become effective at the same time that the Young Plan became operative. Hence Germany legally returned to the gold standard on that date for the first time since the outbreak of the war in 1914, although actually the Reichsbank had freely exchanged its notes for gold at a fixed price and for foreign exchange since the reorganization in 1924.

Blocked marks.   The standstill agreements with foreign short-term creditors, the various regulations for the control of foreign exchange and for the prevention of the flight of capital, and the transfer moratorium decree of June 1933, created a unique currency situation. While there was outwardly no change in the monetary unit, the currency came to be divided into "free" and "blocked" marks (*Sperrmark*). Free marks are balances which may be converted into gold or foreign exchange at the legal value of 1,392 marks for one pound of fine gold, as stipulated in the Bank Law of 1924. The Reichsbank allots free marks (*i.e.*, sells foreign exchange) first to the national government, secondly to importers for approved imports, and thirdly for a part of the foreign debt service.

Blocked marks are mark balances which cannot be freely used by the owners and consequently sell at a discount, which varies directly with the degree of restrictions placed on their utilization. The degree of depreciation and limitation in use divide the blocked marks into the following six main categories:

1. Old deposit marks (*Altguthaben*).
2. Blocked mark-currency (*Notensperrmark*).
3. Blocked credit-marks (*Kreditsperrmark*).

4. Blocked security-marks (*Effektensperrmark*).
5. Registered marks (*Registermark*).
6. Blocked conversion-marks (*Konversions-Sperrmark*).

In June 1934 registered marks were dealt in at a discount of about 40 per cent, blocked credit-marks 55 per cent, and blocked security marks about 70 per cent. The discount on conversion-marks (scrip), representing the untransferred part of interest on external bonds, was fixed for the year July 1, 1933, to June 30, 1934, by the Reichsbank at approximately 50 per cent of the nominal value. Some of the blocked marks cannot be used without specific permission of the Reichsbank, and so long as such permission is refused they are practically of no value. The blocked marks are almost exclusively owned by foreigners, as the scheme was devised primarily to prevent foreign creditors from withdrawing their funds entirely or collecting interest in full.

Reserves against deposits. The influence of the Federal Reserve system on the Bank Act of 1924 is clearly seen in the adoption of the American principle of maintaining legally fixed minimum reserves against the demand deposits of the central bank. While the old Reichsbank was under no obligation to maintain a reserve against its deposits, section 35 of the 1924 Act stipulates that the demand deposits (*Giro Guthaben*) of the Reichsbank must be secured by not less than 40 per cent of liquid assets, consisting of demand deposits at home and abroad, checks on other banks, loans payable from day to day, and bills of exchange of a maturity not exceeding thirty days. This stipulation is less exacting than the statutes of some central banks, which treat sight liabilities as the equivalent of notes in circulation and make them subject to the same reserve requirements.

Banks as well as non-banking concerns and individuals throughout the country maintain balances with the Reichsbank and its 455 offices primarily for clearing purposes. The amount of deposits which banks or others dealing with the Reichsbank maintain is not, as in the United States, fixed by law. To have a "giro," or clearing account with the Reichsbank, depositors other than banks must maintain a minimum balance of 100 reichsmarks. On the other hand, banks which are members of an *Abrechnungsstelle* (clearing office) located in cities where the Reichsbank maintains central offices, must carry a minimum balance of 1,500 reichsmarks. The number of clearing accounts at the end of 1933 was 42,053, as compared with 26,148 at the end of 1913. Owing to the shortage of working capital in Germany, the minimum balances kept by banks with the Reichsbank are at present lower than before the war and amount to about 2 to 3 per cent of their total deposits. The Bank Act stipulates that the Reichsbank may not pay interest on giro accounts. Giro balances (demand deposits) with the Reichsbank are lowest at the end of the month and increase gradually, reaching their highest point usually at the end of the third week in order to meet the month-end requirements. The movement of demand deposits at the Reichsbank is in inverse relationship to the movement of notes in circulation and reflects the demand by the banks for funds from the Reichsbank.

Clearing function. One of the duties of the Reichsbank, according to the Bank Law of 1875, was to develop a better method for financial settlements in Germany. While Great Britain and the United States had already developed the checking system, Germany continued to settle accounts with cash. In the opinion of the Reichsbank, settlements by book transfers from one account to another (*Giroverkehr*) were more suitable for Germany than the checking system. Moreover, its predecessor, the Prussian Bank, and the Hamburg Giro Bank, founded in 1619, had clearing offices which facilitated local payments by transfers on accounts.

The Reichsbank's first clearing office was opened in Berlin on April 2, 1883, under the name of "Check Association" (*Checkverein*), based on an agreement concluded

February 14, 1883, between the Reichsbank and sixteen of the largest Berlin banks and bankers. During the same year the Reichsbank organized clearing offices in six important cities. However, between 1884 and 1909 only nine additional offices were established. The enactment of the check law on March 11, 1908, and the introduction of the postal check system on January 1, 1909, greatly facilitated the development of the clearing system. The postal check system is used by medium- and small-sized businesses and by private individuals. In 1911 the postal check offices became members of the local Reichsbank clearing offices, and thus made possible cashless payments between the two systems throughout Germany.

Clearing takes place in offices provided by the Reichsbank under the supervision of a Reichsbank employee. All clearing members must maintain accounts with the Reichsbank, and their accredited representatives must be present at the daily clearing meetings even though they have no business to transact. The clearing embraces practically all money claims between the members, including claims resulting from security transactions, collection of coupons, etc. Clearing balances are charged or credited to the accounts with the Reichsbank, thus eliminating entirely cash payments. At the end of 1933 there were seventy-four clearing offices (*Abrechnungsstellen*) scattered throughout Germany. During that year they cleared 37,463,000 items (checks, bills, etc.) for a total amount of 52,199,400,000 reichsmarks, as compared with 43,913,000 items for 119,-341,700,000 reichsmarks in 1930.

In post-war years the Reichsbank concluded international clearing agreements with a number of foreign central banks. The first agreements were made in 1927 with Austria, Hungary, Danzig, Switzerland, and Czechoslovakia. By 1930 the Reichsbank had clearing arrangements with over twenty countries.

Discount policy. The discount policy of the Reichsbank in post-war years has been directed to the regulation of the flow of credit, in order to prevent excessive speculation, and to the maintenance of the stability of the German exchange. From the time of the stabilization of the currency up to the banking crisis in 1931, this policy was determined primarily by conditions prevailing in the leading financial centers of the world and by the degree of confidence which the latter had in Germany. Aside from foreign considerations, the Reichsbank's policy was directed toward lowering the prevailing high rates of interest and, in times of great ease on the short-term money market, toward diverting the flow of short-term funds into the capital market. The latter was carried out with the aid of the gold discount bank. To enforce its policy, the Reichsbank has three measures at its disposal: (1) the discount rate, (2) the rationing of credit, and (3) direct action, by forcing the leading banks to follow the course of action desired by the Reichsbank. All three of these measures have been used at times, although credit rationing and direct action have been resorted to only in extreme cases. In contrast to the Federal Reserve banks, which since 1922 have relied mainly on open market operations in regulating the volume of credit, the Reichsbank has relied primarily on its discount rate, which is normally considered as a satisfactory means of credit control.

Discount rate. Shortly after the stabilization of the currency, interest rates in Germany were very high. The average rate for day-to-day money in January 1924 was 87.64 per cent, as contrasted with a 10 per cent discount and 12 per cent lombard rate. Though commercial rates decreased sharply throughout 1924 and the greater part of 1925, the discount rate remained lower than the open market rates.

The discrepancy between the discount and open market rates prevailing during 1924 made it extremely profitable for the various banking, industrial, and commercial establishments to borrow from the Reichsbank. As a matter of fact, the volume of credit granted by the Reichsbank through discount and lombard operations from January 7, 1924, to April 7, 1924, increased from 696,100,000 reichs-marks to 2,093,100,000 reichsmarks. This rapid increase in the volume of borrowing from the Reichsbank would have resulted, under ordinary circumstances, in an increase in the discount rate. However, it was feared that an increase in the rate would have an adverse effect on the economic recuperation of Germany. The Reichsbank therefore decided not to raise its discount rate but, instead, to institute a policy of credit rationing. Accordingly, the Reichsbank fixed the amount of its loans and discounts outstanding on April 7, 1924, as the maximum volume of credit which it would grant in the future. Under this policy the amount of credit extended by the Reichsbank was not based on the amount or merits of the requests for credit, but was arbitrarily limited for each class of borrower to the amount for which that class happened to be indebted to the Reichsbank on April 7, 1924. In view of the prevailing unusually wide spread between the discount rate and the market rates, the privilege of discounting at the Reichsbank amounted practically to receiving a subsidy from the latter.

At the end of 1924, particularly after the effect of the inflow of foreign funds began to be felt on the German money market, the Reichsbank somewhat modified this rigid system of credit rationing. At the beginning of 1926 credit rationing was abolished, and the Reichsbank returned again to the discount rate as the principal medium of credit control. From the beginning of 1926 the Reichsbank, influenced by monetary conditions abroad, steadily reduced its discount rate, until on January 11, 1927, the rate reached 5 per cent.

The influence of foreign funds on the discount policy of the Reichsbank was particularly felt from the time of the legal stabilization of the currency until August 23, 1926, during which period the Reichsbank maintained the mark rate pegged at RM 4.20 per dollar. Banks and industrial establishments needing funds either could discount with the Reichsbank and pay a high rate of interest, or could borrow abroad at a lower rate and sell their foreign bills of exchange to the Reichsbank and, then, repurchase them when the need for funds ceased. Since the exchange rate of the dollar was fixed, the banks assumed no exchange risk. The effect of this situation was a sharp decrease in discounts of domestic bills with the Reichsbank and a sharp increase in its holdings of gold and foreign exchange.

On August 23, 1926, the Reichsbank discontinued the practice of pegging the dollar rate for the mark, and from then on the selling and buying of foreign bills through the Reichsbank involved the risk of sustaining losses from exchange fluctuations. The unpegging of the dollar rate increased the effectiveness of the discount and lombard rate of the Reichsbank particularly at the time of the monthly settlements, since the banks had to return to the normal manner of financing their settlement requirements through the discounting of bills or through borrowing against collateral. The variable dollar quotation caused the banks partially to abandon the method of obtaining marks through the sale of borrowed foreign exchange.

The heavy outflow of funds following the elections in September 1930 forced the Reichsbank to increase its rate to 5 per cent on October 9, 1930,[1] but this was not considered as unusual, for in post-war years a 5 per cent rate was regarded as more or less normal. Early in June 1931, when the German money market was subjected to an unprecedented "run" from abroad and when a substantial flight from the mark set in, the Reichsbank, in the course of two weeks, lost approximately 1,000,000,000 reichsmarks in gold and foreign exchange and was forced to raise its discount rate to 7 per cent. However, owing to the loss of confidence by foreign lenders, the discrepancy between interest rates in Berlin and those of the leading financial centers not only

---

[1] The rate was reduced from 4½ per cent to 4 per cent on June 21, 1930.

has failed to attract funds from abroad but has even been insufficient to stem the further outflow of funds from Germany.

On July 15, 1931, when the reserve ratio of the Reichsbank had fallen below 40 per cent and all German banks had been closed for two days, the Reichsbank raised its discount rate to 10 per cent. At this time credit rationing was adopted only to a limited extent, in order to enable the banks to meet the increased demand for cash from domestic and foreign creditors. During the period of the banking crisis, which extended until August 5, when the banks resumed payments in full within Germany, the Reichsbank's chief aim was to prevent an outflow of funds and to maintain the stability of the exchange. On August 1 it raised the discount rate to 15 per cent and the lombard rate to 20 per cent for a short period and, with the aid of the foreign exchange control instituted by the government, prevented a collapse of the mark. After the crisis had run its course and after the reopening of the banks, the Reichsbank reduced its discount and lombard rates twice in succession. The banking crisis of 1931, the institution of rigid foreign exchange restrictions, the freezing of a large amount of foreign balances through the standstill agreements, and the impossibility of obtaining foreign credits, brought to an end the Reichsbank's policy of regulating the discount rate with a view to conditions in foreign money centers. After the middle of 1931 the discount policy of the Reichsbank was determined entirely by domestic considerations.

Credit rationing. The use of credit rationing as a major policy of credit control has been referred to several times. It is, therefore, necessary to explain this policy in greater detail.

The German money market from 1924 up to the middle of 1931 was closely connected with the international money markets, and the discount policy of the Reichsbank depended to a very large extent upon financial conditions prevailing in foreign centers. So long as foreign markets had confidence in Berlin, an advance in interest rates in that market led to an inflow of funds and the Reichsbank was more a follower than a leader in the Berlin money market.   It was only when the foreign international money markets lost confidence in Germany, and not only refused to make new loans but even withdrew part of those already extended, that credit rationing became effective.   It was exercised by the Reichsbank from April 1924 to the end of 1925, for a short time in the spring of 1929, and in a milder form in July 1931.   In each case the policy of credit rationing coincided with the loss of confidence in the German currency, both by foreigners and by German nationals.   On the one hand, this loss of confidence led to a withdrawal of funds by foreigners and, on the other hand, to an increased demand for foreign exchange by domestic banks and corporations, which endeavored either to cover their forward foreign exchange commitments or to convert part of their assets into foreign currencies.   Since the Reichsbank, under such circumstances, was not the last but rather the first resort for foreign exchange, it was bound to lose a part of its foreign exchange as well as of its gold holdings.   An increase in the discount rate was useless, for under such conditions it could neither lead to an influx of funds from abroad nor stop completely the flight from the mark at home.

The need for credit rationing arose out of the fact that domestic banks and corporations, in order to obtain foreign exchange, discounted a part of their portfolios with the Reichsbank, and purchased foreign exchange with the proceeds thereof.   Through credit rationing the Reichsbank granted to each individual borrower only a fixed amount of credit, and for the rest of the funds the borrowers, notably banks, had to seek accommodation elsewhere.   Banks and business in need of funds were thereby forced to sell foreign exchange to the Reichsbank.   Through this measure the Reichsbank not only prevented the use of its funds for the purpose of buying foreign exchange but also compelled banks and corporations to sell to it a part of their foreign exchange holdings.

Effect of credit rationing. Credit rationing has a grave effect on the national economy as well as on the money market and the banks. It injects an element of uncertainty into business—industry and trade do not know whether they will be able to procure credit through the ordinary channels. Such a central bank policy contradicts the well-established principle that credit must always be obtainable at a price. It deprives the central bank of its function of being the ultimate source of credit through which the banks can increase their liquidity. Since the central bank discounts only a certain amount of bills for individual borrowers, the latter, if they need additional funds, have to sell part of their portfolio in the open market, call some of their loans, or sell foreign exchange to the Reichsbank. The banks, in order to increase their liquidity, immediately curtail the volume of their credits, which action, in turn, results in a general contraction of the total volume of credit outstanding. Credit rationing is a very radical measure and the most drastic step that a central bank may undertake under any circumstances. The Reichsbank has therefore always refrained from adopting this policy whenever it can be avoided.

Policy of direct action. A new element in the credit policy of the Reichsbank was introduced in May 1927, when the president of the Reichsbank forced the large Berlin banks to reduce their loans on securities (report and lombard loans) used for stock exchange operations. This was done to curtail stock exchange speculation financed chiefly with foreign short-term funds and to prevent a rise in prices, which would cause reduced exports, increased imports, and pressure on the foreign exchange holdings of the Reichsbank. The discount rate, the classical and traditional weapon of a central bank, has proved to be ineffective in combating a stock exchange boom. Credit rationing was of no avail so long as, in the words of Dr. Schacht, there

were functioning side by side two Reichsbanks or two
sources of credit—namely, the Reichsbank and foreign
financial centers.

The only means of stopping the flow of funds feeding a
stock exchange boom was direct pressure, brought by the
central bank on the commercial banks. This method was
resorted to by Dr. Schacht, when he announced•to the
members of the Berlin Stempel-Vereinigung that the decisive factor in granting rediscount facilities to each individual bank in the future would be the latter's liquidity as
determined by an examination of the bank. This was a
novel procedure, for the Reichsbank usually looks merely
at the quality of the paper offered for discount and not at
the status and liquidity of the borrowing banks. The latter, therefore, if they wished to obtain additional credits
from the Reichsbank, had to increase their liquidity and
were thus forced to curtail their secured loans, whether or
not they agreed with the Reichsbank. This was particularly the case because the banks could hardly have liquidated the trade bills or outstanding credits without exerting
credit pressure on commerce and industry. The measure
has been criticized by the banks, which have maintained
that the break in the stock market on May 13, 1927, could
have been avoided.

Public funds and the discount policy. In post-war years
and, particularly, shortly after the legal stabilization of the
currency, public funds played an important rôle in the discount policy of the Reichsbank. The administration of the
public funds is of greater importance in Germany than in
the United States or England. This importance is due to
the fact that the volume of public funds is very large, embracing not only the funds at the disposal of the federal
government, states, and municipalities, but also the funds
of corporations owned by the government, notably the
railway company, the post office, and the various government insurance funds. Funds of public corporations which
are operated independently of the government, such as the

Viag, are not considered as public funds. Since the German railroad company is one of the largest single administrative railroad units in the world and since the German post office, through the acceptance of funds for checking and clearing purposes, has a large volume of deposits, it is obvious that the amount of public funds involved is enormous.

In November 1926, Dr. Schacht, then president of the Reichsbank, estimated that the funds at the disposal of the railway, the post office, and the State of Prussia alone amounted to two and one-half billion reichsmarks. The magnitude of this sum becomes more apparent if one considers that, at the end of 1913, the total liquid public funds amounted to about 850,000,000 marks. In addition, the liquid funds of the various social insurance institutions were of great importance. They include the various health (sick benefit) insurance funds, which at the end of 1926 were estimated to have liquid funds of about 493,000,000 marks. In view of the impoverished national economy of Germany, such sums were staggering, and their employment on the Berlin money market had a decided influence on credit conditions.

Administration of funds. Before the war, the administration of these funds was almost exclusively in the hands of two institutions: the Reichsbank and the Seehandlung (Prussian state bank). By far the larger part of the funds was lodged with the Seehandlung, which administered them solely for the benefit of the market. However, after the stabilization of the currency in 1924 each individual government department endeavored to administer its own funds regardless of the effects which it might have on the market, with the result that the disposition made of the various public funds very often counteracted the policy of the Reichsbank. The president of the Reichsbank therefore endeavored to concentrate these funds in the hands of one or two institutions in order to make the Reichsbank policy more effective. At present, the public funds of Germany are administered chiefly by the Reichsbank, the Seehandlung, the Verkehrs-Kredit-Bank, and to a very small extent, the private banks.

Other Public Credit Institutions

In addition to the Reichsbank there are in Germany several so-called public credit institutions which are the outgrowth of the paternalism of the German federal and state governments. Some of these banks were established prior to the war, while others were created after the close of the war for the purpose af aiding in the reconstruction of the German economy.

Gold Discount Bank. This institution was established on March 19, 1924, before the reorganization of the Reichsbank, for the purpose of providing Germany with foreign short-term credits. It was intended to serve as a central institution for foreign transactions, thus supplementing the functions of the Rentenbank, whose currency was limited to domestic transactions only. The bank was also authorized to issue pound sterling currency notes, but the privilege was never exercised and was subsequently withdrawn under section 2 of the Bank Law of 1924.

The capital of the Gold Discount Bank was fixed at £10,000,000, divided into two equal series designated as *A* and *B*. Series *A* was acquired by the Reichsbank and Series *B* by a consortium of the leading banks of the country. Soon after the reorganization of the Reichsbank and the legal stabilization of the mark in 1924, the Reichsbank acquired the interest of other banks in the Gold Discount Bank, and since that time the latter has been operated as a subsidiary of the Reichsbank.

The Gold Discount Bank provided foreign short-term credits for German firms out of its capital funds and through the establishment of a revolving rediscount credit of £5,000,000 in London and of $5,000,000 in New York. The last-mentioned credit, although not used since 1924, was kept open through periodical renewals and was increased to $50,000,000 in 1928.   Finally, it was used to the full extent in the critical days of July 1931.   The bank was originally authorized to discount bills drawn in dollars and sterling only, but on April 1, 1927, it was empowered to discount bills drawn in reichsmarks.

Being controlled by the Reichsbank and not prohibited to pay interest on deposits, the Gold Discount Bank acts as a subsidiary of the former and often performs such functions as the Reichsbank is prohibited by law from undertaking, particularly the shifting of short-term funds into the capital market.   Thus, during 1926 the Gold Discount Bank borrowed short-term funds in the market on its promissory notes and purchased 360,000,000 reichsmarks of 7-per-cent three- to five-year agricultural mortgage notes of the Deutsche Rentenbank-Kreditanstalt (German Central Bank for Agriculture).

The scope of activities of the Gold Discount Bank was considerably broadened by a law of December 1, 1930, which, among other things, authorized the Bank to issue bonds up to five times its capital and reserves.   At the present time its prime function is the financing of foreign trade, particularly where longer credit terms are required, such as in trade with Russia, Turkey, and other countries, and in the administering of blocked marks used to foster foreign trade.   As noted elsewhere, the Gold Discount Bank played an important rôle in the 1932 reorganization of the banks.

State banks.   The four other note-issuing banks in Germany besides the Reichsbank are state banks: namely, the Bayerische Notenbank, the Saechsische Bank, the Badische Bank, and the Wuerttembergische Notenbank.   In addition to these four institutions there are other state-owned banks which do not enjoy the note-issue privilege and which, as a rule, do not operate for profit.   Their principal function is to act as bankers for the several governments, and they are closely supervised by the states.   The most important state bank from the standpoint of the money market is the

Prussian State Bank (Preussische Staatsbank), founded in 1772 and generally known as the "Seehandlung."

The Seehandlung is the largest and, next to the Reichsbank, the most important public bank in Germany. It is not only the fiscal agent of the State of Prussia, the largest political unit of Germany, which owns the total capital of the bank, but also the depository for other public funds. While the Reichsbank is prohibited by law from allowing interest on deposits, the Seehandlung can and does pay interest on deposits. Its huge deposits give it great influence over the short-term money market, where it is one of the largest lenders as well as borrowers of funds. It is the principal lender on stock market collateral to banks and for stock exchange purposes. Its operations are a stabilizing factor in the market, since it is always ready not only to lend but also to absorb surplus funds. While the Seehandlung before the war did business primarily in Berlin, in post-war years it established close contact with banks in Frankfort, Hamburg, Cologne, Munich, and Dresden. Up to 1926 the bank also engaged in the financing of private enterprises, but owing to the losses which it sustained in that year from some of its private transactions (*Barmat-Affair*), the bank has restricted its activities to dealings primarily with banks. All engagements of the Seehandlung are guaranteed by the State of Prussia, which also receives the net profits of the institution.

Reichs-Kredit-Gesellschaft, A. G. Although this institution is usually considered as a commercial credit bank, it is treated in this section because it is indirectly owned by the Reich. The entire capital, in the amount of 40,000,000 reichsmarks, has been underwritten by the VIAG (Vereinigte Industrie Unternehmungen, A. G.) a holding company wholly owned by the government for managing the Reich's interests in business enterprises. The Reichs-Kredit-Gesellschaft is the successor to the Reichs-Kredit and Kontroll-Stelle, G. m. b. H., founded in 1919 primarily as a trust company for corporations owned by the government. In 1922 the name was altered to Reichs-Kredit-Gesellschaft, G. m. b. H., and in 1924 it was changed to a corporation under the present name.

The Reichs-Kredit-Gesellschaft performs all the functions of a private commercial bank and is regarded as one of the leading banks in Berlin. Since it does not have branches, it has attracted the deposits of a large number of small public credit institutions as well as deposits of the smaller provincial banks, which prefer to deal with this institution rather than maintain correspondent relations with large credit banks which, through their branches, compete with them in the provinces.

Deutsche Verkehrs-Kredit-Bank A. G. This institution was organized in 1923 for the purpose of financing deferred freight payments, and in 1924 it passed under the control of the German Railway Company, which acquired about 75 per cent of the capital stock. Since it functions mainly as a depository of the railway company, the bank may for practical purposes be considered as the treasury and finance department of the railway company. Its deposits have averaged around 500,000,000 reichsmarks since 1926, and this large concentration of funds has established it as an important element in the money market because the funds have been partly redeposited with other banks and partly invested in bills. Since the funds were administered primarily with the object of making profit, the distribution of the funds frequently clashed with the policy of the Reichsbank. This situation was remedied through an agreement concluded in January 1928 between the Reichsbank and the railway company whereby the bulk of the funds are deposited with the Reichsbank for account of the Verkehrs-Kredit-Bank, and investments are made by the agreement of both institutions.

In addition to the institutions described above, all of which are important factors in the money market, there are a number of public institutions which have only a minor or indirect influence on the money market. Among these the provincial and communal banks and the public mortgage banks are the most prominent.

Provincial and communal banks.   These are small public credit institutions whose operations are localized in the provinces, cities, and communes throughout the country. Their business resembles that of the state banks (*Staatsbanken*) of the smaller states.   In this group may be included local savings banks, central clearing institutions (*Giro-Zentralen*) and land banks.   The clearing institutions were established to facilitate payments among the local savings banks and to connect them with the two national clearing organizations, namely, the Reichsbank and post office clearing systems.   They also act as reserve banks for the savings banks located in their respective districts, investing the largest part of the guaranty reserves of these institutions in savings banks' acceptances and, since the liberalization of the investment provisions of savings banks in March 1934, in treasury bills and various kinds of securities which can be purchased by the Reichsbank under the October 1933 amendment to the Bank Law.   Mortgage banks are primarily engaged in the granting of long-term mortgage credits.

CHAPTER XV

Berlin—The Private Credit Banks and the Operation of the Market

Private Credit or Commercial Banks

ALTHOUGH the Reichsbank deals directly with the public, its influence is felt principally through the private commercial banks. Trade bills (*Warenwechsel*), the principal credit instruments used in financing trade in Germany, are drafts drawn by the seller of goods on the buyer and are often discounted by the former with a commercial bank. If the bill carries a third signature—say, that of a bank—it becomes eligible for discount with the Reichsbank. As a matter of fact, most of the discounts of the Reichsbank consist of such bills. The volume of trade bills outstanding is itself a good indication of the status of German trade and industry.

Trade bills, in order to be eligible for discount with the Reichsbank, must not run for more than three months. Although the Reichsbank, with the exception of periods when it institutes credit rationing, is not limited in the amount of bills it may discount for an individual borrower, it sees to it that a bank or other customer does not abuse the discount privilege. Since the Reichsbank is not willing to absorb all the bills offered to it for discount, a special market for trade bills has developed. The main sellers of such bills, as a rule, are small and middle-sized banking firms, while the Seehandlung and the Reichs-Kredit-Gesellschaft A. G. are among the largest buyers.

The private credit, or commercial, banks of Germany are divided into two groups: the incorporated and the private banks. From the legal point of view, the incorporated banks are either corporations (*Aktien-Gesellschaften* [A.G.]) or *Kommandit-Gesellschaften auf Aktien.* The characteristic feature of the latter is that, in addition to the stockholders (*Kommanditisten*), whose liability is limited to the subscribed capital, there are partners who are personally liable with all their private property for the obligations of the company. The private banks are either general partnerships or limited companies—*Gesellschaften mit beschraenkter Haftung* (G.m.b.H.).

The credit banks of Germany differ from the commercial banks of the United States and Great Britain in that the scope of activity of the former is much broader. The German credit banks are of the "mixed type," for they engage in both commercial and investment banking; in other words they grant short-term as well as long-term credits to trade and industry. They may and actually do engage in almost every kind of banking business, but refrain from granting mortgage credit. Each of the larger banks has a number of industrial establishments with which it is more or less identified through stock ownership. The various enterprises belonging to the sphere of influence of one particular bank look to the latter for the financing of short-term as well as long-term transactions. The purely investment functions of the banks, such as the issuance of common and preferred stocks and of bonds, have greatly declined in recent years. The banks also perform the functions of brokers on the stock exchanges in buying and selling securities for their own account as well as for third parties. To carry out these transactions, one or two of the senior officers of the banks are usually represented on the bourse. Commissions accruing from trading in securities for third parties are an important item of income to the German banks.

The commercial banking activities are similar to those carried on by commercial banks in other countries: accepting deposits, extending short-term credit, discounting trade bills, and financing stock exchange transactions through collateral loans.

Branch banking is well developed in Germany and, with the exception of the Berliner Handels-Gesellschaft and the Reichs-Kredit-Gesellschaft A. G., all important Berlin banks have a string of branches at home—and some have branches abroad. The banking activities in foreign countries of most of the German banks, however, are carried on through overseas banks or affiliations rather than through foreign branches. In post-war years the German banks were very active in Holland, where they established a number of affiliate banks, but after the crisis of July 1931 the banks adopted a policy of retrenchment, which led to the closing of competitive branches at home and the liquidation of affiliates abroad.

German banking during recent years has been marked by mergers and consolidations which have affected not only the smaller institutions but also some of the largest banks. The mergers undertaken in the process of reorganizing the banking structure following its collapse in July 1931, left the Deutsche Bank und Disconto-Gesellschaft, the Dresdner Bank, the Commerz- und Privat-Bank Aktiengesellschaft, the Berliner Handels-Gesellschaft and the Reichs-Kredit-Gesellschaft A. G., as the most important banks in Berlin. The Reichs-Kredit-Gesellschaft A. G. is regarded as one of the large commercial banks of Berlin, although as explained before, it is treated in this volume as a public credit institution. In addition to the five Berlin banks mentioned above there are three provincial institutions— the Bayerische Hypotheken- und Wechsel-Bank, and the Bayerische Vereinsbank, both of Munich, and the Allgemeine Deutsche Credit-Anstalt (ADCA) of Leipzig, which may be classified as *Grossbanken* (large banks).

Influence of foreign funds. While the capital and surplus of the large Berlin banks shrank considerably in the aftermath of the war, the deposits in 1930 were twice the amount of those before the war. This great increase of deposits in commercial banks since the legal stabilization of the currency was due, to a large extent, to short-term credits obtained from abroad, which appeared as deposits in the balance sheets. These foreign deposits constituted at the end of 1928 about 45 per cent of the total deposits of the commercial banks, about 40 per cent at the end of 1929, and 35 per cent at the end of 1930, in spite of the withdrawal of about 700 million marks of foreign deposits during the latter part of 1930. Against these foreign deposits the German banks maintained considerable balances abroad. According to a study by a German parliamentary committee on money, credit, and finance, the international position of the German banks from the end of 1926 to the middle of 1930 was as shown in Table 45.

TABLE 45

INTERNATIONAL POSITION OF GERMAN BANKS
(In billions of reichsmarks)

DATE	DUE TO FOR- EIGNERS	DUE FROM FOREIGNERS		NET LIABILITY	
		Inclu- sive of Reichs- bank	Exclu- sive of Reichs- bank	Inclu- sive of Reichs- bank	Exclu- sive of Reichs- bank
End of 1926	3.5	2.7	1.8	.8	1.7
End of 1927	5.7	2.7	2.3	3.0	3.4
Middle of 1928	6.0	2.9	2.3	3.1	3.7
End of 1928	7.6	3.7	3.2	3.9	4.4
Middle of 1929	7.2	3.8	3.3	3.4	3.9
End of 1929	8.6	4.4	3.6	4.2	5.0
Middle of 1930	9.2	4.7	3.7	4.5	5.5

Foreign short-term deposits are entirely different from those of domestic origin. In case of any disturbance on the money market, domestic deposits may be withdrawn from some institutions, but unless withdrawn in the form of notes for hoarding they remain in the credit system of the country, for the funds are deposited with other institutions and the total volume of deposits of the banking system remains unchanged. On the other hand, a withdrawal of foreign deposits results ultimately in a loss of foreign exchange and gold by the central bank and, consequently, in a curtailment of credit.

In addition to foreign deposits, German banks have obtained abroad large amounts of acceptance (reimbursement) credits for account of their customers. These credits are known under the phrase *seitens der Kundschaft bei Dritten benutzte Kredite* (credits with third parties used by customers). At the end of 1929 the volume of foreign acceptance credits of the six large Berlin credit banks amounted to 1,877,400,000 reichsmarks, as compared with a total for all credit banks of Germany of RM 2,305,200,000. During 1930, in spite of the general decrease in the demand for credits, acceptance credits obtained abroad by all credit banks increased by about RM 100,000,000—an indication that a number of domestic commercial transactions were financed through such credits.

Since most of the deposits of the German banks are short-term deposits and are subject to withdrawal upon short notice, it is essential that the German banks maintain a high degree of liquidity. This is indispensable especially in case foreigners lose confidence in Germany, as happened in April 1929, in September 1930, and again in June 1931.

The large Berlin banks showed at the end of June 1930 an average ratio of 54 per cent of liquid assets against deposits (domestic and foreign) and acceptances. The ratio at the Danat Bank was 56.2 per cent, *i.e.*, a ratio higher than the average. The liquid assets consisted of cash, balances with domestic and foreign banks (*Nostroguthaben*), bills, report and lombard loans, and advances against merchandise. An analysis of the important items of the balance sheet throws some light on the true character of the liquidity.

Cash. After the stabilization of the mark, the cash and balances with the Reichsbank maintained by the large

Berlin banks amounted, at the height of liquidity, to only slightly above 2 per cent of the deposits (*Kreditoren*) and acceptances, while in July 1914 the cash ratio was 7.2 per cent and was to be raised up to 10 per cent (the average cash reserve of the English joint stock banks) following an agreement between the president of the Reichsbank and the banks.

Bill portfolio. The bill portfolio of the leading Berlin banks represented at the end of June 1930 about 40 per cent of the liquid assets and 23 per cent of the total assets. However, one-sixth of the portfolio consisted of non-rediscountable Treasury notes of the Reich and states, which the banks acquired partly voluntarily and partly involuntarily. To a limited extent the banks could use the notes as collateral for lombard loans with the Reichsbank. As these Treasury notes have always been renewed at maturity, it is not surprising to find that at the end of June 1931 the amount held by the banks was 437 million marks, or almost one-quarter of the total portfolio. It is difficult to estimate the true liquidity value of the bill portfolio of the large banks, because long before the credit crisis, and to a larger degree during the panicky period in 1931, credits on current accounts (overdrafts) were converted into acceptances. The line of demarcation between self-liquidating paper and finance bills grew hazier or, at certain banks, even disappeared entirely. In view of this situation, the Reichsbank unexpectedly informed the banks (three weeks before the fatal July 13, 1931) that it had allotted to each one for discount purposes an acceptance quota in order to stem the rapidly increasing number of acceptances of inferior quality offered to the Reichsbank for discount.

Nostroguthaben. The growing foreign indebtedness of the banks made it imperative to maintain a foreign exchange reserve. In the last few years this foreign exchange reserve was kept in the form of deposits with foreign banks, and these balances made up the largest part of the item *Nostroguthaben.* These balances proved, however, inadequate to meet the foreign run. The Layton Report estimates that, out of three and one-half billion marks withdrawn by foreign creditors during the first seven months of 1931, about one billion marks were supplied by the banks, and the latters' free foreign balances were reduced to 520 million marks. The greater part of these balances could not be drawn upon, as the banks had to maintain abroad certain agreed-upon deposits against the acceptance credits.

Report and lombard loans. The stock exchange loans (report and lombard loans), the liquidity of which was greatly doubted, proved to be truly liquid in spite of the fact that the stock exchange was closed at the outbreak of the crisis and remained so for a long time. Up to the end of July 1931, the report and lombard loans were reduced by one-half, and during the following year they declined from 254 million to 39 million—a 93 per cent liquidation of the amount outstanding at the beginning of the crisis. No other asset could have been realized upon to such an extent as the stock exchange loans, which fact is most probably due to the strict regulations of the stock exchange governing such loans and to the guarantees of the stock exchange clearing offices (*Liquidationskassen*).

Advances on merchandise. The advances on merchandise or the acceptance credits (*Rembourskredit*), which kept on growing after the stabilization of the currency, assumed a different character in 1926. From that year on, the foreign banks granting acceptance credits to German banks required tangible security in exceptional cases only with the effect that these credits did not differ from unsecured loans. Owing to the ease of obtaining foreign acceptance credits, the German banks relaxed their requirements, with the result that in June 1930 only 8 per cent of their advances on merchandise were secured by bills of lading and warehouse receipts and 45 per cent of the credits lacked any tangible security. When the foreign banks began to curtail and cancel the acceptance credits in the spring of 1931, the German banks on their part endeavored to liquidate the advances—a task which, unfortunately, proved to be difficult. In June 1931 the advances amounted to 1,750 million marks, which represented a reduction of only 200 million marks from the highest point. These loans, therefore, were in practice as far as liquidity is concerned no better than the open credits (*Debitoren*).

Debitoren. It is generally known that a large part of the credits on current account have been diverted to fixed investments. From the end of June 1930 to the end of June 1931, the large Berlin banks succeeded in reducing their current account loans (*Debitoren*) only by 523 million marks—*i.e.*, an amount not much above the new loans made during the first half year of 1930. Up to July 31, 1932, the total of these loans had been reduced by an additional amount of about one billion marks, several hundred millions of which, however, represented write-offs in connection with the reorganization of the banks, and a considerable part of which was due to the exchange of book credits into trade bills.[1]

Effects of the 1931 banking crisis on the commercial banks. The elections in September 1930, which showed a decisive trend of the German voters toward both the extreme right and left, caused considerable apprehension abroad. Cancellations of credits and withdrawals of funds by foreigners set in, and these were accelerated after the announcement of the proposed Austro-German customs union. The withdrawals assumed the character of a run in May 1931, when the precarious condition of the Austrian Credit-Anstalt became known. The strain that the German credit structure was subjected to during the first seven months of 1931 is shown in Table 46, taken from the report of the committee (Wiggin Committee) appointed on the recommendation of the London Conference of 1931.

Accompanying the withdrawals of RM 2,900,000,000 were considerable sales of investments in Germany held by for-

---

[1] *Wirtschaftskurve*, Heft III, 1932.

TABLE 46

SHORT-TERM DEBT OF GERMANY
(In billions of reichsmarks)

	Dec. 31, 1930	July 31, 1931*
Short-term debt of public authorities	1.1	.8
Short-term debts of banks:		
Current account and acceptance liabilities	7.0	
Other liabilities	.2 7.2	5.1
Other short-term liabilities	2.0	1.5
Total	10.3	7.4

* Exclusive of the $150,000,000 foreign credits of the Reichsbank and the Gold Discount Bank.

eigners and a flight of German capital abroad, bringing the total outflow of funds up to an estimated amount of RM 3,500,000,000.   On June 25 the Reichsbank obtained a 20-day credit of $100,000,000 from the Bank for International Settlements, the Federal Reserve banks, the Bank of England, and the Bank of France.   This credit, and the $50,-000,000 granted to the Gold Discount Bank on July 7 by a syndicate of American institutions, were soon exhausted.   These loans could not restore confidence or stem the tide of foreign withdrawals.   The collapse of the "Nordwolle," the largest German textile concern, dealt a severe blow to confidence in the solidity of German business and caused a domestic run on the Danat Bank, which was heavily involved in the Nordwolle Company.   Attempts to save the Danat Bank failed because of the lack of foresight of the Berlin banking community, which did not fully realize the contagious character of a run.   The Danat Bank suspended payments on July 13, and within a few hours the banks throughout the country were confronted with runs in spite of the government guaranty of the deposits of the Danat Bank.   When it became evident that no adequate assistance would be forthcoming from the Bank for International Settlements, the government decided to resort to a drastic step not taken even during the chaotic monetary conditions of 1922 and 1923. An emergency decree issued on July 13 ordered all banks to suspend cash payments and interbank clearings during July 14 and 15. The government utilized this short respite to issue various emergency decrees designed to protect the banking system from domestic and foreign runs and to prevent the flight of German capital. A decree issued on July 15 concentrated all foreign exchange transactions and payments abroad in the hands of the Reichsbank or institutions designated by it as agents. On July 16 the banks were permitted to open for limited payments, and on August 1 restrictions on domestic withdrawals of commercial bank deposits were completely abolished. On July 29 a temporary agreement to prevent further withdrawals of short-term funds was reached in Berlin between representatives of the British and American banks and representatives of the German debtors. The "standstill' agreement concluded in September with the foreign creditor banks provided for a six-month (subsequently renewed) continuation of outstanding credits.

Measures to strengthen banks. Before the banks were permitted to resume unlimited domestic payments, two institutions were set up to reinforce the banking structure in general and, more particularly, to aid weak banks. A new clearing association (Ueberweisungs-Verband) was created which embraced the most important banks of the country, including the principal private banks, the labor banks, and the provincial clearing houses. The object of this association was to offset, by loans from banks gaining deposits to those losing them, the losses of deposits of individual banks. The other institution called into being was the Acceptance and Guaranty Bank of Berlin, capitalized at RM 200,000,000. The Reich subscribed RM 80,000,000 directly and, through five banking institutions controlled by the Reich, RM 46,-000,000 indirectly; the Gold Discount Bank subscribed RM 20,000,000; and the remainder was underwritten by five large Berlin banks. The bank was established primarily for the purpose of accepting bills not in themselves eligible for rediscount with the Reichsbank and, secondarily, to pave the way for the resumption of the private discount market.   By accepting drafts of banks and by discounting bills not suitable for discount with the Reichsbank, the Acceptance and Guaranty Bank enabled the banks to convert some of their open credits into acceptances, and in turn, to discount such acceptances.   The bank thus provided the third signature necessary to make the bills eligible for rediscount at the Reichsbank.   In doing this, it performed a function which the banks themselves had previously performed but which the stronger institutions were now reluctant to undertake for the weaker ones.   The endorsement of the Acceptance and Guaranty Bank eliminated the practice of exchanging acceptance signatures by the individual banking institutions, and created acceptances which were readily taken by all leading banks because they were backed by the joint liability of all participating institutions up to the amount of their capital subscriptions.   By the end of 1931 the institution had acquired more than RM 1,600,000,000 of acceptances, the bulk of which was rediscounted with the Reichsbank.   The name of the bank was changed in the spring of 1932 to the Acceptance Bank, and at the same time its statutes were amended to allow it to function more widely.   In March 1934 the directors of the bank decided to take on no more new business and proceeded to liquidate its affairs, which action may be taken as an indication of the improvement in the banking structure since the 1931 crisis.

Banking supervision.   A decree of September 19, 1931, instituted government supervision of banks, establishing for this purpose the office of a Reichs-Commissioner for Banking and a Banking Board.   The board consists of five members, namely, the president of the Reichsbank as chairman, the vice-president of the Reichsbank, the Banking Commissioner, the Secretary of the Ministry of Economics, and the Secretary of the Ministry of Finance.   The banking commissioner is an administrative officer responsible to the Ministry of Economics. He is charged with the duty of supervising general banking policies from the standpoint of the public interest. Within the limits prescribed by law and in accordance with the rules adopted by the board, the commissioner has the power to dictate regulations in case the representative organizations of banks, savings banks, coöperatives, and other financial institutions cannot agree in matters of competition, uniform policy as to deposits and interest rates, etc. The commissioner also has the power to veto or to terminate such agreements in the event that they should prove to be unsatisfactory. He may demand information from the banks about their business activities; he has the right to examine the books of the banks; he may address the general meetings of stockholders and those of the supervisory board and may demand the calling of such meetings (see pages 410–413).

Reorganization of banks. The emergency measures described above prevented a major catastrophe and made possible the functioning of the banks. However, with the exception of the Berliner Handels-Gesellschaft and the government-owned Reichs-Kredit-Gesellschaft, the illiquidity of most other large banks made a thorough reorganization imperative. The government announced the reorganization plan on February 22, 1932. It involved the restoration of liquidity by the application of reserves, a reduction of capital, and the assumption by the government of the greatest part of the losses.

The plan also provided for new capital and reserves. The Danat Bank was absorbed by the Dresdner Bank, the new institution bearing the name of the latter. The RM 33,000,000 of the Dresdner Bank's shares and the RM 35,000,000 of the Danat Bank's original shares held by the two banks themselves were cancelled, and the remaining capital stock of the merged banks was reduced from RM 92,000,000 to RM 20,000,000. The RM 300,000,000 of preferred stock of the Dresdner Bank which the Reich had subscribed to in July 1931 were reduced to RM 200,000,000 of ordinary capital stock; RM 64,000,000 reserves of the two institutions were wiped out.   In addition, the Reich put at the disposal of the merged banks RM 115,000,000 in Treasury notes to be applied toward losses and depreciation of assets, and RM 85,000,000 in Treasury notes to provide liquid funds.   Moreover, the Reich, out of its holdings, turned over without any compensation to the Dresdner Bank RM 55.5 million stock of the Dresdner Bank, of which the latter sold RM 48 million to the Gold Discount Bank for RM 50.4 million and used the remaining RM 7.5 million to exchange the privately held RM 25 million stock of the Danat Bank at the ratio of 10 to 3.   The Reich has also guaranteed the Danat Bank's foreign obligations, which amounted to RM 400 million.   However, the Reich's guaranty of the domestic liabilities of the Danat Bank ceased with the latter's absorption by the Dresdner Bank.

The reorganization of the Deutsche Bank und Disconto-Gesellschaft was accomplished without assistance from the Reich.   Out of the RM 105 million of shares held by the bank, RM 33 million were cancelled and the RM 180 million of shares outstanding were reduced at the ratio of 5 to 2 to a nominal amount of RM 72 million, which, together with the remaining RM 72 million held by the bank, made up RM 144 million of the new capital stock.   The Gold Discount bank purchased from the bank RM 50 million of shares at RM 115 per RM 100 nominal amount.   The reserves have been reduced from RM 160 million to RM 25.2 million, which, together with the reduction of the capital by RM 141 million, represented a shrinkage of RM 275.8 million in the bank's own funds.

In the case of the reorganization and merger of the Commerz- und Privat-Bank A. G. with the Barmer Bank-Verein Hinsberg, Fischer & Co. Kommanditgesellschaft a.A., the aid of the Reich and of the Gold Discount Bank was invoked.   The RM 37.2 million of its own stock held by the Commerz- und Privat-Bank A. G. were bought at par by the Reich.　Then the total capital stock of RM 75 million was reduced on the basis of a 10-to-3 ratio to RM 22.5 million, of which the Reich received RM ·11.2 million of shares for its RM 37.2 million.　Subsequently the capital stock was increased by RM 57.5 million of new shares to RM 80 million.　Of the RM 57.5 million of new shares, RM 45 million were taken over by the Gold Discount Bank at 115 and the remaining RM 12.5 million were exchanged at the ratio of 1 to 1 for the outstanding stock of the Barmer Bank-Verein.　The RM 23.5 million of stock of the Barmer Bank-Verein held by the latter were cancelled. Tables 47 and 48 indicate the magnitude of the reorganization and the great influence which the government now exercises over the private commercial banks.

TABLE 47

REORGANIZATION OF THE LEADING BANKS
AS OF JANUARY 1, 1932
(In millions of reichsmarks)

	Nominal Amount of Original Capital Stock	Original Published Reserves	New Capital Stock—Nominal	New Reserves	Shares Held by Reich	Shares Held by Gold Discount Bank	Percentage of Stock Held by Reich and/or Gold Discount Bank
Deutsche-Disconto Bank..	285	160	144*	25.2	...	50	35
Dresdner Bank.	100	34 ⎫	220†	30†	151†	48	90
Danat Bank ..	60	60 ⎭					
Commerz Bank	75	40.5 ⎫	80	30	11.2	45	70
Barmer Bank..	36	18 ⎭					
Adca	40	11	19	6	...	13	68
	596**	323.5	463	91.2	162.2	156	69

* Reduced in 1933 to RM 130 million through repurchase and cancellation of RM 14 million from the Gold Discount Bank.
† Reduced July 1, 1933, capital to RM 150 million; reserves to 15 million; shares held by Reich to RM 103.1 million.
** The purchase by the Reich of RM 300 million of preferred stock of the Dresdner Bank prior to its merger with the Danat Bank brings up the total to RM 896 million.

The funds required by the Gold Discount Bank for the acquisition of the stock of the reorganized banks were supplied by the Reichsbank, which placed RM 200,000,000 at the disposal of the Gold Discount Bank, for which the latter issued to the Reichsbank RM 200,000,000 of new-class "C" shares.

In the annual report for 1931, the Reichsbank justified its rôle in the reorganization of the banks in the following words:

> The Reichsbank is aware of the extraordinary character of the measures undertaken. . . . If the Reichsbank—after the distribution of its previous customary dividend—had not used these funds in the manner described in this report, corresponding sums would have had to be applied to reserves or writing down assets. The Reichsbank preferred to create a sound eco-

TABLE 48

ASSISTANCE OF THE REICH AND REICHSBANK IN THE RECONSTRUCTION OF THE BANKS

(In millions of reichsmarks)

	Reich (Direct)	Reich (Guaranty)	Gold Discount Bank	Total
Dresdner Bank and Danat Bank..	576.8	400.0*	50.4	1,027.2
Deutsche-Disconto Bank	....	....	57.5	57.5
Commerz- und Privat-Barmer.....	77.2	....	51.8	129.0
Adca	16.0	....	15.0	31.0
Norddeutsche Kreditbank	35.0	88.0	....	123.0
Landesbank der Rheinprovinz	120.0	....	....	120.0
Deutsche Orientbank A. G.........	15.3	7.7	....	23.0
Berliner Bank fuer Handel & Grundbesitz	12.3	20.5	....	32.8
Clearing Center of the German Civil Service Bank..............	....	1.3	....	1.3
Industrial Coöperatives	....	47.6	....	47.6
Deutsche Girozentrale	....	100.0	....	100.0
Coöperative Shops	....	8.5	....	8.5
Handelsbank A. G., Berlin........	....	.5	....	.5
Gewerbebank A. G., Treves	....	.5	....	.5
Acceptance and Guaranty Bank...	80.0†	66.0	....	146.0
Other banks	....	7.9	....	7.9
Total	932.6	748.5	174.7	1,855.8

* Represent foreign obligations of the Danat Bank.
† Additional RM 46 million were subscribed indirectly through government-owned banks.

nomic position by strengthening the German banking system rather than merely to correct its balance sheet items.

The recent condition of the important commercial banks is shown in Table 49.

TABLE 49

SOME BALANCE SHEET ITEMS OF THE FIVE LARGE BERLIN BANKS* AND OF PRIVATE CREDIT BANKS PUBLISHING MONTHLY STATEMENTS

(In millions of reichsmarks)

	FIVE BERLIN BANKS		PRIVATE CREDIT BANKS PUBLISHING MONTHLY STATEMENTS	
	Feb. 28, 1933	July 31, 1934	Feb. 28, 1933	July 31, 1934
ASSETS				
Cash and cash items......	132	159	61	53
Treasury bills	462	491	49	184
Other bills	1,274	1,349	460	431
Balances with banks (Nostroguthaben)	235	140	114	147
Reports and lombard loans	28	20	5	5
Loans on commodities....	941	526	98	95
Investments	621	668	330	278
Syndicates and participations	313	279	69	61
Debtors (mainly secured and unsecured loans in current account)	4,427	3,843	981	912
Total assets	8,674	7,704	3,717	3,801
LIABILITIES				
Capital	512	428	664	654
Reserves	115	82	158	163
Liability on credits opened with third parties for customers	1,073	552	68	42
Deposits of German banks.	1,257	1,067	226	288
Other deposits	4,828	4,694	1,257	1,204
Deposits payable within 7 days	2,853	2,648	571	719
Deposits payable within 3 months	2,550	2,514	456	502
Deposits payable after 3 months	682	600	456	270
Acceptances	746	737	85	81
Long-term loans	128	86	1,207	1,276

* Deutsche Bank und Disconto-Gesellschaft, Dresdner Bank, Commerz- und Privat-Bank A. G., Berliner Handels-Gesellschaft, Reichs-Kredit-Gesellschaft A. G.

In addition to the incorporated credit banks there are a number of important private banking firms which operate along the same lines as the credit banks. The most important of these are Mendelssohn and Co., S. Bleichroeder, and Delbrueck Schickler & Co., of Berlin; M. M. Warburg & Co., of Hamburg; Gebrueder Arnhold, of Dresden; Sal. Oppenheim, Jr. & Cie., of Koeln; and Simon Hirschland, of Essen. The private banking firms do not publish their balance sheets, and therefore it is impossible to state what their financial status is.

Bank associations. The Berlin banks are grouped together into an association known as the Vereinigung von Berliner Banken und Bankiers, usually known under the name of Stempelvereinigung. This association was established in 1883 in consequence of the disputes concerning stamp duties prevailing in those days in Germany. In addition to this original purpose the association undertook to eliminate unsound practices among the large Berlin banks and particularly to prevent cutthroat competition among them. This program in turn led to agreements concerning interest rates, commissions, and other matters affecting the banking business and policies. The last mentioned are, at the present time, the most important functions of the Stempelvereinigung. The authority and influence of the Stempelvereinigung on methods and policies of banking throughout the country have been recognized by the Reichsbank, and it is this body to which the latter communicates its wishes regarding changes in the credit policy, *i.e.*, so-called "direct action." For example, it was the Stempelvereinigung which decided on radical curtailment of stock exchange loans on May 13, 1927, in compliance with the request of the Reichsbank.

The Stempelvereinigung is an important factor in the regulation of the rate on acceptances and in the fixing of the rate on report loans. Its influence is particularly felt on the stock exchange. For a number of years it was composed of twelve members. At the present time, its membership includes: Deutsche Bank und Disconto-Gesellschaft, Dresdner Bank, Commerz- und Privat-Bank A. G., Berliner Handels-Gesellschaft, S. Bleichroeder, Delbrueck, Schickler & Co., and Mendelssohn & Co. As a rule, members of the Stempelvereinigung borrow day-to-day money as well as longer-term funds without security.

In addition to the Stempelvereinigung, there are throughout Germany a number of other bankers' associations which, in their localities, perform more or less the same functions as the Stempelvereinigung in Berlin. Since the end of the inflation period a number of *Kassenvereine* have also been established in Germany. Originally the main purpose of these organizations was to provide local clearing facilities, but at the present time they are also important factors in stock clearing. The most important of the *Kassenvereine* is the Bank des Berliner Kassen-Vereins, which since its organization in 1823 has been active in developing clearing facilities in Berlin. The technical apparatus for clearing stock exchange transactions devised by this institution proved to be very successful, and the stock exchange transactions are almost exclusively cleared through it.

Bank Law of 1934. The Bank Law promulgated by the government on December 5, 1934, constitutes in its main features a continuation and broadening of the banking supervision instituted in September 1931. The law applies to all credit institutions except the Reichsbank, the Gold Discount Bank, the Reichspost (postal check accounts), and housing financing institutions. All domestic credit institutions and branches of foreign credit institutions operating in Germany are subject to supervision by the authorities created by this law.

Credit Supervision Board. Supervision over the banks is exercised by the Credit Supervision Board (Aufsichtsamt fuer das Kreditwesen) and the Reich Commissioner for Credit (Reichskommissar fuer das Kreditwesen), who replace the banking board and banking commissioner established in September 1931. The Credit Supervision Board is attached to the Reichsbank. It consists of seven members: (1) the president of the Reichsbank as chairman, (2) the Reichsbank vice-president as deputy chairman, (3) a person to be appointed by the Chancellor, and (4) the state secretaries of the Ministries of the Interior, Finance, Economic Affairs, and Food. The Reich Commissioner for Credit is not a member but is entitled to attend sessions in an advisory capacity.

Authority to make decisions and issue orders is vested in the Chairman of the Board. The functions of the other members are chiefly of a consultative character. Doubtful cases, however, or cases in which the decision of the Chairman is opposed by a member of the Board, are referred to the Reichs Cabinet for decision. Certain decisions of the Commissioner may be appealed by the banks to the Board, and such appeals are decided, by a simple majority vote, by the members.

Besides the specific duties and powers of the Board relating to capital structure, liquidity, and the clearing system, the law gives the Board a blanket authority over all banking affairs. Section 32 of the act states that it is the duty of the Board to eliminate abuses in banking, to take proper measures when a bank gets into difficulties, and to require independent auditing of the yearly balance sheets of all credit institutions. The Board may issue basic rules governing the management of the banks and is given the authority up to the end of 1935 to order cessation of certain or all operations by any credit institution whenever such action is deemed necessary for "a more purposeful organization of the credit system."

Reich Commissioner for Credit. The Commissioner is an administrative official appointed by the Chancellor upon consultation with the president of the Reichsbank. In addition to the duties and powers vested in his predecessor, the banking commissioner, the Reich Commissioner for Credit is intrusted with the administration of the licensing system introduced by the Bank Law.

The law requires a license issued by the Reich Commissioner for the establishment of new banks, branches and agencies, and clearing institutions. The existing credit institutions, with the exception of those established after June 30, 1934, need no permit. A license may be refused (1) for personal unfitness of the management, (2) when the resources are not available within Germany, (3) when general economic conditions do not justify the organization of new banks. The Commissioner may close a bank (1) when the information supplied with the application for the license is false, (2) on the ground of insufficient reliability of the management, (3) for violation of public interests, and (4) for insufficient guaranty of the safety of deposits and investments. Appeal against refusal or revocation of a license and against an order for discontinuation of business may be taken to the Credit Supervision Board.

Liquidity provisions. The law stipulates that the total liabilities of a credit institution, less liquid assets of the first and second class, must not exceed a certain percentage of the capital. The ratio varies for the different types of credit institutions, but all banks are permitted to maintain a ratio of five times the amount of their capital. The law defines "first class liquid assets or cash reserve" as cash on hand and deposits with the Reichsbank and with the postal checking system, while liquid assets of second class are 90-day trade bills and securities acceptable as collateral by the Reichsbank. Balances due from banks (*Nostroguthaben*) are not considered liquid assets. The cash reserve is not to fall below a stipulated percentage of total liabilities less savings deposits. The percentage fixed by the Board may vary for different classes of banks but may not be fixed higher than 10 per cent. The secondary reserve is similarly fixed by the Board but may not be set higher than 30 per cent.

Holdings of stocks, except those representing permanent participation in a company, and of bonds not listed on German stock exchanges, are limited to a certain percentage of total liabilities less deposits. The percentage is to be fixed by the Board but may not be fixed lower than 5 per cent. The total investments in real estate and permanent participations may not exceed the capital of the institutions.

Loans. Unsecured credits exceeding RM 5,000 may be made only when the borrower reveals his financial condition, and credits granted to a single borrower must not exceed a certain percentage of the bank's capital. The percentage is fixed by the Board. The law considers all affiliated companies as a single borrower. When the total indebtedness of a borrower at one credit institution exceeds the sum of RM 1,000,000 during a month, it is termed "large credit" (*Grosskredit*) and must be reported monthly to the Commissioner. When a borrower has obtained credits at several institutions, the Commissioner may inform these institutions of the total indebtedness of the borrower and of the number of institutions involved.

Savings deposits. The law defines "savings deposits" as deposits for investment purposes. Withdrawals may be made only against presentation of the savings book, and withdrawals through the clearing system or by check are prohibited. Withdrawals without notice are limited to RM 300 per month per passbook. The Board is authorized to issue instructions regulating the investment of savings deposits.

The Money Market

The Berlin money market is well organized and consists of a number of individual markets, each performing a certain more or less well-defined function. These markets may be broadly divided into four groups. The first group constitutes the acceptance market, which embraces the dealings in bankers' acceptances and trade bills with a bank endorsement. This market is generally referred to as the private discount market and the paper traded in is known as *Privatdiskonten*. The second group is the loan market, in which short-term funds are lent by one bank to another. This market in turn is subdivided into (1) the day-to-day money or money at call (*taegliches Geld*); (2) monthly money or loans for not less than thirty days; (3) ultimo money, which represents a loan from any day to the stock exchange settlement day; and (4) report money, which represents short-term loans for stock exchange purposes—usually for carrying securities from one settlement to another. These various loans may be made with or without securities as collateral. Usually the members of the Stempelvereinigung borrow without collateral, while others are requested to put up security for their loans. The third group is the lombard loan market, in which collateral loans are granted by banks to others for certain defined periods. In this market the Reichsbank has acquired considerable importance in the post-war period. The fourth component part of the money market is the foreign exchange, or *Devisen*, market, which owing to the foreign exchange restrictions is not functioning at present and, therefore, is of no importance. Since the 1931 banking crisis the foreign exchange business has been practically monopolized in the hands of the Reichsbank.

In spite of the absence of legal restrictions, the various markets of Berlin are under the control of the larger banks, notably the members of the Stempelvereinigung, which in a number of cases fix the rate of interest on the various transactions. Rates so fixed are called *kartelliert*, in contrast to free rates. With the exception, however, of the discount and lombard rate of the Reichsbank, all other rates are not considered as official. Transactions on the Berlin money market are carried out primarily over the telephone. The various markets are closely related, and the movement of interest rates is more or less uniform. The rate of interest of one individual market does not in itself, however, determine the policy of a bank as to whether it will place its funds in that particular market.   For example, although the rate for monthly money may be substantially higher than that for bankers' acceptances, or for day-to-day money, a bank will often prefer to invest in the last two markets because of their greater liquidity.

Acceptance market (private discount market).   The private discount market is the market for prime bankers' acceptances—*i.e.*, bills accepted by the large incorporated banks and private banking houses, trade bills with bank endorsement, and Treasury bills of short maturity.   There are less than 100 houses in Germany whose signatures are considered as prime.   Of this number only about 50 appear as regular acceptors.   Bankers' acceptances dealt in on the Berlin market are divided into two classes: (1) those of short maturity (*kurze Sicht*), running from 30 to 55 days; and (2) those of long maturity (*lange Sicht*), running from 56 to 90 days.   Both classes of bills are traded in amounts of RM 5,000 or over.

In the post-war years the importance of the Reichsbank to the acceptance market increased tremendously, because the Reichsbank is the principal sponsor and supporter of the market.   As a matter of fact the bill rate is fixed by agreement between the Reichsbank and the large banks. The Reichsbank does not buy acceptances directly from the accepting banks, since it prefers to hold in its portfolio bills with three signatures.   Consequently banks will often exchange their acceptances in order to give them the additional signature and thus make their bills eligible for sale to the Reichsbank.

Before the war the Berlin acceptance market played an important rôle at home as well as abroad.   At the end of 1913, the acceptances of the large banks amounted to 1,856 million gold marks, which amount was reduced to about 230 million in 1918.   During the inflation period, bankers' acceptances in marks almost completely disappeared, and it is only since April 1, 1925, that the acceptance market in

Berlin has again become important. Although substantial progress has been made in the development of the acceptance market since the stabilization of the currency, the volume of bankers' acceptances outstanding in 1930 was estimated at approximately RM 1,000,000,000, of which RM 670,000,000 were created by the large German banks. The volume of acceptances at that time was therefore about 40 per cent of the volume outstanding before the war.

Although the law does not limit the amount of acceptances which the individual banks may create, an agreement was reached in the spring of 1925 by the members of the Berlin Stempelvereinigung to restrict their acceptance liability to 50 per cent of their capital and surplus. This policy is in contrast with the pre-war practice, under which banks accepted up to about 100 per cent of the capital and surplus. The reason for the restriction is the fact that the number of purchasers is small and that it was desired to avoid flooding the market with acceptances and consequently raising their rate.

In addition to the self-imposed limitation of acceptance credit, the small volume of bankers' acceptances outstanding in Berlin is due to the high rate of interest on German acceptances as contrasted with the rate on bankers' bills prevailing in other countries. The high rate makes the creation of a mark bill rather expensive. This fact has induced a number of German importers and exporters to finance their transactions through foreign acceptances. Large Berlin banks, in order to meet this demand, have arranged acceptance credits abroad (*Rembourskredite*). Thus, at the end of 1930, the large Berlin banks reported that they had arranged abroad for the acceptance of bills of their customers to an amount of about RM 1,980,000,000. Since 1931, when foreigners ceased buying mark acceptances, the Reichsbank and the Seehandlung have been the largest buyers of acceptances.

In addition to bankers' acceptances, trade acceptances with bank endorsements are traded in the acceptance market.   At times these bills are sold above, and at times below, the private discount rate.   When such bills are sold above the discount rate, it is indicated that they have not met the eligibility requirements for discount or purchase by the Reichsbank.   It may also mean that the Reichsbank has restricted the volume of credit that it will extend to one individual customer, which in this case may be the acceptor or, more likely, the endorser.   Trade bills with bank endorsements usually sell at a higher rate of interest than prime bankers' bills.

Short-term Treasury notes of the Reich and of the State of Prussia are sold in the open market like bankers' acceptances.   Before the war, trading in Treasury bills of the Reich and of the State of Prussia was equal in importance to that of bankers' acceptances.   In the post-war years up to November 1933, however, since the amount of Treasury bills which the Reichsbank could acquire was limited to RM 400,000,000 and since these bills had to have an additional signature of a bank of good standing before they could be sold to the Reichsbank, the volume traded in the open market was comparatively small.   Treasury bills traded in the open market usually run for a period of not more than three months.   They may also be used as collateral with the Reichsbank, in which case the latter usually grants a loan up to 95 per cent of the market value of the bills.

Day-to-day money.   Day-to-day money represents funds which have been loaned for one day.   The loan is not necessarily repaid the following day, but may be renewed for one-day periods as long as the arrangement is satisfactory to the parties.   The loan may be terminated by either borrower or lender within twenty-four hours, but loans may not be called after one o'clock and repayments are made before 12 o'clock on the next stock exchange day. If the day is a stock exchange holiday, payment is made the following day.   Settlement is made through the clearing house.   Large lenders usually do not call their loans without the consent of the borrowers. In the case of small and middle-sized firms, on the other hand, it is quite common for the lenders to call their loans without first obtaining the consent of the borrower. The reason for this situation is that important lenders, such as the large banks, usually have considerable amounts of funds which they can place on the market daily and, hence, when money is tight they simply do not make any new loans.

Day-to-day loans are made with or without security, either on the stock exchange or over the counter. Members of the Stempelvereinigung, which as stated before includes only the most important banks and bankers of Berlin, obtain day-to-day loans unsecured (*blanko*), while non-members are usually required to pledge collateral as security (*gedeckt*), the market value of which is at least 125 per cent of the amount of the loan. Interbank loans of large institutions are not carried on the books as loans but as "due from banks" (*Nostroguthaben*).

There is no official interest rate for day-to-day money. In Berlin the rate is agreed upon by borrower and lender and remains in force until the following day, when the loan is repaid or extended for another day at a newly agreed-upon rate. In Frankfort, on the other hand, the rate of interest is fixed by the members of the clearing house. This procedure, however, applies only to loans without security. The rate on secured loans is fixed by the borrower and lender.

Day-to-day loans, particularly those that are unsecured, are used by banking institutions as marginal credits to meet temporary cash needs or for the temporary employment of surplus funds. The need for funds for short periods arises out of the bank's activities. It frequently happens that unusually large demands for funds are made on a bank by its clients. The bank will meet the demand, and in turn will borrow in the day-to-day market from an institution which has a surplus of short-term funds. The borrowing bank thereby obtains the necessary funds until it can re-discount eligible paper at the Reichsbank or convert other assets into cash. The Seehandlung usually stands ready to borrow, in the day-to-day market, large amounts which it employs in discounting bills of coöperative associations.

Secured day-to-day loans are used by brokerage houses and smaller banks for stock exchange transactions because, in addition to stocks which are traded for delivery on settlement day, many securities are sold for immediate delivery and payment is made the day following the transaction. Very often the funds to make such payments are borrowed on a day-to-day basis. The lenders are chiefly the large Berlin commercial and public banks.

The market for day-to-day money is the reservoir for the cash surpluses of the banks. Thus, whenever a bank has a momentary surplus of funds, it will place the funds in the day-to-day market. This market is in close contact with other markets, particularly with the private discount market (acceptance market).

Although the day-to-day rate is usually lower than the private discount rate, banks prefer to lend their surplus funds on a day-to-day basis, especially when an increase in the bill rate is expected. This preference is due to the fact that when a bank has loaned money on the day-to-day market, it can withdraw the funds whenever it desires without incurring any loss. On the other hand, when a bank which has invested its surplus funds in acceptances is compelled to sell its bills in order to meet unexpected withdrawals or demands, it may suffer a loss if the bill rate has gone up in the meantime. The day-to-day rate usually increases at the end of the month and when stock exchange settlements take place, and at times it rises above the acceptance rate, since borrowers would rather pay a comparatively high rate of interest for a few days than a moderate rate for monthly money. As a rule, large borrowers first endeavor to obtain day-to-day money. If the rate on this type of loan is too high, they then endeavor to obtain funds from the Reichsbank. If the latter refuses to discount or lend, then borrowers revert back to the open market.

Money for one day (Eintagsgeld). This type of loan is very similar to the Federal funds market in the United States. It represents a loan for one day only. Usually the transaction is carried out through the exchange of checks. The lender gives the borrower a check which can be cashed immediately, and obtains from the borrower a check for an equal amount, plus interest for one day, due the following day. The object of such a loan is to wipe out a debit balance at the clearing institution, the rules of which strictly prohibit overdrafts.

Time loans (Termingeld). To this category belong monthly money (*Monatsgeld*), semi-monthly money (*Halbmonatsgeld*), loans of a longer maturity ranging up to six months, and report loans. Loans which appertain to the money market are transacted only among banking institutions. In many respects these loans are not unlike time loans secured by stock exchange collateral used in the New York money market. In Berlin, however, in the case of the larger banks no security is offered as collateral, while in the case of smaller banking institutions collateral ranging from 10 to 50 per cent over and above the market value of the security is requested. As a rule the market value of the collateral amounts to not less than 125 per cent of the loan. Monthly loans (*Monatsgeld*) are obtained for a number of purposes, and the proceeds are used for stock exchange as well as for commercial transactions. The rate of interest is not fixed by general agreement among the banks but is determined by the borrower and lender. The banks cooperate, however, in fixing the rate of interest on these types of loans. Loans of the type described above are widely used by medium- and large-sized banking institutions for the placing of part of their liquid funds. The lenders are careful in the selection of collateral and, as a rule, will accept stocks traded in for future delivery (*Terminpapiere*) and bonds which have an active market.   Whenever time loans are renewed, the borrower pays only interest on the maturity date.   In contrast to day-to-day loans, which are usually made between institutions in the same locality, time loans are often made between institutions in different cities.

Ultimo loans. Very similar in character to the loans described above is the market for ultimo money, which is used by banks at times for the purpose of obtaining short-term funds either up to the ultimo or for a few days more. In the latter case, the rate of interest is somewhat higher. Ultimo money may range for a month, in which case the loan is contracted from the end of one month to the end of the next month; or it may range for a shorter period— *i.e.*, from any day during the month to the ultimo date. The Seehandlung is a large lender of ultimo money.

Lombard loans. Lombard loans are loans made by banks to customers and other financial institutions, collateralled by securities or merchandise.   Before the war, the securities which were offered as collateral for lombard loans consisted almost exclusively of bonds, notably those of the Reich, of the states, and of municipalities.   At the present time, security collateral consists to a large extent of stocks. Thus, for example, of the total lombard loans made in recent years by the Seehandlung, one of the largest lenders of such funds, between 80 and 90 per cent have been secured by stocks.   The funds obtained by the borrower may be used for a number of purposes.   The rate of interest is usually above the lombard rate of the Reichsbank and fluctuates in accordance with the lombard rate.   The Reichsbank and other banking institutions have established certain rules concerning the margin at which they will accept individual securities as collateral.

Report loans. Similar to lombard loans are report loans, which are secured exclusively by stock exchange collateral, which are used solely for the purpose of carrying securities on margin from one settlement day to another, and which run usually for a period of thirty days.   While the lombard loan is a straight collateral loan, in the case of a report loan the lender assumes a stock exchange obligation of the borrower with the agreement that the latter will reassume this obligation at a future date.   The operation of report loans may best be explained by the following example.

The banking firm A purchases for a customer securities to be delivered on the ultimo of June.   The customer of A is not able to pay the full amount and requests A to carry the securities for one month.   If A itself is not in a position to finance the transaction, it borrows from B report money on the exchange.   The loan is transacted as a sale of the securities involved by the borrower (A) to the lender (B), delivery ultimo June and repurchase per ultimo July.   The Liquidations-Kasse (the stock exchange clearing house), which guarantees all future contracts of its members, is notified of the transaction.   On the ultimo June settlement, the Liquidations-Kasse takes up the securities purchased by A and delivers them to B against payment of the purchase price.   On the ultimo July settlement, B delivers the securities to the Liquidations-Kasse for account of A and receives back the amount of the loan plus the agreed-upon interest for one month.   All transactions are cleared by the clearing house at the liquidation price fixed for each security at each settlement date, and the difference between the price at which the security was purchased or sold and the liquidation price is charged or credited to the accounts of the parties.   The customer of A is charged for the interest and may arrange for another extension or sale of the securities.

While the lombard lender must watch the margin of the securities, the report lender has the guaranty of the Liquidations-Kasse that the borrower will take back the securities for the amount of the loan plus interest.   Report loans are usually made on securities which are subject to future trading (*Terminpapiere*).   The rate of interest on report money is higher than on lombard loans, partly because users of lombard loans are usually regular customers of the bank and maintain with the latter a larger deposit than do borrowers on report money.   The large brokerage houses therefore finance their stock exchange transactions through lombard, and not report, loans.   Also, since report money is used exclusively for stock exchange purposes, the rate of interest depends to a considerable extent upon the conditions of the stock market.   During a rising market, report money rates are generally relatively high.   On the other hand, when there is considerable short selling of certain securities, the sellers may have difficulties in borrowing the securities for delivery.   The borrower of securities who is at the same time the lender of report money not only may be compelled to forego interest on the report money in order to obtain the securities for delivery on his short sales, but also may be compelled to pay a premium (deport-money) to the lender of the securities.   The lenders of report money are primarily the members of the Stempelvereinigung and public credit institutions.

CHAPTER XVI

Amsterdam—The Dutch Banking System

Historical survey.   The history of Amsterdam as a center of international commerce and finance dates back to the beginning of the commercial revolution initiated by the explorations of the Portuguese and Spanish in the last decade of the fifteenth century.   The Dutch, driven to sea by the limited resources of their narrow strip of coastland, early began to participate in the growing volume of international trade.   In the sixteenth century their activities centered chiefly on European trade, and it was not until the close of the century that they began to make voyages to India and the New World.

The first years of the seventeenth century witnessed the succession of the Dutch to a large part of the colonial empire of Portugal.   Throughout the seventeenth century the Dutch almost monopolized the trade from Asia as well as that between southwestern Europe and the Baltic countries.   The large profits derived both from this trade and from their colonial possessions greatly increased the liquid wealth of the country.   The national wealth was further augmented in the sixteenth century by the influx of *marranos* from Spain, who brought with them not only part of their movable property but also their international connections.   In addition, the Thirty Years' War resulted in an inflow of capital from Germany and the neighboring countries, and a large volume of the banking business formerly transacted in Antwerp was shifted to Amsterdam.

The natural outgrowth of the expansion of the Dutch colonial empire was the evolution of Holland into a great commercial and trading nation and the development of

Amsterdam as an international financial center. The Amsterdam Beurs, organized in 1608, soon became the most important European exchange—not only for securities but also for commodities. The Amsterdamsche Wisselbank, one of the famous early banks, was established in 1609. In the middle of the seventeenth century the acceptance business had already begun to flourish, and the low rates of interest prevailing in Amsterdam made it one of the chief centers for international financial transactions.

The frequent contact of the Dutch with other countries and the lack of adequate investments at home produced a natural tendency toward the investment of capital abroad —a tendency not confined to a few capitalists, but extending to the small "rentier" class. Although Dutch commercial supremacy was supplanted by England's rise, toward the end of the seventeenth century, as the world's greatest colonial and trading nation, the Dutch had become so accustomed to making foreign investments that they continued to hold a place of importance in that field. For example, it has been estimated that about one-third of the shares of the Bank of England and the British East India Company, and 40 per cent of the total public debt of Great Britain, were at one time held in Holland.

The Napoleonic wars left Holland exhausted and with its financial resources at a low ebb. But William I, who ascended the throne in 1814, set about vigorously to promote the revival of trade and commerce. In the first year of his reign he established the Netherlands Bank, and in 1824 he took the initiative in the organization of the Netherlands Trading Society (Nederlandsche Handel-Maatschappij), which is now the leading financial institution in Holland. The country recuperated rapidly from the war, and toward the middle of the nineteenth century the Dutch, again seeking profitable investments abroad for their surplus funds, turned to American railways and other American enterprises. Amsterdam thus regained a part of its former financial prestige, although its importance as an international financial center was overshadowed by London, New York, Paris, and Berlin.

War and post-war periods. The World War and its influence on the leading European money markets caused a change almost revolutionary in nature both in the international position and in the organization of the Amsterdam money market. Since the Netherlands remained neutral during the war, the Dutch florin was not subject to the disturbances which caused the depreciation of so many European currencies in the post-war years, and it remained comparatively stable throughout the entire period of currency chaos. Amsterdam became a convenient and safe place of refuge for foreign capital seeking to escape from depreciating currencies and high taxation at home, with the result that the foreign exchange business transacted on this market greatly increased.

With the passing of extraordinary conditions after the Armistice and with the stabilization of the principal currencies of Europe, the money markets of London, Paris, and New York resumed their normal functions, and a considerable volume of foreign funds was withdrawn from Amsterdam. The Amsterdam market, however, retained a large part of the ground gained during and immediately after the war. It continued to finance the foreign trade of the central European countries which had been diverted to it by the war. A number of foreign banks, particularly German institutions, were established in Amsterdam to participate in this business and to administer foreign funds invested in Holland. The Amsterdam acceptance market steadily developed, and at the present time remains among the most important in continental Europe.

The financial disturbances in Europe beginning in May 1931 had serious consequences for Holland. At first the unsettled state of affairs in Germany led to an inflow of German funds to Amsterdam, strengthening the guilder. The situation, however, became serious when England abandoned the gold standard on September 21, 1931; first, because of the loss suffered by the Netherlands Bank on its sterling assets; and second, because of the danger to Dutch trade and shipping from the competition offered by the depreciation of the pound.

Although the first shock of the abandonment of the gold standard by Great Britain was well absorbed by the Amsterdam market, the crisis was by no means over. Rumors developed to the effect that Holland, too, would abandon the gold standard. These were promptly and consistently denied by the Netherlands Bank, and the denials were effectively supported by the Bank's weekly statements. On September 30, 1931, Dr. Vissering, the Bank's president, announced that the holdings of sterling bills on the part of the Bank would in no way impede its fullest functions as a bank of issue, that the gold standard would be maintained, and that there would be no inflation of the currency. This attitude was maintained by the Nederlandsche Bank even after the abandonment of the gold standard by the United States. The maintenance of a stable currency and of a more or less free gold market, together with the fact that the large Dutch banks had withstood without any failures the financial panic of 1931–33, further strengthened the position of Amsterdam as an international financial center.

The Banking System

The Dutch were among the pioneers in the development of modern banking in Europe. The Amsterdamsche Wisselbank, established by a decree of January 31, 1609, was one of the most famous of the early European banks. The business of this bank, like that of the early English goldsmiths, was to receive deposits of bullion and coin for safekeeping. The receipts issued for deposited bullion came to enjoy extensive circulation and were known as bank money. Later the Amsterdamsche Wisselbank and similar institutions began to make loans and advances, until gradually, during the last quarter of the nineteenth century, modern banking practices were evolved.

Bank concentration. Up to the beginning of the present century most of the Dutch banks (the Netherlands Trading Society being a notable exception) were comparatively small and of merely local importance. However, shortly before the war a concentration movement similar to that which took place at earlier dates in England and Germany made itself felt in Dutch banking, with the result that at the present time by far the largest portion of the country's banking business has become centralized in the hands of a few leading institutions. This concentration has partly consisted in the absorption of the smaller, provincial institutions by the larger banks and partly in the maintenance of informal alliances between banks which continue their separate existence but which are actually under the same control.

Ratio of capital to deposits. A peculiarity of the Dutch banks is the small amount of their deposits in relation to capital and surplus. This peculiarity may be illustrated by a comparison of capital and reserves with deposits for five leading banks as of the end of 1932 (see Table 50). In 1929 the ratio of capital and surplus to liabilities (excluding acceptances and sundry accounts) for the principal

TABLE 50

RELATIONSHIP OF CAPITAL AND RESERVES TO DEPOSITS
FOR LEADING DUTCH BANKS AT END OF 1932
(In millions of guilders)

	Capital and Reserves	Current Accounts and Time Deposits	Ratio of Capital and Reserves to Deposits (per cent)
Nederlandsche Handel-Maatschappij	100	301*	33.22
Amsterdamsche Bank	104	169	61.53
Rotterdamsche Bank-Vereeniging	70	204	34.31
De Twentsche Bank	55	190	28.94
Incasso-Bank	39	76	51.31
Total	368	940	39.14

* Includes deposits in East India offices.

commercial Dutch banks was 28 per cent, compared with that of 7.4 per cent for the principal British banks and 9.5 per cent for the chief French institutions.   The capitalization of the Dutch banks is large in relation not only to the deposits but also to the financial needs of the country. This fact explains the endeavor of the banks to employ a part of their resources in international business.

The paucity of bank deposits in Holland is attributable to a number of peculiarities in Dutch financial practice. In the first place, it has long been the custom in Holland for business concerns as well as individuals to place their liquid resources in prolongatie loans on the stock exchange rather than in banks (see page 460).   Again, the Dutch have shown a traditional propensity toward placing their savings in securities rather than in bank deposits, so that the wealth of the people is administered not by the banks, as is the case in the United States, but generally by the people themselves.   Another factor is the lack of a well-developed checking system at the banks, owing to the competition of the postal check and transfer service which has practically monopolized the business of transferring funds.   In addition the postal savings system has gained great popularity, attracting funds which in other countries would have been deposited with the banks.   The facts that some municipalities, and Amsterdam in particular, have established a transfer and deposit system of their own, and that the international character of Dutch business has forced many concerns to maintain deposits in foreign countries, have also adversely affected domestic deposits.

In the Netherlands, as in several other European countries, there is no general banking law.   Banking institutions other than the central bank have much the same legal status as any other business enterprise.   They are not subject to any governmental supervision and are under no legal obligation to publish periodical balance sheets.   Dutch banks on the whole operate more or less along the lines of the continental European system; i.e., they are engaged in commercial as well as investment banking. However, the banks in Holland are not so closely tied up with industry as those elsewhere on the Continent, and they do not exercise the same influence on the policies of corporations as do the banks in Germany, Austria, Hungary, and Belgium. In addition to their commercial and investment banking business, the banks also perform the functions of stock exchange houses, executing orders for their customers.

The Dutch banks may be classified as follows:

1. General banks.
2. Provincial banks.
3. Colonial banks.
4. Cashiers.
5. Private bankers.
6. Foreign banks in Amsterdam.
7. Acceptance banks.
8. Other institutions.

The Netherlands Bank

The Netherlands Bank (De Nederlandsche Bank) was organized at Amsterdam by a royal decree of March 25, 1814. This decree not only called for the establishment of a bank of issue but also presented the economic reconstruction program of the government after the Napoleonic wars. The decree declared it to be the duty of the government to restore trade, the "nerve" of the Netherlands, which had been destroyed by the Napoleonic wars and the continental blockade. To this end a sound monetary system was held to be indispensable, and this in turn could be achieved and maintained only through the functioning of a strong central bank. The original charter, which expired after twenty-five years, was renewed through a royal decree on August 21, 1838, and again by an act of the legislature on December 22, 1863. This act was subsequently amended and finally codified in the Bank Act of 1919, according to which the present charter will remain in force until April 1, 1937.

The Bank is a private institution incorporated as a limited company with a paid-up capital of fl. 20,000,000.

Only Dutch citizens may be voting shareholders. No person may, either for himself or for others, or for himself and others collectively, return more than six votes.   The management of the Netherlands Bank is vested in a managing board composed of a president and a secretary—appointed by the Crown for a period of seven years out of a list, containing two names for each appointment, submitted by a combined meeting of the managing board and the commissioners—and of not less than two directors, elected by the shareholders for a term of five years.   The managing board is assisted by an advisory committee of five members, elected by the shareholders for five years, and by a board of not less than fifteen commissioners, also elected by the shareholders. The supervision of the Bank on behalf of the government is exercised by a royal commissioner appointed by the Crown.   The management must publish once a week in the *Netherlands Staatscourant* (State Gazette) a concise bank return in a form sanctioned by the Crown.   The annual balance sheet must be submitted for approval to the government, which may reject it if it has been prepared contrary to the terms of the charter.

The operations of the Netherlands Bank may be conveniently considered under two general headings: (1) note-issue function and (2) banking functions.

Note-issue function.   Up to the end of the seventeenth century, various coins were in circulation in the Netherlands.   The resultant confusion was so great that the government found it necessary after 1516 to issue, from time to time, public notices (*plakaats*) stating the mutual exchange values of the different coins.   Through the eighteenth century and down to 1806 the silver gulden was, generally speaking, the Dutch monetary unit.   From December 15, 1806, to September 26, 1847, Holland was on the bimetallic standard, but on the latter date she adopted the single silver standard, to which she adhered up to May 21, 1873, when a decline in the price of silver resulted in the suspension of the free coinage of silver.   During the following two years the Dutch currency was not linked to any metal, but on June 6, 1875, a new monetary unit (the gold florin) was introduced, with a metallic content of 604.8 milligrams of fine gold, equivalent to about $0.4020 of United States currency (old parity). Free coinage of gold was provided, the gold florin (or guilder) was made full legal tender, and the larger silver coins (half-florin, florin, and 2½ florins, called *rijksdaalder*) remained legal tender, as they had been under the régime of the silver standard. The free coinage of silver, however, continued to be prohibited.

The original bank law contained no stipulations regarding the note cover, the regulation of the latter having been delegated to the Crown. A royal decree of April 16, 1864, renewed on June 20, 1880, ordered the Bank to maintain a metallic reserve of at least 40 per cent against notes, demand deposits, and bank assignations. There are no provisions regarding the cover of the remaining 60 per cent, and the Bank consequently has a free hand in its choice of assets. The Netherlands Bank was one of the first, if not the first, of the central banks obligated by law to maintain a metallic reserve against demand deposits. Current accounts and assignations represent, however, only a small percentage of the total liabilities of the Bank and therefore exercise no influence on its policies. The assignations mentioned above are drafts of the Bank on its branches payable at sight, at not more than three days after sight, or not later than eight days after date. The law of July 18, 1904, made the notes of the Bank legal tender to any amount, and the government ceased issuing paper money. A clause in the Act provides that the government will lose its share in the profits of the Bank if: (1) any other institution should be permitted to issue bank notes and put them in circulation; (2) the government should resolve to issue notes after October 1, 1904. The Bank may not issue notes for a smaller amount than ten guilders. In case of war or danger of war, the obligation of the Bank to redeem its notes may be suspended by Order in Council.

The metallic reserve of the Bank may consist not only of gold but of silver coin and bullion. In fact, up to 1906 more than half of the total reserve usually consisted of silver. Foreign exchange holdings and balances with foreign correspondents may not be considered as part of the metallic reserve. Gold deposited with banks of issue abroad and gold in transit are, to the extent that the Netherlands Bank has free disposal of it, counted as part of the metallic reserve, provided that not less than 80 per cent of the obligatory 40 per cent cover shall actually be in the vaults of the Bank itself.

A peculiar feature of the Dutch currency system is that the central bank is required to redeem its notes only in other legal tender currency. Since other legal tender currency consists of both gold and silver coin, the Bank may at its option effect redemption in silver. Thus Holland is not and never has been legally on the gold standard, but rather, like France before the war, on the so-called "limping" standard. In practice, however, the Netherlands Bank, although not legally obligated to do so, has maintained the Dutch currency on what amounts to the gold standard.

The Bank Act amendment of August 7, 1888, authorized the Bank to invest in foreign bills, which authority eventually gave rise to the practice of selling foreign exchange whenever the guilder exchange approached the gold export point. Thus the law passed for the purpose of enabling the Bank to find profitable employment for its funds became an instrument of the gold and discount policy. However, the small amount of foreign exchange holdings limited the effectiveness of this policy, and the Bank adopted the practice of selling gold whenever the exchanges touched the gold export point. The Bank adhered voluntarily to this self-imposed practice, but in connection with the renewal of its charter in 1903 it made the formal statement—at the urgent request of the government and the States-General— that, as long as it can, it will continue to sell gold for export at 1,653.44 florins per kilogram of fine gold. The Bank also, although not legally obligated to do so, made it a practice to buy at a fixed price all gold offered to it.

Although Holland remained neutral during the World War, the outbreak of hostilities in 1914 caused such grave disturbances and extreme uncertainty that on July 31, 1914, the export of gold was prohibited. This prohibition of course necessitated the suspension of the central bank's policy of selling gold for export, and the Bank was formally released by the government from the obligation assumed in 1903. At the same time the minimum metallic reserve requirement of the central bank against its notes and other demand liabilities was reduced from 40 to 20 per cent. This measure was designed to give the Bank greater latitude in view of the unusual circumstances then prevailing; however, the reserve fell below 40 per cent only during the first few months of the war. The government was also authorized to free the Bank of the obligation to redeem its notes in specie, but no use was made of this authority nor did the Bank find it necessary to apply for the suspension of specie payments.

The note circulation of the Netherlands Bank increased from 310,437,000 florins at the end of July 1914 to 1,068,-947,000 florins at the end of 1918, chiefly as a result of heavy gold imports and the marked increase in discounts of domestic bills and advances on securities. However, a large amount of notes, estimated at 200,000,000 florins at the end of 1918, was hoarded, so that the actual note circulation at the close of the war was about 850,000,000 florins. In August 1914 the note circulation of the Netherlands Bank was augmented by currency notes known as "silver bonds" (*zilverbons*), issued by the government in agreement with the central bank. These emergency notes were legal tender up to any amount and were issued in denominations of 1, 2½, and 5 florins to replace the silver coins, which were being hoarded and had almost disappeared from circulation. At the end of 1918 the maximum amount of silver bonds in circulation was about 70,000,000 florins. They have since been gradually withdrawn, and at the present time only a nominal amount of them remains in circulation.

Although the demand liabilities of the Netherlands Bank increased rapidly during the war period, the metallic reserve increased even more rapidly. From the end of July 1914 to the end of December 1918, the Bank gained 527,-328,000 florins ($211,986,000 of the old parity) in gold, and the total metallic reserve increased from 170,341,000 to 697,986,000 florins. The reserve ratio on the latter date was 60.3 per cent, as compared with 54.0 per cent on the former.

When the embargo on gold exports from Holland was lifted on April 29, 1925, simultaneously with the return of Great Britain to the gold standard, the Netherlands Bank was in a position to resume its pre-war policy of maintaining the florin within the gold points. The Bank was bound again by its formal statement of 1903, with the modification that the Bank was under no obligation to sell gold for export to countries whose banks of issue were not required to give up gold for export whenever their currency fell below the gold export point. The metallic reserve had declined considerably from the high level of 1918, but a very large volume of foreign bills had been acquired. Both notes in circulation and deposits had declined to more normal levels and, on the date when redemption was resumed, the Bank had a reserve ratio of 53.5 per cent. A royal decree of January 4, 1929, restored the legal minimum metallic cover to 40 per cent, as was in force from 1864 until July 31, 1914. Inasmuch as the reserve ratio had been maintained at more than 40 per cent except for a short period in the latter part of 1914, this measure was of purely theoretical importance.

The year 1925 witnessed in the monetary policy of the Bank two innovations, both of which, however, had to be abandoned in 1931. In the first place, the Bank began to play an active rôle in the regulation of foreign exchange rates. This policy had its inception before the war, but at that time the foreign bill holdings were so small (the average portfolio did not exceed 15,000,000 florins in the five years immediately preceding the war) that an effective policy was impossible. The way for an increase in holdings of foreign bills was paved in 1919 with the removal from the Bank Act of the clause stipulating that the Bank should not hold for more than a fortnight an amount of foreign bills larger than the amount by which the metallic reserve exceeded the minimum legal requirement. After the war the Bank began to acquire foreign bills on a much larger scale, and by April 1925 the foreign exchange portfolio was almost ten times as large as the average before the war. Prior to the suspension of the gold standard by Great Britain on September 21, 1931, the holdings of foreign bills averaged more than 200,000,000 florins. With these huge resources, the Bank was able to exert great influence in the foreign exchange market.

The task of regulating the exchange rates in the post-war period has been much more difficult than before the war, partly because of the accumulation of large foreign balances in Amsterdam and partly because of Holland's increased importance as a foreign lender. In discussing the foreign exchange policy, the annual report of the Netherlands Bank for 1925–26 commented as follows:

> It is therefore obvious . . . that our foreign bill portfolio must be much larger than it formerly was in order to enable us to continue to control the exchange market. . . . There is no doubt that large sums from abroad have found a safe refuge in the Netherlands and . . . this foreign capital also explains the abundance of money which has almost constantly prevailed in this country. This plentifulness, however, is a warning that the Netherlands may, for reasons entirely beyond its control or intention, be exposed to sudden and large drains on its funds from abroad. A very large foreign bill portfolio

with an ample stock of gold will therefore, also for the near future, have to .form an indispensable counterweight to permit under all circumstances the maintenance of the guilder within the steady atmosphere lying between the so-called gold points.

This policy of maintaining a large foreign bill portfolio was followed up to the outbreak of the German banking crisis in July 1931, and, as shown in Table 51, was definitely abandoned when Great Britain suspended the gold standard on September 21, 1931.

The losses incurred by the Bank on its foreign balances in connection with the abandonment of the gold standard by Great Britain have shown in glaring light the extraordinary risk inherent in such assets, and have to a considerable extent disqualified foreign exchange not only as a basis for currency but also as a suitable means of maintaining the exchange parity of a currency. Dr. G. Vissering, the head of the Netherlands Bank since November 1912, who had sponsored this policy, resigned on October 12, 1931, and Holland began to convert its New York balances into gold.

When Great Britain abandoned the gold standard, the Netherlands Bank had sterling balances to the extent of £10,760,795. Of this amount £2,496,795 were sold at an average rate of fl. 9.55 per pound (the gold parity is fl. 12.10½ for one pound), and £7,839,000 (with the option of increasing this amount by the remaining £425,000, which were on deposit with the Bank for International Settlements), were sold for future delivery to the Dutch East Indian Government at the rate of the day of delivery, with a minimum of fl. 9.25 and a maximum of fl. 9.45 per pound sterling. The Dutch East Indian Government used these sterling balances for the redemption of its two sterling loans on their first calling dates—July 15, 1933, and August 15, 1933, respectively. This arrangement was amended by an Act of March 15, 1933, whereby the Netherlands Bank delivered to the Government of the Netherland Indies the total amount of £8,264,000 at the rate of fl. 9.25. Thus the loss incurred by the Netherlands Bank on the sterling

TABLE 51

FOREIGN BILL PORTFOLIO AND METALLIC RESERVE, 1930–1933

(In millions of florins)

End of	1930		1931		1932		1933	
	Foreign Bills	Metallic Reserve	Foreign Bills	Metallic Reserve	Foreign Bills	Metallic Reserve	Foreign Bills	Metallic Reserve
January	217.1	466.0	250.7	463.3	83.7	900.0	73.4	1,054.1
February	200.7	464.1	227.2	476.9	84.3	905.1	73.4	1,045.7
March	204.2	459.8	217.9	480.2	84.4	904.0	72.8	972.4
April	213.2	457.9	220.9	485.4	88.6	931.5	73.2	952.7
May	236.2	458.7	223.7	486.8	88.6	978.7	73.4	860.2
June	237.7	458.4	228.5	535.8	68.7	1,001.8	73.2	791.8
July	240.6	417.3	228.7	621.5	69.0	1,034.2	21.5	797.1
August	234.3	415.3	230.0	683.0	71.3	1,050.8	1.2	850.9
September	242.9	414.2	218.8	734.8	71.3	1,052.7	1.2	866.7
October	250.5	449.9	99.8	865.6	71.3	1,053.9	1.6	919.9
November	249.4	451.4	66.4	928.7	71.3	1,053.2	1.4	948.5
December	246.8	450.3	86.3	914.0	71.3	1,056.1	1.4	948.3

balances amounted to fl. 29,889,408.15, or slightly below one and one-half times the capital of the Bank. An Act of May 27, 1932, authorized the Netherlands Bank to charge to the government the sterling exchange loss sustained by the Bank during the financial year ending March 31, 1932, to the extent as such loss was not made good by reducing the reserve fund and the special reserves of the Bank to a total of fl. 8,000,000. By applying fl. 4,255,-558.41, representing the net profits of the current year, and fl. 6,302,654.57 taken from the reserve fund and the special reserves, the loss was reduced to fl. 19,331,195.17, which amount was charged to the Netherlands Government on a special non-interest bearing loan.

The above-mentioned act provides for gradual amortization of this account out of the profits of subsequent years. Accordingly, the clauses of Articles 8 and 31 of the Bank Act of 1919 as amended by the Act of June 25, 1929, referring to the distribution of profits of the Bank, have been suspended as of April 1, 1932, and the new scheme of distribution of profits will remain in force until the claim is wiped out. The claim was reduced by fl. 1,000,000 out of the profits of the Bank for the year 1932/33, and by fl. 1,334,103.80 out of the profits for the year 1933/34, bringing down the amount to fl. 16,996,491.37 as of March 31, 1934. This arrangement greatly curtailed the profits to the state and the dividends to the stockholders for years to come, but on the other hand it enabled the Bank to retain its full capital and part of its reserves. For the first time since the establishment of the Bank in 1814, the financial year (ending March 31, 1932) closed with a deficit and no dividends were paid to the stockholders. During the twelve years 1919–20 to 1930–31, inclusive, the earnings of the Bank derived from foreign bills and balances amounted to fl. 86,690,033, or 63 per cent of the total net profits. After the deduction of the loss incurred on the pound sterling balances, there remains a net profit of about fl. 56,000,000 for the period.

The other innovation witnessed in 1925 was the experiment with the use of gold coin for internal circulation. Before the war it had been the policy of the central bank to concentrate the gold of the country in its vaults—a policy which it was able to make effective because it had the option of redeeming its notes in either gold or silver. Moreover, the gold stock of the Bank before the war amounted only to about 162 million guilders, an amount too small to permit the maintenance of gold in circulation. After the gold stock reached a total of over 450 million guilders, however, the Bank considered that it was in a sufficiently strong position to meet any demand for gold from the public, and in November 1925 it commenced to pay out gold coins for internal circulation. At the same time it lowered its fixed buying rate for gold from 1,648 florins to 1,647.5 florins per kilogram of fine gold. From November 17, 1925, to March 31, 1927, the bank issued about 31,500,000 florins in ten-guilder gold pieces. However, it was found that the greater part of the gold coins issued for internal circulation were sold to foreign countries at a premium. Consequently the Bank gradually restricted the issue of gold coins and finally, on March 31, 1931, ceased to issue them at all.

Banking functions. The Netherlands Bank, besides carrying on its functions as the sole bank of issue, conducts a general banking business. It is required by law to maintain a branch office at Rotterdam, at least one agency in each province, and correspondents in certain other places. At the end of March 1934 the Bank had one branch office, seventeen agencies, and seventy-nine correspondents.

The operations in which the Bank may engage are clearly defined in the Bank Act and in the statutes. The government, however, may authorize the Bank to undertake in the public interest transactions not mentioned in the Bank Act. The Bank is authorized to discount bills, notes, and debentures; to make advances (lombard loans); to purchase and sell precious metals, bills, checks, and telegraphic transfers and other commercial paper payable abroad; to receive deposits on current account; to provide transfer, clearing, and collection facilities for its customers; to receive securities and other valuables for safekeeping; and to sell "assignations" (drafts) on its offices and correspondents. It also acts as fiscal agent and banker for the government and certain government institutions, such as the Post Office Savings Bank. The Act stipulates that the Bank "shall not grant to any person whomsoever any credit or advance without security." The Bank is not permitted to grant loans on mortgage deeds. It does not engage in open market operations, and its investments are restricted by law to the amount of its capital and reserve funds. There are no restrictions as to the parties with whom the Bank may deal, and an important part of its business is transacted with private firms and individuals.

Discounts. By the terms of the Bank Act the Netherlands Bank is authorized to discount:

1. Bills of exchange, drafts, and promissory notes bearing the signature of two or more persons or firms who are severally liable for the whole amount, with a maturity which is not longer than is required by the customs of the trade; and

2. Debenture bonds redeemable within six months, accompanied by the full guarantee of the discounter for the whole amount.

During the war and the immediate post-war years, bills arising out of transactions between the Netherlands and foreign countries or between foreign countries were not eligible for discount at the Netherlands Bank except where the Bank was previously consulted and had approved the creation of the bills. As a rule the approval was granted when the underlying transaction involved Dutch commercial or shipping interests. Thus the soundness of the bill itself was not sufficient to give access to the Bank. Domiciled bills, as a rule, were barred by the Bank.

The provision requiring previous approval by the central bank in each individual case worked hardships on all the parties concerned, and consequently, in April 1922, the Bank declared the following acceptances as, in principle, eligible for discount without prior sanction of the Bank:

1. As regards bankers' acceptances:

    a. Bills financing the importation of goods in the Netherlands or the Dutch Indies, drawn by the exporter abroad on a Dutch bank and accepted by the latter, provided it has been shown to the satisfaction of the accepting bank by means of documents or declarations that the goods which represent the countervalue for the bill have been delivered in, or shipped to, the Netherlands or the Dutch Indies.

    b. Bills drawn under a reimbursement credit granted by a Dutch bank to a Dutch or foreign firm and accepted by the said bank, provided, however, that the reimbursement credit results from the firm's current business and does not amount to too large a sum, and that the total of the acceptances falling under this category does not, under the circumstances, assume too great a volume for the accepting house.

2. As regards acceptances of Dutch acceptors other than bankers:

    Bills relating to the importation of goods in the Netherlands, drawn from abroad on the importing firm in the Netherlands, accepted by the latter, and presented for discount by a Dutch bank or banker, provided that the accepting firm is a Dutch firm established in the Netherlands and that it has been shown to the satisfaction of the Dutch bank, by means of documents or declarations, that the goods which represent the countervalue of the bill have been delivered in, or shipped to, the Netherlands.

These regulations are designed to exclude all but genuine self-liquidating commercial bills. The Netherlands Bank, however, must still be consulted beforehand as to the eligibility of acceptances arising out of other types of transactions between Holland and foreign countries or between foreign countries. On March 10, 1925, the Bank modified that condition of eligibility which stipulated that Dutch commercial or shipping interests must be involved, by requiring only that the transaction should not be in conflict with any Dutch interest. The acceptances of the three accepting houses established in Holland by Dutch and foreign bankers in 1924 were admitted to discount on this basis. With the object of developing an international acceptance market in Holland, in March 1926 the Netherlands Bank declared eligible for discount self-liquidating commercial paper accepted by foreign banks or bankers established in the Netherlands after 1914, provided that they operated in Holland as Dutch companies. However, the Bank had to be consulted beforehand with regard to each acceptance. This provision was abolished in April 1927, and the foreign banks were admitted to the 1922 arrangement with the Dutch banks.

When the shrinkage of international trade in 1932 and 1933 reduced drastically the number of acceptances, and thus closed up an important outlet for the investment of short-term funds by the banks without impairment of the banks' liquidity, the Netherlands Bank declared certain foreign treasury bills eligible for rediscount. The annual report of the Bank for 1933/34 states:

> In certain cases when requests from bankers to that effect reached us, we have declared eligible for rediscount a number of three months' French and Belgian Treasury Bills, made out in guilders and payable in Amsterdam, as well as some similar bills of colonies and enterprises guaranteed by the French or Belgian Government. We have only granted the eligibility for rediscount when a marked scarcity of paper manifested itself in the money market and made it difficult for the banks to employ their liquid funds remuneratively.

The discounting banks are obliged to send regularly to the Netherlands Bank their balance sheet and profit and loss statement, together with proper explanations. The Bank has the right to inspect certain documents and books at the offices of the discounting banks. The Bank may, without stating reasons, reject any bill offered for discount.

Advances. Normally, about 30 per cent of the operating capital of the Netherlands Bank is employed in advances, or collateral loans, as compared with about 20 per cent invested in domestic bills. These advances are of three principal types: ordinary advances, advances in current account, and advances to the government.

Ordinary advances are made on securities, goods, warrants, coin and bullion, and paper eligible for discount, usually for a period of one month. If, two days before maturity, neither party has given notice, they are automatically renewed for the same period. The larger part of the advances are usually renewed. However, borrowers occasionally requiring money for short periods find it convenient to maintain deposits of collateral at the Netherlands Bank against which they may obtain advances in current account in the form of overdrafts. While short lombard loans run for a minimum of eight days, overdrafts in current account may be repaid every day. The Bank Act requires the Netherlands Bank to make advances in current account to the State Treasury against the security of Treasury notes. Advances not exceeding fl. 15,000,000 bear no interest, except when the government issues currency notes (the "silver bonds" of August 1914 were not considered notes in the sense of this clause) and when the metallic surplus—namely, the amount of specie and bullion in excess of the 40 per cent legal minimum—falls below 10,000,000 guilders.

The daily average amount of advances in the last six years is shown in Table 52.

Discount and loan rates. The rates charged by the Netherlands Bank for credit extended by it have been comparatively low and stable for many years. Even in the fall of 1929, when the great demand for credit for security speculation in New York raised interest rates throughout the world to abnormally high levels, the Netherlands Bank was able to maintain its discount rate at 5½ per cent, while the discount rate of the Bank of England was forced up to 6½ per cent and that of the Federal Reserve Bank of New York to 6 per cent.

The rate quoted for the discount of domestic bills is

TABLE 52

DAILY AVERAGE ADVANCES OF NETHERLANDS BANK, 1928-34

(In thousands of florins)

	1928–29	1929–30	1930–31	1931–32	1932–33	1933–34
Ordinary advances	88,036	73,750	57,644	57,429	48,180	36,841*
Advances in current account	20,752	24,477	33,747	44,887	36,121	35,324
Advances to the government	7,079	7,541	4,919	1,263	853	2,167
Total advances	115,867	105,768	96,310	103,579	85,154	74,332

* Exclusive of the loan made to the Dutch East Indies in connection with the liquidation of the sterling balances.

445

generally termed the discount rate, but a separate rate is
quoted for the discount of promissory notes. This is normally ½ per cent above the rate on bills. The lombard
rate (loans secured by stock exchange collateral) is usually
somewhat higher than the rate on promissory notes. On
March 25, 1929, the Bank discontinued the practice of
quoting on foreign securities a separate lombard rate, usually ½ per cent higher than that on domestic securities.
The differentiating rate instituted in December 1865 to
curb the then-growing speculation in foreign securities was
no longer required, since the Netherlands Bank admits only
a very small portion of the foreign securities traded in on
the Amsterdam Stock Exchange as collateral for loans.
During periods of monetary stringency, the rate for advances in current account is often as much as one per cent
above the rate for ordinary advances, but when money is
easy the rates are usually the same.

Table 53 shows the average rates charged for the different types of discounts and advances during recent years.

TABLE 53

AVERAGE RATES OF INTEREST, 1926–34

	1926–7 (per cent)	1928–9 (per cent)	1929–0 (per cent)	1931–2 (per cent)	1932–3 (per cent)	1933–4 (per cent)
Discount rate:						
Bills	3.50	4.52	4.96	2.57	2.52	2.87
Promissory notes	4.00	5.02	5.46	3.07	3.02	3.37
Loan rate:						
Domestic securities	4.08	5.02	5.47	3.32	3.05	3.37
Foreign securities	4.58	5.51	5.47	3.32	3.05	3.37
Goods	4.00	5.02	5.47	3.32	3.05	3.37
Specie	4.00	5.02	5.47	3.32	3.05	3.37
Advances in current account	5.08	6.02	6.18	3.32	3.05	3.37

Deposits. The Netherlands Bank accepts deposits on
current account from the public, banks, and the government, but the volume of public deposits has always been
comparatively small, while government deposits are negligible. Total deposits normally average less than fl. 40,-

000,000, or about twice the capital of the Bank, while the
Bank of France at times holds public deposits alone
amounting to about 44 times its capital. The general
Dutch banks (described below) are not required to maintain reserve balances with the Netherlands Bank and, since
it is more profitable to place their liquid resources in prolongatie loans, they have adopted the practice of maintaining only small balances with the central bank. As the
Bank pays no interest on these balances, heavy deposits
either are an indication that the surplus funds of the banks
and the public cannot find profitable employment, or reflect
caution on the part of commercial banks, which strive for
high liquidity. The "balances in current account" grew
steadily after the German banking crisis in July 1931,
reaching an amount of over 300 million guilders in January
1933. During that year the balances fluctuated between
300 and 200 million guilders and fell off to less than 100
million guilders in April 1934, only to reach again the mark
of 200 million guilders in October 1934.

Other Banking Institutions

General banks. The bulk of the banking business of the
Netherlands is done by several large institutions, which by
reason of the broad scope of their activities have come to
be known as general banks. Of these general banks, those
having a capital and surplus of over 50 million florins are:
the Nederlandsche Handel-Maatschappij, the Amsterdamsche Bank, the Rotterdamsche Bankvereeniging, and
the Twentsche Bank. Although somewhat smaller, the
Incasso-Bank also belongs to this group. The relative positions of these institutions as of the end of 1932 may be
seen from Table 54.

The Nederlandsche Handel-Maatschappij N. V. (Netherlands Trading Society) was established by a royal decree
in 1824, at the initiative and with the capital participation
of William I, for the purpose of reviving the Dutch over-

TABLE 54

RELATIVE POSITIONS OF THE LEADING GENERAL BANKS, 1932
(In millions of guilders)

	Capital and Reserves	Current Accounts and Time Deposits	Cash; Due from Banks; Daily Money	Bills and Treasury Notes	Total Assets
Nederlandsche Handel-Maatschappij*	100	301	87	108	447
Amsterdamsche Bank..	104	169	116	22	295
Rotterdamsche Bank-Vereeniging	70	204	48	92	292
De Twentsche Bank...	55	190	27	62	286
Incasso-Bank	39	76	11	26	121

* Includes East India offices.

seas trade and developing the Dutch East Indies.   In 1842 the Society obtained a legal monopoly in the Netherlands as agents of the East Indian Government.   From an ordinary commercial enterprise it developed gradually into a so-called Cultuurbank, financing the various plantations in the Dutch colonies.   In 1880 the Batavia branch, which acts as head office for the East, began to execute international banking transactions.   Shortly thereafter the Society ceased trading entirely on its own account and entered the general banking business.   This transition became complete in 1903, when the Society commenced to accept deposits from the public in Holland.   It is, at the present time, the largest financial institution in the country. Besides the head office in Amsterdam it maintains two branches in Holland, sixteen offices in the Dutch East Indies, and nine offices in British India, the Straits Settlements, China, Japan, and Arabia.

The Amsterdamsche Bank was organized in 1871 by German, Austrian, and Dutch banks to act as a connecting link between the German and Dutch money markets.   The bank participated in 1924 with the Twentsche Bank and with Swedish, German, and British banks in the organization of the International Bank at Amsterdam, an institution for financing international transactions.

The Rotterdamsche Bank-Vereeniging was founded in 1863 as the Rotterdamsche Bank, with the object of financing private enterprises in the East Indies. The latter were being organized at that time in connection with the government's withdrawal from plantation enterprises and with the gradual transfer of this business to private initiative. In 1872 the bank withdrew from the East Indies, where it suffered heavy losses, and directed its activities mainly to the financing of trade and industry. In 1911 it merged with the Deposito en Administratie Bank of Rotterdam, and in 1929 it absorbed its affiliate, the Nationale Bankvereeniging. The paid-up capital of the bank grew from the original 5 million florins to 30 million in 1913 and 75 million in 1919. However, as a result of the post-war deflation the capital was decreased in 1924 to 50 million, and the surplus was reduced from 37 million to 20 million guilders. On January 1, 1934, the capital and surplus amounted to 65 million florins. The bank maintains about 150 offices, which are scattered throughout the country.

The Twentsche Bank was established at the end of 1916 to take over the affairs of the Twentsche Bankvereeniging, B. W. Blijdenstein & Co., established in 1861 mainly to finance exports to Java. The house of B. W. Blijdenstein & Co., established in 1858 in London, operates at the present time as a branch of the Twentsche Bank, but for certain reasons continues under its own name. The Twentsche Bank has always paid particular attention to the development of industry in Holland. It maintains about 70 branches throughout the Netherlands.

The Incasso-Bank was established in 1891 to carry on, mainly, a regular commercial banking business. Its initial capital of fl. 104,000 was increased during the first ten years to fl. 5,000,000, and reached fl. 30,000,000 in 1928. The bank engaged even before the war in the security business, which was further developed during and after the war. The bank maintains about 40 branches throughout the Netherlands.

Provincial banks. These banks are local in character and are consequently of less importance to the Amsterdam money market. The more important of the provincial institutions are the Geldersche Credietvereeniging, with a capital of 12.4 million florins, and the Friesche Bank, with a capital of 4 million florins.

Colonial banks. The colonial banks have played an important rôle in the Amsterdam money market and have greatly contributed to its international position. The importance of these institutions lies in the fact that they are large borrowers at the time of the financing of crops and, after the marketing of the latter, appear as large lenders of short-term funds. The colonial banks may be divided into two groups: (1) note-issue institutions, which comprise the Javasche Bank and the Surinaamsche Bank, and (2) the other colonial banks, which have no note-issue privilege.

The Javasche Bank is the oldest and most important of the colonial banks. It was established by royal decree in 1827, for the purpose of carrying on a banking business in Java. It was given the exclusive privilege of issuing banknotes in denominations of not less than 25 florins and was authorized to discount bills, to make advances on securities and merchandise, to deal in gold and silver, to act as fiscal agent for the government and all public offices, and to engage in such banking transactions as are usually common to note-issuing institutions. Up to 1864 the activities of the Bank were restricted to Java, but in that year a branch was established in Sumatra, and in 1865 another was established in Celebes. Since 1891 the bank has had a branch in Amsterdam. Prior to that time most of its European business was carried out through the Nederlandsche Handel-Maatschappij. Besides the head office in Batavia, during 1933 the bank maintained seventeen agencies in the main cities of the archipelago. The Javasche Bank carries out most of its European business, including foreign exchange transactions and the investment of its temporary funds, through the branch in Amsterdam.

The other colonial bank enjoying the note-issue privilege is the Surinaamsche Bank, established in 1864 to provide currency and banking facilities in Surinam (Dutch Guiana). The main office is located in Amsterdam; two resident directors administer the branch in Paramaribo, the capital of Dutch Guiana. The functions of the Surinaamsche Bank are identical with those of the Java Bank; however, the volume of business and, consequently, the importance of the bank in the Amsterdam money market are much smaller.

In addition to the above-mentioned colonial banks, three institutions not having the note-issue privilege are important in the Amsterdam market. These are the Nederlandsch-Indische Handelsbank, the Nederlandsch-Indische Escompto Mij., and the Koloniale Bank. All three institutions have offices in Amsterdam and therefore contribute greatly to the importance of Amsterdam as an international money center. The most important is the Nederlandsch-Indische Handelsbank, established in Amsterdam in 1863. Originally it was primarily an agricultural bank and devoted itself to the development of plantations in the Dutch East Indies. In 1884, however, its agricultural business was turned over to the Nederlandsch-Indische Landbouw Maatschappij, and the bank restricted its activities to purely banking transactions. It maintains, besides offices in Rotterdam and in The Hague, a score of branches in the Dutch East Indies and also branches in Japan, China, British India, and Straits Settlements.

The Nederlandsch-Indische Escompto Mij. was established in 1857 in Batavia. The Amsterdam branch was opened in 1896 to facilitate its growing business. From its inception this institution limited its activities to a general banking business. The Koloniale Bank, established in 1881, devotes itself primarily to financing the large—notably sugar—plantations in Java and Sumatra. As of the end of 1932 the three institutions had capital and reserves in the amount of 147,000,000 guilders.

Cultuurbanks. Similar to the colonial banks, but more restricted as to operations, are the cultuurbanks. They engage primarily in financing the development of plantations and the marketing of crops. They operate with their own capital, which is relatively large, and have also obtained long-term funds through the issue of bonds. They not only manage their own plantations but also, for compensation, administer those belonging to others. Strictly speaking, the cultuurbanks can be classified not as banking institutions but rather as financial management organizations. Their importance to the Amsterdam money market arises from the fact that, after the harvesting of the crops, they place large amounts of funds in the Amsterdam market. In recent years a considerable portion of their liquid funds has been placed in acceptances.

Amsterdam cashiers. An institution peculiar to the Amsterdam money market is the "cashiers" (*kassiers*). They have been in existence in Holland for several centuries; the cashier business has been mentioned in government decrees as far back as 1604. Originally the functions of the cashiers were similar to those of the early London goldsmiths. They accepted for safekeeping the cash of the merchants and held it at their disposal. They charged a commission for this service, since they were prohibited from investing or lending the intrusted funds. The commercial law code of 1838 gives the following definition: "Cashiers are persons to whom, for consideration of a specified compensation or commission, money is being intrusted for safekeeping and repayment."

Following the decree of the City of Amsterdam of June 1621, which regulated the cashier business, the number of cashiers increased rapidly. Between 1770 and 1780 there were 54 cashiers in Amsterdam alone. There were 80 cashiers in the years 1860/61, 216 in 1878/79, and 250 in 1890/91. In the second half of the eighteenth century payments between Amsterdam merchants were effected through the cashiers, and these payments led to the establishment of a clearing system between the cashiers long before the organization of the London Bankers' Clearing House. The cashiers began gradually to use the deposits of their customers for discounting bills and making secured loans. Thus they became bankers, limiting their activities to receiving deposits, discounting trade bills, and making advances against goods and securities.

At present there are only two cashier institutions in Holland, the Associatie-Cassa and the Kasvereeniging N. V., both located in Amsterdam. The Associatie-Cassa, established in 1806, remained a cashier within the legal definition of the word. It pays no interest on deposits which are being kept in cash. It uses its own funds for granting short-term secured loans. In 1864 the Associatie-Cassa organized an affiliate institution, the Rente-Cassa, which is permitted to pay interest on deposits. It invests these deposits in bills, prolongatie loans, and (not more than 25 per cent) in securities.

The Kasvereeniging was organized in 1865 out of a private cashier firm, with the purpose of performing functions similar to those of the London joint stock banks. It accepts deposits in current account and on time, paying interest on the latter only. It discounts bills and makes advances on merchandise and securities. In 1929 the Kasvereeniging absorbed the third cashier institution, the Ontvang-en Betaalkas, founded in 1813 and reorganized into a corporation in 1874. Neither of the two cashier institutions maintains branch offices.

Unlike the commercial banks and banking firms, the cashiers do not undertake the flotation of security issues, and by their statutes they are not allowed to grant credits without security. They act as collecting agencies for the other banks and for the Amsterdam stock exchange brokers. The latter, in addition to cash balances, maintain with the cashiers large blocks of securities on which they can obtain short-term loans. This has been the outgrowth of the fact that the cashiers held a large volume of the deposits of the important merchants and banking institutions of the country and became clearing centers for them.

The cashier institutions in recent years have played an increasingly important rôle in the Amsterdam money market, and now hold a position more or less comparable to that held by the discount houses in the London market. The banks not unfrequently maintain accounts with both cashiers. The cashiers in turn have accounts with the Nederlandsche Bank, and checks drawn on the cashiers (*kassiersbriefjes*) are accepted by the central bank as cash; this is not the case with regard to checks drawn on the other banks. The liquid position of the cashiers may be seen from the accompanying balance sheet (Table 55) of the Kasvereeniging N. V. as of the end of 1932.

TABLE 55

KASVEREENIGING, N. V.

(In thousands of florins)

ASSETS		LIABILITIES	
Cash	3,302	Capital	11,500
Dutch Treasury bills	19,020	Surplus	3,385
Discounts	17,052	Pension fund	1,765
Prolongatie and day-to-day loans	13,114	Deposits	22,894
Securities	11,510	Creditors in current account	50,608
Secured current account loans	25,567	Other liabilities	843
Building and inventory	1,430		
	90,995		90,995

Private bankers. In addition to the incorporated banks, private bankers still are influential in the banking structure of Holland. This position is due to the fact that the average Hollander still considers the small banker as his financial adviser and prefers to do business with him rather than with an employee of a large bank. The most important private banking firms are Hope & Co., established in 1732; R. Mees & Zoonen, established in 1720; Lippmann, Rosenthal Co., established in 1859; and Pierson & Co., established in 1875. These institutions are prominent in the

Amsterdam money market, particularly as issuing houses.

Miscellaneous institutions. Like every other important international money market, Amsterdam has a number of special financial institutions engaged in international transactions. To this group belong the following classes of institutions: (1) the international acceptance corporations; (2) the Wool Bank; (3) foreign banks; and (4) Dutch overseas banks, established with the aid of domestic and foreign capital.

International acceptance corporations. The most important of these are The Netherlands Acceptance Company, the International Bank at Amsterdam, and the International Credit Company. These institutions, all of which were established in 1924, are chiefly engaged in the creation and discounting of acceptances arising out of international trade.

Wool Bank. This institution was established in October 1924 as successor of the Wolfinanciering Maatschappij. Its chief purpose is to finance imports of wool into Amsterdam, from which center the wool is distributed throughout a large part of the continent. Owing to the activities of the Wool Bank, an increasing amount of bills covering wool shipments have been stated in guilders. This fact has greatly aided the development of florin bills. In 1926, two years after its organization, the bank accepted over 59,-000,000 florins in florin acceptances and also a number of pound sterling bills.

Foreign banks. Of the foreign banks some, such as the Banque de Paris et des Pays Bas, had already been established before the war, but most of them were established during the war and post-war periods. Of these the German banks have a preponderant position. Following the end of the war, and particularly after the stabilization of the reichsmark in 1923, almost every important German bank organized an affiliate in Holland, acquired an interest in an existing bank, or participated in the establishment of new banks in Amsterdam. The affiliates were to assume the rôle played before the war by the London branches of German banks. This development was of a magnitude to cause anxiety on the part of the Dutch authorities. However, the financial crisis of May–September, 1931, not only brought that movement to a stop but also initiated the liquidation of some German affiliates and interests in Amsterdam banks.

Of the German banks and banking houses which have established affiliates or subsidiaries in Amsterdam, the following are the most important: (1) The house of Mendelssohn & Co. of Berlin established in 1920 an affiliate in Amsterdam which developed very rapidly and plays an important rôle in that market. (2) The international banking house, M. M. Warburg & Co., established in 1929 a firm in Amsterdam under the name of Warburg & Co. (3) The Deutsche Bank opened a branch in Amsterdam which, upon the merger between the Deutsche Bank and Disconto-Gesellschaft, was absorbed by the Handel-Maatschappij H. Albert de Bary & Co., an affiliate of the Disconto-Gesellschaft established in 1919. (4) Similarly, the firm of Proehl & Gutmann, organized in 1918, acted as agents for the Dresdner Bank. (5) The International Bank in Amsterdam was closely connected with the Darmstaedter und Nationalbank. As a matter of fact, every important banking house in Germany has some sort of subsidiary or affiliate in Amsterdam. In addition, banks of some other countries, including several American and South African institutions, are represented in the Amsterdam market.

Dutch overseas banks. The great importance of foreign trade in Holland, and the fact that the Dutch have been a trading nation for many centuries, have led to the development of overseas financial institutions. (1) The Hollandsche Bank voor Zuid-Amerika (Netherlands Bank for South America), was established in 1914. It maintains branches in Argentina and Brazil. In 1933 the bank absorbed the Hollandsche Bank voor de Middellandsche Zee (Netherlands Bank for the Mediterranean Sea), which was organized in 1919 by the above institution together with the Rotterdamsche Bank-Vereeniging and certain non-banking firms. (2) The Nederlandsche Bank voor Zuid-Afrika (Netherlands Bank for South Africa), founded in 1888, has its head office in Amsterdam and maintains about 20 branches throughout South Africa.

CHAPTER XVII

Amsterdam—Operation of the Money Market and the Stock Exchange

THE TWO important markets for short-term money in Amsterdam are the market for loans on securities and the acceptance, or discount, market. There are of course other financial markets, such as the market for promissory notes and that for Treasury bills, but the two first mentioned are dominant from both a domestic and an international viewpoint.

Security Loans

Loans on securities, and particularly prolongatie loans, have for many years been very popular in Holland as a medium for the investment of short-term funds. Before the war the market for such loans completely overshadowed the other financial markets and gave employment to the bulk of the short-term funds of the country. The great importance of prolongatie loans in Holland before the war may be seen from Table 56, which is based on a special inquiry made by Dr. Vissering, president of the Nederlandsche Bank, shortly after the outbreak of the World War. Out of a total of fl. 345,000,000 in security loans 325,000,000, or 94 per cent, represented prolongatie loans.

The popularity of security loans was of course somewhat dampened by the "freezing" of a large volume of loans during the period from July 29, 1914, to February 9, 1915, when the stock exchange was closed and notice of recall of loans, with few exceptions, could not be given. This event, together with changed conditions brought about by the

TABLE 56

COLLATERAL LOANS TO MEMBERS OF ASSOCIATION OF
SECURITY DEALERS AT AMSTERDAM AT END OF JULY 1914

(In florins)

	Prolongatie	On Call	Advances	Current Acct. Loans	Total
Obtained from:					
1. Lenders outside the stock exchange	201,000,000	3,500,000	200,000	5,300,000	210,000,000
2. Members of the exchange	124,000,000	4,500,000	5,300,000	1,200,000	135,000,000
Total	325,000,000	8,000,000	5,500,000	6,500,000	345,000,000

war, has lessened the relative importance of security loans, so that today this market no longer enjoys the dominant position of former years.

Loans against securities are divided into three groups: (1) call loans (day-to-day loans); (2) loans for one month (prolongatie); (3) loans for three months (*beleening*). The principle underlying these classes of loans is the same, the only difference being the time element.

Call loans (day-to-day loans). As the name implies, these loans are made for one day and the loan contract may be terminated by either party at any time up to 2:15 p.m. If the loan is not called or repaid up to that time, it cannot be cancelled until the next day. There are three classes of day-to-day loans. The first class is that of non-secured loans made between banks, which usually are carried out through an exchange of checks on the central bank. Through such loans, the marginal demand and supply of short-term funds by the banks is met. This market is similar to the Federal funds market in New York. The second class of day-to-day loans is loans against security made to brokers. These are similar to call loans made in the United States. The third class is loans against acceptances, in which the acceptances are not turned over to the lender but are held in trust by a trustee, usually one of the cashiers. Loans to brokers are secured by securities having at least a value of 110 per cent of the amount of the loan. In case securities decline in price, additional collateral must be delivered before 12 o'clock noon the next day. The rate of interest is agreed upon between borrower and lender and is paid on termination of the loan.

Loans for one month (prolongatie). This is the oldest and the most important individual market in the Amsterdam money market, for even today prolongatie loans overshadow all others. In its importance it is equal to the call market in New York prior to 1930, and to the bill market in London. As the name implies, such loans are made for a period of one month, during which the lender is not allowed to call the loan. The borrower, on the other hand, may cancel the transaction at any time at his option but must pay interest for at least fifteen days. If the borrower avails himself of this privilege, he may repay the loan and interest and demand the return of the securities between 9 and 12 o'clock in the morning. The prolongatie loan does not necessarily mature at the end of the month. On the contrary, in order to terminate the loan, the lender must give notice to the borrower, or vice versa, the borrower to the lender. If notice of cancellation of the loan is not given by either party before 2:30 p. m. on the day of maturity, the loan is automatically extended for another month; hence the name prolongatie (prolongation = extension).

The rate of interest on the renewed loan is the rate prevailing in the open market on the maturity date. In case the last day is a holiday, then the rate of interest of the previous stock exchange day is applicable. In case of prolongatie loans, the month is figured at thirty days. When a loan has been renewed, the lender is not allowed to call the loan before maturity. The borrower, however, may cancel it, and he pays interest only up to the day on which he has given notice of cancellation. The fifteen-day interest rule, therefore, does not apply to loans which have been renewed.

The loans are generally made in multiples of 10,000 florins. The rate of interest is fixed daily, on the basis of all transactions which have taken place during the day, and is published in the official quotation list of the stock exchange. The rate, therefore, is uniform for all borrowers. The borrower is under obligation to pay, in addition to the rate of interest, a small commission fixed by a stock exchange committee.

Lenders of prolongatie loans. These may be divided into two groups: (1) lenders outside of the stock exchange and (2) lenders on the stock exchange. Lenders outside the stock exchange comprise practically the entire well-to-do class in Holland, owing to the fact that until recently the Dutch public did not place their liquid funds on deposit with banks but preferred to lend them out on prolongatie. As has been pointed out before, a considerable part of the liquid assets of commerce, trade, industry, and agriculture are placed in prolongatie loans. Various factors have contributed to this development, the most important, perhaps, being the fact that for many years the wealth of Holland has consisted to a large extent of securities. In the second place, the traditional thrift of the Dutch has led them to invest their money in securities and in prolongatie loans because the interest yield on these is higher than that on deposits. Aside from the liquid funds of commerce, industry, and agriculture, the government Post-Office Savings Bank, the Government Insurance Office, shipping and life insurance companies, and particularly the large plantations in the Dutch East Indies, appeared and still appear as lenders of prolongatie money.

The lenders on prolongatie on the stock exchange are stock exchange brokers acting, as described above, as middlemen for the lenders outside of the exchange, and banks and bankers. In this connection it should be noted that the security brokers and dealers still have an important part in the financial structure of Holland.

The borrowers of prolongatie money may also be divided into the same two groups: (1) borrowers on the stock exchange and (2) borrowers outside the stock exchange. Borrowers on the stock exchange are primarily stock exchange brokers who borrow either for their own account or for the account of their customers. Provincial security dealers and brokers also appear as large borrowers in the prolongatie market.

Borrowers outside the stock exchange may be divided as follows: (1) owners of securities who are in immediate need of cash but who, instead of borrowing from banks, use their securities as collateral for prolongatie loans; (2) purchasers of securities who are unable to pay in full and obtain a prolongatie loan for the balance, pledging the purchased securities as collateral; and (3) provincial security dealers who borrow on prolongatie in Amsterdam, using the securities pledged with them by customers for prolongatie loans. Through this reborrowing the provincial dealers avoid tying up their own funds.

Prolongatie loans are rather costly and cumbersome for business needing cash for very brief periods of time. The borrower must not only pay full commission and interest for at least fifteen days, even though he is able to repay the loan within a few days; he must handle securities each time he negotiates or terminates a loan. These circumstances caused the Amsterdam stock exchange to permit its members to grant loans in current account to their customers against pledged stock exchange securities. The rate of interest charged on such advances is about one per cent above the average prolongatie rate prevailing at the time of the making of the loan.

The study of Dr. Vissering previously mentioned gives a good indication of the classes of borrowers of prolongatie loans before the war:

Prolongatie loans made through the aid of brokers to:

	Florins
Government and private institutions	3,000,000
Individuals, firms, etc.	179,000,000
Provincial brokers	128,000,000
Others	15,000,000
Total	325,000,000

Thus individuals, firms, and provincial brokers were borrowers of 94 per cent of total prolongatie loans made by brokers. While more recent figures are not available, it is believed that the proportion of the borrowers is still more or less the same as given here.

The fact that a large part of the liquid funds of the country is placed on prolongatie has an adverse effect on the Amsterdam money market, particularly in times of a crisis when security prices are declining. At such times lenders are more apt to cancel their loans, thereby forcing a number of margin traders to liquidate their security holdings, which action in turn results in a further decrease in security prices. The Dutch security market in this respect is not unlike that of New York, where a decline in security prices leads to margin calls and, if these are not met, to liquidation of securities and a further decline in prices. It is also of interest to note that New York and Amsterdam are the only money markets of importance where the bulk of security transactions are settled daily.

Although trading for future delivery is carried out on the Amsterdam bourse, few securities are so traded in, and their volume is relatively small. The experience of New York and Amsterdam indicates how daily settlements on the stock exchange affect the money market and lead to the overwhelming importance which security loans assume on this market. In periods of financial or economic crisis or of political disturbance, this large volume of short-term funds, which represents a considerable part of the working capital of the country and the liquidity of which depends

on the marketability of the collateral, is likely to become
frozen and cause an acute panic.

> During a stable or rising market the prolongatie system func-
> tions regularly, but in years such as the present [1903], when
> the prices of the securities pledged for the prolongatie money
> fall precipitously, it augments the pressure for liquidation,
> which does not restrict itself solely to the securities which
> have suffered, a drop in price but spreads to other prolongatie
> collateral. In such times the great disadvantages of the pro-
> longatie system become apparent and one asks himself how
> the system could maintain itself for such a long time.[1]

Three months' loans (beleening). These loans run for
three months, during which period the lender has no right
to call the loan. The borrower may do so, but he is under
obligation to pay interest for the whole current month.
At the end of the three-month period the loan is considered
extended for another three months at the rate of interest
prevailing on date of maturity, unless explicitly terminated
by either party. The required minimum margin is 20 per
cent, or twice the margin for call and prolongatie loans.

The Acceptance Market

The acceptance market of Amsterdam is for the most
part a development of the war- and post-war periods. Although florin bills were used to a considerable extent before
the war in financing Holland's imports and exports, such
bills were almost unknown for the financing of trade between two foreign countries. As a matter of fact, a large
portion of Holland's external trade was financed through
London because of the better facilities offered there.

There are a number of reasons for the absence of an
international acceptance market at Amsterdam before the
war (and some of them continue at the present time to
hinder the full development of the market). Probably the
chief handicap was the lack of short-term funds to be invested in acceptances. The Dutch, as mentioned before,
have long preferred to place their short-term surplus funds

---

[1] *De Economist,* 1903, p. 1000.

in security loans (prolongatie) rather than in banks or commercial paper. As in a number of continental European countries, the Dutch banks have not developed their deposit function and so were not in a position to employ substantial funds in the acquisition of acceptances. In short, almost the entire financial machinery of the country was adapted to the financing of stock exchange operations and to investment in long-term securities, rather than to the financing of international trade. To this most fundamental factor should be added the fact that London, and to some extent Berlin and Paris, offered ample facilities for the financing of international trade, so that there was neither a necessity nor an inducement to develop a discount market in Amsterdam.

War and post-war changes. The World War and the post-war conditions in Europe, however, caused a revolutionary change in the position of Holland in international finance, necessitating a readjustment of the financial machinery of the country. The war and its aftermath brought to Holland a volume of international trade and international financial transactions unknown before the war. After the cessation of hostilities the Dutch currency remained more or less stable, particularly as compared with other European exchanges, and this stability made the florin a desirable medium of exchange in international transactions. Furthermore, the political unrest prevailing in several European countries and the heavy burden of taxation, coupled with the rapid depreciation of some of the currencies, made Holland a safe refuge for foreign capital.

Up to the end of 1923 a considerable portion of the capital which left Germany was temporarily invested in Holland and, similarly, a large amount of capital from the old Austro-Hungarian Empire as well as from the Balkans was invested in Holland. This inflow of foreign funds increased the volume of short-term capital seeking temporary investment and added greatly to the expansion of the market. After 1923 Italian and, particularly, Belgian and

French money found its way in increasing amounts into
Holland, thereby more than replacing the German and
Austrian capital, which was partly withdrawn after the
stabilization of the respective currencies. Furthermore,
Amsterdam became a very important foreign exchange
market for the currencies of Central Europe, a number of
central banks maintaining large balances there for the purpose of supporting their exchanges. The war also had
brought about a shift from London to Amsterdam in the
international banking operations of the Central Powers.
Before the war the Austrians and Germans had financed a
large part of their international trade through London,
where the leading German banks maintained branches.
After the war, partly because during the war the assets of
the branches of the German banks in London had been
seized and liquidated, and partly because, for a short period
after the war, the former enemies did not have access to
the London money market, the Germans shifted their international transactions to Amsterdam.   As a result, a number
of German banks opened branches there while others established Dutch affiliates, which played an important rôle
in the development of the Dutch acceptance business.
Some of the German institutions were liquidated after the
banking crisis of 1931; others severed their connections
with the German home offices.

Holland's geographical position, its neutrality during the
war, the comparative stability of the guilder, and the growing importance of Amsterdam as an international financial
center, favored the establishment of acceptance institutions for the purpose of financing Central European trade.
During the first two months of 1924 the Netherlands Acceptance Company, the International Bank at Amsterdam,
and the International Credit Company were founded.
These three accepting houses commenced business with a
fully paid-up capital of 22,000,000 guilders, subscribed by
Dutch, German, British, Swedish and Swiss banks and
bankers.   In addition, the fact that a number of commodi-

ties traded in internationally were quoted in Dutch guilders
in post-war years also favored the development of an acceptance market. Thus, for example, in the entire post-
war period an increasing volume of grains used for consumption in central Europe, as well as tobacco and wool,
were quoted in guilders. Whereas before the war the center of the wool trade for the continent of Europe was
located at Antwerp, after the war it was shifted to Amsterdam; the establishment of the Wool Bank (Wolbank) in
1924 further tended to concentrate the wool trade in
Amsterdam. All these factors, coupled with the comparatively low rates of interest prevailing in Holland, contributed to the rapid growth of the Amsterdam discount
market.

The passing of the abnormal war conditions and the
stabilization of the currencies of Europe did not cause a
decline in the Dutch acceptance business. In spite of the
withdrawal of a part of the foreign balances from Amsterdam, the bill market was not deprived of the necessary
funds, since Dutch banks and business concerns have finally
recognized the advantages of keeping a part of their liquid
resources in acceptances, so that the gradually increasing
demand from these quarters has more than counteracted
the decreased demand on foreign account. As was the case
in other countries, the banking crisis in Germany and in
other central European countries affected the Dutch acceptance market adversely. A number of German bills became
frozen under the standstill agreements and the volume of
guilder acceptances declined rapidly.

Regulation of acceptance market. The volume of bills
created by Dutch financial institutions and outstanding at
the end of 1926 has been variously estimated at 270,000,000
to 350,000,000 florins. The Netherlands Bank has published figures for later years on the amount of bills of the
acceptance of which it was notified. These figures, which
include practically all of the bills accepted in Holland, are
shown in Table 57.

TABLE 57

ACCEPTED BILLS IN CIRCULATION
(In florins)

End of	Amount
1927	324,600,000
1928	300,900,000
1929	325,800,000
1930	282,200,000
1931	140,600,000

The strict supervision of the acceptance business by the Netherlands Bank has been an important factor in the development of the Amsterdam bill market. By requiring all transactions involving the creation of bills to be submitted for its preliminary approval before bills are drawn, except bills eligible on principle, the central bank has obtained complete control over the character of the bills created in Holland. There is no market for ineligible bills in Amsterdam as there is in London, and no Dutch bank of renown would accept or discount such bills. The Netherlands Bank has exercised this control to restrain any undue expansion which might become detrimental to the stability of the market. It has discriminated against so-called finance bills, but has created no opposition to bills financing trade between two foreign countries provided they are genuine self-liquidating commercial bills. However, since it is impossible in most cases to ascertain beyond doubt whether or not a bill is a bona fide commercial bill, the attitude of the central bank authorities toward the large number of doubtful cases influences to a great extent the volume of bills in the market. By its control over the acceptance market the Netherlands Bank has been able to benefit domestic trade by keeping bill rates low without thereby provoking an abnormal increase of foreign acceptance credits, which would eventually lead to a rise in discount rates. Unlike the Federal Reserve banks, the Nederlandsche Bank does not buy acceptances in the open market for its own account, but makes such open market purchases for the account of foreign central banks. Following the enactment of the Law of December 29, 1928, relating to the investment of balances of government funds and institutions, the Netherlands Bank, in agreement with the Chairman of the Central Investment Council, commenced to buy bills in the open market and to make call loans on collateral of bills for the account and risk of the government funds and institutions.

The regulations of the Netherlands Bank regarding the eligibility of bills for discount are set forth below:

For the acceptance to be discountable, it is required:

1. That the acceptant be established in the Netherlands and be of Netherlands nationality or registered as a Netherlands firm or body corporate;

2. That the Netherlands Bank shall be consulted with regard to each acceptance before its issue (for smaller amounts the Netherlands Bank is on principle prepared to make an arrangement by virtue of which it will be sufficient to submit to the Bank a list of the bills after their acceptance);

3. That the bills shall be purely reimbursement bills for the financing of imports into the country of the party for whose account the bill is accepted (hence no extension bills and no bills for the financing of exports from the country of the seller for whose account the bills would have to be accepted, or for warehousing or industrial purposes);

4. That the proofs that an acceptance complies with the above requirements shall be submitted to the Netherlands Bank on demand (the applicant shall, at the request of the Netherlands Bank, permit the inspection and perusal of all the necessary vouchers at the office of the accepting party);

5. That a report shall be sent in to the Netherlands Bank immediately after acceptance of every bill which is discountable on principle, stating date, amount, and marks agreed upon, and also a description of the transaction in goods on which the bill is based;

6. That the acceptant shall regularly send his/their balance sheets and profit and loss accounts with a proper explanation to the Netherlands Bank.

When declaring whether an acceptance is on principle discountable, the Netherlands Bank leaves the strength of the bill signatures out of consideration for the time being; a decision is taken on this point only at the moment that the bills are presented to the Bank for discount; attention will, however, be paid to the proportion of the acceptant's own funds in relation to the total of his acceptances.

In order to be admitted to discount it is required:

1. That the discounter be established in the Netherlands, and be of Netherlands nationality or registered as a Netherlands firm or body corporate;

2. That the discounter shall regularly send his/their balance sheets and profit and loss accounts with a proper explanation to the Netherlands Bank. (The Netherlands Bank shall be entitled, if desired, to inspect certain documents or books at the office of the discounter).

The Netherlands Bank reserves the right to reject, without stating reasons, any paper presented for discount; reasons for such rejection, may, *inter alia*, be the following:

a. Too little variation in the paper discounted as regards amount and signatures;

b. The standing of the signatory parties on the day on which the bills are presented;

c. Too great a degree of similarity in the bills presented for discount.

Through these regulations the Nederlandsche Bank prevented as far as possible the development of abuses which are noticeable in other financial centers.

Acceptors. The acceptors in the Amsterdam money market may be divided into three main groups: (1) Dutch banks; (2) German banks; and (3) international acceptance institutions established with the aid of capital from a number of countries. While no legal limit is fixed by law as to the amount of acceptances which the individual banks may create, the volume of acceptances created by the banks is not very large, and as a rule does not exceed capital and surplus. The accepting institutions have voluntarily limited not only the amount of acceptances created by them but also the volume of bills which they will accept for an individual country. Combining the capital and surplus of the leading banks engaged in the creation of acceptances, the acceptance capacity of the various institutions may be estimated at between fl. 400,000,000 and fl. 500,000,000. In addition there are a number of private banking firms engaging in the creation of acceptances whose capacity to create acceptances cannot be determined.

The Dutch banks not only act as acceptors but also appear as large buyers of acceptances in the open market. It has been estimated that, in 1926, between 80 and 85 per cent of the total volume of acceptances outstanding in Holland were held by the large banking institutions. Acceptances created by a bank are usually put into the market through brokers. Although the banks have at various times attempted to eliminate the services of brokers, thus far they have not succeeded. Once a bank has sold its own bill in the open market, as a rule it does not re-purchase it until maturity. In recent years the bill brokers as well as the banks have made a serious effort to divert to the acceptance market a part of the funds which were usually placed on prolongatie.

Bill brokers. Bill brokers in Amsterdam perform the same function as those in London, but their number is comparatively small. Originally the bill brokers concerned themselves primarily with foreign exchange transactions, particularly during the period of wild currency fluctuation at the time when Amsterdam was the center of foreign exchange dealings for a number of continental European currencies. Most bill brokers still act in both capacities— namely, as bill brokers and as foreign exchange dealers, while the "cashiers" (described on page 452) act at the present time in a capacity similar to that of the discount houses in London.

Bill brokers operate partly with their own funds and partly with funds borrowed in the open market. Whenever bill brokers borrow funds, they put up the bills as collateral security. The bills, however, are placed not in the custody of the lender but in the custody of the cashiers, who act as trustees for the lender. The lender merely receives a photostatic copy of the bill which enables him to compare and verify signatures. In case the lender calls

the loan, the bill broker endeavors to obtain the amount
from another lender, but the bills remain in the possession
of the cashier in trust for the new lender. Through this
mechanism Dutch bill brokers do not have to carry their
bills from the one lender to the other, and the practice of
turning over bills to a broker under a trust receipt is also
eliminated. The cashier usually receives a commission for
services rendered. Bill brokers do not endorse the bills
which they sell.

The Amsterdam Stock Exchange

Historical review. The Amsterdam Stock Exchange is
one of the leading international securities exchanges of the
world. The first Amsterdam Stock Exchange building was
erected in 1611. It was a city-owned and supervised institution in which all kinds of business were transacted. As
late as 1838 the Commercial Law defined the Exchange as
a meeting place of traders, shippers, brokers, cashiers, and
of other people having relations with commerce. It was
a free exchange, and everybody could enter the premises
and transact business.

In about 1785, following the war of 1780–84 between
Holland and England, the Collegie tot Nut des Obligatien-
handels (Association for Promoting Trading in Securities)
was organized for the purpose of reviving the security business.   The Association began to issue its own list of security prices, and since 1795 these have appeared regularly
twice a week under the name *pryscourant der Effecten*.   In
1833 another security dealers' association, composed of
dealers and brokers, was organized under the name *Nieuwe
Handels-Societeit* (New Trading Association), with the
object of giving its members an opportunity to transact
business outside the regular Exchange hours. This association obtained in the Exchange building rooms exclusively
reserved for trading in securities. Both associations existed
side by side up to 1857, when they merged under the name

Effectensocieteit opgerigt door het Algemeen Beurs-Comite (Security Association Organized by the General Stock Exchange Committee). In January 1857 the Association issued a set of rules for dealing in securities which became binding upon its members.

The present Vereeniging voor den Effectenhandel te Amsterdam (Association for Trading in Securities in Amsterdam), usually referred to in English as the Association of Security Dealers in Amsterdam, was organized in 1876 following the dissolution of the General Exchange Committee for Securities and of the General Stock Exchange Committee. In December 1876 the Association prepared a new set of rules for dealing in securities which, with subsequent amendments, is still in force. In connection with the opening of the new Stock Exchange building in 1903, the Association was successful in bringing about a division of the Exchange into a security, a commodity, and a general department. The Association rented the premises of the security department, from which it excluded non-members and thus obtained for its members a practical monopoly of security trading. In January 1914 the Association opened its own building, and the Amsterdam Stock Exchange became a private institution to which only the members of the Association have access.

From July 29, 1914, to February 9, 1915, the Stock Exchange was closed as a result of the outbreak of the war. The closing tied up a large amount of loans secured by stock exchange collateral, and the lenders could not be compelled to accept the settlement proposed by the Association. To make the reopening of the Exchange possible, on September 4, 1914, the Stock Exchange Law was enacted. This put the exchange under government supervision—exercised at first by the Ministry of Commerce and later by the Ministry of Finance. The law prohibited until further notice the cancellation of prolongatie loans, and this prohibition made possible the reopening of the Exchange. However, the control of the government over the Exchange is more theoretical than actual and is exercised only in emergency cases, as on September 21, 1931, when it closed the Exchange upon the announcement of the abandonment of the gold standard by Great Britain.

Organization. The Vereeniging voor den Effectenhandel is a private autonomous organization which, according to the law of the country and like any other association, must submit its statutes and their amendments to the government for approval. In this respect the Amsterdam Stock Exchange, which is identical with the Association, differs from the London Stock Exchange, over which the government exercises no control. As indicated before, the Association has an actual but not a legal monopoly of trading in securities on the Stock Exchange. Since only members of the Association can transact business on the Exchange, public auctions of securities—which according to the law must take place on the "Exchange"—are held in a room open to the public.

Membership. The following persons and corporations are eligible for membership in the Association: (1) dealers, brokers, and bankers actively engaged in the security business and resident in Amsterdam; (2) corporations with main offices in Amsterdam engaged in the security business, provided their managing directors are members or are simultaneously applying for membership; and (3) managing directors of corporations, provided the corporation is a member or is simultaneously applying for membership. Since December 11, 1916, it has been required that applicants for membership be Dutch citizens. Naturalized citizens must have resided without interruption in Holland during the ten years immediately preceding their application. Physical persons applying for membership must prove that they have engaged for at least two years in the securities or banking business in Holland or in the Dutch colonies. A candidate for membership must be endorsed by at least twenty members. He must deposit with the Association as a guarantee fund fl. 6,000 in 4 per cent bonds of the Association; or—in case these bonds are not available at below 103 per cent—in listed bonds of the Netherland Government, provinces, or municipalities; or in cash. A rejection of an applicant by the Stock Exchange managing board may be appealed by the endorsing members to the general meeting of the members, who decide by a majority vote. Each member pays a yearly contribution, the amount of which is proposed by the board and voted upon by the general meeting. In recent years the contribution has amounted to about 80 florins per annum. Since January 1, 1912, newly admitted members have paid an entrance fee, the amount of which is determined by the general meeting on the proposal of the board. This fee fluctuates around fl. 2,000. Employees of members are admitted to the Exchange according to special rules for the admission of employees, and are classified as those authorized to transact business and those not so authorized.

Membership may be lost (1) through resignation; (2) when one of the principal prerequisites of admission ceases to exist; (3) through expulsion by a decision of the managing board. In case of bankruptcy, the expulsion may be permanent; it may be temporary in case of the violation of rules or failure to meet contractual obligations. An excluded member has the right to appeal within fourteen days to the general meeting, which by a majority vote may change the decision of the board, provided there is a quorum of 25 per cent of the members present.

Administration. The Amsterdam Stock Exchange is governed by the managing board, consisting of fifteen members elected by a majority vote of the general meeting of the members. The membership of the board may be increased by a vote of the general meeting. Five members drawn by lot retire yearly, but may be reëlected. Not more than one member of the same firm may serve on the board at any one time. The members of the board are organized in the form of the following five committees, which are permanent:

1. Committee for Daily Management (Commissie van Dage-lijksch Bestuur).
2. House Committee (Huishoudelijke Commissie).
3. Committee for Admission of Securities (Commissie voor de Fondsen).
4. Quotation Committee (Commissie voor de Noteering).
5. Committee for Disputes (Commissie voor de Geschillen).

In contrast to the autocratic powers of the Committee for General Purposes of the London Stock Exchange, neither the special committees nor the managing board have absolute powers in important matters. Such powers are exclusively in the hands of the general meeting of the members.

Admission of securities. The requirements for the admission of securities to trading on the Amsterdam Exchange are contained in the *Reglement voor het opnemen van fondsen in de Prijscourant*. Netherland Government bonds and Netherland East Indian Government bonds are admitted and listed by the managing board on its own initiative and without examination. The admission application for other securities must be signed by a member of the Association. Pending investigation of the application, the board may admit a security to provisional listing. The committee for admission of securities may refuse admission without stating its reasons. It must refuse the admission of securities issued by corporations in default on previous obligations or when certain requirements of the Reglement have not been observed. When the listing of a security has been refused, no new application will be considered before the expiration of six months from date of refusal. The Minister of Finance has the right to prohibit the admission of certain securities to official quotation, but he cannot force admission against the decision of the Association.

Quoting of securities. In the quotation list (*Prijscourant*) issued daily by the Association, securities are classified as follows:

Government loans
Provincial and municipal loans
Reclamation and other bonds of public bodies
Ecclesiastical and charitable institutions
Bank and credit institutions
Mortgage banks
Industrial enterprises
Electric, gas, telephone, telegraph, and waterworks companies
Trade enterprises
Mining enterprises
Petroleum enterprises
Rubber enterprises
Shipping companies
Sugar enterprises
Tobacco companies
Tea companies
Colonial enterprises
Miscellaneous enterprises
Railroads, tramways
Premium loans

Each group is subdivided into domestic and foreign issues. About 3,000 securities are officially quoted on the Amsterdam Stock Exchange, and the larger part of them are of foreign origin. The bulk of the securities are quoted in percentages of par, and others in currency units per security. Foreign securities are quoted in their respective currencies at a fixed parity with the florin (so-called Amsterdam Usance) which is published in the daily quotation list; for example, the United States dollar is equal to fl. 2.50; the pound sterling, to fl. 12.0; the Swiss franc, to fl. 0.50. The difference between the fixed conversion rates and the actual daily exchange rates of the various currencies in Amsterdam is reflected in the prices of the securities. Thus, the quoting of an American stock at $10 means that it is being dealt in at fl. 25, which, converted at the current rate of exchange of the florin in New York and allowing for the cost of the certificate and the tax, will equal approximately the quotation of the security in New York on the same day.

Securities for which application has been made for admission to official quotation are quoted in a separate group under the heading "provisionally quoted securities," and after all conditions for admission have been complied with, they are transferred to the group of "officially quoted securities." The provisional quotation is annulled as soon as the definite listing has been granted or declined. Bond issues of less than fl. 500,000 and stocks of companies capitalized at below that amount are not admitted to the group of officially quoted securities.

The daily quotations are divided into three groups: (1) The first group embraces the most actively traded stocks which are quoted seven times (*zeven tijdvakken*) during the trading session. The first six quotation periods (*tapes*) last ten minutes each, and the seventh fifteen minutes. (2) The second group includes all other stocks which are quoted twice during the session, the first tape lasting thirty minutes, from 1:30 to 2:00 p.m., and the second tape until 2:45 p.m. (3) The last group is composed of bonds which are quoted once, from 1:30 to 2:30 p.m.

Trading on the Stock Exchange. On the floor of the Exchange each group of securities is assigned a definite space called a "corner" (*hoek*), and the members specializing in a certain security or group of securities are called *hoeklieden.* This specialization is not official but free and voluntary. Every member may become a "cornerman" or specialist (*hoekman*) in one or more groups of securities, but in practice newcomers find it difficult to establish themselves in this position. The specialists are divided into (1) those trading in a single corner; (2) those who deal in more than one corner; and (3) daily traders (*daghandelaren*), who usually trade in a single security for their own account and, as a rule, take no position for the next day. The specialist acts as a clearing medium by offsetting orders, taking a position for unmatched orders. Members may deal directly with other members in the "corner" instead of giving the orders to the specialist. The specialist is obligated by the statutes of the Association to charge a commission for each transaction. The Association prescribes officially the commission rates (*Provisie-Reglement*) which members must charge for deals transacted on the Amsterdam Stock Exchange.

The bulk of transactions on the Amsterdam Exchange are for cash and actual delivery of securities. As a rule they are cleared through one of the two cashiers for a moderate fee. In this respect the Amsterdam Exchange differs from most other European exchanges and resembles the New York Stock Exchange. Securities must be delivered officially within four days after the date of the transaction, except where the deal was made with the stipulation *op levering* (on delivery), in which case the securities must be delivered not later than twenty-one days after the date of the transaction. Trading in options is confined to active stocks, and transactions are in lots of not less than fl. 2,000 (nominal amount of the stock). There is no official machinery for short sales, such transactions being made by special arrangements with the brokers.

Foreign stocks, notably American, dealt in on the Amsterdam Exchange are usually deposited with and transferred in the name of an Administration Office (*Administratie-Kantoor*), a special organization which issues its own bearer certificates, called *Certificaten van Administratie Kantoren*. A fee varying between ¼ per cent to ½ per cent of the nominal amount plus the tax stamp is charged by the administration offices for the issuance of certificates against stocks or bonds. This arrangement does away with the registration of securities and simplifies the transfer of ownership and the collection of interest and dividends. The certificates have no voting rights and are provided with talons and coupons, the latter being paid in florins at exchange rates fixed by the administration offices. Certificates are also issued against a combination of stocks of different corporations—*e.g.*, certificates of three French banks. The administration offices usually act also as trustees. The cash transactions, as well as the contracts for future delivery and options, are financed through (1) call money, (2) prolongatie, and (3) *beleening* (described before).

Contracts for future delivery (*tijd-affaires*) are made for settlement at a certain fixed date (*affaire op zekeren termijn fixe*); or either the buyer or the seller may reserve the right to demand fulfillment of the contract on any day from the date of the transaction or from an agreed later date up to the specified final date (*levering in koopers of verkoopers keuze.*)   The customary dates for "futures" are the first and the middle of the month.   The exact dates, so-called *rescontre-dagen* (settlement days), are fixed yearly by the Stock Exchange managing board.

CHAPTER XVIII

The Swiss Money Market

by

Ernest Schwarzenbach

SWITZERLAND is a small country, but for its size has attained considerable importance in international finance as a lender of short- and long-term funds and as a place of refuge for nervous capital. In 1930 Swiss short-term loans to foreign countries were estimated at 2,000,000,000 Swiss francs, and Swiss investments abroad at an additional 2,000,000,000 Swiss francs. Public offerings of foreign securities in Switzerland from 1924 to 1933 alone totaled about 1,320,000,000 francs (exclusive of refunding operations). Foreign investments in Swiss securities were estimated in 1930 at about 1,000,000,000 Swiss francs. Before the war Swiss investments abroad were larger, but they were of a more indirect and longer-term nature.

Switzerland emerged from the war with a sound currency and with most of its national wealth intact. In the neighboring countries, however, the war and inflation destroyed much of the existing working capital. Hence the relative financial position of Switzerland in Europe, and that of the Swiss banks as holders of large amounts of liquid wealth, were greatly enhanced. Zurich and Basle replaced Vienna and Berlin to a certain extent as lenders of short-term funds in central Europe, and the Swiss banks participated actively in the long-term lending operations incident to the stabilization of the various currencies. Switzerland has a comparatively large national wealth, estimated at 50 billion Swiss francs, or about 12,500 francs per capita. It will undoubtedly continue to play an active part in the international money market even though its relative importance may decline somewhat with the withdrawal of the large foreign deposits and the return of more stable conditions in central Europe.

While the position of the Swiss banks was strengthened, that of Swiss commerce and industry, which were largely responsible for the accumulation of the large capital wealth, did not improve to the same extent during the war and postwar period. The country's central location, the poverty of its soil, and the lack of natural resources, except for abundant water power, forced the Swiss at an early date to develop manufacturing (cotton and silk textiles, chemicals and dyes) and, particularly, the making of products requiring fine workmanship, such as watches, machines, and precision instruments. They also developed the tourist and transit trade and an international insurance business. The development of new industries during and after the war in markets to which the Swiss had been selling for the preceding fifty years, and the establishment of protective tariffs all over the world, made the position of Swiss trade and industry increasingly difficult. Today the Swiss export trade, like that of England and Germany, is facing many problems, and its outlook is uncertain. The position of the banks and of the Swiss money market is naturally tied closely to the fortunes of industry and trade, and their future development will be strongly dependent upon the general trend of business in Switzerland.

In contrast to the other financial centers heretofore described, the money market in Switzerland is not concentrated in any one city. This fact is chiefly due to the political organization of Switzerland as a confederation of twenty-five states (cantons) which have wide powers of local government. As an outgrowth of territorial and historical factors, a strong local individualism exists which is responsible for a lack of uniformity in the social and economic structure of the various states. Consequently there has developed in Switzerland no single preponderant business or financial center such as Paris in France, London in England, or Amsterdam in Holland. This individualism is also the reason for the great variety of Swiss banking institutions, for the diversity of their business, and for the variations in the practices of the different banks.

The Swiss National Bank

Early history. The establishment of the Swiss National Bank was authorized by the law of October 6, 1905, and the central bank opened for business on June 20, 1907. Prior to its creation, the issuance of bank notes was largely in the hands of the cantonal banks and the so-called "discount banks." The latter were local institutions most of which had been established during the first half of the last century for the purpose of financing local trade. Most of these discount banks had disappeared toward the close of the last century because they were unable to compete with the cantonal banks, which, owing to the state guarantee of their liabilities, were able to offer better terms or better security. Their elimination was further hastened by the establishment, during the second half of the last century, of the strong *banque d'affaires* type of commercial banks under the sponsorship of large industries.

The history of central banking in Switzerland is in many ways similar to that in the United States. Because of the absence of rediscounting facilities, the currency circulation was inelastic and failed to expand in times of emergency when the need was greatest. The note issue lacked uniformity and, since each bank redeemed only its own notes, the circulation was purely local. There was no coöperation among the various issue banks, and as a result there was no effective discount or foreign exchange policy. Prior to 1881 there were 36 different banks of issue.

Finally, in 1881, a Federal law was passed which subjected all issue banks to government supervision, required a 40 per cent precious-metal reserve (the balance to be covered by bills and securities), taxed notes in circulation, limited their total to twice the paid-up capital, provided for uniform bank notes, and required the acceptance of these notes by all banks of issue. The new law improved the situation and stimulated coöperation between the various banks to a certain extent; but it still had many shortcomings, the most important of which were the lack of elasticity and the absence of rediscount facilities. In 1891 the Federal Constitution was amended so as to permit the establishment of a single bank of issue with a monopoly of the note issue. In 1894 a bill providing for the creation of a government-owned central bank was introduced in Parliament, but the law, as finally passed by the two Houses, was rejected by the people in a referendum vote. Other attempts were made, until finally the law of 1905 was enacted and the National Bank established. The law has since been repeatedly amended and revised; and the Act under which the Bank now operates is dated April 7, 1921.

Organization and administration. The Swiss National Bank ("Schweizerische Nationalbank," "Banque Nationale Suisse," "Banca nazionale svizzera") is a private corporation domiciled in Berne, with a paid-in capital of 25,000,000 Swiss francs represented by 100,000 shares of 500 francs par value, one-half paid up. The original law provided that 40 per cent of the Bank's shares were to be issued to the public, 40 per cent to the states (cantons), and 20 per cent to the old issue banks. At the end of 1933, 8,286 individuals owned 46.3 per cent of the shares, 23 states held 38.2 per cent, and 24 cantonal banks held 15.5 per cent. The shares may not be transferred to other than Swiss citizens, partnerships domiciled in Switzerland, or corporations that have their head office in Switzerland.

The Bank is administered by (1) the Bank Council, (2) the Bank Committee, (3) the Board of Management, and (4) Local Committees.

The Bank Council consists of 40 members, elected for a period of four years. Fifteen members are elected by the stockholders and 25 are appointed by the Federal Government. The chairman and the vice-chairman are also appointed by the Federal Government. The Bank Council elects five members of the Bank Committee, appoints the local bank committees, submits proposals for the election of officers, and passes upon, among other things, all transactions in excess of 5,000,000 francs and all credit lines in excess of 3,000,000 francs.

The Bank Committee corresponds to the executive committee of a large American bank. It supervises and exercises the immediate control over the Bank's management. It consists of seven members, five of whom are appointed by the Bank Council, the other two of whom are the chairman and the vice-chairman of the Bank Council. The Bank Committee meets at least once a month. It examines all important transactions and approves all business in excess of 1,000,000 francs. It acts in an advisory capacity when changes in the discount and the collateral loan rates are considered, and elects all junior officers and department heads.

The management of the Bank is in the hands of a Board of Management of three members, each of whom heads one of the Bank's three departments and each of whom is assisted by the necessary number of deputies. These "directors," who are the chief executives of the Bank, and their deputies are appointed by the Federal Government upon recommendation of the Bank Council for a period of six years. The president and the vice-president of this board are selected by the Federal Government.

The Local Committees, consisting of three to four members, are set up in all the larger cities where the Bank has branches. They assist in the establishment of credit and discount lines.

It is clear that, while nearly one-half of the Bank's stock is privately owned, the Federal Government exercises a strong control over the bank through its right to appoint the officers and a majority of the members of the Bank Council, and to approve the annual report, the statements, and the Bank's regulations.

Operations. The Swiss National Bank is, by the law of April 7, 1921, entrusted with "the main task of regulating the currency circulation of the country and of facilitating payments. It also handles, free of cost, the Treasury operations of the Federal Government, as far as they are entrusted to it." The seat of the management is Zurich. The business of the Bank is handled by three departments, two of which—one concerned with discounts, foreign exchange, and secured loans, and the other with giro and auditing—are in Zurich, while the third—concerned with note issue, administration of cash reserves, and business with the Federal Government and the Federal railways— is in Berne. The Bank operates ten offices in the most important cities and has fifteen agencies; most of the latter are administered by cantonal banks. It collects bills and makes payments through correspondents in 340 bank places and 143 sub-banking places.

Note issue. The National Bank Law confers on the Bank a monopoly of the note issue, renewable every ten years with the approval of Parliament. The present period runs until June 20, 1937. The Federal Government has the right to acquire the Bank's assets and liabilities at the expiration of any period, subject to due notice and the reimbursement of the stockholders.

The Bank is required by law to maintain in Switzerland a gold reserve against notes in circulation of at least 40 per cent in gold bars, or domestic or foreign gold coins at mint value. The balance necessary to constitute a 100 per cent reserve against notes may consist of (1) bills of exchange, checks, or bonds payable in Switzerland; (2) bills of exchange, checks, or sight balances payable abroad, and foreign government treasury notes; and/or (3) advances on current account callable at 10 days' notice and secured by bonds and/or by precious metals.

The amount of notes that the Bank may issue is not limited. The notes are not legal tender except in times of war when they are so decreed by the government. The Bank and the Federal Treasury, however, are required to accept them whenever presented. Article 20 of the National Bank Law provides that the notes must be redeemed upon demand (except in time of war when so authorized by the government) on the following basis:

> As long as the central banks of countries considered by the Bank's authorities to be of foremost importance, do not redeem their notes in gold coin, the National Bank is to redeem its notes upon presentation, at par, at its option in:
>
> (a) Swiss gold coins;
>
> (b) gold bars of the customary weight (about 12 kg.) at the legal mint parity; or
>
> (c) gold exchange (payments or checks) in an amount of the then market value, calculated in gold, of a currency that is based upon a free gold market. Such gold exchange may, however, not be calculated at an amount higher than the export point for Swiss gold coins to the respective foreign banking center. The choice of such exchange rests with the National Bank.

Thus, the Swiss currency is legally based upon the so-called "gold exchange standard," even though in practice it functions as a gold standard currency. The amendment to the bank law putting the currency on this basis is dated December 20, 1929, and it was felt at that time that a country as small as Switzerland could not return to an outright gold standard while some of the much larger neighboring countries, whose nationals had large deposits (representing exported capital) in Switzerland, were on a gold exchange standard. Developments since 1931 have given some support to this view but, contrary to the intent of the above permissive provisions of the law and perhaps to the wishes of the management, they have also forced the Bank to adopt in practice what amounts to a gold standard: it meets demands for gold with drafts on Paris, for which it has usually supplied cover through the release of gold held abroad or through the export of gold. During the last few years the central bank has held very little foreign exchange.

Banking operations. The Swiss National Bank is authorized by law to transact a broad, general central banking business. It may discount bills of exchange and checks drawn to order, bearing at least two independent, solvent signatures and maturing in not more than three months. It may also discount acceptable domestic bonds for periods of not more than three months. The Bank makes loans collateralled by bonds ("lombard loans") either for fixed periods of not more than three months, or on current account subject to the right to obtain repayment on at least ten days' notice.

Authorized open-market operations consist of purchases and sales of bills of exchange, checks, and sight balances in foreign countries, and of treasury bills of foreign governments, all of which must be of maturities of not more than three months. Bills must bear at least two independent and solvent signatures. In addition, the Bank is permitted to purchase readily marketable interest-bearing bearer obligations of the Federal Government, of the states, and of foreign governments, but only as temporary investments.

The Bank accepts deposits from the banks, the public, the government, and government-controlled institutions. No interest is paid on deposits, except on those of the government and of the government-controlled institutions. One of the important functions of the Bank is arranging for giro and clearing transactions and also the handling of orders of payment and collections. The Bank has been very active and successful in organizing and developing the giro system and in facilitating clearings.

Other authorized operations of the Bank consist of: (1) the purchase and sale of precious metals and the extension of loans secured by such metals; (2) the issuance of gold certificates; (3) the acceptance, custody, and administration of securities and of valuable objects; (4) the purchase and sale of securities and the handling of subscriptions for account of third parties; and (5) participation in the placing of loans of the Federal Government and the acceptance of subscriptions to loans of the government and the states, in both cases with the exclusion of any participation in the underwriting of the bonds.

The National Bank since its inception has pursued a conservative discount policy. It was announced in the beginning that only such bills would be discounted as were based upon commercial transactions which would provide funds for payment before the maturity of the paper. This policy has been adhered to by the Bank ever since. It has refused to discount bills or notes secured by collateral, the so-called "lombard loans," and it has carefully examined all bills submitted to it in an attempt to exclude finance bills. As a result, the quality of the bills submitted for discount has improved considerably. Naturally the central bank could not prevent the commercial and cantonal banks from continuing to create finance bills, but its firm attitude has tended to discourage them from doing so.

During the World-War period, when many commodities could be imported only on the basis of long-term credits, a large percentage of the bills held by the central bank lost their self-liquidating character, but after the war the Bank lost no time in reverting to its pre-war discount policy. This policy proved to be sound, but because of the large inflow of foreign funds there was comparatively little need for the commercial banks to rediscount with the National Bank.

Since the Bank does only a very limited amount of open market buying and discounts only at the official rate, its volume of bill holdings remained comparatively low and its discount policy was rather ineffective. Its principal contact with the market was through its foreign exchange operations. The steady offerings of foreign exchange while

funds were flowing into Switzerland involved the issuance
of bank notes or credits to the giro-accounts; these issues
increased the money supply, while exchange movements in
the other direction had a tightening effect upon money market
conditions. The comparatively lower volume of bills
was probably due also to a greater scarcity of real commercial
paper and to the growing use of other methods of payment
such as the bank check, the postal check, transfers
through the National Bank, and postal transfers.

The discount rate of the Swiss National Bank is fixed by
the three members of the Board of Management in consultation
with the Bank Committee. It is the Bank's policy
to keep the rate as stable as possible and to change it
only if the spread between the official and the private rate
becomes too great.

The National Bank discounts both trade bills and acceptances
directly for commercial and industrial concerns that
keep accounts with it. Such bills may include small "no
protest" paper with a maturity of not more than 45 days.
As a result the Bank often receives many small or second-rate
bills which meet the eligibility tests but which the commercial
banks or cantonal banks are not anxious to take.
Sometimes these bills are in amounts of less than 2,500
francs. The central bank takes them simply as a matter
of accommodation.

As pointed out above, the Swiss National Bank as a rule
does not operate in the open market. The supply of short-term
government obligations in Switzerland is usually very
small. From time to time in the past the Bank has discounted
so-called "rescriptions" of the Federal Treasury,
the Federal railways, the states and municipalities, which
are usually three-month bills, but the amount has been
small and only during and shortly after the war did the
total reach any sizable figure. In 1933 the largest amount
of such bills held at any one time was 31,275,000 francs
for a period of six days, and it seems probable in this
case that the Bank did not buy these certificates in the

open market but discounted them upon the solicitation of a customer.

The Bank during the depression. The events of the last few years have, of course, caused extensive changes in the situation of the Swiss National Bank. One of the most striking developments was the tremendous increase in the gold holdings of the Bank from 595,000,000 Swiss francs at the end of 1929 to 2,346,800,000 francs at the end of 1931. This reflected chiefly the inflow of foreign capital and the repatriation of Swiss funds from abroad as a result of the international financial panic of 1931, the depreciation of many currencies, and the uncertainty as to the stability of other currencies. To some extent, however, it was the result of the conversion into gold of the Bank's gold exchange holdings, which declined from 352,900,000 francs at the end of 1929 to 103,000,000 francs at the end of 1931.

The inflow of funds abroad during 1931 and 1932, together with the decline in business activity, created a marked ease in the Swiss money market. This was evidenced by a sharp decline in the central bank's discounts and advances and a tremendous increase in deposits. At the end of 1932 total discounts of both bills and bonds amounted to only 20,700,000 francs. Giro deposits increased from 171,700,000 francs at the end of 1929 to 922,-300,000 francs at the end of 1932. Since the Swiss banks are not required to maintain reserves with the central bank, a considerable part of the large volume of giro deposits accumulated during the depression may be considered as the equivalent of the excess reserves of the Federal Reserve member banks in the United States.

In view of its very large gold holdings and its high ratio of coverage, the Bank's currency position seems to be very strong. The government has taken a definite stand against the abandonment of the gold standard or currency devaluation. Switzerland has been an active member of the so-called "gold bloc," maintaining that any change of its present currency policy would be contrary to the best interests of the country. The cost of living in Switzerland is very high—in proportion to the national income, probably too high. The question is whether it can be brought down to a level that will permit the Swiss industries again to compete for foreign business. This adjustment is largely a political problem. If its solution should be delayed, the faith in the currency might become seriously undermined, in which case a large flight of capital would seem likely. There was some loss of confidence abroad in 1933 and 1934, and a substantial amount of foreign deposits was with-

TABLE 58

PRINCIPAL ITEMS OF THE BALANCE SHEET
OF THE SWISS NATIONAL BANK

(End of year; in millions of Swiss francs)

Assets	1929	1931	1932	1933	1934
Gold in Switzerland	558.8	1,526.0	2,224.1	1,687.9	1,734.8
Gold held abroad	36.2	820.8	247.1	310.1	175.0
Total gold	595.0	2,346.8	2,471.2	1,998.0	1,909.8
Foreign gold balances	352.9	103.0	86.6	17.2	7.1
Domestic discounts:					
Bills	134.2	28.1	14.0	34.3	(*)
Bonds	15.1	6.5	6.7	16.7	(*)
Total discounts	149.3	34.6	20.7	51.0	26.3
Advances on securities	75.2	64.7	48.7	94.7	118.0
Liabilities					
Notes in circulation	999.2	1,609.4	1,612.6	1,509.5	1,440.3
Giro deposits	171.7	883.2	922.3	629.6	(*)
Government deposits	28.5	40.1	51.0	9.4	(*)
Other deposits	7.1	44.9	67.9	51.4	(*)

* Not available.

drawn, particularly after the devaluation of the United States dollar. At the same time the large Swiss banks and wealthy individuals converted considerable cash balances into gold, and thus encouraged hoarding. As a result the National Bank's gold holdings were materially reduced, in spite of the almost complete liquidation of the gold exchange reserve, and there was some tightening of the credit situation in Switzerland. It seems reasonable to assume that, should France or some of the other important members of the gold bloc devalue, Switzerland would follow.

These changes in the position of the Swiss National Bank are shown in Table 58.

The Swiss Banking Structure

General survey. Prior to 1935 there was no general banking law in Switzerland and, with the exception of the state-owned banks and some savings banks, banking was not subject to governmental regulation or supervision. This long freedom from governmental restriction, combined with strong local individualism, has resulted in the development of a great variety of banking institutions which cover the widest possible range of banking activities. An outstanding characteristic of the Swiss banks is the universality of their business. State-owned institutions compete with privately owned banks, and mortgage and savings banks do a commercial banking business; large commercial banks handle mortgage loans, do a large stock-exchange brokerage business, and accept savings deposits. Even finance companies, or financial holding companies, accept certain deposits. Practically all banks render fiduciary banking services.

Two main groups of banks can be distinguished: (1) the large commercial banks and (2) the "cantonal," or state-owned, banks. The large commercial banks handle most of the important commercial and industrial banking transactions and practically all the international business, while the state-owned banks handle the bulk of the agricultural mortgage credit and distinctly local and state-wide commercial and retail business. Both groups operate through a great number of branches and deposit agencies, and thus keep in contact with local traditions and conditions. Neither of the two groups has a monopoly in its own field. The commercial banks have competition from the cantonal banks and from many local banks in their local commercial business, and from the private banks in some of the phases of trust business, such as custody, personal trust, and investment. The cantonal banks share their mortgage-loan business with many local savings, coöperative, and mortgage banks.

Investment credit is furnished by all of the large banks, either directly or, in the case of large loans, through a syndicate of the large commercial banks in conjunction with a syndicate of the cantonal banks. The granting of such long-term credit is facilitated by the existence of many holding and investment companies. There are two central mortgage-bond institutions, one organized by the cantonal banks and the other operating on behalf of the other mortgage banks, which obtain cheap long-term funds by the sale of bonds and relend them to what might be called their "member banks." Issue bank credit is supplied by one central bank which, like the Federal Reserve System, acts as a bankers' bank. For emergencies there is the Federal Loan Institution, similar to the American Reconstruction Finance Corporation, which was created during the war and was revived again in the summer of 1932.

With a population of only 4,000,000 people, Switzerland has some 3,000 banking establishments (head offices, branches, agencies, etc.), or one establishment per 1,333 inhabitants. This is probably a greater "banking density" than exists in any other country in the world.

Types of banking institutions. The Swiss banks may be classified for statistical purposes into seven principal groups: (1) the large commercial banks; (2) the cantonal, or state-owned, banks; (3) the large local banks; (4) the small or medium-sized local banks; (5) the Association of "Raiffeisenbanks," or coöperative credit societies; (6) the savings banks; and (7) the finance, or holding, companies. The number of institutions in each group, together with their total capital funds and total assets, is shown in Table 59.

TABLE 59

SUMMARY OF SWISS BANKING STATISTICS AT END OF 1933
(In millions of Swiss francs)

	Number of Institutions	Capital and Reserves Amount	Per Cent of Total	Total Assets Amount	Per Cent of Total
Cantonal banks	27	821.3	24.2	7,767.2	37.5
Large commercial banks	7	1,001.4	29.5	5,546.9	26.7
Large local banks....	81	432.3	12.7	3,490.2	16.8
Other local banks....	108	65.5	1.9	553.3	2.7
Raiffeisenbanks	1*	14.8	.4	340.7	1.6
Savings banks	97	86.4	2.5	1,451.1	7.0
Finance companies ..	43	980.5	28.8	1,587.9	7.7
Totals	364	3,402.2	100.0	20,737.3	100.0

* An association of 591 banks.

The total capital funds of the 364 Swiss financial institutions in operation at the end of 1933 amounted to 3,402,-200,000 francs, and their assets totaled 20,737,300,000 francs. Excluding resources of the finance companies, the total resources of the banks increased from $1,225,000,000 in 1906 to $4,203,000,000 in 1930, but declined to $3,696,-000,000 at the end of 1933 (conversions at the old par of exchange). The increase was continuous to 1930, except in 1914 and in 1921 and 1922. The decline since 1930 has been due, to the extent of some $62,000,000, to the failure of one of the large commercial banks, but the chief factor of course has been the general deflation of bank credit.

The deposits of all the banks, exclusive of the finance companies, aggregated about 16,307,000,000 francs at the end of 1933, or somewhat more than the combined deposits (at the present rate of exchange) of the three largest New York banks. About 17.3 per cent of the total deposits were current accounts payable at sight, 6.5 per cent commercial time deposits, 34.6 per cent "cash debentures," 5.4 per cent mortgage and other bonds, and 36.2 per cent passbook and savings deposits. It is obvious from these figures that the large proportion of time deposits in the form of cash debentures is the outstanding characteristic of the Swiss banking system.

The relative importance of the different groups of banks is roughly indicated by the distribution of the total banking assets.   Thus, the cantonal banks hold more than one-third of the total banking resources of the country, while the seven large commercial banks with a larger capitalization hold slightly more than one-fourth.   The large local banks rank third, with 16.8 per cent of the total at the end of 1933.   The small local banks and the Raiffeisenbanks are of minor importance in the banking system, and the savings banks hold only about 7 per cent of the total banking assets. The finance companies, with a larger total capitalization than any group except the large commercial banks, hold 7.7 per cent.

A study of the relative importance of the various groups over a period of 25 years indicates that the commercial banks and the cantonal banks have greatly strengthened their positions in their respective fields at the expense of the other groups.   The large commercial banks' share in the country's aggregate current account deposits increased from 42 per cent in 1906 to 63 per cent in 1930; in that of "cash debentures" it increased from 18 to 27 per cent, in that of savings deposits from 5 per cent to 10 per cent, and in that of acceptances and drafts from 80 per cent to 92 per cent.   Their loans and discount showed corresponding increases, and their only asset item which declined was security holdings and syndicate participations, which fell from 32 per cent to 27 per cent while the corresponding item of the cantonal banks increased from 25 per cent to 36 per cent of the total of all the Swiss banks.

The current account deposits of the cantonal banks declined during the above period from 27 per cent of the total to 19 per cent, and their acceptances and drafts from 6 per cent to 4 per cent.   On the other hand, their share of the savings deposits increased from 26 per cent to 41 per cent. The cantonal banks' share of the total cash resources declined, chiefly as a result of the transfer of the note-issue business to a new central bank, from 53 per cent in 1906 to 22 per cent in 1913 and to 13 per cent in 1930. Their bill holdings declined from 32 per cent in 1906 to 18 per cent in 1930, while their mortgage loans increased in the same period from 30 per cent to 42 per cent of the aggregate loans of all banks.

The large commercial banks. The group of seven large commercial banks comprises the following institutions: Schweizerische Kreditanstalt (Crédit Suisse), Zurich; Schweizerischer Bankverein (Société de Banque Suisse), Basle; Schweizerische Bankgesellschaft (Union Bank of Switzerland—Union de Banques Suisses), Winterthur; Eidgenoessische Bank A. G. (Banque Fédérale S. A.), Zurich; Basler Handelsbank (Banque Commerciale de Bâle), Basle; A. G. Leu & Cie. (S. A. Leu & Cie), Zurich; and Schweizerische Volksbank (Banque Populaire Suisse), Berne. It is interesting to note that, of these seven banks, five have their largest offices in Zurich and two in Basle; and that one of them, the Volksbank, is a coöperative enterprise and not a corporation. This latter bank, since its reorganization in 1933, has greatly contracted its international activities.

With the exception of A. G. Leu & Co., which was founded in 1755, all of these banks were established during the second half of the last century for the purpose of financing the development of railways and industries, and they functioned as typical *banques d'affaires,* like the old type of Austrian and German commercial banks or the French Banque de Paris et des Pays-Bas. Without these banks the considerable development of the Swiss economy up to the beginning of this century would have been impossible. As the domestic industries became more firmly established, the banks gradually solidified and consolidated their positions on a stabler and more permanent basis and eventually developed into institutions of a type somewhere between the old German "D" banks and the French deposit banks.

Fundamentally they differ little from the large New York banks, except for a slightly closer tie-up with industry and with holding companies or investment trusts.

The large Swiss commercial banks, like the large New York banks, accept demand and time deposits, but the bulk of their time deposits take the form of so-called "cash debentures." They also accept deposits on passbooks and, in some cases, savings deposits. They make loans, discount bills and acceptances, open letters of credit, and make stock exchange loans and, in some cases, even mortgage loans. They make investments, sometimes of a permanent nature, and participate in the underwriting of securities. In some

TABLE 60

COMBINED BALANCE SHEET OF THE LARGE SWISS BANKS
(In millions of Swiss francs)

| | December 31, 1931 * | | September 30, 1934 | |
| | | Per Cent | | Per Cent |
Assets	Amount	of Total	Amount	of Total
Cash and with banks	1,713.3	23.9	1,064.3	20.9
Bills of exchange	950.8	13.3	563.2	11.1
Loans on current account	2,646.8	36.9	1,934.3	38.0
Time loans	940.0	13.1	734.1	14.4
Mortgage loans	363.8	5.1	387.4	7.6
Securities and permanent participations	280.6	3.9	188.1	3.7
Syndicate participations	103.1	1.4	65.4	1.3
Other assets	172.9	2.4	153.3	3.0
Total assets	7,171.3	100.0	5,090.1	100.0
Liabilities				
Capital and reserves	1,205.8	16.8	986.8	19.4
Due to banks	469.7	6.5	305.5	6.0
Demand deposits	1,520.4	21.2	1,131.7	22.2
Time deposits	889.1	12.4	513.9	10.1
Savings and passbook deposits	892.5	12.4	603.2	11.9
Cash debentures and certificates	1,614.0	22.5	1,195.4	23.5
Loan obligations	122.0	1.7	97.0	1.9
Bills and acceptances	339.1	4.7	131.3	2.6
Other liabilities	118.7	1.8	125.3	2.4
Total liabilities	7,171.3	100.0	5,090.1	100.0

* Eight banks in 1931 and seven in 1934.

cases they control investment trusts, but they practically never control industries or participate in their management, except temporarily when loans become frozen. Table 60 is a combined balance sheet of the large banks as of September 30, 1934, compared with that for December 31, 1931.

The total capital and reserves of this group of banks are equivalent to about 27 per cent of their total deposits— a much higher ratio than that for the British joint stock banks, the large French deposit banks, or the American commercial banks. Only about one-third of their total deposit liabilities consist of demand deposits; another third is represented by cash debentures, and the balance consists of time and savings deposits. The comparative figures show the marked declines in all deposit items since 1931, and it is particularly interesting to note that the cash debentures, which have fairly long maturities, have declined proportionately as much as the other types of deposits. The reduction in deposits since 1931 is due chiefly to the repayment of loans, to withdrawals from abroad, and to domestic hoarding.

A brief explanation of some of the principal items in the balance sheets of the large commercial banks may contribute to an understanding of their operations:

Cash debentures. The so-called "cash debentures" are debenture bonds issued by the banks for periods of from three to five years, but sometimes for longer periods, in denominations of 500, 1,000, and 5,000 francs. They are called "cash debentures" because they are issued at any time upon deposit of cash at the bank window and are repaid in cash at maturity. Except in a few instances they are not issued through a public offering in blocs or series, but are sold daily. This means that there are usually no large maturities of these bonds on any one date, but, instead, regular daily maturities according to the issue dates. None of these bonds are quoted on a stock exchange, nor is there an over-the-counter market for them.

In theory one could reason at length against the issuance of such bonds by commercial banks. One criticism is that such large maturities might embarrass the obligor banks. However, as pointed out above, the debentures are issued daily and the maturities are therefore well distributed. The debentures are a well-established and well-regarded credit instrument in Switzerland and are willingly taken by all classes of investors. The proceeds from the sale of the cash debentures are not used for loans to industrial concerns to finance the creation of capital goods, but are normally used for strictly short-term loans.

The most valid objections to the issuance of three- to five-year debentures are, first, that some of the banks (mostly non-commercial banks) have used the proceeds for mortgage loans which, because of their shortness, create instability in the mortgage-loan market; and, second, that in times of declining and continued low money rates the earnings of the banks are affected by their inability to adjust the interest rates on the debentures to the lower yield on their earning assets. For instance, the average interest paid by the large banks on such cash debentures decreased from 4.89 per cent in 1930 to only 4.23 per cent in 1933, while debit rates declined much more drastically.

The first of these objections has been met during the last few years by the establishment of a so-called central mortgage-bond institution for the cantonal banks and a similar institution for the other banks. These institutions issue long-term mortgage bonds and relend the proceeds to their members against a corresponding amount of long-term mortgages. This procedure obviates the necessity of having to finance long-term loans with medium-term funds. There is no remedy for the second difficulty except careful and prudent management which shortens maturities in periods of declining money rates and extends them in times of rising rates. It is obviously difficult to forecast the trend of money rates over a period of years, but the banks seem to feel that in the long run the fluctuations tend to balance each other.

Deposits. Deposits are usually classified as "creditor current-account," "bank creditors," "checking accounts," "short-term deposits," "deposits maturing in more than six months," and "deposits on passbooks" or "savings deposits."

The creditor current-account is the most common type of deposit account. It is used mostly by industrial and commercial firms and is distinguished from the checking account (which is also used by the same types of firms) by a slightly higher interest rate and the charge of a turnover commission of about .05 to .125 per cent for each six-month period, whereas no commission is charged for the turnover in the checking accounts. The "bank creditors" item represents balances of local and foreign correspondent banks which normally bear interest at a rate at least ¼ per cent to ½ per cent below the rate for prime commercial paper. They are subject to withdrawal on call. The "short-term deposits" and "deposits maturing beyond six months" are time deposits either maturing on a fixed date or subject to withdrawal only after due notice. The "deposits on passbooks" are the current accounts of officials, employees, artisans, etc., and differ from savings deposits in that they are subject to less stringent restrictions and that, in some instances, orders of payment may be drawn against them and they may be transferred to other accounts.

Cash. The item "cash" in the bank statements includes domestic and foreign currency holdings, balances on giro-account with the National Bank, and coupons and called bonds held for collection. The bulk of the cash item consists of balances with the central bank which bear no interest.

Bills of exchange. This item includes both domestic and foreign bills. Although the exact proportions are not known, it is believed that the holdings of domestic commercial bills are small at present and that the bulk of the portfolio consists of domestic finance bills and of foreign bills affected by the German and Hungarian standstill agreements.

Lombard loans. Advances on securities, or "lombard loans," are advances for periods of from one to six months secured by collateral. Under the rules of the Swiss National Bank these loans are not rediscountable.

Securities and participations. The total security holdings and participations of the large Swiss banks (including permanent and syndicate holdings) represented at the end of September 1934 only about 5 per cent of their total assets, and of the total less than one-tenth consisted of Federal Government and Federal railway bonds. The small proportion of government security holdings of the Swiss banks is due to the fact that the market for government bonds in Switzerland is very narrow and that the supply of Treasury bills is quite limited. As a result the banks are unable to use government securities as a secondary reserve, except to a limited extent, and are forced to maintain under the present uncertain conditions large amounts of unproductive deposits with the central bank. The permanent investments consist largely of blocks of stock in affiliated banks or holding companies, and the syndicate transactions represent participations in syndicates for the underwriting or marketing of securities, which have not as yet been completed.

Loans. Loans on current account, both secured and unsecured, constitute from 35 to 40 per cent of the total assets of the large Swiss banks. A break-up of these loans into domestic and foreign loans unfortunately is not available, but it seems reasonable to assume that foreign loans represent a considerable part of the total and that their proportion is probably greater than before the war. Probably a large share of the foreign loans are to German and Central European concerns, and some of them are undoubtedly frozen. At the end of 1933 about 80 per cent of the total loans were secured. Before the war the percentage of unsecured loans was much higher, reaching in some cases as high as 50 per cent. The interest rates on secured loans are usually about ½ per cent to one per cent above the official discount rate, and those for unsecured loans about ¾ per cent to 1½ per cent higher.

Mortgage loans. The mortgage loans of the large commercial banks are nominal, except in the case of the Schweizerische Volksbank and A. G. Leu & Co.

Branches and associated financial concerns. Branch banking in Switzerland is highly developed. Most of the large commercial banks have established a large number of branches, agencies, and offices accepting deposits. The total in 1934 was 199, which is a comparatively high figure in view of the fact that there are not more than 25 cities with a population in excess of 10,000. This dense network is a commentary upon the active industrial and commercial life of the country and upon the easy ebb and flow in the money market. The branching out of the large banks into other parts of the country was done largely at the expense of the local stock or private banks, many of which were taken over and converted into branch offices. In some cases their independence was conserved, but on the whole the concentration process has been fairly complete. It should, however, be noted that many of the small local banks lacked capable management and that the branching out of the large banks probably created greater stability and, in any case, resulted in a better distribution of the risk—a consequence of importance in a country where each center has its specific important industries.

An interesting characteristic of the large Swiss banks is their large financial interest in holding companies or investment trusts with which they coöperate. The majority of these companies were established before the war for the purpose of financing the sale of railway and electrical equipment by Swiss and German manufacturers to the Balkan and other undeveloped countries. In some cases, these companies were investment trusts of the general man-

agement type. During and after the war many of them
suffered heavy losses and had to be reorganized because of
currency depreciation in the various countries and the lack
of careful geographical diversification of their investments.
It should not be assumed that these investment trusts serve
merely as storehouses for undigested security offerings of
the banks, although there may have been cases where the
banks tried to unload securities on them. The most important of these companies, grouped according to the banks
with which they are associated, together with their capitalization and year of establishment, are as follows:

Bank	Holding or Investment Company	Established	Capital Stock (in francs)
Crédit Suisse	Bank für elektrische Unternehmungen.	1895	75,000,000
Swiss Bank Corp.	Schweizerische Gesellschaft für Anlagewerte.	1907	20,000,000
	Schweizerische Gesellschaft für Metallwerte.	1910	25,000,000
Union Bank of Switzerland	"Thesaurus" Continentale Effekten Gesellschaft.	1927	15,000,000
Basler Handelsbank	Bank für Transportwerte.	1894	11,000,000
	Schweizerische Gesellschaft für elektrische Industrie.	1896	40,000,000

In addition, the Swiss Bank Corporation has a branch
office in London and the Credit Suisse has an interest in
the Swiss Argentine Mortgage Bank, which does a mortgage
business in Argentina. Otherwise the Swiss banks have
no close banking affiliates abroad, nor are there many
branch offices of foreign banks in Switzerland.

Cantonal banks. The cantonal banks, which play a very
important rôle in the Swiss banking system, are state-owned
institutions. Most of them were established during the
last three decades of the past century in order to provide
cheap agricultural credit. Practically all of them issued
notes until 1907, when the central bank was established.

The issue business brought many of the banks into close contact with industry and trade; some of the banks succeeded in maintaining these valuable connections and thus conserved a good-sized commercial banking business (Zurich and Berne). This business is state-wide, and the banks maintain an extensive system of branch offices and agencies which collect savings from all corners of the states. Early in 1934 these offices and agencies of the 27 cantonal banks numbered 877. The cantonal banks are thus in very close contact with local business, particularly with the small local trade and the business of the craftsmen and the farmers.

The state guarantee which the cantonal banks enjoy, and the fact that they are practically exempt from taxation, makes it easy for them to compete for deposits. It is perhaps an unfair competition, but it exists and is effective, as is indicated by the fact that the savings and pass-book deposits of the cantonal banks have increased some 30 per cent from 1930 to 1934, while those of the seven large commercial banks have decreased nearly 40 per cent. The difficulties of one of the commercial banks which holds large savings deposits (the Volksbank) and the fact that the average interest rate allowed by the commercial banks was, in 1933, only 2.59 per cent, as compared with 2.98 per cent in the case of the cantonal banks, may explain part of this decrease. On the other hand, the average interest paid by the cantonal banks on cash debentures in 1933 was only 4.03 per cent, as compared with 4.23 per cent for the commercial banks; yet their cash debentures increased while those of the commercial banks decreased sharply. In any case the cantonal banks hold nearly one-half of the total savings deposits of the country and are responsible for the issuance of about one-half of the cash debentures outstanding.

The cantonal banks use these semi-long term deposits largely for intermediate and long-term lending. Their mortgage loans amount to nearly 90 per cent of their savings and time deposits (inclusive of cash debentures), and a sizable part of their other loans consist of advances to municipalities. They supply over one-half of all the mortgage credit, and for this reason they are the most important factor in the semi-long-term and long-term agricultural and building credit market. They do not maintain as high a degree of liquidity as the large commercial banks. Their demand deposits are less than one-half of those of the large commercial banks, and their aggregate commercial banking business is probably not more than one-fourth or one-fifth of that of the large commercial banks. Their commercial loans are probably slower but better diversified than those of the large banks. Their bill holdings consist largely of trade bills and promissory notes under lombard loans. From an international point of view they are not a deciding factor in the money market. Table 61 is a combined statement of the 27 cantonal banks.

TABLE 61

COMBINED STATEMENT OF THE 27 CANTONAL BANKS
(In millions of Swiss francs; End of October)

	1932		1934	
Assets	*Amount*	*Per Cent of Total*	*Amount*	*Per Cent of Total*
Cash and due from banks.....	374.1	4.9	322.8	4.1
Bills of exchange..............	217.2	2.9	180.2	2.3
Debtors on current account....	1,032.6	13.6	1,014.7	12.9
Time loans	626.6	8.3	715.9	9.1
Mortgage loans	4,523.4	59.5	4,823.4	61.4
Securities and participations....	691.7	9.1	667.3	8.5
Other assets	130.7	1.7	131.6	1.7
Total assets	7,596.3	100.0	7,855.9	100.0
Liabilities				
Capital and reserves...........	804.8	10.6	820.8	10.4
Due to banks.................	96.5	1.3	118.2	1.5
Demand deposits	590.3	7.8	553.3	7.0
Savings and passbook deposits	2,551.4	33.6	2,691.8	34.3
Time deposits	336.0	4.4	358.5	4.6
Cash debentures	2,681.8	35.3	2,639.7	33.6
Loan obligations	365.0	4.8	408.9	5.2
Other liabilities	170.5	2.2	264.7	3.4
Total liabilities	7,596.3	100.0	7,855.9	100.0

Other types of financial institutions. The other types of Swiss banks are of little importance from an international standpoint. All of them issue cash debentures and accept savings deposits and make mortgage loans. Most of the local institutions are commercial banks of the same type as the American small-town bank, except that about 50 per cent of their assets consist of mortgage loans and about 60 to 70 per cent of their liabilities are cash debentures and savings deposits. The finance companies resemble the investment trusts of the Anglo-Saxon countries, but they accept certain deposits and make short- and medium-term loans.

Recent banking legislation. Because of losses suffered on its foreign commitments, coupled with the freezing of loans made to domestic industries which were seriously affected by the depression, the Swiss Discount Bank of Geneva (one of the large commercial banks) failed in April 1934. Serious difficulties of the Banque Populaire Suisse due to the same causes were averted only by timely intervention on the part of the government, the National Bank, and the Federal Loan Office. The latter and the other commercial banks had also tried to help the Discount Bank but had been unsuccessful. As pointed out before, the Banque Populaire is a coöperative institution, and legally the members of the society are responsible for its liabilities. Most of them are small business people, artisans, farmers, employees, etc., who considered the investment in participating certificates as equivalent to savings deposits. When the threat of liability suddenly arose (or the question of a reduction of the existing nominal value and of a subscription to new stock), a wave of dissatisfaction swept over the country. A wide popular demand for government supervision of the banks developed, and there was little else that the government could do but to heed this demand. On November 8, 1934, a Federal Banking Law was enacted to take effect early in 1935.

In substance the law requires the maintenance of certain

minimum ratios of liquidity and of capital funds to deposits; it makes annual independent audits and periodical publication of statements compulsory, and requires notification of the National Bank with regard to all large foreign loans, short- and long-term. It creates a certain preferential position for savings deposits in case of failure, and requires notification of the central bank of any increase in the rates on new cash debentures. Supervision of the banks is placed in the hands of a Federal Bank Commission.

The new law actually makes few changes in the established practices, but it puts them in an amplified form on the statute books. Practically all of the banks have in the past published their statements at regular intervals, and the banks have notified or consulted the central bank, at its request, concerning large transactions involving an export of capital. The large banks have also furnished the central bank with periodic statements and have published quarterly balance sheets. The notification of increases in interest rates on new "cash debentures" was required because of the effect of such changes upon the money market.

The following is a summary of the various provisions of the new banking law:

> *Sec. 1.* The law applies to all types of banks, public and private (including the cantonal banks but excluding the central bank), and to all financial concerns that publicly invite deposits. Foreign banks and their representatives also come under the bill, and the Federal Government may establish special regulations covering their activities, including the issuance of a guarantee, conditioned upon reciprocal treatment.
>
> *Sec. 2.* Calls for distinctly separate management, auditors, and comptrollers for the large banks and the submission of by-laws of new banks to the Bank Commission.
>
> *Sec. 3.* Provides for the establishment of minimum ratios of capital funds to deposits and of current assets to current liabilities, and for annual contributions of 1/20 of net profits to the reserve fund until the latter reaches 1/5 of the capital stock.
>
> *Sec. 4.* Requires publication of statements by all banks annually; by banks with resources of 20,000,000 francs and more, semiannually; and by banks with resources of 100,000,000

francs and more, quarterly. This section does not apply to private bankers who do not publicly solicit deposits.

Sec. 5. The Swiss National Bank is to receive copies of the annual statements of all banks and may obtain from banks with resources in excess of 100,000,000 francs any statement or information it desires. It must be notified prior to conclusion of all external loans or credits maturing in twelve or more months or of any transactions involving an export of capital, if they amount to 10,000,000 francs or more. If the money market or economic conditions require it, they must notify the Central Bank even if smaller amounts are involved. If the National Bank feels that these operations are against the interests of the money market or the general interest of the country, it may veto them and the banks may not carry out the transactions. The National Bank is to be notified of proposed increases in the rate of interest on cash debentures.

Sec. 6. This section deals with reduction of capital stock and with repayment of share interest in coöperative banks, and prohibits formation of commercial banks on a coöperative basis.

Sec. 7. In case of bankruptcy, savings deposits up to 5,000 francs for each depositor will enjoy a preferential position and will rank in the so-called "third class" of debts, provided they are not subject to a state guarantee. The states may require the setting aside of certain assets for the protection of savings deposits up to 5,000 francs for each depositor.

Sec. 8. This section provides that the approval of the owner of securities has to be obtained before securities are used for margin requirements.

Sec. 9. Calls for a detailed annual audit by independent accountants. Infractions which are called by the auditors to the bank's attention and which are not remedied must be reported by the auditors to the Bank Commission. Secrecy of banking transactions is guarded.

Sec. 10. The Federal Council nominates a Federal Bank Commission of five members, including a president and a vice president. They must be bank experts, but may not be officers of any bank or of any auditing firm. The Commission supervises the enforcement of the law. Certain of its decisions may be appealed to the Federal Supreme Court.

Secs. 11, 12, 13, and 15. These contain permissive provisions concerning banks subject to large withdrawals of deposits (moratoria may be decreed if liabilities are covered and earnings are sufficient to pay interest), appointment of administrators for solvent but frozen banks which continue operations, bankruptcy and reorganizations, and introductory regulations.

Sec. 14. Deals with penalties. Cantonal banks are subject to relative provisions of state laws. Officers, auditors, and controllers of banks are liable to shareholders or creditors for any loss caused by negligence.

The Money Market

This brief survey of the Swiss banking and currency system indicates that the country has the financial prerequisites of an international financial center. First, the banking structure is sufficiently well developed and sufficiently flexible to permit the ready movement of funds to and from the country. Second, the Swiss banks have large resources which under normal conditions are available for lending. Third, the Swiss currency has been one of the most stable currencies in the world during the last thirty years. Fourth, the Swiss banks have the equipment and experience for the handling of foreign exchange transactions. The central location of the country facilitates arbitrage, and the steady exchange of commodities, services, and funds with nearly all European countries necessitates trading in their currencies.

The fact that Switzerland has not become a more important international financial center is due to the lack of an adequate economic basis for a broad money market. There are no important commodity or securities markets in Switzerland in the financing of which a large amount of short-term funds may be employed. The demand for funds to finance domestic commerce is readily met through ordinary banking channels. Switzerland is not a great trading nation, and there is comparatively little outlet for short-term funds in the financing of the country's foreign trade.

For these reasons the Swiss National Bank has not favored or encouraged the development of an international money market. It has been more interested in the development of a strong banking system and in making credit available for domestic business at low interest rates. The central bank authorities have felt that foreign funds come to Switzerland not primarily because of the country's outstanding qualifications as an international money market, but rather for the sake of safety, and that they are therefore subject to instant withdrawal. In view of the developments during 1931–35, this policy seems to be a sound one.

Most of the large commercial banks naturally disagreed with the position taken by the Swiss National Bank during the period 1924–31. They felt that one of the Swiss markets—say, Zurich—should actively strive to become an international center in competition with Amsterdam. It was an understandable desire, but the National Bank gave it little support. On February 5, 1924, it circularized the banks to the effect that it would not discount any foreign bills except those resulting from the export or import of merchandise from or to Switzerland, but it later interpreted this rule rather liberally. In the spring of 1925 it again discounted foreign bills of exchange that met its statutory discount requirements, provided they matured within not more than 20 days; but at the same time it limited them to a certain percentage of its total portfolio. These restrictions resulted in the application of a higher rate for foreign bills than for Swiss bills. At the beginning of 1929, when the rise of the money rates abroad tended to lift the Swiss rates, the National Bank tightened its discount requirements for foreign bills by limiting them to 25 per cent of the domestic bills presented, while still insisting upon the 20-day maximum maturity. The central bank's holdings of foreign bills dropped from 23 per cent of the total portfolio in February 1929 to 4 per cent in May of the same year. Shortly afterwards the rates tended to ease, and in July 1929 the Bank admitted foreign bills up to 50 per cent of the total bills presented. In January 1930 the percentage was raised to 75 per cent. In March 1930 the limit on foreign bills was lifted entirely, and on January 15,

1931, the maximum life of bills discountable was extended from 20 to 30 days.

These restrictions of the Swiss National Bank illustrate its policy toward foreign bills. Before the World War it had been a frequent practice, particularly in the watchmaking industry, to issue acceptances on foreign countries payable in Swiss francs and to domicile them in Switzerland. While the statutory restrictions permit the National Bank to discount these bills, the Bank's management always felt that, since they carry only one Swiss signature, the acquisition of such bills involves a certain risk. Hence, when the custom of creating such bills spread to other branches of the export trade after the war, the management insisted that the Swiss drawer of the bill should represent a "prime name" and that the acceptor should be a known solvent firm located in a country with a stable currency. Furthermore, only a fraction of the bills presented for discount could consist of bills of this type.

The acceptance market. The policy of the central bank gave little encouragement to the development of an international acceptance market in Switzerland. Nevertheless such a market developed because of the attractiveness of this business for the large commercial banks. The steady inflow of foreign funds made the commercial banks fairly independent of the National Bank, and they were at times quite liberal in discounting foreign bills, particularly German and other Central European bills. A substantial portion of these bills were frozen under the German standstill agreement of 1931 and, as a matter of fact, the Swiss banks were proportionately more heavily involved in Germany than the institutions of any other country.

The supply of acceptances originating in the Swiss markets is very limited. The principal domestic source of bills is the financing of imports of raw materials for the large manufacturing concerns—as for cotton, silk, and wool, or other commodities such as grain, etc.—and the financing of certain exports.. The only other local acceptances available to the market are the relatively small number of bills originating in connection with domestic trade transactions and the drawings of industrial or large commercial firms upon the banks in order to cover their seasonal requirements or for temporary working capital. The banks accept bills of the latter type, which have become quite common in Switzerland although it is at times difficult for the uninformed to ascertain whether such advances (which are put in acceptance form because of the lower discount rate) are really of a self-liquidating nature or are merely finance bills.

Before the war the volume of finance bills was relatively large, particularly in the portfolios of the cantonal banks, but the insistence of the National Bank on scrutinizing all bills, and its firm refusal to discount doubtful ones, eliminated a good many of them. At that time the Swiss banks financed not only local industry but also the textile industry of Northern Italy, of the South of Germany, and of Alsace-Lorraine. In the post-war period the place of the Lombardy and Alsace-Lorraine industries was taken by certain North German, Austrian, and Hungarian industries which in many cases, as the Swiss banks later learned to their regret, used the proceeds for plant investments or as permanent working capital.

Acceptances have always had a ready market in Switzerland at rates usually below the official discount rate of the National Bank. In the case of foreign bills, the rate is normally somewhat higher than that for domestic bills. The official discount rate remained unchanged at $3\frac{1}{2}$ per cent from October 1925 to April 1930, when it was reduced to 3 per cent. In July 1930 it was reduced to $2\frac{1}{2}$ per cent, and in January 1931 to 2 per cent, where it has remained ever since. By an agreement between the commercial banks, the minimum private discount rate (bill rate) has been fixed at $1\frac{1}{2}$ per cent since February 1932. The trend of the annual average of the bill rate (private discount rate) since 1926 is shown in Table 62.

TABLE 62

PRIVATE DISCOUNT RATE IN SWITZERLAND

(Annual average rate on prime
bills and acceptances)

Year	Rate
1927	3.27
1928	3.33
1929	3.31
1930	2.01
1931	1.44
1932	1.52
1933	1.50
1934	1.50

The bill rate, or private discount rate, is "private" in a literal sense. The published rate is not a uniform rate, since each bank fixes and varies its own rate according to its needs and the quality of the paper offered. The relative narrowness of the market is thus indicated. The Swiss National Bank does not buy at any rate other than the official rate, which it publishes regularly. Since the discount rate is usually higher than the bill rate, the National Bank's portfolio never contains large amounts of bills, except in periods when the banks are in urgent need of cash and must rediscount at the official rate.

The principal buyers of acceptances are the banks and insurance companies, and in view of the limited opportunities for short-term investment in Switzerland, they have been very eager in recent years to absorb all bankers' bills offered. However, the banks are reluctant to discount their own acceptances. The volume of bills has greatly declined during the depression, and thus the earning capacity of the banks has been further reduced.

Trade bills. The market for trade bills, like that for bankers' bills, is primarily a bank discount market. There are no discount houses or brokers to maintain an open market and quote uniform rates. The discount rate on each item is determined by the discounting officer of the bank to which it is presented, who tries to obtain the best possible terms for the bank but must be careful not to charge rates which would drive future discounts into the hands of competitors. Next to bankers' acceptances, the lowest rates are on prime trade bills, followed by second-grade trade bills or, at times, by finance bills at rates which are usually still slightly below the central bank's official discount rate. Prime trade paper must normally amount to at least 5,000 francs, but in times of a scarcity of such paper even smaller bills are gladly purchased.

The largest buyers of these bills are the big commercial banks and the various cantonal banks, particularly those located in the larger cities. Many of the small local trade bills are discounted with the independent local banks or the local branch offices of the large commercial banks, which, because of the dependence of these small local industries upon them, may charge rates even as high as or higher than the existing official rate, or may offset a somewhat lower rate by high collection or commission charges. Finance bills are frequently bought by the local banks, and at times by the cantonal banks, which often rediscount them for the small local banks provided the latter also supply them at the same time with a reasonable percentage of their good commercial paper.

The supply of trade bills naturally depends upon trade conditions, and in times of commercial or industrial inactivity the volume outstanding is very small. In 1930 total bill holdings of all the Swiss banks reached an all-time high of slightly over two billion francs, but at the end of 1933 this figure had declined to somewhat less than one billion francs, of which nearly 70 per cent were held by the seven large commercial banks, 20 per cent by the cantonal banks, and about 10 per cent by the local banks. During 1934 the total volume of bills again declined sharply.

There is no single large discount center in Switzerland. Zurich undoubtedly handles the largest volume of bills, but business is also transacted in Basle and, to a limited extent, in Geneva. This distribution of the limited volume of business in a small country makes the formation of a strong and uniform market more difficult, but distances fortunately are so small and the telephone service between the various cities is so well developed that there are only minor inequalities in rates.

Day-to-day money market. The day-to-day money market in Switzerland corresponds to the "Federal funds" market in the United States. When one of the large commercial banks finds itself temporarily short of funds, possibly as a result of adverse clearings, it simply calls up one of the other banks and borrows overnight in amounts of 500,000 or 1,000,000 francs on an unsecured basis at a rate mutually agreed upon. This rate is usually below the private discount rate, but it may at times be higher. However, it is never in excess of the so-called "lombard rate" of the National Bank, since it would otherwise be less expensive for the banks to borrow from the central bank on a lombard basis. The operation of the day-to-day market may be briefly described as follows: Upon receipt of a telephone request, the lending bank puts the funds at the disposal of the borrowing institution through a transfer from its giro account at the National Bank to that of the borrower, or by remitting a check on the National Bank, and it receives a return check or transfer, due the next day, together with a cash payment for the interest. .

Report loans. Report loans, as in other continental European countries, are used to finance stock exchange transactions. If a speculator has purchased shares for delivery at the end of the month and, because he anticipates a higher price during or at the end of the following month, does not desire to take up the shares, he may carry over his position by a report transaction. He simply resells the shares purchased at the end of the first month to his bank or stock exchange house at the market price and repurchases them at the same price for delivery a month later. The price that he pays to the bank for its part in the transaction is called the "report interest." It varies in accordance with money market conditions and the supply and demand for "reports."

Likewise, if a speculator sells shares for delivery at the end of the month in anticipation of lower prices and wishes to carry over his position, he may purchase from the bank shares for immediate delivery at the existing price, and may resell them to the bank at the same price for delivery a month later. In such a case he is entitled to a so-called "deport interest" for the month period. In each of these cases the purchase or sale is a firm transaction subject to delivery or acceptance of the same number of like shares a month later, and the bank may therefore, in the interim period, do with the shares whatever it pleases. In other words the shares are not held as collateral for a loan, as in the case of collateral loans in which the identical collateral is to be delivered upon repayment of the loan.

Cash debenture market. The issuance of cash debentures by the banks always has a decided effect upon conditions in the money market. These debentures are often issued in sizable blocks, and their sale naturally reduces the floating supply of money. Likewise large maturities which are not immediately re-invested increase the floating supply. The interest rates on new issues of debentures are particularly important for the money market because they serve as an indication of the trend of rates on medium-term investments, savings deposits, and mortgage loans. If the banks increase their rates on these debentures, the savings and mortgage rates will immediately have a tendency to rise. For this reason the National Bank has in the past insisted that it be notified of any contemplated changes in the rates, and the new bank law makes it compulsory for the banks to advise the central bank of any contemplated increase two weeks in advance and authorizes the bank to negotiate, if necessary, for a modification of the contemplated terms of issue if the interests of the money market should require such action.

Lombard loans. Advances on collateral, or "lombard loans," are loans for periods of from one to six months secured by collateral which, in Switzerland, usually consists of securities. Lombard loans secured by bills of exchange or merchandise are not customary in that country. The difference between a secured current account loan and a lombard loan is that there is a continuous business relationship in the former while a lombard loan is as a rule a single, non-recurring transaction (at least theoretically, although renewals are frequent in practice) effected for a specific purpose and evidenced by a promissory note of the borrower which the lending bank discounts. Under the rules of the Swiss National Bank these notes are not rediscountable. Such "lombard" loans are often used by stock exchange firms (under the name of "ultimo moneys") for the purpose of covering their requirements from one end-of-the-month settlement to the next. Private speculators or industrial firms who have but temporary needs sometimes have recourse to this type of credit for periods of from three to six months. The collateral margin is normally 10 to 25 per cent. The interest rate on such loans depends, of course, upon money conditions, but it is very often 2 per cent above the official discount rate. As a rule no commission is charged against these accounts. The amount of lombard loans has been more or less stationary in recent years. Their total amounted in 1934 to approximately 2 per cent of the aggregate assets of the large commercial banks, which figure confirms the view that they are of little importance from the standpoint of the money market.

The large commercial banks carry so-called "lombard accounts" with the Swiss National Bank. These are current accounts secured by the deposit of bonds, largely government and Federal Railway bonds, against which the banks may borrow temporarily (up to ten days' notice), often in order to cover month-end requirements. The rate charged by the National Bank is the same as for three-month secured loans, *i.e.*, one per cent above the official discount rate. The central bank insists that credits obtained on such a secured basis be used for commercial purposes and not for the speculative purchase of securities.

The Swiss Stock Exchanges

There are seven stock exchanges in Switzerland—those of Zurich, Basle, Geneva, Lausanne, Berne, Neuchatel, and Chur—but only the first three are of importance, and the present discussion is therefore limited to them.

The Swiss stock exchanges are small as compared with the stock exchanges of New York, London, Paris, Amsterdam, and Berlin, but in relation to the size of the country they are important and handle a considerable amount of foreign business. A comparatively large number of foreign securities are listed, and there is a steady volume of trading for foreign account. In pre-war years foreign holdings of Swiss securities were estimated at about 1½ billion Swiss francs, of which about one billion were for French account. During the war the bulk of these foreign holdings were repatriated, and in the post-war period, as has been pointed

TABLE 63

TOTAL TURNOVER
(In millions of Swiss francs)

	Zurich	Basle
1926	5,291	2,634
1927	9,456	1,410
1928	10,121	2,632
1929	6,769	1,409
1930	6,772	1,270
1931	6,280	1,124
1932	3,701	598
1933	3,918	687

out, Switzerland lent abroad on long-term an aggregate of at least 1,300 million Swiss francs. These various foreign issues are all listed on the Swiss stock exchanges and most of them are actively traded in. The inflow of foreign capital seeking investment during the period of currency depreciation and political and economic instability in the neighboring countries stimulated the activities of the Swiss stock exchanges.   As a result the turnover increased rapidly up to 1928; it decreased thereafter, as indicated by the figures in Table 63 for the stock exchanges of Zurich and Basle.   The corresponding figures for Geneva are not available.

Government supervision.   For some time Federal regulation of all stock exchange activities has been under consideration, and the government has already prepared a bill to establish such regulation.   The bill has not been published, but early in 1935 it was expected that it would soon be introduced into the Swiss Congress.   At present a description of the stock exchanges must be based upon the respective state laws, which are dated as follows: Zurich—Law of December 22, 1912, and regulations of Association of Stock Exchange Brokers regarding admission of securities; Basle—Law of April 8, 1897, and regulations of October 15th and December 29, 1897; Geneva—Law of December 20, 1856, and regulations of September 2 and November 5, 1930.   Generally speaking, these various laws and regulations are fairly liberal, and the new law will undoubtedly be much stricter, although probably not so drastic, as the American Securities Exchange Act of 1934.

In each of the three cities the state government supervises the activities of the stock exchange.   In Zurich and Basle this is done by the Department of the Interior through an official supervising office consisting of a supervisor and a secretary and their assistants, and through a Stock Exchange Commission consisting of the head of the Interior Department and six members, of which two have to be members of the Association of Stock Exchange Brokers.   The supervisor's office is responsible for the strict enforcement of the laws and regulations; it keeps the records and issues the daily quotation list.   The Stock Exchange Commission supervises the stock exchange in a general way and is consulted in connection with any modification of the existing regulations or of the law. In Basle it also passes on applications for listing. In Geneva the state supervision is less stringent, and there is only one supervisory body composed of *commissionaires* who supervise the trading and quoting.

Brokers. In Zurich and Basle a broker must be licensed by the state government. In Zurich the license is issued by the Department of the Interior, which consults with the Stock Exchange Commission, the Stock Exchange Commissioner, and the governing board of the Association of Stock Exchange Brokers. In Basle the license is issued by the Stock Exchange Commission. In Zurich, brokers of unlisted securities must also be licensed. In both Zurich and Basle, but not in Geneva, banks may obtain licenses to act as brokers. Applicants must be able to exercise their citizenship rights and must have a good reputation. In Zurich an applicant must be a resident of the state.

Both states require a license fee, the size of which depends upon the annual turnover. They also require the furnishing of surety bonds, which for a banking firm aggregate 100,000 francs in Basle and 30,000 francs in Zurich. In all three cities an additional bond is required to be given to the local association of stock exchange brokers. In Zurich, for instance, this bond amounts to 100,000 francs. In addition, annual payments have to be made to the state, the amount being 10,000 francs in Zurich and, in Basle, depending upon the turnover. In Geneva a state tax of .01 per cent is levied on all transactions in listed securities, regardless of whether they are executed on the floor or over the counter.

Brokers may act either as agent for their customers in executing orders or, unless the customer expressly stipulates to the contrary, as principal.

The powers of the various stock exchange associations differ. In Zurich, for instance, the association may establish broad rules, including listing regulations, subject to approval by the state government. In Basle most of these powers rest with the Stock Exchange Commission. In Geneva the association has more or less the character of a self-governing body, establishing practically all of the rules and regulations of the exchange.

Listing. The listing requirements on the Swiss stock exchanges are not as drastic as in New York. In Zurich applications must be approved by the Stock Exchange Association and are then submitted to the Department of the Interior of the state for final approval. In Basle the decision is made by the Stock Exchange Commission, and in Geneva it rests with the Association of Stock Exchange Brokers. Firms whose securities are listed must publish annual statements. In Basle a prospectus must be published prior to the listing. Domestic issues below 500,000 francs are not listed in Zurich or Basle, while the minimum for foreign issues is 1,000,000 francs. In Basle, applicants for securities listing must agree that the listing will be maintained for at least five years.

Trading hours. The Zurich Stock Exchange trades between 10:45 a. m. and 1:00 p. m. and from 4:00 p. m. to 4:30 p. m. In Basle the trading hours are 10:45 a. m. to 12:00 noon and 4:00 p. m. to 4:30 p. m.; in Geneva they are 10:45 a. m. to 12:30 p. m. and 3:30 p. m. to 4:00 p. m.

Quotations. Prices are quoted continuously during trading hours on all three stock exchanges. All purchases and sales must be immediately reported to the secretary, who enters them on his books and later publishes the official quotation list. The quotations in Zurich and Basle are, for bonds, in percentage of their par value plus accrued interest, and for stocks, in francs per share, inclusive of the dividend warrant attached. In Geneva both bonds and stocks are quoted on a per-bond or per-share basis, inclusive of the accrued interest or dividend, except that government and Federal railway bonds are also quoted on a percentage basis.

Cash transactions. Purchases and sales on a cash basis in Zurich involve deliveries against payment in cash or checks not later than four o'clock the next day. Business may also be done in Zurich on a cash basis, subject to payment and delivery "within a few days." In Basle and Geneva delivery and payment on cash transactions must be completed not later than five days after the date of execution.

End-of-month settlements. All listed securities, except those of companies capitalized at less than 1,000,000 francs, may be dealt in on the "term" market. Settlements on the Swiss stock exchanges are only at the end of the month; there is no mid-month settlement. These so-called "ultimo" settlements work as follows: On the fourth day before the end of the month non-members of the clearing association and holders of options have to notify those with whom they have contracts concerning the securities and amounts which they intend to settle. On the next day the settlement sheets are prepared. On the third day, at 11:00 a. m. the settlement sheets are turned over to the secretary's office, and at 4:00 p. m. on the same day payment is made at the same office. An hour later the securities themselves are delivered. On the last day of the month, at 10:00 a. m. the settlement balances are paid out and the deliveries are completed.

"Premium" and "stella" transactions. The so-called "premium" business has at times been fairly important. It is the equivalent of the American "put and call market." A buyer or seller agrees with another party, upon the purchase or sale of securities, that within not more than two months one of the parties has the right to cancel the contract against the payment of a premium. The so-called "stella" transactions are similar. They arise when a right is granted to deliver, or call for, certain shares at some future settlement date at a definite spread, or *écart,* above or below a fixed price. The *écart* represents the premium for the risk involved.   These transactions used to be quite frequent in Basle, but in recent years both have become less common.

Financing of stock exchange transactions.   A very large part of the end-of-the-month settlements are financed by means of "lombard" accounts.   The National Bank frowns upon this type of loan if it is for speculative purposes, but the commercial banks are only too glad to discount these promissory notes secured by stock exchange collateral at rates which are usually $1\frac{1}{2}$ per cent to 2 per cent above the official discount rate.   Such loans may run from one to six months but are usually granted on a monthly basis.   The margin ranges between 10 per cent and 25 per cent.   Speculative transactions are financed chiefly through report loans, which play an important rôle in the market for stock exchange funds.

Selected List of References

Chapter I

BOOKS

Cassel, Gustav, *The Crisis in the World's Monetary System*, 2nd edition, 1932, The Clarendon Press, Oxford.

Gregory, T. E., *The Gold Standard and Its Future*, 1932, E. P. Dutton & Co., Inc., New York.

Halasi, Dr. Adalbert, *Die Goldwaehrung*, 1933, Carl Heymanns Verlag, Berlin.

Hawtrey, R. G., *The Gold Standard in Theory and Practice*, 2nd edition, 1931, Longmans, Green & Co., New York and London.

Keynes, J. M., *A Treatise on Money*, 2 vols., 1930, Harcourt, Brace and Co., New York.

Keynes, J. M., *Essays in Persuasion*, 1932, Harcourt, Brace and Co., New York.

Le Branchu, Jean-Yves, *Essai sur le Gold Exchange Standard*, 1933, Librairie du Recueil Sirey, Paris.

Lombard, Leon, *L'Or Regulateur de la Production*, 1933, Librairie du Recueil Sirey, Paris.

Mlynarski, Dr. F., *Gold and Central Banks*, 1929, the Macmillan Co., New York.

Mlynarski, Dr. F., *The Functioning of the Gold Standard*, 1931, published by the League of Nations (Document #F 979).

Puxley, H. L., *A Critique of the Gold Standard*, 1934, Harper & Brothers, New York.

Rogers, J. H., *America Weighs Her Gold*, 1931, Yale University Press, New Haven.

Royal Institute of International Affairs, *The International Gold Problem—Collected Papers*, 1931, Oxford University Press, New York.

Warren, G. F., and Pearson, F. A., *Prices*, 1933, John Wiley & Sons, Inc., New York.

REPORTS, PAMPHLETS, AND DOCUMENTS

Gold: A World Problem, Addresses delivered at the Institute of Public Affairs, University of Virginia, July 1932, the Academy of World Economics, Washington, D. C.

Gold Clause, by Madden, J. T., and Nadler, M., 1929, Bulletin #27, Institute of International Finance, New York.

Report of the Gold Delegation of the Financial Committee of the League of Nations, Official No. C. 502, M. 243, 1932, II A, Publications Department of the League of Nations, Geneva, Switzerland.

Chapters II and III

BOOKS

Conant, C. A., *The Principles of Banking,* 1908, Harper & Brothers, New York and London.

Hawtrey, R. G., *Currency and Credit,* 2nd edition, 1923, Longmans, Green & Co., New York and London.

Hawtrey, R. G., *The Art of Central Banking,* 1932, Longmans, Green & Co., New York and London.

Hobson, K. C., *The Export of Capital,* 1914, Constable & Co., Ltd., London.

Lavington, F., *The English Capital Market,* 2nd edition, 1929, Methuen & Co., Ltd., London.

Madden, J. T., and Nadler, M., *Foreign Securities,* 1929, The Ronald Press Co., New York.

Melchett, H. M., *Modern Money,* 2nd edition, 1933, Martin Secker, London.

National Industrial Conference Board, Inc., *The International Financial Position of the United States,* 1929, National Industrial Conference Board, Inc., New York.

REPORTS, PAMPHLETS, AND DOCUMENTS

America as a Creditor Nation, Academy of Political Science, Proceedings, Vol. XII, No. 4, January 1928.

Annual reports of the Bank for International Settlements, 1931–1934, Basle, Switzerland.

Commercial Banks, 1913–1929, League of Nations, Economic Intelligence Service, 1931, Geneva.

Commercial Banks, 1925–1933, League of Nations, Economic Intelligence Service, 1934, Geneva.

"Die deutsche Zahlungsbilanz," *Verhandlungen und Berichte des Unterausschusses fuer allgemeine Wirtschaftsstruktur,* E. S. Mittler & Sohn, 1930, Berlin.

Sale of Foreign Bonds or Securities in the United States, Hearings before the Committee on Finance, United States Senate,

72nd Congress, 1932, U. S. Government Printing Office, Washington, D. C.

"Some Major Forces in the International Money Market," Anderson, B. M., *The Chase Economic Bulletin,* Vol. VII, No. 4.

World Economic Survey, 1931–32, League of Nations, 1932, Geneva.

World Economic Survey, 1932–33, League of Nations, 1933, Geneva.

World Economic Survey, 1933–34, League of Nations, 1934, Geneva.

Chapter IV

BOOKS

Einzig, P., *Behind the Scenes of International Finance,* 1931, Macmillan & Co., Ltd., London.

Einzig, P., *The Sterling-Dollar-Franc Tangle,* 1933, Macmillan & Co., Ltd., London.

Einzig, P., *Germany's Default,* 1934, Macmillan & Co., Ltd., London.

Einzig, P., *Exchange Control,* 1934, Macmillan & Co., Ltd., London.

Hantos, Elemer, *La Monnaie: ses Systèmes et ses Phénomènes en Europe Centrale,* 1927, Marcel Giard, Paris.

Jack, D. T., *The Restoration of European Currencies,* 1927, P. S. King & Son, Ltd., London.

Lehfeldt, R. A., *Restoration of the World's Currencies,* 1923, P. S. King & Son, Ltd., London.

Mlynarski, F., *Credit and Peace,* 1933, George Allen & Unwin, Ltd., London.

Nadler, M., and Bogen, J., *The Banking Crisis,* 1933, Dodd, Mead & Co., New York.

Peddie, J. T., *The Crisis of the Pound,* 1932, Macmillan & Co., Ltd., London.

Royal Institute of International Affairs, *Monetary Policy and the Depression,* 1933, Oxford University Press, New York.

Schacht, Dr. H., *The End of Reparations,* 1931, Robert O. Ballou, Publisher, New York.

REPORTS, PAMPHLETS, AND DOCUMENTS

Financial Reconstruction of Austria, Report of the Financial Committee of the Council of the League of Nations, 1921, Constable & Co., Ltd., London.

Index, Monthly publication of the Svenska Handelsbanken, Stockholm, Sweden.

Monthly Review, Barclays Bank, Ltd., London.

Quarterly Report, Skandinaviska Kreditaktiebolaget, Stockholm, Sweden.

Quarterly Review of International Conditions, by J. Henry Schroeder & Co., London.

Westminster Bank Review, monthly publication of the Westminster Bank, Ltd., London.

Chapters V, VI, VII, and VIII

BOOKS

Burgess, W. R., *Reserve Banks and the Money Market,* 1928, Harper & Brothers, New York.

Currie, L., *The Supply and Control of Money in the United States,* 1934, Harvard University Press, Cambridge.

Goldenweiser, E. A., *Federal Reserve System in Operation,* 1925, McGraw-Hill Book Co., New York.

Griffiss, B., *The New York Call Money Market,* 1925, The Ronald Press Co., New York.

Hardy, C. O., *Credit Policies of the Federal Reserve System,* 1932, The Brookings Institution, Washington, D. C.

Harris, S. E., *Twenty Years of Federal Reserve Policy,* 2 vols., 1933, Harvard University Press, Cambridge, Mass.

Laughlin, J. L., *A New Exposition of Money, Credit and Prices,* 2 vols., 1931, The University of Chicago Press, Chicago.

National Industrial Conference Board, Inc., *The Banking Situation in the United States,* 1932, National Industrial Conference Board, Inc., New York.

The National Industrial Conference Board, Inc., *The New Monetary System of the United States,* 1934, National Industrial Conference Board, Inc., New York.

The New York Money Market, 4 vols., edited by B. H. Beckhart, 1931–32, Columbia University Press, New York.

Pasvolsky, L., *Current Monetary Issues,* 1933, The Brookings Institution, Washington, D. C.

Reed, H. L., *Federal Reserve Policy, 1921–1930,* 1930, McGraw-Hill Book Co., New York.

Riefler, W. W., *Money Rates and Money Markets in the United States,* 1930, Harper & Brothers, New York.

Steiner, W. H., *Money and Banking,* 1933, Henry Holt and Co., Inc., New York.

Strong, B., *Interpretations of Federal Reserve Policy* (speeches and writings of Benjamin Strong), edited by W. R. Burgess, 1931, Harper & Brothers, New York.

Warburg, P. M., *The Federal Reserve System*, 2 vols., 1930, the Macmillan Co., New York.

Willis, H. P., Chapman, J. M., and Robey, R. W., *Contemporary Banking*, 1933, Harper & Brothers, New York.

Willis, H. P., and Chapman, J. M., *The Banking Situation*, 1934, Columbia University Press, New York.

Reports, Pamphlets, and Documents

Acceptance Bulletin, issued monthly by the American Acceptance Council, New York.

Annual reports of the Comptroller of the Currency, U. S. Government Printing Office, Washington, D. C.

Annual reports of the Federal Reserve Board, U. S. Government Printing Office, Washington, D. C.

The Balance of International Payments of the United States, 1922–1933, published annually by the U. S. Department of Commerce, U. S. Government Printing Office, Washington, D. C.

Circulation Statement of United States Money, issued monthly by the Treasury Department, Washington, D. C.

Daily Statement of the U. S. Treasury, issued by the Office of the Secretary of the Treasury, Washington, D. C.

Economic conditions, governmental finance, U. S. securities, *Monthly Bulletin of the National City Bank of New York*, New York.

Federal Reserve Bulletin, Monthly publication of the Federal Reserve Board, Washington, D. C.

The Guaranty Survey, published monthly by the Guaranty Trust Co. of New York.

New York Stock Exchange Bulletin, monthly publication of the New York Stock Exchange.

Operation of the National and Federal Reserve Banking Systems, Hearings before a Subcommittee of the Committee on Banking and Currency, U. S. Senate, 71st Congress, 1931, U. S. Government Printing Office, Washington, D. C.

Stabilization, Hearings before the Committee on Banking and Currency, House of Representatives, 1927, U. S. Government Printing Office, Washington, D. C.

Monthly Review of Credit and Business Conditions, Federal Reserve Bank of New York.

NEWSPAPERS AND PERIODICALS

The American Economic Review, New York.
The Bankers Magazine, New York.
Banking (journal of the American Bankers Association).
The Commercial and Financial Chronicle, New York.
Harvard Business Review.
The Journal of Political Economy, Chicago.
The Quarterly Journal of Economics, Cambridge, Mass.

Chapters IX, X, and XI

BOOKS

Acres, W. Marston, *The Bank of England from Within,* 1931, Oxford University Press, London and New York.

Andreades, A., *History of the Bank of England,* 1909, P. S. King & Son, London.

Armstrong, F. E., *The Book of the Stock Exchange,* 1934, Sir Isaac Pitman & Sons, Ltd., London.

Bagehot, Walter, *Lombard Street,* 14th edition, 1922, John Murray, London.

Butson, H. E., "The Banking System of the United Kingdom," in *Foreign Banking Systems,* by H. P. Willis and B. H. Beckhart, 1929, Henry Holt & Co., New York.

Clare, George, *A Money Market Primer,* 1914, Effingham Wilson, London.

Feaveryear, A. E., *The Pound Sterling,* 1931, The Clarendon Press, Oxford.

Greengrass, H. W., *The Discount Market in London,* 1930, Sir Isaac Pitman & Sons, Ltd., London.

Killik, Sir Stephen H. M., *The Work of the Stock Exchange,* 2nd edition, 1934, Stock Exchange, London.

Lavington, F., *The English Capital Market,* 2nd edition, 1929, Methuen & Co., Ltd., London.

Minty, L. Le Marchant, *English Banking Methods,* 1925, Sir Isaac Pitman & Sons, Ltd., London.

Spalding, W. F., *The London Money Market,* 3rd edition, 1924, Sir Isaac Pitman & Sons, Ltd., London.

REPORTS, PAMPHLETS, AND DOCUMENTS

Banking and Trade Financing in the United Kingdom, Trade Information Bulletin #636, 1929, U. S. Department of Commerce, Bureau of Foreign and Domestic Commerce, Washington, D. C.

Monthly Review, 1930–1934, Lloyds Bank, Limited, London.

Monthly Review, 1927–1934, Midland Bank, London.

Report of the Committee on Finance and Industry (Macmillan report), June 1931, H. M. Stationery Office, London.

"The Stock Exchange," special number of the *Financial News*, London, issued November 13, 1933.

NEWSPAPERS AND PERIODICALS

The Banker, London.

The Bankers' Magazine, London.

The Economist, London.

The Financial News, London.

The Financial Times, London.

The New York Times, New York.

The Statist, London.

The Stock Exchange Gazette, London.

Waehrung und Wirtschaft, 1933–1934, published monthly by the Waehrungs-Institut, Berlin.

Chapters XII and XIII

BOOKS

Conant, C. A., *A History of Modern Banks of Issue*, 1927, G. P. Putnam's Sons, New York.

Lemoine, R. J., "The Banking System of France," in *Foreign Banking Systems*, by H. P. Willis and B. H. Beckhart, 1929, Henry Holt & Co., New York.

Meliot, M. et A., *Dictionnaire Financier*, 1910, Berger-Levrault & Cie., Paris.

Robert-Milles, S., *La Grammaire de la Bourse*, 1928, Flammarion, Paris.

Montarnal, H., *Traité Practique du Contentieux Commercial de la Banque et de la Bourse*, 1928, Librairie des Sciences Politiques et Sociales, Paris.

Montarnal, H., *Manuel des Opérations Commerciales et Financières de Banque et de Bourse*, 1929, Librairie des Sciences Politiques et Sociales, Paris.

Page, L., *La Bourse Classique Modernisée*, Michel, Paris.

Parker, W., *The Paris Bourse and French Finance*, 1920, Columbia University, New York.

Ramon, G., *Histoire de la Banque de France*, 1929, Grasset, Paris.

Vigreux, P. B., *Le Crédit par Acceptation*, 1932, Librairie des Sciences Politiques et Sociales, Paris.

REPORTS, PAMPHLETS, AND DOCUMENTS

Annual reports of the Bank of France.

Annual reports of the large French banks.

Banking System and Practices in France, 1931, U. S. Department of Commerce, U. S. Government Printing Office, Washington, D. C.

Commercial Banks, 1925–1931, 1934, League of Nations, Geneva.

Lois et Statutes qui Régissent la Banque de France, 1926, Dupont, Paris.

The Paris Bourse, U. S. Department of Commerce, U. S. Government Printing Office, Washington, D. C., 1930.

NEWSPAPERS AND PERIODICALS

The Annalist, New York.

The Economic Journal, London.

The Economist, London.

European Finance, London.

Journal des Economistes, Paris.

La Situation Economique et Financière, Paris.

La Vie Financière, Paris.

L'Economiste Français, Paris.

Révue d'Economie Politique, Paris.

Chapters XIV and XV

BOOKS

Blum, Dr. Eugen, *Die deutschen Kreditmaerkte nach der Stabilisierung*, 1929, Industrie-Verlag Spaeth & Linde, Berlin.

Conant, Charles A., *A History of Modern Banks of Issue*, 6th edition, 1927, G. P. Putnam's Sons, New York and London.

Quittner, Paul, "The Banking System of Germany," in *Foreign Banking Systems*, by H. P. Willis and B. H. Beckhart, 1929, Henry Holt & Co., New York.

Riesser, J., *Die deutschen Grossbanken und ihre Konzentration*, 1912, Gustav Fischer, Jena.

Schacht, Dr. Hjalmar, *The Stabilization of the Mark*, 1927, The Adelphi Company, New York.

Whale, P. Barrett, *Joint Stock Banking in Germany*, 1930, Macmillan & Co., Ltd., London.

REPORTS, PAMPHLETS, AND DOCUMENTS

Allgemeine Bestimmungen fuer den Verkehr mit der Reichsbank, December 1931, published by the Reichsbank, Berlin.

Annual reports of the Reichsbank, 1922–1933.

Annual reports of the large German commercial banks, 1924–1933.

Fuenfzig Jahre Abrechnungsstellen der Reichsbank, 1933, by Volkswirtschaftliche und Statistische Abteilung der Reichsbank, Berlin.

Germany's Economic Development, semiannual reports of the Reichs-Kredit-Gesellschaft A. G., Berlin, 1926–1934.

"Die Reichsbank," *Verhandlungen und Berichte des Unterausschusses fuer Geld-Kredit und Finanzwesen*, 1929. E. S. Mittler & Son, Berlin.

Reparation Commission Official Documents: *The Experts' Plan for Reparation Payments*, 1927, H. M. Stationery Office, London.

Reports of the Agent General for Reparation Payments and of the Commissioners and Trustees for the period September 1924 to May 1930, published by the Office for Reparation Payments, Berlin.

Report of the Committee appointed on the recommendation of the London Conference, 1931.

Verhandlungen des VI Allgemeinen Deutschen Bankiertages zu Berlin, 1925, Walter De Gruyter & Co., Berlin.

Verhandlungen des VII Allgemeinen Deutschen Bankiertages zu Berlin, 1928, Walter De Gruyter & Co., Berlin.

Reports of Reichs-Kredit-Gesellschaft Aktiengesellschaft, Berlin.

NEWSPAPERS AND PERIODICALS

Die Bank, Berlin.

Der deutsche Volkswirt, Berlin.

The Economist, London.

Frankfurter Zeitung und Handelsblatt, Frankfurt a/M.

German Institute for Business Research, *Weekly Reports*, Berlin.

Weltwirtschaftliches Archiv, Kiel.

Wirtschaftsdienst, Hamburg.

Die Wirtschaftskurve mit Indexzahlen der Frankfurter Zeitung, Frankfurt a/M.

Chapters XVI and XVII

BOOKS

Brenninkmeyer, Dr. Ludger, *Die Amsterdamer Effektenboerse*, 1920, G. A. Gloeckner, Leipzig.

Eisfeld, Dr. Curt, *Das Niederlandische Bankwesen*, 1916, Martinus Nijhoff, The Hague.

François-Marsal, F., *Encyclopédie dè Banque et de Bourse*, Vol. V, Part II, Imprimerie Crete, Paris.

Harthoorn, P. C., *Hoofdlijnen uit de ontwikkeling van het moderne bankwezen in Nederland voor de concentratie*, 1928, Rotterdam.

Hirschfeld, Dr. H. M., *Nieuwe stroomingen in het Nederlandsche bankwezen*, 1925, J. J. Romen & Zonen, Roermond.

Houwink, Dr. A., *Acceptcrediet*, 1929, N. V. H. Van der Marck's Uitgevers-Mij., Amsterdam.

de Jong, A. M., "The Banking System of Holland," in *Foreign Banking Systems*, by H. P. Willis and B. H. Beckhart, 1929, Henry Holt & Company, New York.

de Roos, Dr. R. Brandes, *Industrie, Kapitalmarkt und Industrielle Effekten in den Niederlanden*, 1928, Martinus Nijhoff, The Hague.

Smith, Dr. M. F. J., *Tijd-Affairs in Effecten aan de Amsterdamsche Beurs*, 1919, Martinus Nijhoff, The Hague.

Theyse, J. S., "De Effectenhandel," in the series *Het Bankwezen*, 1921, G. Delwel; Wassenaar.

Westerman, Dr. W. M., *De concentratie in het bankwezen*, 2nd edition, 1920, Martinus Nijhoff, The Hague.

REPORTS, PAMPHLETS, AND DOCUMENTS

Annual Reports of the Netherlands Bank, published by Blikman & Sartorius, Amsterdam.

The Bank Act and the statutes of the Netherlands Bank.

Bankboek, published yearly since 1924 by the daily newspaper *De Telegraaf*.

"Divers Aspects des Questions Bancaires aux Pays-Bas," by Dr. G. Vissering, excerpt from the *Révue Economique Internationale*, June 1922.

Gedenkboek, 1876–1926, published in 1926 by the Vereeniging voor den Effektenhandel te Amsterdam, Holland.

"The Netherlands Bank and the War," by Dr. G. Vissering, reprinted from *Grotius*, Annuaire International pour 1915, Martinus Nijhoff, The Hague.

Statuten der Vereeniging voor den Effectenhandel te Amsterdam, Vereeniging voor den Effectenhandel te Amsterdam, Holland.

Reglement voor den Effectenhandel, Vereeniging voor den Effectenhandel te Amsterdam, Holland.

Reglement voor het opnemen van fondsen in de Prijscourant, Vereeniging voor den Effectenhandel te Amsterdam, Holland.

Reglement voor de Noteering, Vereeniging voor den Effectenhandel te Amsterdam, Holland.

Provisie-Reglement, Vereeniging voor den Effectenhandel te Amsterdam, Holland.

Chapter XVIII

Books

Einzig, P., *The Fight for Financial Supremacy*, 1931, Macmillan & Co., London.

Hoeweler, Dr. Kurt, *Der Geld und Kapitalmarkt der Schweiz*, 1927, Julius Springer, Berlin.

Kurz, H., *Die Schweizer Effektenboersen*, 1931, Schulthess & Co., Zurich.

Kurz, H., und Bachmann, Dr. G., *Die Schweizerischen Grossbanken*, 1928, Orell Fuessli Verlag, Zurich.

Schneebeli, H. M., *La Banque Nationale Suisse, 1907–1932*, 1932, Swiss National Bank, Zurich.

Steiger, Dr. J., *Schweizerisches Finanz-Jahrbuch*, 1934, Zimmermann & Cie., A. G., Berne.

Schwarzenbach, E., "The Banking System of Switzerland," in *Foreign Banking Systems*, by Willis, H. P., and Beckhart, B. H., 1929, Henry Holt & Co., New York.

Reports, Pamphlets, and Documents

Annual reports of Banque Nationale Suisse, Zurich.

Bulletin Financier, issued by Credit Suisse, Zurich.

Bulletin of Société de Banque Suisse, Basle.

Monthly bulletin of Banque Nationale Suisse, Zurich.

Das schweizerische Bankwesen, published annually by Mitteilungen des statistischen Bureau der Schweizerischen Nationalbank, Art. Institut Orell Fuessli, Zurich.

Index

A

Abnormal movement of funds, distinguished from normal movement, 52
Acceptance and Guaranty Bank of Berlin, 402, 403
Acceptance liabilities, classification of banks reporting (*table*), 165
Acceptance market:
Amsterdam, 164
Berlin, 415
Federal Reserve banks in, 166
London, 254
New York, 161
Paris, 341
Acceptances:
dollar exchange, 164
export and import, 162
freezing, 163
held by Federal Reserve banks (*table*), 219
Nederlandsche Bank policies concerning, 442
New York:
classification of, 162, 163
distribution of, 168, (*table*) 169
outstanding (*table*), 162
purchasers of, 166
Accepting institutions:
Amsterdam, 466, 470
Berlin, 415
international, 455
London, 254
New York, 164
Paris, 341
Affiliates:
German, in Holland, 455
United States, elimination of , 153
Agricultural Adjustment Act of 1933, 141
Amsterdam:
acceptance institutions, 466, 470
acceptance market, 464
regulation of , 467
acceptances (*table*), 468
buying of, 471
acceptors, 470
banking system, 427
classifications, 430

Amsterdam (*cont.*) :
beleening. 464
bill brokers, 471
call loans, 459
capital and deposits (*table*), 428
cashiers, 452
importance of, 454
collateral loans (*table*), 459
colonial banks, 450
concentration of banks, 428
day-to-day loans, 459
deposits, 428, 429
development of, 425
financial disturbances in Europe, affected by, 426
foreign banks, 455
foreign capital, 465
general banks, 447
position of (*table*), 448
German banks, 455, 470
gold coin circulation, 440
history of, 424
international acceptance corporations, 455
legislation, banking, 429
miscellaneous institutions, 455
money market and stock exchange operation, 458
Nederlandsche Bank (*see also* Nederlandsche Bank), 430
overseas banks, 456
post-war period, 426
private bankers, 454
prolongatie loans, 458, 460
borrowers, 462
Dutch preference for, 464
lenders, 461
made through aid of brokers (*table*), 463
provincial banks, 450
reserves, 428
security loans, 458
stock exchange, 472
war period, 426, 434, 465
Wool Bank, 455
Amsterdamsche Bank, 448
Amsterdam Stock Exchange, 472
administration, 475
admission of securities, 476
foreign stocks, 479
futures, 480

Index